"In the Public Interest"

Oral Histories of Hoosier Broadcasters

"In the Public Interest"

Oral Histories of Hoosier Broadcasters

Compiled and Edited by

Linda Weintraut and Jane R. Nolan

John Warner, Assistant Editor

Indiana Historical Society

Indianapolis 1999

The paper in this publication meets the minimum requirements of American National Standard for Information Sciences—Permanence of Paper for Printed Library Materials, ANSI Z39. 48-1984

Library of Congress Cataloging-in-Publication Data

"In the public interest" : oral histories of Hoosier broadcasters /
   [edited by] Linda Weintraut and Jane Nolan.
     p. cm.
   Includes bibliographical references and index.
   ISBN 0-87195-131-2 (alk. paper)
   1. Broadcasting–Indiana–History. 2. Broadcasters–Indiana–Interviews. I. Weintraut, Linda. II. Nolan, Jane R.
PN1990.6.U5I5 1999
384.54'09772–dc21   98-40701
                                  CIP

Contents

Foreword

Broadcasting has had such a profound effect on our nation as a whole that we, the broadcasters of Indiana, consider it an honor to tell the story of Hoosier broadcasting. Not only has the state been a training ground for nationally known broadcasters such as "Red" Skelton and David Letterman, but it has also originated programs, such as the Indianapolis 500-Mile Race, that have been broadcast worldwide. Who has not heard of the Indiana High School Boys Basketball Tournament?

Radio in Indiana began when fifteen stations set up operations in towns and cities across the state during the 1920s. The frenzy to pick up stations on rigged-up receivers and earphones attracted a wide variety of people to this new means of communication.

The early entrepreneurs did not get involved in radio stations to make money. They were dreamers and tinkerers who foresaw the kind of entertainment and service that this new invention could provide for communities, large and small. When the government set up a federal agency to license these stations, it became apparent that public service was one of the purposes of radio.

The first generation of broadcasters has died with few of their experiences recorded, making it imperative that a history of broadcasting in Indiana be written. Since 1920 there have been many changes in broadcasting. We have gone from the crystal set to digital electronics and high-definition television (HDTV). If we had not endeavored to record how radio began in Indiana, the early pioneers and those who followed and made the transition into the new era of electronics would quickly have been forgotten.

In 1992 a small group of second-generation broadcast pioneers decided to record the history of our profession. We had established the Indiana Broadcasters Pioneers' Hall of Fame to recognize those who had worked in broadcasting in the state and who had helped at the Indiana State Museum with an exhibit that told some of the story. We wanted to do more. Because much of the history was being lost as our pioneers died, we began conducting oral history interviews with living members of the "Hall of Fame." I was in a small group, which included Ken Coe and Jim Phillippe, that started this project. Several other individuals soon joined our oral history committee. By 1997 twenty-seven interviews had been completed.

I am honored to have been asked to write the foreword for this book. Down through the years, I have had the pleasure of knowing most of those who were interviewed, plus some of the early pioneers who died before this project began. It has been an exciting experience to read about the impact of broadcasting on their lives. Their stories have convinced me more than ever that this book and these interviews were worth the time and struggles we all experienced. There have been those from Indiana who chose to enter the arena of "big-time" broadcasting, and we are proud of their accomplishments and the recognition they have brought to our state. But this book tells the story of those who chose to pursue their dreams in broadcasting while remaining in Indiana. Their memories and experiences will illuminate the sense of responsibility that guided many of these early broadcasters to broadcast "in the public interest." I am thankful to have lived during those formative years.

REID G. CHAPMAN

Fort Wayne, Indiana
January 1998

Acknowledgments

This project would never have reached fruition had it not been for the valiant efforts of the history committee of the Indiana Broadcasters Pioneers Foundation, Inc., led by Reid Chapman and Michael Corken. Chapman served as the chairman for nearly four years and gave unstintingly of his time and talent. Corken, the present chairman and current president of the Foundation, has proven to be a superb leader in the final stages of preparation for the book. Through the years, however, there have been many who have donated untold hours to this project; we would be remiss if we did not thank those who have participated on the committee. While Reid Chapman and Jim Phillippe have served all five years, others have moved on and off the committee but have contributed ably: Ken Beckley, Charlie Blake, Barbara Boyd, Howard Caldwell, Helen Campbell, Ken Coe, Jim Hetherington, Ruth Hiatt, Bob Kaltoff, Dick Lingle, Dave McGhee, Dale Ogden (ex officio), Doug Padgett, Bob Petranoff, Ed Roehling, and Dave Smith. Jeff Smulyan spearheaded an advisory committee that included Dick Fairbanks and Durward Kirby.

In the course of preparing this book, the editors have relied on many people. Robert M. Taylor, Jr., director of education at the Indiana Historical Society, has acted not only as liaison to the Society, but his wise counsel has also been invaluable during the interviewing process and writing of the book. Susan Sutton, Pam Tranfield, and Wilma Gibbs at the Indiana Historical Society Library helped with photo research, as did Martha Wright at the Indiana State Library. In addition, Dick Gantz at the Indiana State Museum allowed us the use of its files and photographs on broadcasting. Howard Caldwell tirelessly researched photographs in the central Indiana area and provided background information and citations. If we were stumped, we called Howard. The narrators gave us access to their personal collections, and many others generously sent pictures and mementos that enriched the book: Ken Beckley, Helen Campbell, Anne Clark, Jack Conolly, Rae Gates, Mary Lou Holland, Paula Katt, Durward Kirby, Dick Lingle, Bob Petranoff, Gene Slaymaker, Julie Slaymaker, Ruth Spencer, and Adelaide Walton sent photos from their private collections. Others provided us with photos from their companies or institutions: Nancy Alexander, Butler University; Dave Bailey, WTHI-TV; Claudia Burgess, AgDay; Julius DeCocq and Jim Freeman, WSBT; John Escosa, Stedman Studio in Fort Wayne; Scott Hainey, WISH-TV; Claudia Johnson, Fort Wayne PBS; Robert Klingle, WKJG-TV; Gene Kuntz, WITZ; John Long, WTTV; John McDaniel, WBCW; Leslie McGuire, McGuire Photography; Frank Moore, WANE-TV; Lou Pierce, WNDU; Rod Porter, WTHR; John Rekis, WISH-TV; Robin Rene, Emmis Broadcasting Corporation; Tony Richards, WMEE; Larry Shores, the *Muncie Star-Press;* Dave Smith, DRMS, Inc.; Morris Smulevitz, WIBC; Gus Stevens, Lewis Historical Collections, Vincennes University; Kurt Swadener, WRTV-6; Debra Taylor, Hall of Fame Museum at the Indianapolis Motor Speedway; and the *Indianapolis Star* and *News.*

We are especially indebted to the committee that read and critiqued the manuscript several times and whose attention to technical detail has been invaluable: Howard Caldwell, Reid Chapman, Mike Corken, and Jim Hetherington, all former broadcasters. They have given up other activities for our lengthy meetings; we will miss the camaraderie. In addition, we must thank Andrew Kerr and John Warner, our associates. Andrew's dedication and careful work has made a major contribution to the project, and John's attention to detail and knowledge of history helped us during our intense brainstorming sessions in working through the first draft of the commentaries. Paula Corpuz, Shirley McCord, Kathy Breen, and George Hanlin, our editors at the Indiana Historical Society, guided us through the final stages of the preparation of the manuscript. Finally, our husbands, Tom Weintraut and Alan Nolan, advised and encouraged us during the long process. To all those many, many people who have made this book a reality, thank you.

Linda Weintraut

Jane R. Nolan

"In the Public Interest"

"It was more of a lark for most of the bunch than anything else," wrote K. D. Ross of the broadcast in 1924 that inspired Fred Zieg to start WOWO. An opera singer from Bluffton, Indiana, the treasurer of Allen County who did "old time fiddling," and some other "prominent people who were musicians" put together a few songs for an experimental radio broadcast from the home of Harold Blosser on South Wayne Avenue in Fort Wayne, Indiana. The low-budget program transmitted on a five-watter had a limited range, but it was a hit. According to Ross, Zieg received "hundreds" of calls. Zieg had been searching for a way to promote the sale of Dayfan radios, one of the product lines sold at his store, Main Auto Supply. When Ross convinced him that for a mere $150 he could build a radio station above his store, WOWO was born.[1] WOWO came to be known as "The Voice of a Thousand Main Streets." It was destined to become one of Indiana's best-known stations, but it was not the first. Others, such as WSBT (1921) in South Bend and WBAA (1922) in West Lafayette, associated with Purdue's electrical engineering student laboratory, had preceded it.

The significance of WOWO's beginning extends beyond its status as an early station to suggest several points about radio in the 1920s. Much was happenstance; little thought went into programming. For performers and owners, this was a time of creativity and experimentation; there were few rules. Performers would try anything, and people were so amazed that words and music came across the airwaves and into their homes that they would listen to *anything*. For those living in rural areas, radio became their connection with other people and to new ideas. For all, it became a way to gain access to a wider

world, one that previously had been available only through the written word. It stirred imaginations and passions and united the nation in a way that no other medium had been able to do. Few other innovations had the impact of radio. It changed people's lives more dramatically than any other means of communication since the invention in the 1440s of Gutenberg's printing press, which had made the printed word available for wider distribution.

Radio did not remain unsophisticated for very long. The same year that WOWO made its first broadcast, General Electric, Westinghouse, and RCA organized the National Broadcasting Company (NBC) to provide programming.[2] Stations that signed on for those few hours a day when they could secure live local talent soon sought network affiliation to fill the empty hours. Entertainment remained a mainstay, but before long broadcasters explored the possibilities of transmitting sports and local and national news. Newspaper owners felt threatened: would they lose readers and advertisers? The radio provided a personal, ongoing connection with the outside world that newspapers could not. "News was immediate," in the words of Tom Carnegie, one of the narrators in this book. Few who lived through World War II would ever forget learning of the bombing of Pearl Harbor or of the death of President Franklin D. Roosevelt over the radio. Gradually, radio became inextricably woven into people's memories and the nation's culture.

In the 1950s television vied with radio for audiences. Not only could people hear distant voices, but now they also could *see* events as they happened. Television captured people's wonder in much the same way that radio once had. At first, television was as unsophisticated as radio had been; the main networks rushed to fill the hours with the same kind of variety, dramatic, and comedy programs that had excited radio listeners. Television also carried news; it was through this medium that the nation viewed unfolding national events: racial confrontations, the death of a president, campus protests, the war in Vietnam, the wonders of space flight. As television claimed more and more of the audience, some questioned the longevity of a strictly audio means of broadcasting. By necessity, radio executives became more creative. In the late 1970s and 1980s, entrepreneurs began to experiment with the concept of format radio,[3] which has set the stage for a resurgence of this medium. Radio has survived and flourished even though—and because—it is different from television.

As this brief overview of broadcasting illustrates, radio and television have served the public as they have adapted to meet the needs of their audiences. They have provided entertainment and sports coverage. They have informed people about news events and issues, sometimes arousing anger and inspiring change. They have encouraged an active listening audience through the format of talk radio. Beyond that, local stations are involved members of their community. They give station time and money to public affairs and tell us about the happenings in our community. On many levels, stations operate "in the public interest."

This concept of the public interest arose out of federal legislation and self-regulation. In the words of one of our narrators, Jeffrey H. Smulyan, president of Emmis Broadcasting Corporation, broadcasters have a "unique compact" with the public because they utilize the airwaves, which are both public and free. Since the 1920s, when President Calvin Coolidge first called for federal regulation, the airwaves have been labeled a "public medium." Stations are granted licenses from the government, and they do not pay for use of the air. The Radio Act of 1927 and later the Communications Act of 1934 set forth the conditions for licensees: they must operate "in the public interest, convenience and necessity," but the concept of "in the public interest" was left open to interpretation. Since that time, the Federal Communications Commission (FCC) has strived to maintain a delicate balance between the needs and desires of the listening audience and the First Amendment rights of the owners.[4]

The industry recognized its unique position in American society, and broadcasters took a giant step toward professionalization of the industry by forming the National Association of Broadcasters (NAB) in 1928. The organization established a "code" that stressed voluntary adherence. A more extensive industry-wide code was established in 1937 and revised in 1945, which set "guideposts" for children's programming, advertising, contests, and news. Most problematical was the definition of these standards. For example, in defining acceptable content for children's programming, the code said that it "should be presented with due regard for its effect on children." Perhaps because the language was fairly broad, it was open to interpretation as the definition of morals and values evolved in the postwar era. The profession was addressing the issue of public interest independently of the FCC.[5]

The first era of FCC regulation (1927–1981) has been called the "Trusteeship Model." With the release of the "Blue Book" in 1949, the commission required "balanced program fare," which led to the "fairness doctrine" three years later. That doctrine stated that licensees needed to broadcast opposing points of view on controversial issues. In 1960 the FCC began reviewing content, mandating that stations "discover and fulfill the tastes and desires" of their listening area. It was at this time that the commission began requiring stations to originate a certain amount of local programming. The FCC was, in effect, encouraging stations to operate as public trustees.[6]

The 1980s saw a different environment in broadcasting. At a time when some stations and individuals advocated fewer government restrictions, the FCC began to favor another model in which the marketplace would dictate programming content: the "Marketplace Approach." In early 1981 the commission weakened the concept of "equal time" for political candidates, which had been established in 1957 in Section 315 of the Communications Act. Then in 1985 the commission issued the "Fairness Report," which said that the fairness doctrine "violates the First Amendment and contravenes the public interest." Two years later, the fairness doctrine was eliminated. Further, in 1982 the Justice Department initiated a lawsuit charging that the NAB advertising code was unconstitutional. The NAB did not appeal and dropped its code entirely. This has led to a gradual reduction in the regulation of the broadcasting industry.[7]

Since the early 1980s the "Marketplace Approach" has fostered a change in the structure of the industry itself and permitted a resurgence in entrepreneurial opportunities in broadcasting. In 1970 the FCC instituted "the duopoly rule," which stated that no operator of an AM, FM, or TV station could acquire another like station in the same market. This rule was based on the premise that the number of stations was limited because there were only so many frequencies available on the spectrum in a given area. Concerned that operators might monopolize the dissemination of information, the FCC ruled against cross-ownership of television and radio with newspapers in 1975. This philosophy changed somewhat in 1982 when the commission ruled that operators no longer had to wait three years from the date of purchase to sell a station, a rule that had been established to prohibit profit taking. Then Docket 80-90 provided for an additional 689 new FM stations nationwide, opening up opportunities for new ownership. Further, in 1984 the FCC allowed a single operator to own a greater number of radio and television stations in a market, as long as no more than one operator covered more than 25 percent of the total radio market. Newspapers that already owned broadcasting stations were grandfathered until the station was sold.[8] The effect of this lessening of restrictions has allowed entrepreneurs to flourish in the broadcasting industry.

The concept of public interest has received renewed attention in recent years, yet few studies focus on the ordinary people who really created the industry and who interacted with the public on a daily basis. Jon T. Powell and Wally Gair's *Public Interest and the Business of Broadcasting* (1988), a series of essays written and edited by broadcasters, examines how the federally mandated concept of public interest was internalized and translated into public service by the broadcasting industry. The editors say that "what may have begun as a legal concept has evolved into a social one." In a strikingly simplistic fashion, they accept the idea that there was a "golden age" of radio broadcasting in the 1930s and 1940s, during which children were presented positive role models on programs, programs that taught conventional, middle-class values, even when it was not mandated by the FCC. What may seem "golden" to some in terms of programming content is revealed in George Lipsitz's *Time Passages* (1990) to be fraught with complex and contradictory messages. Lipsitz discusses the role of popular culture (i.e., television programs) in creating and sustaining public

memory and asks questions about messages embodied in programming and its effect on society that Powell and Gair do not contemplate. Still, Powell and Gair's essays touch upon some of the collective meanings of the concept of public interest and the role of the federal government in creating a definition.

Depending upon their professional, personal, and generational backgrounds, individual broadcasters interpreted the public interest differently. For some of those who came into the business in the late 1930s and 1940s, this concept was quantifiably defined by the FCC. For some, public interest meant a good "bottom line," a philosophy that the station that meets the needs of the community will prosper. However, there evolved a different meaning, which included an involvement in, and a sensitivity to, the local community, whether it was serving on boards, interfacing with listeners, or adapting programming to fit special interests. It seems clear that over time public interest came to mean much more than the mandated definitions, although not all broadcasters had the same sense of dedication to this responsibility. These people felt that broadcasting was more than a job; it was a way of giving back to the community—and it was fun. They loved the profession.

This love of the profession led a small nucleus of radio and television pioneers to initiate this oral history project. The members of the group saw that industry standards and ways of doing business were changing rapidly, and they were acutely aware that the memories of their industry were being lost. Their past would go unrecorded if they did not take the initiative to document it. In the early 1990s they began to talk among themselves at the Indiana Broadcasters Pioneers' annual "prune breakfast": someone ought to record the stories of the members of the Indiana Broadcasters Hall of Fame and write the history of their industry for posterity. The Pioneers had contributed to an exhibit at the Indiana State Museum, but its members wanted to do more. By 1992 we, the compilers and interviewers, were contacted about the possibility of establishing a formal oral history project that would culminate in a book.

Two years later, the broadcasters, through the Indiana Broadcasters Pioneers Foundation, Inc., had raised enough money to begin oral interviews. Fund-raising was not always easy. Some members of the committee became ill, and in the early 1990s, when the broadcasting industry experienced hard times, it was difficult to convince people to donate funds for an oral history project. However, the "history steering committee" persevered and eventually raised the necessary funds believing that it was imperative to proceed with the interviews. The urgency of the project was underscored by the deaths of pioneers such as Jim Shelton and Luke Walton. That this book has been written is a tribute to the vision and tenacity of men and women who were true pioneers.

The scope of these oral histories is remarkably broad despite limitations of the sample. At first only members of the Hall of Fame were to be interviewed. However, the committee soon realized that if we were to write a representative history of Hoosier broadcasting, the sample would have to be broadened. Although the number of women and African Americans involved in the industry historically has been proportionately small, their oral histories tell an important facet of the larger story. The scope of the project was enlarged further to include broadcasters from all areas of the state who were involved in a variety of occupations from 1926 to the present. As a result, the narrators range from forty-six to eighty-seven years in age, and from support personnel to on-air personalities, engineers, managers, and owners. The sample is limited in that these twenty-seven oral histories are of men and women who have achieved success. Although they experienced their share of failure along the way, these are people who are highly regarded by their peers. This regard is based in no small part upon their sense of responsibility to the public.

Although we did not set out to write a book about the public interest, it was a theme that arose in the interviewing process. These were broadly based interviews. We asked questions about the broadcasters' early lives and interests and about what led them to their chosen careers. We tried to elicit information about individual stations and about the people who worked there, especially deceased members of the Hall of Fame and well-known broadcasters who were not being interviewed. We also traced the evolution of technology and the regulation of the industry by government. We were concerned about the ethics of broadcasters and how they learned these ethics. Who were their mentors? We asked thought-provoking questions about station philosophy and the impact of broadcasting upon the public. Had they made a difference? Was there a "golden age" of broadcasting? Had it passed?

What is the future of broadcasting? These questions produced varied and sometimes surprising responses.

Oral historians are fond of saying that the memories shared in oral history interviews fill in the "gaps in the written record." But whose record? And whose memories? According to David Lowenthal, "error and self-interest warp evidence and interpretation."[9] It is undeniably so. Painful memories of death and defeat are eased by time. Who of us has not read a letter or a journal account that we ourselves wrote about an experience and thought, "I do not remember feeling that way at all." There are many versions of any event and of the remembered past. Recognizing such, we, the compilers/interviewers, caution you to read these oral histories with a certain measure of skepticism. For example, the broadcasters interviewed did not remember women serving as announcers, but photographs from WOWO in the 1930s clearly show women at the microphone. Thus, the following interviews must be read as stories or tales. Memory is selective and subjective, allowing people to reorder and remember the past in a way that makes sense to them. Memory is the truth according to how one person interpreted and reinterpreted his or her past over time.

Nevertheless, this is an important study. The people interviewed had a measurable impact on Hoosier culture. Their moral and ethical principles have influenced how we perceive ourselves individually and collectively, even though the broadcasters do not always discern it as such. Their story is not a simple one; it presents many versions of the reality of the broadcasting profession over time. The narratives also show how the participants redefined their memories as they pursued their careers. Beyond that, there is a wider story here. Although these broadcasters are Hoosiers, we suspect that there is much in their experience that is typical of broadcasters in general, as certain trends were replicated across the United States. The FCC mandates and the NAB codes were national in scope. While all broadcasters were responsible to the federally inspired definition of civic responsibility, each station was responsible to its audience. If it was not, people would not listen and it would not survive. As these stations provided entertainment, news, sports, and services, they became integral to their communities. To read the story of WTLC in Indianapolis in the 1970s and 1980s is to understand the power of the media in effecting social change and in sustaining a sense of the African-American community. While few others have had as dominant a role as WTLC, many stations were, and continue to be, important parts of their listening areas. Thus, these oral histories can be read as descriptions of the impact of governmental regulations upon a public industry, as expressions of media's impact over the course of life in the twentieth century, and, perhaps foremost, as personal narratives.

What follows are *short* excerpts from the oral histories. They are intended to give the reader a sense of these individuals, their notions of public interest, and their memories of the changes in broadcasting. In the course of this project, more than three thousand pages of oral history interviews have been transcribed from tape. These interviews are from one to five hours in length and tell a wide-ranging story of the development of broadcasting in Indiana. For the purposes of this book editing changes have been kept to a minimum. The interviewers' questions have been omitted, some passages have been moved to ease transitions between time periods, and some distracting idiosyncrasies of speech have been reduced. If words have been added to make a passage clearer, they are set off by brackets. When we have written introductory material or a transitional line, italics have been used. In making these editing changes, we have tried to maintain the integrity and intent of the original interview.

Because some of the pioneers had died prior to the beginning of this project, we have included a few interviews conducted by others. R. Dale Ogden, curator of history at the Indiana State Museum, and Darrell E. Wible, a retired professor from Ball State University, have generously allowed us to include their interviews of broadcast-

ers in the 1980s. Helen Campbell has permitted us to use an oral interview of her husband, Eldon Campbell, conducted by Westinghouse. Unfortunately, a few of these interviews had not been transcribed. The tapes were so old that some of them had deteriorated; as a result, we had only part of the interview with which to work. In addition, these narrators were asked different kinds of questions, and sometimes the concept of "the public interest" comes through in an oblique way. However, the inclusion of these interviews makes this a richer book.

"*In the Public Interest*" reveals much about the history of a profession. The interviewers'/compilers' voices appear in the commentaries; most of the text consists of the stories of the individual broadcasters. Part Two tells the story of the beginning of the industry. Part Three looks at the changes in the perception of the public interest for on-air personalities, those who came into the business during the 1940s. Part Four discusses the responsibility of broadcasters in delivering the news and establishing community identity. Part Five examines the role of the public interest in operating a station. A concluding commentary ties the excerpts together and raises some questions for future research. Our division of these oral histories into sections was somewhat arbitrary; the histories could be ordered and reordered in a multitude of ways. Our ordering is an attempt to give a sense of cohesion to diverse points of view. In no way is this to be construed as a definitive history of the broadcasting profession; rather, it is the story of Hoosier broadcasters told in their own words. As broadcasters relate their life stories with warmth, humor, and, for the most part, candor, we gain insight into their collective sense of the public interest.

"Radio Makes a Neighborhood of a Nation"

"**R**adio makes a neighborhood of a nation." This comment by a prescient Hilda Woehrmeyer at WOWO in the 1930s reminds us that before the United States was united by radio, it was a far-flung nation of communities informed by daily or weekly local newspapers. Woehrmeyer is perhaps unique among that first generation of broadcasters in her appreciation of the impact of radio. Many of these broadcasters were drawn to the profession by a love of the new and uncharted. Motivated by a desire to perform, our first group of narrators took the initial steps on a long, eventful journey in a dynamic new industry. Not professionally trained but energetic and incorrigibly innovative, the kids of the twenties and thirties brought music and words into our homes.

The Great War had thrown open the door to a world previously unknown. "How 'ya gonna keep 'em down on the farm after they've seen Paree?"[10] was a popular song that captured the prevailing sense of adventure, possibly heightened by the soldiers' contact with the larger world. After the war, the economy expanded for many, while others suffered severe hardship. Farmers who had profited during the war years now faced a society with a shrinking demand for their crops. Young men and women looked for jobs in town, where opportunities existed for employment. The short skirts and wild dancing of the flappers, the clandestine drinking in speakeasies, and the rampant speculation in the stock market were balanced by the cries for prohibition and law and order and anti-union sentiments. On the one hand, American workers feared mechanization and advances in technology that might lead to the loss of industrial jobs; on the other hand, they recognized that this same evolutionary process was expanding their world in remarkable and unintended ways. It was into this society that the early broadcasters' careers were launched.

This first group of broadcasters matured during the First World War and its aftermath. True pioneers, they were willing to try something new, a choice that would determine the direction of their lives for decades to come. Don Burton gave up his dreams of a career in engineering to start a station in his mother's living room. Some, including Tommy Longsworth and Luke Walton, got into the business through their interest in music and bands. Others, such as Bob Sievers and Les Spencer, were bitten by the radio bug early, tinkered with crystal sets, and longed to be on the air. Still others such as Eldon Campbell were captured by the business side of broadcasting. All were unaware of how radio would change people's lives.

Radio was experimental—one learned by doing. Programming was done on an ad hoc basis; the cardinal rule, followed by most stations, was to fill airtime with anything. The on-air hours were erratic because of frequency overlaps and stations' limited material. Informality characterized programming. No schools of broadcasting taught delivery technique, production, or ethics. In this wide-open and freewheeling environment, if opportunity knocked, our narrators answered.

As the frenzied times of the 1920s gave way to the austerity of the 1930s, the perceptive realized that radio had a responsibility beyond entertainment. During natural disasters, broadcasters organized relief efforts and gave on-the-spot reports, forging the public's collective recollection of such events. They mustered support, calmed fears, and rallied folks to work together, reaffirming bonds of community. Public officials from President Franklin D.

When WSBT (W South Bend Tribune) first went on the air in 1921, its call letters were WGAZ (World's Greatest Automotive Zone). A stage in the Tribune *'s building served as its first studio.* WSBT STATIONS

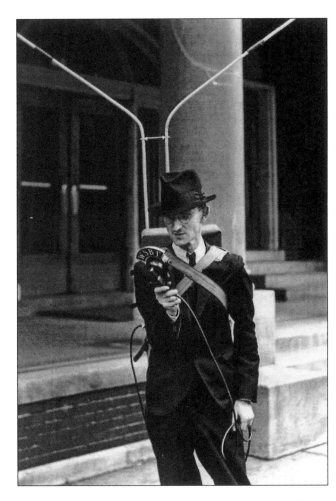

Reporters went out of their studios in search of an audience on WSBT (ca. 1930s). WSBT STATIONS

Roosevelt to Governor Paul V. McNutt recognized the potential of radio for reaching the masses and the power of the spoken word to persuade or dissuade in a personal yet public manner.

Radio went out of the studio in search of an audience. Men such as Don Burton, Luke Walton, and Les Spencer slogged through the mud in inclement weather, doing play-by-play of high school football games. Bands broadcast from local dance halls, and orchestras brought music by the great masters into living rooms. With cumbersome equipment on their backs and microphones in hand, broadcasters such as Eldon Campbell roamed city streets, providing entertainment and sampling opinions about issues of local interest. In addition, stations tapped a need for a spiritual connection by scheduling religious programs from local churches each Sunday.

Radio brought women and children into the studios in the early 1930s. Women left their kitchens to watch homemaking demonstrations and to hear fashion tips presented by personalities such as Jane Weston and Jane Day. Live programming ran the gamut from purely educational pursuits, including spelling bees for schoolchildren, to purely entertainment-related activities, such as talent shows and reading the Sunday comics. Daytime programs were not targeted toward men, who were more likely to be employed away from their homes during daylight hours. However, farm directors and county agricultural agents did broadcast daily market reports and advice on farm-related matters in the early morning and during the noon meal.

The seven narrators in this section are representative of many of the pioneers of broadcasting. As they speak of the creativity of the early days, they infuse their words with excitement. Public interest was not uppermost in their minds, but in exercising their profession, they exhibited a sense of individual responsibility to their listeners. Their concept of the public interest, indeed, evolved with their personal growth and the maturation of the industry toward a more institutionalized ethos. Regardless, these early broadcasters shepherded radio through its infancy with a real sense of style.

Howard D. "Tommy" Longsworth
(ca. 1938)

Tommy Longsworth

(1909–)

Howard D. Longsworth, almost universally known by the nickname "Tommy," was a spry eighty-four year old with a lively wit and a wry sense of humor when he was interviewed at his home in Fort Wayne in March 1994. He had debuted on WOWO fifty-eight years before, while still in high school. His quartet had won the first prize in a competition, which was the opportunity to perform on the air. Within two years he was a regular performer at the station, playing on such programs as Hoosier Hop, *which was broadcast on seventeen stations. For four years during the Great Depression he traveled with big bands, including those of Whitey Kaufman and Henry Lang. In 1936 Westinghouse purchased WOWO and hired Longsworth as a musician with the staff band. He became music librarian for WOWO/WGL in 1939, and four years later he went into management, moves he made because he saw the era of staff musicians drawing to a close. By 1946 he was promoted to general sales manager for WOWO, a position that he held until his retirement in 1972. A lifelong broadcaster, Longsworth felt that radio had "created a whole new life for everybody that was associated with it."*

I was born on a farm in Ridge Township, Van Wert County, Ohio. My daddy was a farmer. One year he had a whole bunch of hogs, and they got cholera. It killed them all, and this put him out of business. Back then, you depended on either grain or meats for your living or your sales. He just couldn't cut this; so he got a job with the railroad. He became an auditor with the railroad, and he was transferred from this little town, Ohio City, Ohio, to Fort Wayne.

And that is how I came to Fort Wayne. In fact, my parents moved to Fort Wayne a year before I did. I stayed in Ohio City and went to school, and I stayed with a doctor there, Dr. Jacob Wiggers. He was a graduate of Ohio State. He came from Holland, Michigan, however; he was a Dutchman. He and his wife were wonderful people, and I stayed with them. I fixed the fires and helped cook and did the housework and drove his cars for him and [did] a lot of his office work. I did the things that you had to do. I had to go downtown every morning and build a fire because they had no electric heat or gas heat there. It was all coal stoves or wood stoves. That is how you got your heat back then.

There were only two or three stations that you listened to back at that time, like from St. Louis and Detroit and New York . . . Los Angeles, and New Orleans, and the station out in Missouri—Kansas City—that used to broadcast from a prison out there. Harry Snodgrass was his name, and he was a wonderful piano player, but he had done something in his life that got him incarcerated. They broadcast him regularly. That was one of the things we listened to, a man playing a piano from a prison in Missouri. We didn't have a radio. We had about three or four people in this little town that had superheterodyne radios that you could pick up anything with.

The people that had enough money in town were, of course, the first ones that bought them. My family did not happen to be classified with them. When we wanted to hear something, we went to their house or got invited or invited ourselves in for some reason or another. One fellow was a grain dealer there, and he bought this set because he wanted to get the price of grain, which they gave over the radio from Chicago at that time. He was ahead of everybody else. He would get the grain price, and I don't know how much money he made knowing the price ahead of everybody else, but I'm sure it must have been pretty profitable for him.

Finally, more people got sets . . . back in my home the first radio we had, had earphones with it. It didn't have any speaker. We would put the earphones in a bowl so that two or three people could listen to the thing at one time. . . . They had a set in the drugstore, and we used to go down there and listen to whatever came over the air anytime this guy would let us in and didn't get tired of us hopping around and breaking up his showcases and stuff. That is where I was first introduced to the old Edison cylinder phonograph, too. They had one of those, and they sold these cylinders of the old artists, and I think that probably there were more phonographs in the city than radios. But I'm sure that wasn't a very profitable business, either, because I think we wore his machine out [laughs].

There wasn't a whole lot of educational information. It was a matter of slip-bang, you know. "This is what we'll put on," and I'm sure that they didn't know until about an half hour before it came on the air what they were going to put on. Things were not planned. This is how it all came about. It was just through trial and error that these things happened. We really didn't have any other entertainment. This was so new; we would put up with anything, even if it was only crickets chirping—anything.

I graduated from high school, and I went to work for Perfection Biscuit Company. I worked there for a short time, and I decided that was not for me. I worked sixty hours a week from five o'clock at night until five o'clock in the morning—Monday through Friday—which was sixty hours and got $12.50 a week. I figured that I wasn't just too interested in making that a career. I made the ingredients for the sugar wafers. They used mixes, and I spilled a couple of vats full of the inside stuff they used in these things. The foreman wasn't too happy with me anyhow. I just decided that wasn't for me. I finally got in with a bunch of people that were just going around different places and playing for entertainment. No pay involved or anything else. Finally wound into where I got involved in radio.

Well, it [WOWO in Fort Wayne] was on the second floor above the Main Auto Supply Company. So, you had these little narrow stairs that you had to go up, and every time you did—according to what kind of an instrument you were carrying—you would generally bang it on the wall, because there wasn't any light going up there. You finally got up to the end of this, and then you came into a hall. At the end of one hall was what they called Studio A and the other end of the hall was Studio B.

I played with one band called Earl Gardner, and he had the nickname of the "band with a million friends." He played for all the universities in the area from the University of Michigan to the University of Illinois—out of Fort Wayne. Purdue, Indiana, you name it. We hit all the circuits from . . . I don't know whether there's anybody old enough to remember those days or not, but it was a great circuit that we had. Played for a lot of fraternities and sororities.

At times, if things got slow, I would come back, and I would have to look for work someplace else, because you couldn't support yourself. This is back in the pre-depression days when things were bad. That's the reason I started to get involved with the radio station, because the one band, Earl Gardner especially, played for commercials. The first commercials ever aired for Alka-Seltzer were broadcast over WOWO.

The Kroger Country Club . . . consisted of Fred Tangeman, Maury Cross who became a great big band leader later on, Dick Galbreath, who played on the staff band eventually (he was a great photographer), and myself. And, we had a program; I think it was three times a week in the morning. It was the first program that Kroger ever put on. We had a vocalist by the name of Mary Berghoff. She was sort of a socialite in Fort Wayne. She came from the Berghoff Brewery people. She married John Berghoff who was the president of Berghoff Brewery. They started the Haufbrau Brewery when they sold their interest in the Berghoff Brewery. Mary was a wonderful person, a good

In the 1920s listening to radio was a collective experience in which people shared earphones.   TOMMY LONGSWORTH

*In the 1930s radio stations broadcast remotes from a variety of places, including meetings
and dance halls. Eldon Campbell directed the popular "Phil (or Fill) Spitoonly Dinner Ensemble"
with Tommy Longsworth as vocalist, Mel Ott on the trumpet, Guy Fitzsimmons on the saxophone,
and Bob Pumsky on the drums.*   TOMMY LONGSWORTH

singer, and that was really the first, or one of the first, commercials that we ever played on the station, where we actually were guaranteed that we would be paid "X" amount of money for playing and didn't have to worry about anything else and actually had a contract for it.

One thing I do remember that was funny; we were putting on a program for something—I can't remember what it was for. They had a window in this studio, and they would open up the window because it was so hot in there you couldn't stand it. When they would open up the window, there was a guy down there with an old automobile. He would start it up, and it would make all kinds of racket. So this went over the air, too. We would have to go over there real quick and slam the window down so it wouldn't drown us out. It was mostly hit and skip.

You just thought of it as you went along. It wasn't planned at all. I was too dumb to think of that. You know, we just didn't worry about it. Even if we had to get in there and yell, when we got on, we'd do something. Oh, I whistled, barked like a dog. Wayne Dog Food, which was Wayne Feed, had a program where Earl Gardner's band, again, played for them. Back in that time, they didn't have any sound effects like they have now or had later. At the opening of the program, why, I barked like a dog, and I got paid more for barking like a dog than I did for playing on the program, which I always thought was the highlight of my career.

Well, it was just mostly entertainment at that time, and then they finally came around to where they had a program called *Calling All Poets*, of all things. Who in the world would want to listen to a program of poetry? But it so happened that the advertising manager, a man by the name of Oliver Capelle for Miles Laboratories, was interested in poetry, and he made himself available to read the poetry while we furnished the background music. So we sort of had that built in.

Generally, you would have a theme song. Everybody had a theme song so you could identify yourself or what group you were. You would come on with that, and then the program was on for fifteen minutes, a half hour, or whatever. And you had a script. These were planned programs. Hilda Woehrmeyer was an employee of the Auto Supply Company at that time, and she wrote the continuity for it. So, you would have a format that you filled out, and you would start out with your theme song. An announcer

would come in and identify who you were broadcasting for and probably a short tag to get you there. Then you played the first tune and then had a thirty-second or a minute commercial that they would come in and sell the product. Then you would go on and play more music. When the end of the program came, then you started your theme song again and you faded out elegantly [laughs].

Carl [Vandagrift], of course, became the general manager. He started out as a rewrite man, back in the old Zieg days.[11] A person by the name of Bob Valentine was the newsman. They hired him especially just to do the news on the stations. We only had one newsman; so you know how much news they put on (about like TV today). Carl was a rewrite man for him. Most of the rewriting was done from newspapers. They would pilfer from the newspapers, see. Then they bought the syndicated news from AP and UP and such as that, and we called them the "rippin' readers." They would rip it off of the machine and take it in and read it, you know. There was no editorializing or anything else on it. You read it just as it came over the wires. Finally, they got their rewrite guy, and that was what Carl did, although he did it out of a newspaper, but we had the other people that did that at WOWO. Then a different guy would read the news, not the one that wrote it all. But then that way, these news people would go out get the news themselves, too.

Nobody knew who you were because they couldn't see you . . . until finally you started making personal appearances. After you made personal appearances, then they, of course, would know who you were, see. Of course, that was what your livelihood was built on, the personal appearances. By appearing on the radio station, then you got a lot of personal appearances. If it hadn't been for the radio, you wouldn't have ever been exposed to that. That helped the old pocket book a little, too, you know. You could get a pretty price. But there again they were thinking maybe you were a celebrity. But, it was a great way for us to make additional money.

[Zieg] was sort of a funny guy. If he didn't like what he heard on the air, it didn't go on again—one of those things. He didn't like tenor singers, for instance. It didn't make any difference if you were a Caruso or what you were. He didn't like tenor singers, so you didn't go on the air. Just other things like that . . . he was a forward-thinking person. He had to be to do the things he did with the help

Bob Shreve conversed with a cow in 1938 as Uncle (or Cousin) Elmer on the Hoosier Hop. *He also played opposite Shirley Bowersocks on the popular comedy program* Sari and Elmer, *broadcast by WOWO.*   TOMMY LONGSWORTH

of other people nudging him along, I think. I don't know why he sold out as soon as he did. He probably could have made a fortune had he contained the businesses together.[12] But, finally, he sold the Main Auto Supply business.

During the Great Depression, Longsworth traveled with big bands. There wasn't enough going on at the radio station to keep me there. You had a chance to make more money and, by doing that too, you gained experience. And that was a very popular thing in 1932. The "big band era" was like radio coming in. It was something new where people were exposed to you or you were exposed to people, and it was a way of making money first. That was the main reason. You had to make a living, you know. You went wherever you could make the most money.

We were doing the remotes there and doing the remotes in Savannah. And we did them in Cleveland. When I was with the band in Saratoga Springs, why we did remotes from there even. That was over the Schenectady station. Then I think the remotes sort of dribbled out a little later after that.

Originally, the first *Hoosier Hop* was on, and it was just the studio show. It was on in the 1920s; it started in 1929, I believe, [and went] on up through about 1935, or somewhere around there. What happened to it, I just can't remember now. It faded out like it did, and then when Westinghouse bought the stations, they renovated this because they had about sixteen country-western people that they were using for programming on WOWO. They decided to make it into one big show and make a feature out of it. That's the way the *Hoosier Hop* was renovated again. Then it went network, and we broadcast it quite a long time from the studios at WOWO until they hired the auditorium, and Harry Smythe promoted it. It became a community-involved thing where we had all the people from all the area to come and pay to get in the show. So it was a commercial venture for Harry, see, and the station, too. The station got a certain amount of the profit, and he had to pay all of the talent, of course.

They didn't have any soap operas until Westinghouse bought the stations, and then Westinghouse did produce *Friendly Neighbors.* It was a program for Alka-Seltzer who bought the series, and it was running in like seventy or eighty markets. We produced it here. They shipped it out to the other stations then. That was one of the first soap operas, I think. Proctor and Gamble used to have a lot of soap operas. . . . There were soap operas going before *Friendly Neighbors.* That was not the first soap opera. Let's just say, *The Days of Our Lives* and things like that were on. Well, it's like television today. They had a whole afternoon full. One would follow the other, and big companies, like Proctor and Gamble or soap companies, would come along, and they could buy them on what they called a contingency rate. If you bought two programs together, you got a better rate than if you bought one here and bought the other one there. It was cheaper for them to have two programs that they sponsored rather than one here and one there.

There was a program called *Sari and Elmer.* Shirley Bowersocks and Bob Shreve . . . and this was a fifteen-minute program. It was a great program. It was sort of like a *Fibber McGee and Molly* program. And it was very popular. Sponsored by the Bluffton Grocery Company for years. Then these things sort of died out, you know. I mean they lost their popularity. Again, the cycles that you go on. So, it was a good thing for our station for a while there. And then, a few other people tried to be funny at times on different programs, you know, by doing different things and, of course, you couldn't be seen. So it all had to be—people had to imagine what you were doing. So you tried to create funny situations.

It was established what the—they use the word "criteria" so much now, I hate to use it, but I mean—what a programmed radio station would be like and what the rules and regulations were according to what the FCC would permit you to do and things like that . . . all in good common decency. Well, at first, in the old days, I don't think anybody ever knew it existed, because it really didn't exist. It was even under a different name. At the time when Westinghouse bought the station, it was a big factor. They were great sticklers for protocol. They just never deviated from what the rules and regulations of FCC were. You had to have, for instance, the politicians that would come along and if you gave "X" amount of time to one guy, why you damn well better be sure to do it for the other guy. All kinds of public service programs—the FCC required that you do so much public service. You really did public service to the best of your ability. The FCC was a great guidance. Now, with the commercialism as it is now, it infringes on some of their rules, I'm sure. It was a good thing for radio, because it kept it in line.

Westinghouse was really involved in community service. They had all kinds of things going for them. Again, the FCC required you supposedly to do so much, but they had the capabilities of doing it and the money to do it with. They had a lot of town meeting business and such. They would go out into the communities—not only just in Fort Wayne, but also all the territory that they served—and they would have town meetings out there. If there was some kind of a thing that was bothering a community, why they'd take our facilities out there and expose it to more people. You could only get so many people in the [town] hall, you know. And by broadcasting that, well, they thought they'd get it to the minds of a lot of people. I'm sure that they helped build a lot of community buildings and everything else back in those days.

Many features that we put on were not necessarily too commercial, but we figured they had to be on because we wanted to serve the community. And people, such as Jay Gould and Jane Weston,[13] those type of people were well-educated. Jay Gould had three degrees from three different universities; he was no slouch.[14] Although people never knew that and some of them thought he was a pile of wind, like they do a lot of people, but Jay was a great philosopher. He got through to the communities, and I'm sure that they followed a great many ideas that he had. I'm sure they have changed today, because people are better educated today. You don't have to listen to many people; your university graduates, your farmers are smart. They don't need a lot of the information that they had to have back in those days.

Community interest—we tried to make the communities better to live in. That followed through with a lot of things that we did that ordinarily most stations wouldn't have done because they didn't either have the personality to do it or didn't have the money to go through with the things or couldn't spare the commercial time to do it. So that's about the best way that I can explain that.

We had beer, but we never would sell it near a religious program. We would never sell beer—now this is early—never sell beer until after six o'clock at night, figuring, you know, the kids—seven o'clock, I guess it was. So if they would buy the news or sports or whatever we had at that time, but we never allowed spot announcements for a long time for beer. It's sort of silly to think of it now, why, because, exposure is exposure, and the kids who like

television, listen any time. But the management at that time didn't want to create an unfavorable impression for the kids. They didn't want them to drink beer, you know. [In later years] Westinghouse was the first group to throw cigarette announcements out. Man, I mean, that broke my heart, in that I knew it was good that we threw them off, but we had thousands and thousands of dollars that we got as revenue, and I had to make that up someplace else, see. So, it was a tough decision, but a good one.

I think Eldon [Campbell] had a lot to do with making WOWO what it was in those days. We had a lot of great managers. Steve [J.B.] Conley was a great business manager. He got us off on the business part more than anything else. A guy by the name of W. C. Swartley was a great educator. He became a vice president of Westinghouse, and he was transferred to Boston and became a vice president of the Boston TV and Radio Division. We had Franklin Tooke who was also a very smart chap when he started. Carl Vandagrift was a broadcaster from A to Z.

Eldon came here from a little station in Illinois. He graduated from the University of Illinois and came over here from working at the station while he went to school there. When he started, he had a patch on the seat of his pants. He presumably was a poor boy, you know. You thought he was poor because he had a father that, like so many fathers back in those days, didn't give his boy too much money. He paid for his boy to go through college maybe, but with a little help from Eldon working at the radio station. When he died—Eldon's mother was dead and had been dead for quite some time—when he died, why he had a little more money than what anybody thought. So, it sort of helped Eldon along a little bit. He was able to get a couple of new suits.

Eldon Campbell met his wife, who was Helen Jones from Garrett, Indiana. Helen started singing with us—how he ever run onto her, I don't know. She auditioned, and she was great. She was a great singer, as good as any singer in any of the bands today, or of the big bands at that time, or any pop singer that you'd have now. So, we had a jewel there, and she sang always with the Melody Spinners or with the Swing Quartet, all this type of music she sang. And Eldon Campbell, who was at that time program manager got a liking for Helen. Helen also liked another guy in one of the other organizations, and she didn't know who she liked the best. But it turned out that Eldon won

Helen Jones (far right), a young singer, had stars in her eyes as she stood next to her future husband Eldon Campbell in the studios of WOWO. Taken on the day they first met, this photo shows the cast of Hoosier Hop. *Tommy Longsworth is playing the bass.*

As part of a promotion, Tommy Longsworth, sales chief, and Hilda Woehrmeyer, promotion manager, counted dimes sent to the station to purchase a "weather wheel." In 1955 WOWO received ninety thousand pieces of mail.

out. Eldon married Helen. That's how Eldon got his wife, see. But a funny thing, after Eldon became involved in New York City, they moved to White Plains, New York. He commuted back and forth from New York City. I was up there one time on a sales trip, and Eldon was out of town. So I called Helen and knowing her like I did (she was just like a sister of mine) I said, "Come on in to town, and I'll take you to dinner. We'll go to the Old Astor Hotel where Sammy Kaye is playing." So we went up there, and I knew a couple of guys in the band. I talked those guys into talking the director into letting her sing a couple of songs, and she brought the house down. Now, here's a little country girl from Indiana who went to New York City and was on the stage and could have, if she had wanted to, probably become a big shot in the entertainment field. But that's the way that she started. She started with us at WOWO.

There were many, many, many people that became very famous after they left here, that started on WOWO. A funny thing about Chris Schenkel.[15] When I was playing on the station, he used to come up and he played guitar, see, and he tried to get a spot on WOWO. They wouldn't hire him. They told him that he should go to some other station and get more experience, see. Of course, this guy could buy and sell them now. That was always sort of funny to me. He went to work for Les Spencer down in Richmond, Indiana, and, of course, Chris became a very famous sports announcer, but a lot of things like that.

I think I was a very fortunate person. Everything just seemed to work well for me. I know so many musicians that had a bad time. Everything just seemed to correlate, you know. I wasn't really involved in any of the real bad times that the musicians had. And a lot of them had a lot of bad times, as the other populace did, too, with their jobs. They were not making any money or not even having a job,

you know. So everything looked—the best thing that happened to me, I guess, was when I got back in Fort Wayne that Westinghouse did buy these stations. I'm sure it never would have turned into the thing it did if Mr. Zieg had continued to operate them. It would have just been a local organization. But by it being this big chain of radio stations that Westinghouse owned, it gave all of us a great opportunity. And then by becoming a musician, I was exposed to these people that ran the station. They asked me if I didn't want a chance to go from music into the commercial department. I thought the "big band era" was coming to an end; so I thought maybe this might be the smart thing to do.

We didn't have any salesladies [in the commercial department]. Now, we had a sales promotion woman, Hilda Woehrmeyer, who was great, but she'd been there forever, too, and she knew exactly what was going on all the time. She had a great many ideas and all. No, I must admit that I think it was wrong, but it just wasn't a principle that they hire a woman. Would you believe that at one time in the big city we went to a private club that was a old boys' club, you know, and the sales promotion lady, who was Hilda, had to ride up on a different elevator than we did even?

Ours was a challenging thing where you got to do so many different things. It just never got boring. It was always a delight to go to work. The people that you worked with and the product that you had . . . it was a delight to go to work. So, I always enjoyed myself. I never, never hated to go to work or anything. Sure, I was ready for a vacation when it came, but when the time came for me to retire, I was a very sad person. I knew it was time, and I just couldn't keep up with the traveling that I had to do and everything else at that time. So that's the way I exited from broadcasting.

*Donald A. Burton in press box
(ca. 1930)* MARY LOU W. HOLLAND

Don Burton

(1906–1990)

Darrell E. Wible, former professor at Ball State University, interviewed Donald A. Burton in his office at WLBC in Muncie, Indiana, on 5 August 1986, at the request of the Indiana Broadcasters Association. Burton founded WLBC in his parents' living room in 1926, initially operating the station alone and without much capital. Within just four years WLBC boasted three employees, two studios, its own transmitter, and a business office downtown. Known for his play-by-play, Burton could be found along the sidelines at sports events even in the worst weather. Innovation, tenacity, and long days eventually paid off; WLBC became a Muncie mainstay in broadcasting. With WLBC prospering throughout the 1940s, Burton founded a television station, Channel 49, in May 1953. Battling the vagaries of technology in an infant industry, he succeeded in keeping that station afloat for more than ten years, selling it in 1972 to the Ball State University Foundation. He kept the radio station until 1986 when he retired. According to the Muncie Evening Press *(13 November 1986), Burton said, "We have always tried to be the best small-market station in the country."*

I had a ham station, and I was acquainted with another ham in Logansport who had applied to the Department of Commerce and got a broadcasting license. He was making the fabulous sum of one hundred dollars a week with the operation of that little station. And he convinced me that I should apply, which I did. But at about that same time there was a litigation taking place, which I believe ended up in the Supreme Court. It prevented the Department of Commerce from issuing licenses for a very long period. And I had nearly forgotten about this application for a broadcast license. One day in the mail, I received communication from Herbert Hoover, who later became president of the United States but then was secretary of commerce. In it was a license for radio station WLBC, and that's how it began.

I was pretty much set for a music career, believe it or not. I played several musical instruments. In fact, was signed to go on a Chatauqua tour in Canada when I got the license for this radio station. My real ambition was to be an electrical engineer, and I had made preliminary arrangements to enroll at Purdue University. But, of course, that never came about when I got this license. That's another thing my parents thought I made a big mistake about—not going to college. But I had to make a choice. I couldn't do both.

I lived with my parents at 2224 South Jefferson. That's the next to the last house between 15th and 16th Street on the east side of the street. And my dad had built me a shack on the back of the lot where I had installed my wireless station, and that's where WLBC began. My

Many early broadcasts occurred in private residences. WLBC first broadcast in 1926 from the living room of Don Burton's mother.

Burton's car advertised the Muncie Broadcasting Company as a small station that gets results.

parents were very lenient with me, and the parlor of our home became the studio for whatever live programs we originated. On Sunday afternoons, we usually had a big crowd there with many kinds of entertainers for a three-hour program, and my poor mother had to clean house every Sunday after that was over. That's how it started. It was quite a while that [my family] didn't even have a radio.

[We operated] only about thirty minutes a day. Monday through Friday. Nothing on Saturday. And a three-hour Sunday afternoon program which was sponsored by the Chamber of Commerce. The weekday broadcasts consisted of market reports, butter and egg markets, the livestock reports, and what other market information we could glean. [I got this information] from principally two sources: the Meadow Gold Company and from the Muncie Stockyards. I made daily trips to those locations and gathered the information for the broadcasts.

We had a few [church programs] originate from the parlor. We were unable to lease telephone line circuits for broadcast loops in the early days, so another man and I strung wire for about six blocks from where I lived to 12th and Walnut, where the Walnut Street Baptist Church was then located. We did the Sunday morning church services until someone tore our wires down.

My first engineer was a man by the name of Roy Smith, who still resides in Muncie, and was the communications officer for the Muncie Police Department for many years. And then I scrambled around and, believe it or not, I had a lot of applicants. I hired a man by the name of Herschel Miller to sell advertising. That was the staff for many months.

I think the Cooper Commission Company at the Muncie Stockyards was one of the earliest [sponsors]. We had the Campbell Ice Cream [which] was an early sponsor, but I can't remember any more. None of the companies are still in operation.

I think that by 1930, I believe by that time we were located on the mezzanine floor of the Delaware Hotel. We had two studios, our transmitter and control room, and a very small office there. And we were there for three or four years. Later, we moved to a temporary site on the west side of Walnut Street, on the second floor, between Adams and Jackson Street. [There we] began building studios in what then was called the Anthony Building. It's the second floor above where Pazols Jewelry Store is now

located at Jackson and Walnut. In about 1933 we moved into those quarters and stayed there until we moved out here, where we are now located, in January of 1942.

Chris Schenkel, of course, was here in the 1930s while we were still downtown. And a man whose name was Mcdlin, but who became a figure at Channel 6 using the name of Harry Martin, was a broadcaster here for several years. Don Hancock, later with network in New York, and another one whose name doesn't come to mind at the moment.

In the early days, in the 1930s, we signed on with International News. We couldn't afford to have the teleprinters in our studios. In those days the Indiana Railway Company operated what were called interurbans, electric railways between many points in Indiana, [with] frequent cars between Muncie and Indianapolis. I made a deal with the motorman of one of those cars to pick up copies of the teleprinter news in Indianapolis and bring it to Muncie. We picked it up at the interurban station, and that is how we got our early news on the station. Prior to that, at one time, we did have a remote in the offices of the *Muncie Press*, and did a fifteen-minute news broadcast from there once a day. Later, we put our teleprinters in the office. [By] 1935 we had wire service at our station and still with International News.

[During the Great Depression, radio was] very difficult. Advertising sales were about nil, and we traded lots of things: gasoline for the car, groceries for food, for rent, for living quarters. Almost anything that you could imagine would be tradable; we traded in lieu of cash because there was very little cash circulating in those days. I think my salary was eight dollars a week for several years. But the dollar certainly bought a lot more than it does now.

My workday usually began with arising at 4:30, eating a hurried breakfast, and going to the station, arriving about 5:15. And I was the announcer and transmitter operator, then until about 10:30 or 11:00 when I got relief. And then did desk work. Quite often I departed in the middle of the afternoon for an out-of-town basketball game, sometimes as far away as Hammond, Indiana, Akron, Ohio, Evansville, always driving back that night and opening up the station the next morning and repeating the day's work. I did that for a great many years.

Well, as I mentioned we did not have authority from the telephone company to lease their circuits. That involved the paying of a royalty for a patent license to use the circuits that the AT&T had patented for transmitter operation. The telephone company was charging five hundred dollars for that patent, and you couldn't lease wires unless you had that license. We finally scraped together the money and got the license. But in the early days we would install a business telephone at the arena site, and I sent a man to the game. Before the game he would pass the lineups of both teams to me, and I would write them down. When the game started he would tell me who got the tip-off. And then if a shot was attempted [he would tell me] who attempted the shot and whether or not it was made. I would ad lib in between those bursts of information making a phantom description of the ball being passed about the floor from one player to another. In the early days, for several years, all of our basketball games were broadcast in that manner.

One of the most interesting things we did at a later time was in the 1930s. We had a very interesting [high school] game scheduled between the [Muncie] Bearcats and the Marion Giants. Something had happened in Marion between the local radio station and the school board which had the effect of prohibiting any broadcasts from Marion. So I sent two court reporters from Muncie to Marion along with a man who could tell them who had the ball and who made the shot and whether it was hit or missed. And in the first half of the game, one of the court reporters made shorthand notes and went to the Western Union and telegraphed those first half reports to Muncie where we had installed a telegraph set in our studio. And when the first half was done I had a record with crowd noise on it. I played the crowd noise and described the first half of the game. And then when the second half was received, after a suitable interval for halftime, we described the second half. As a side issue, the Bearcats in those days always visited a local restaurant, called the Polly Parrot, after they came back from a game. And the counter man was a Bearcat fan and their radio set was down in the kitchen. And he was dashing back and forth between the counter and the kitchen to keep up on the scores. And late in the second half he returned from downstairs hearing the last minute of the game and came upstairs. And there was the whole Bearcat team seated around the counter. He couldn't understand how they got from Marion to Muncie so quickly.

We investigated FM in the 1940s when it occupied a different frequency band than it now does. We did file an application for the older frequencies. But before that could be considered by the FCC, there was another long delay due to litigation. And finally, new frequencies were assigned. We were issued a license for our present frequency, 104.1. [We then] built the station and put it on the air in the fall of 1947.

It was [a big decision]. We began to try to separately program that station. And after about a year and a half, without success in the way of advertising sales, we switched it to a simulcast. Operated as a simulcast station until about 1958 or 1959 when we installed the first automation system, and began to try to separately program it with what I call "elevator music," and had a very minimal success in selling advertising. And it wasn't until the 1960s, when we put hard rock on the air, that we began to have some advertising success with the FM station. During that time we did increase its power to the maximum power, which was one of the best guesses I ever made.

We had a UHF [television] station on Channel 49, and began operating in May. I believe it was May 8, 1953. Continued until 1972 when the station was sold to Ball State University. During those years it was a terrible struggle because the market was a little too small for a commercial TV station. But we did manage to keep our head above water all those years. And the times I spent on many roof tops in Muncie, moving antennas around, trying to find what we called the "hot spot," in order to get a signal that people could watch. Of course, one of the early problems was the converter that was in most receiving sets. It had to do a double converting job. And as the vacuum tube aged, its efficiency lessened. After a while it would not convert the UHF frequency, although it worked fine at VHF. Many of the viewers wouldn't spend the money to have their set looked after to continue to receive the UHF [signal], so we faced a diminishing audience all of the time. The advent of cable has overcome that problem, of course.

The industry certainly has made tremendous progress. You only have to walk by the magnificent headquarters for the National Association of Broadcasters in Washington [D.C.], or to visit the offices of the Federal Communications Commission, one of whose principal occupations is dealing with, and enforcing regulations for the broadcast

Burton crouched along the sideline of a high school football game as he broadcast play-by-play.

Don Burton worked in broadcasting for sixty years. Here he is shown at station WLBC in 1986 shortly before its sale to Jim Davis and DRMS Communications. MUNCIE EVENING FRESS

industry, to see how it has grown. I think there's something close to nine thousand stations on the air in the United States now. And you can hardly go through a village or a hamlet anywhere, at least in this part of the world, without seeing a transmitting antenna. Each one [of these stations is] doing their very best to try to serve the public, to bring the issues of the day to the public, to try to make the public better understand what they are. Many times, [they are] editorializing or having panel discussions, trying to throw light on many sides of the issues. I think broadcasting has contributed a great deal in that area. Most certainly, on-the-spot news has probably been the greatest development of AM, FM, and TV news. We have seen that grow. Our station was one of the very first stations in the United States to have a news service.

I feel better about [the FCC] now under their present leadership than I did a few years back, when they were more antibusiness than they are now. But in the early days the broadcast field was very chaotic under the operation of the Department of Commerce. The Federal Radio Commission was created to license stations. And then later, the newer set of laws were passed, which created the Federal Communications Commission. Of course, there are hundreds and hundreds of laws and regulations. There are several volumes up there on the book shelf which contain the rules and regulations. And hardly a day goes by that we don't have some occasion to delve into those. I spent some time yesterday with our chief engineer going over some regulations pertaining to remote broadcasts. Nowadays, many of our remotes are done by shortwave. And there have been some changes in those regulations. He and I were getting ourselves up-to-date on that yesterday.

I think I have enjoyed seeing the station grow and mature, and being able to improve our programs, to make sure that we had good equipment, that we had a good sound on the air. I've always been proud of that, and that we've made a profit over most of these years. Those are the things that I've been proud of accomplishing.

Lester Graham Spencer
(ca. 1929) RUTH SPENCER

Les Spencer

(1911–1997)

Lester Graham Spencer's interview took place in a series of short sessions over a period of two days in February 1995 at his sunny home in Florida. Although he had suffered a stroke prior to the interview, his comments suggest a sense of his distinguished career in broadcasting. Spencer started out in 1929, at the age of eighteen, as a part-time announcer in Columbus, Ohio. Later that year he moved to WOWO in Fort Wayne, where he remained until 1936. After forsaking Indiana to broadcast in Ohio for eighteen years, he returned to Richmond, Indiana, in 1952, as manager of WKBV. He organized the Central Broadcasting Company, and within a few years had acquired stations in Celina and Chillicothe, Ohio, Adrian, Michigan, and Beaumont, Texas, as well as Marion and Richmond, Indiana. Even after he became president of the company, Spencer continued to do play-by-play sportscasting of high school football, basketball, and baseball as a sideline. An original supporter of the Indiana Broadcasters Association (IBA), he served as its president in 1957. When he retired in 1978, Spencer had been president of the Central Broadcasting Company for twenty-six years.

I was fascinated by what went on in radio . . . especially the on-the-scene news, the live, active programming. I was a good listener. I listened to a lot of radio, and I was a fan of radio—not just one radio station or one piece of talent, but all of it. There were very, very few who didn't have radio in their house.

[My first radio experience was in] Columbus, Ohio. It was WCAH. Those were the call letters then—WCAH. It was my first day, really afternoon, at work so I got there in plenty of time. The boss handed me a stack of records. He didn't explain any of them or say why—just a stack. He said, "All you have to do is go down through the stack. I've got it all arranged the way I want it." We used an old Brunswick Panatrope to play them on. (It was just a fancy record player. It was all in a big cabinet that they didn't need—a rich, elaborate cabinet.) Well, there was one record I was not familiar with at all, because I wasn't an operatic fan and I didn't know anything about opera. But the boss came rushing into the studio because I had said, "Now we have excerpts from the opera *Aida* by—." I forget the author's name. Well, to me A-i-d-a is "ada." I called it "ada." Well, seconds after I said, "Ada," here comes the boss flying through the door. He was upset and said, "Don't you know how to pronounce those words? If you don't know how, you ought to find out."

[In those days] I used a two-button carbon mike. It uses carbon, and every so often you'd have to hit it on the back to keep it working. [Later], Jenkins & Adair put out microphones—

condenser mike they called it. That was the first switch from the first two-button carbon mike. It was a big square—looked like a big square dice—a lot bigger, but squared off like that. Then Jenkins & Adair put together one, and RCA put together one. Eventually, over a period of time, RCA locked the other people out. They used condenser mikes; then they got to using velocity microphones. Ribbon velocity. It looks almost like a camera would today.

[Radio was] definitely an entertainment mode. The big influence was provided by long variety hours, dramatic hours—like one of the last ones to make it was the *Lux Radio Theater.* You may remember that. It was not a soap opera. I just remember it was called *Lux Radio Theater.* DeMille directed it; a lot of people don't realize that Cecil B. DeMille did things like that.

We broadcast from hotels, dance halls, that sort of thing. In our case, we had these small-size bands that played locally. Then, there were downtown organizations that really had big bands. We had Guy Lombardo in. We had Rudy Vallee for the first concert he ever had. It was there at Valleydale at Columbus, Ohio. Rudy Vallee became a sensation. He was always very popular, so we knew we had something in Vallee. Incidentally, the fans were parked outside along the driveway because there wasn't any more parking. It was an overwhelming success.

Spencer moved from WCAH-Ohio to WOWO in 1929. I had written out three or four letters saying that I would like to have a job. And I got one at Fort Wayne. Fred Zieg was our president; he was a little different [laughs]. He was also the head of Main Auto Supply. Main Auto Supply was on the ground floor, and the broadcasting division was up on the second floor, because the building was that kind of a building. So, you could go up the steps, which were not enclosed at all, and that was our broadcasting division. In fact, when they started into the radio business, it was kind of a good thing for the Main Auto Supply. [Fred Zieg] actually hired a chief engineer, Art Rekart, to keep the station operating and to keep it up to date on equipment. But they had no idea of really going into it as a business until a couple of farmers walked from their car up to the station. One farmer had an overage on green beans and didn't think he was going to get rid of them. He was trying to figure how cheap he could get rid of them. So, he took them up there and asked Fred what

could be done about it. The two together cooked up this plan of using radio [for advertising].

I thought WOWO was very friendly. We had regular social affairs. It became a habit at one time, for instance, to get together with the men playing cards—poker or some card game. While the men did that, their wives and the women got together like the men did. Instead of playing cards, they'd go to a show. In other words, they'd decide, "Let's go to the Emboyd Theater and see so-and-so." They'd decide that, and then everybody was set. The men would go to one party, and the women could go to another. That lasted quite awhile. I was kind of surprised—all men getting together and all women getting together—and these were people who saw each other all the time anyhow. It was kind of surprising. Of course, the men liked it because they were all poker players [laughs].

As competition grew, WOWO was one of the old, old-time stations. It had some definite rules. You did it this way. They used the term "the WOWO way." One thing that I never did get over—WOWO had the ability to get people to like it. It's hard to explain.

From WOWO, Spencer left Indiana and went to WHIO-Ohio in Dayton for eighteen years. One of Spencer's favorite stories of his experience in radio is about the flood of 1937. The Ohio River runs by Portsmouth, and flooded everything. The whole town was underwater. So, I went to my boss and told him that a couple of us would like to go down and cover it as a news story. Well, he didn't want to do it. He said, "You guys will drown down there, and I don't want you to do that." Well, he changed his mind, because [the river] didn't show any signs of going down or changing, and we already had other stations taking [broadcast] feeds from us. We had been prompt enough and smart enough to get in on it. They were taking it from us and . . . rebroadcasting it. We got into boats. Some of the local people were willing to let us use their boats to haul the equipment around. . . . In an emergency if we were out somewhere and didn't have a mike, we would use the telephone to get the story across. . . . This was news—our idea of on-the-spot, live news—which it was. There were four of us—two crews of two each. This included announcing, running the control panel, changing anything that had to be changed.

World War II radio was really one of the first major projects that kept radio on the alert all the time, twenty-four

The two-button carbon microphone was used in most radio stations in the 1920s. Sometimes Les Spencer had to hit it on the back to keep it working.

WOWO staff

hours a day, day after day. During the world war, radio grew up. Actually, it *expanded* and grew up during the war. As far as what world war radio did, I think they did fairly well at covering the news and covering the war. I think they learned more things. In the first place, I think they had more material to work with. They had more manpower. One of the troubles with news for years had been manpower. Starting back when they could depend upon correspondence reporters and moving on up, reluctantly the top brass arranged to provide more manpower, more announcers, and more script readers. Ed Murrow. Edward R. Murrow was one . . . and Eric Severeid was one of the early ones over there.

I'll tell you where I was when Pearl Harbor was bombed. I was in a hospital room, and my wife [Ruth] had had a child. This is the way I know what day it was. I was at the hospital because she was having a baby. So, I was there, and they were not supposed to put through calls for me. Well, the phone rang anyway. They put through a call, and Ruth gave me the news. I went immediately to the station when I heard this. I tore off right away and went to the station and never got back from the station for twenty-four hours. Once you got on, you kept getting new information. The whole thing was a tremendous news story.

I did sound tracks during the war—did sound tracks for Wright Field [at Dayton, Ohio]. The air force had this branch at Wright Field and didn't have men for audio. So, they wanted to hire somebody . . . to handle the audio. Well, they asked me if I'd do it, and I said, "Sure." So, I did radio only. What happened was that the script would be all ready. All I had to do is rehearse it, time it, cut it if I had to—that kind of a thing—before it was recorded. [The scripts] ranged a wide area. One of them, I remember, was nothing but carburetors, showing how the M-1 carburetor was to fit in such and such a place—instructions for the air force. I would go from the station out to Wright Field, do what I had to do there, and then go back to work. I was lucky that my boss allowed me to do it.

I had done about all I could do at WHIO, because the manager there was going to stay until he died. They needed a manager in Richmond, Indiana . . . in 1952, and I was going to be able to buy stock in the company. (I was hired as the manager because the board members fired a guy—Jerry Albright. My real motive by then was to own and operate a station.) I had had some management posi-

tions and had some management experience. What I really wanted was to manage a station—WKBV. It was at the old Leland Hotel on Main Street. We had studios and offices in the hotel, and then later we built a building—built a separate building for the studio and offices. The hotel was one of those buildings where you have offices all around on the ground floor. It works out pretty well.

At the time I got there, the manager could buy stock. The men on the board, who invested in the company, pretty much let me be my own boss. Then I went from there. We bought acreage and built our own building. Later . . . I became president [of Central Broadcasting Corporation], and I acquired stock. For a while I concentrated on management and did just what had to be done. Decisions had to be made. Officially, we had a station manager, and he didn't have to acquire stock, but I decided that I would like to do it. When something [stock] turned up, I'd pick it up.

Actually, when we started to acquire stations, we had an idea of how much potential income we should have based on the market, market size, type of operation, and everything. We would pin it down with the markets, and we usually wouldn't buy a station that was sick. We bought stations that were making a profit. Well, we made some changes, but not too many. We planned to buy well stations. Let's see. [Central Broadcasting] had WKBV, Richmond; we had WBAT, Marion; we had WBIW, Bedford; we had Beaumont, Texas . . . Adrian, Michigan . . . Chillicothe, Ohio, and WCSM, Celina, Ohio. We were really interested in smaller markets. What we felt was that our type of operation, our method and type of operation, fit right in with the other stations we had. We went down on the number of people to about fifteen. We didn't have as much power as WOWO, and there were some things that were not paying off. We kind of wanted to weed out the things that were not making it.

I think we imposed a sense of responsibility on our stations through the public service programming of all kinds. I think we've come a long way in broadcasting programs that can be used and can be heard, and we still give the viewer or listener some latitude. I would hate to see any more restrictions or regulations put on either of them— radio or television. They need to do public affairs programming. I think they're very necessary.

Radio quit being an entertainment medium. Radio, you remember, had the big bands and the big variety shows—

When the Ohio River overflowed its banks in 1937, it caused devastating damage. Les Spencer broadcast updates on the flood from the scene.

Well known for his play-by-play, Les Spencer often called games even after he became a broadcasting executive.

Perry Como, Bing Crosby, all your list of people—but they were expensive, high-priced entertainment. Television took over those shows right away, because that was the kind of thing they could do and do well. The radio broadcast management all over began to understand that it had new competition.

Let me put it this way. [Radio has] become a personal medium. You used to think of a radio loud speaker that you set up in the living room and everybody went into the living room to listen to the radio—sit and watch the old Crosley or old radio. Now radio is primarily a personal medium, as I said—car radio, the bedroom radio, clock radio.

Radio helped neighbors to communicate; it increased the power of communication; it began to be an exchange of ideas and helped expand markets. I enjoyed every day. Every day was different. That's one reason I liked it.

Marthabel Geisler (1964)
COURTESY OF INDIANA STATE MUSEUM/PHOTO BY RAY CONOLLY

Marthabel Geisler

(1911–)

Marthabel Geisler saw many changes in the broadcasting industry. From her first position, as secretary to Frank Sharp at WFBM in 1930 to her last, as administrative assistant to the general manager at WRTV in the 1970s, Geisler watched Indiana's radio and television industry grow and prosper. She served as WFBM's traffic manager for twenty-four years, during which time the company established its television station. An active member of the Hoosier Chapter of American Women in Radio and Television (AWRT), Geisler was named Woman of the Year by that organization in 1961. Capping a lifetime of volunteer service that began with the American Red Cross Canteen Corps during World War II, Indianapolis mayor Richard G. Lugar declared 7 July 1975 "Marthabel Geisler Day." After her retirement in 1976, Geisler remained actively involved with coordinating the activities of the Indianapolis 500 Festival Parade Network, which telecasts the parade to more than 190 stations. The following excerpt combines interviews conducted in 1986 by R. Dale Ogden of the Indiana State Museum and in 1997 by Jane R. Nolan at Geisler's home at Riley Towers in downtown Indianapolis.

I was born in Louisville, Kentucky, and there were five girls in our family. . . . When I was eight we moved to Indianapolis. Went to Tech [Arsenal Technical] High School and graduated from there. Did not go to college. Went right out of high school. My sister used to work for Blythe Hendricks, who became manager of WFBM radio. He asked her if she would like to be his secretary, and she had a nice job at the time. She said, "No, but I have a sister who is just out of high school and maybe you'd like to interview her." So, I went up there, and I was hired. I turned eighteen that fall when I started working with WFBM.

Well, I started working there on July 7, 1930, as secretary to Frank Sharp. He had just been promoted to program director. He had been a radio engineer earlier, and we had just joined the CBS network and had a small staff. They weren't on the air all day or evening, but they did share time with the station in South Bend, WSBT. I remember every day we had to sign off at 3:00 so they could go on the air, and they came back on later on in the evening. They had a lot of local talent, so they had a lot of local programming on and off. They had Jim and Walt [Bullock], a comedy team. Jim played the piano, and he was blind, and they both sang. They were very popular in town.

I think that when I first went [to WFBM], we had all of these wonderful bands on that you got for nothing, no commercials in them, and wonderful singers. . . . I thought that was the best time of radio. Of course, I had no idea what TV was going to be like. We didn't even talk about it then. It wasn't even on the horizon. But I think myself—I don't know what other people said [about the golden era], but [for me it was] those days when we had the New York Philharmonic on Sunday afternoons for two hours, and Columbia Masterworks at night, and in between some other nice shows, and then at night we'd have the *Lux Radio Theater* and we'd have *Fibber McGee and Molly* on radio, and you used your imagination. That's what Jim Mathis always said, "Use your imagination as to what they're saying on these shows."[16] You don't need pictures; you do it in your head, and you can imagine what it would be like and then you enjoyed that.

We had news 12:00 to 12:15 or something like that with Gilbert Forbes . . . a fine gentleman. I have a picture of him someplace, when he was a war correspondent with his uniform. Well, we used to laugh at him; they'd introduce him on the air; the announcer would say, you know, the news is coming on, "And here's Gilbert Forbes." He'd just be coming walking down the hall, leisurely walking down the hall and go in and sit in his chair and start. Couldn't hurry him. Couldn't hurry that man. He'd always get there, but it scared the announcer to death.

And [Mr. Sharp] was sort of a right-hand man to whoever was the manager. He was acting manager during the war. Everybody went off to war, and he was appointed acting manager. There was always someone in his office to talk to him, bringing their troubles. Sharp encouraged many young people to move on from the station if he felt that they could benefit, like Dick Powell [and] Durward Kirby. And I know Harry Martin mentioned when he wanted to do his Rural Radio Network, he encouraged him with that.

In 1937 we [WFBM] moved to Monument Circle. And it's interesting to note that there's going to be a broadcasting group there. Building it right now where we were on the fourth floor, right above the Canary Cottage.[17] Mr. [Harry] Bitner had bought the station in 1937, and we moved there. We were very crowded even with our little group, and then when television came in, we still tried to work out of those studios.

I was appointed traffic manager in 1942, and that became a little more hectic because I had the salesmen around my desk all the time wanting to know what was available. Traffic manager . . . means, you worked partly in programming, and partly in sales, because I had to sched-

ule the spots between the half-hour shows, or the fifteen-minute shows. And the salesmen had to go out and come to me and find out what was available. I had to keep track of everything that was sold on this big long ledger. We called it our "bible." So, I think my salary came partly from sales and partly from programming. And we had half-hour shows on the network, or fifteen-minute shows. And we always said on our rate card that we would have fifteen-minute separations from a competitive product, and we did that, and that was one of my worst worries was keeping those spots separated. You know how they do now; they're back to back.

Your copy was all written by continuity men and women. And we did have women in continuity; I'd forgotten that. And then they read it. So we had quite a lot of copy to put in together every day to match the log. And I would really help, you know. We worked that out. Bill Kiley and I worked that out as to how we were going to do it, and a lot of stations copied our method.[18] We thought it was foolproof.

We belonged to the NAB [National Association of Broadcasters], and I think that WFBM just abided by [the code]. I don't recall that they ever fussed about it. I never heard anyone fuss about it. We had a plaque in our lobby. That code said that everything was to be—we would have good morals in the programs; good language, no swearing; and, of course, in television, proper dress. We had to have so much public service on. You had to have so much public service on each day to counteract your commercials. You know, some of this stuff they have on now that people don't like and are always writing in about and complaining and what they should do is just turn off their set. That's all I could tell them to do, because it's going to be on there.

The [FCC] would make regulations, and then if it didn't work, they'd change them. That happened too. They were really in your hair a lot in those days. I don't think they are any more. Just picky-picky. You had to just submit so many things for a license renewal. You had reams and reams of paper to send to them about what you did, especially in public service during the year. [Public service was] anything that was noncommercial; let's see, the Red Cross or a church program that might be coming up, or any of them like Big Sisters now, or something like that. That was all public service. We gave that to this organiza-

Marthabel Geisler was still a teenager when she began her long career at WFBM in 1930. One of Geisler's first assignments was to work as secretary to Frank O. Sharp. They posed for this photograph in 1936. WRTV-6/PHOTO

BY RAY CONOLLY

Durward Kirby, who began his career in Indiana, shared a light moment with Dick Lingle in the dressing room of the Murat Theater when he returned to emcee a telethon in the early 1950s. WRTV-6/DICK LINGLE

tion. They would give us specifics as to what would be used in the spots, you know, as to what they actually did for the community. [People] would contact us and say, "We're going to run a campaign, and we need, . . . " or, "We need people to come in and do so-and-so, and we'd like to be on the air." I'm sure that's how it happened. And that's gone by the boards now that I know of. Anything goes now, so it doesn't make any difference.

I remember during the war that they lengthened our hours. That is, the government did. We had to work forty-eight hours a week instead of forty. We got more money. And the nice part about it, when the war was over, Mr. Bitner did not change our salary back. He changed our hours back to forty [from] forty-eight hours—we got a raise, in a way, you know. He was off to the navy, and Bill Kiley was off to the army, and I think Frank Sharp was acting manager, and then Hazel Gaston—I think Sharp somehow found her. She's a real vivacious person and laughed a lot and was real nice. And she came in and did the announcer shift. Yes. We had some announcers left—I mean men announcers, but she was there, and I think she probably stayed on after the war. And Mr. Bitner's wife became program director while Mr. Sharp was the manager. I'm sure Hazel [stayed on after the war], and then we did have Carolyn Churchman on, and we had Ann Wagner, Ann Wagner Harper. She was our first lady disc jockey.

We were getting ready for television for a couple of years, because we knew it wasn't going to come until after the war was over. And Mr. Bitner had in mind that we'd have to build a new station, a new facility. But the thing was, we really started in 1949 with television with the 500-Mile Race. That was the first broadcast, May 30, and we were so crowded in that little studio on the Circle, we were practically in

each other's laps. We had to get more engineers. We imported people from New York to run the place, and they were just every place. So it was really wonderful in [April 1951] when we moved up to 1330 North Meridian, where they are now.

We were the first [television] station in Indiana. In 1949 there were no other TV stations. So, there were networks vying to get into these markets. We had DuMont; we had NBC programs and CBS and ABC; we had it all. There wasn't any, what they call, interconnected [direct network service] at that time. It was all kinescope. Those films were just flying in and out of our studio. We had to send them back to another station at that time. And we'd get news two days late. We had what they'd call "telenews." When it came in, it was old news, but it was something to see on TV so we used it, of course. They made it as up-to-date as they could.

You remember *Ed Sullivan, the Toast of the Town*? That was one of our good ones. We had Milton Berle, where he'd dress up like a woman so many times. Maybe you don't remember him. But, oh yeah, we had a lot of good shows, a lot better than they are now, more fun; they were cleaner; they were just homey; they were for the family. And then television when it first came on, we were only on from six o'clock 'til ten o'clock at night. And we might have a baseball game out here from Victory Field out on 16th Street, or we might have orchestras or something from another city, and so it wasn't very long—six o'clock to ten o'clock at night.

Eldon Campbell came to WFBM in 1957. He did promotions that involved the public. Like we had what they called the "Zoo Train." We had a train, a real train, and it went to Cincinnati. And people bought space on there to ride, to take their kids to go over there, and it was a promotion put on by WFBM

Frank O. Sharp

Marthabel Geisler remembers Frank Sharp as a quiet and unassuming man whose door on executive row was always open; many of those who worked at WFBM respected him and sought his advice, including manager Eldon Campbell. Sharp's uncanny ability to recognize and develop talent made him one of the most revered broadcasters in Indiana. While many local broadcasters considered him a mentor, he unselfishly sent others on to national acclaim. An Anderson native, Sharp came to work at the Indianapolis Electric Company, which later acquired WFBM. He was associated with WFBM from the day it signed on the air in 1924 until he retired in 1967. As the station's remote engineer, he broadcast from such places as the Indiana Theater, the Wheeler Mission, the old Cow Barn at the State Fairgrounds (then the site of the boys state basketball finals), and the 1929 Indianapolis 500-Mile Race. In 1930 Sharp became program director, and during World War II he served as acting manager while the manager was in the service. He became personnel director and program manager at WFBM and WFBM-TV before it was purchased by Time-Life, Inc. Sharp ended his long career as administrative assistant coordinating the departmental activities of all WFBM operations. He died in 1987.[19]

When Harry Bitner bought WFBM in 1937 it was located above the Canary Cottage on Monument Circle in Indianapolis. During his twenty years of ownership, he acquired a television license and moved the station to new quarters at 1330 North Meridian Street. WRTV-6

Carolyn Churchman interviewed Howdy Bell, a popular Indianapolis-area announcer, at the Marott Hotel in the mid-1960s for her WFBM program. WRTV-6

Jerry Chapman, shown here with Congressman Gerald Ford and Howard Caldwell, started at WIRE as a radio personality before moving into management at WFBM. He worked there until his death in 1987. WRTV-6

[WRTV]. And then another one we had was the "Antique Auto Tour." Have you seen that one here? That was one of his good ideas. And we had a promotion manager, Casey Strange, who came up with real clever ideas about something that the public could—we had what we called "Christmas in July" one time, and they could bring broken toys into our parking lot into big boxes, and they would be repaired and given to children—and things like that to involve the public—or a remote at some automobile place and give away so-and-so, give away tickets to this or that and always some promotion going on. [The rest of the staff] enjoyed it; they all pitched in and helped. I went to those "Zoo Trains." And then finally we went to buses, and they had the people in charge of one bus to be sure that the people were back on the bus when we came home. And I had charge of a bus for two or three years, and it was fun going over to King's Island.

In 1966 I was appointed secretary to Don Menke. He was called station manager. That was under the general manager. He did all kinds of things the general manager didn't do. He was sort of in between a program director and a general manager. And I became his secretary in 1966, and then he retired in 1970, and then Mr. Campbell retired [in 1973], and Jerry [Chapman] became general manager of television and took me with him as his secretary, and I stayed there then until 1976. That was six years. I had to work. I wasn't married, and I just had to work, and I liked my work. I loved my work, loved the people I worked with and besides that I did other things. I played the organ at my church. I loved my work at WFBM, and I didn't see any sense in quitting. I was waiting until I was sixty-five. The last five years, I'll tell you, I was ready to retire.

Ralph Luke Walton (ca. 1941)
WISH-TV/PHOTO BY RAY CONOLLY

Luke Walton

(1907–1990)

Ralph Luke Walton, or "300 Words a Minute" Walton, was interviewed at his Indianapolis home in 1986 by R. Dale Ogden of the Indiana State Museum. Although his health was declining, he still had his feisty spirit. Walton was diminutive in stature but monumental in ability. He broke into professional broadcasting in 1931 as a sports announcer at WGBF in Evansville doing sideline commentary during a local Thanksgiving football game. His reputation for excellence led him to move to WBOW in Terre Haute, where he spent the next eight years. Soon after moving to WISH in Indianapolis in 1941, Walton took a leave of absence to serve in the navy from 1942 to 1946. Stationed at the Great Lakes Naval Training Center and in the Pacific, he worked as an announcer for sports events dedicated to raising and maintaining the morale of our servicemen. Following the war he returned to WISH, where he worked for the next ten years. Although he left WISH in 1956 to form his own advertising firm, Walton continued to announce for the Indianapolis Speedway Radio Network for thirty years. When inducted into the Hall of Fame, Walton was acknowledged as Indiana's "Dean of Sportscasters."

My senior year in high school they had a course in journalism, and while I was in that class I went down to the newspaper and got a job. I didn't know what I was going to do. I just got a job, and the city editor assigned me to cover the high school football game. So that is how I got started in writing sports. [Then] I went to DePauw [University] the first year with a boy who lived across the street from me.

Well, I came up [to Indianapolis] with a dance band from DePauw, and we played in the Columbia Club. . . . We had a contract for that summer. And just before Labor Day, when our contract was up, the club wanted us to play the winter. We played for dinner in the dining room and had two dances. We had dances on Friday and Saturday night up on the tenth floor. So I stayed and transferred to Butler [University]. While I was at Butler we used to put on a Campus News Broadcast from WGBF every Sunday afternoon. That is how I got the bug. Then when I got out of school, I didn't have any idea of going into radio. The summer after I got out of college, I went out on the road out in Iowa, selling syndicated newspaper material to newspapers. And just about that time the banks closed.[20] The depression really hit with the banks.

You couldn't sell anything. Nobody had any money—couldn't do anything about financing. So I came back here [to Indianapolis], and I applied for a job in broadcasting. Didn't know anything about it. And this GBF was owned by a couple here that had stations in Indianapolis, Terre Haute, Evansville, and Decatur, Illinois. Jim Carpenter, who is the manager of GBF, sent

Luke Walton interviewed passers-by on Wabash Avenue in Terre Haute for his Man in the Street *program broadcast on WBOW in 1939.*

me over to Terre Haute to talk to the manager over there—Bill Behrman. And he called up the president of the company who owned the station and asked him if they needed another man down there at Evansville. "Well," the man said, "send him on down." So, I went down there and worked about a month. Then, they sent me back to Terre Haute, which pleased me. I didn't particularly like Evansville.

On Thanksgiving day in Evansville, there was an Annual Turkey Game between Central and Bosse. They only had two high schools then, and there weren't any sports announcers. I was the newest employee there, and nobody wanted to go to that football game—none of them around the radio station. So Lyle Ludwig . . . and I were assigned to go out and do that football game; Lyle to do the play-by-play, and I to use the telex. Lyle was a graduate of Central, and in his broadcast . . . you wouldn't know that Bosse was in the game. Central could do no wrong, and Bosse could do no right. Well, it was a bad, miserable, trashy day—Thanksgiving, snow on the ground and sleeting. The field was a quagmire.

Well, I am ahead of my story. It was a miserable day. A couple of days before that this owner, the president of the station [WGBF, Evansville], called me in and fired me. He said, "Walton, I don't believe you are adapting to radio." I said, "Well, [this] doesn't displease me at all. I have about had it up to my ears on this merry-go-round around here anyway. Everybody running around trying . . . to impress you and not doing a darned thing." He said, "Well, give me a couple of weeks notice . . . if you want to." I said, "You don't have to. I don't care." So I went out on this football broadcast and—I always tell them about Central and Bosse. They had a formation when they received a punt almost like a flying wedge. They form that "V" and put the ball in the middle, [and Lyle] didn't pick that up at all.

And the day was awful; it was terrible, nobody could do a good job running along the sideline. You had to run along the sideline with a long wire [on] the microphone in that mud and the sleeting. It was awful. We got chilled to the bone and wet all the way through. Came to the half [and Lyle] turned it over to me. So I told the folks about that wedge formation and some of the other highlights of the game, which was practically nothing. It wasn't a good football game. It couldn't be in that mire. The teams came out on the field ready to start the second half, and I was look-

ing for Lyle. And you know, he went home to get warm. He went home and left me stranded with that microphone. So I did the play-by-play . . . and when that game was over I got in my car and went back to the station.

I said to myself, "Enough of this. I don't want any broadcasting." The station's studios were located on the second floor in a downtown business building—two-story building. I started up those steps to the studios, and here was the president standing at the head. I was really teed off, and he said, "Walton, I want to see you." And I said, "I want to see you, too." So I went in his office, and I sat down, all wet. He said, "Walton, I have changed my mind about you." And I said. "Well, I haven't changed my mind about this place at all." He said, "Well, how would you like to go to Terre Haute with Bill Behrman?" I knew Bill, and I said, "Well, that would be all right." He said, "Well, you can go up there anytime in the next two weeks. When you get ready to go, just go ahead." Well, I didn't know something. When I went out in the lobby, the girl on the PBX board told me that her board had been lighted up like a Christmas tree all during the second half of that game— nothing but high compliments. "Where did you get that guy?" "Where did he come from?" and that kind of stuff, you know. Well, that is the reason he met me at the top of the stairs. If I had known that, I would have told him how much the price was. But I didn't.

When I first went [to WBOW in Terre Haute], it was on the corner of Sixth and Wabash on the second floor of that business building there. And we had the whole second floor. Two, three years later we moved catawampus down Sixth Street to what was known as the Root Building—the Root Store owned it. The Root Store was a big department store there, and we had some space up on the second floor of that building—not the whole second floor. In those days, there were no specialists, no announcers or copywriters or salesmen per se. You were in radio. You did everything. You went out on the street and sold and came back and wrote the copy for it and then went in the studio and announced it. There weren't any what you just call "radio announcers." You were in radio. And if you couldn't handle all those facets for the business, you didn't have a job. It was that way all over. Well, we had to paint the studios and the offices; so we painted them. We were [at the Root Store building] for about three years. Moved farther down Sixth Street to the corner of Sixth and Poplar and

While on active duty, Walton announced a game between the Great Lakes baseball team and the Shipyard team in 1943. He was sports information director for the Great Lakes Naval Training Center from 1942 to 1946. COURTESY OF INDIANA STATE MUSEUM

Known for his rapid-fire delivery, Walton was the voice of Indianapolis Indians baseball over WISH Radio from 1948 to 1955. He later posed with the Indianapolis Indians mascot on the set of WISH-TV. COURTESY OF INDIANA STATE MUSEUM/WISH-TV

bought a house—three-story brick house. It was there when I left Terre Haute.

Well, in those days ASCAP [American Society of Composers, Authors and Publishers] and the NAB were having a feud over the amount of money that radio was to pay ASCAP.[21] So ASCAP just pulled out, and said you can't play any ASCAP music at all. So that eliminated the playing of any phonograph records on the stations. We had no records to play. We didn't have a network and no news service. Everything was live. So I came back up to Terre Haute, and I was only supposed to be there for about thirty days because the station was in trouble—supposed to stay long enough to get it out of trouble. Well, it was always in trouble. I was there eight years. And as I look back on it, it was a good experience.

We would take an office room, a pretty large one, and hang burlap sacking all around the walls. You know what gunny sack is? Burlap—draped the walls with that burlap to deaden the sound. In those days in broadcasting the engineering opinion was that you had to deaden the room to broadcast. One day, we took all those down and this new acoustical tile came in. That replaced the burlap bags.

We had a control board . . . just right beside the studio. It wasn't very large, but we had a control panel. We had to have a piano because everything was live. We had a woman who was the program director, but there wasn't much that she did in the way of programming. But what programming we had, she did. About 90 percent hillbilly music.

We had, I imagine, about four dozen hillbilly groups with guitars . . . singing country music. We had so many that we couldn't handle all of them. So we gave out tickets to all the groups with numbers on them. They would bring their fiddles and guitars and come to the station and stay out in the hall. If number "four" were on today, we called number "four." That group would come on, and they would play a program for fifteen minutes.

We had an engineer, and his title was chief engineer. But he was the only engineer. [If there was a problem] he would get his pliers and his baling wire and go shoot the trouble. He also made [the equipment]. Our control panel was composite. That means he made it—homemade. Our control panel was composite, and our transmitter was composite. He made the transmitter. We didn't have any frequency monitor, and you could get the station at 1310 one day, 1400 the next day, or 1230 the next day. We were all over the

place, but we didn't have any control monitor at all. And the oven—you know what the oven is? The oven holds the crystal, and has to keep it at a good temperature. Well, our oven was a tin cigar box, and our antenna was one wire stretched between two telephone poles out on the Rose Poly campus [Rose Polytechnic Institute]. [We had] store-bought microphones—carbon microphones. For a stand we would have a lead pipe that we had plated with chromium with a ring at the top with four little hooks on it. And this carbon microphone was suspended in that ring by rubber bands.

We had terrific staff in Terre Haute. There was a fella by the name of Farrington that went to NBC. Guy Boteau went to CBS from there. And we had a young fella who was at Indiana State who strummed the guitar and sang some songs at five o'clock every evening. He was studying voice under Madam Bloomfield—voice teacher there. And on Sunday nights, he sang a half-hour show from the Indiana Theater in Terre Haute with the organ—classic stuff, long-hair stuff. He went down to New York and was aiming to get in the Metropolitan Opera. [At the time] CBS had soap operas all morning long. And the program director, Vic, I think his name was, decided that they should have a little musical interlude right in the middle of the morning, along about ten o'clock—just to sort of split up the soap operas. Guy said, "I know just the thing. I know a guy that can put on a little musical program, singing." And [they] said, "Well, let's hear it." So Guy called up this [young man]. He was washing dishes at the International House. So he came over to CBS, and he had all this longhaired music under his arm. Guy looked at him and said, "Where is your guitar?" "Guitar?" And the young man's jaw fell about four feet. CBS guy said, "Yeah, we want you to sing a little song and want you to play the guitar." So he went back and got his guitar and auditioned. They hired him, and [he] sang those songs on the network. Since then he has been in the movies, made records and [has been] on Broadway. He was Burl Ives. And he has never been in the Metropolitan Opera. The folk songs that he had were unique. Nobody ever heard of them before on that network.

I was home in Terre Haute, and early Sunday morning the telephone rang. It was the head of the American Legion in Terre Haute, Oscar Jensen. He told me that they were having a flood at the Ohio River [1937 flood] and that the people down in New Albany and Jeffersonville were out of food. . . . They needed clothing and food. And he had some

Taxicabs sported advertisements for Walton's broadcasts of the Indians baseball games.   WISH-TV/PHOTO BY RAY CONOLLY

trucks, great big semitrailer trucks to haul from Terre Haute to Evansville. The Terre Haute Brewing Company had provided the trucks. We needed a call to the people in Terre Haute to bring food to the truck to send down there. And [Jensen asked if] I would put something on the air about it.

Well, I got up out of bed and put on my clothes and went down to the studio and started pitching for those poor starving people down in Jeffersonville and New Albany. In thirty minutes there were so many people outside in the street, outside the studio bringing food, that it was a traffic hazard. And I called up Jensen and told him. He said, "Well, I will have forty men there in ten minutes to handle the traffic." And he did. That situation kept going on all day and up into the night—people bringing food. And before dark we had one of those big semis full of food. I don't know how many tons it had. I think about twelve. Before we got through, we had twelve of those trucks down there full of food for New Albany. And I think we took in, on, something around $100,000. And that was pretty big for Terre Haute in those days. It was a monstrous thing for Terre Haute—quite an activity.

Then Evansville put in a call for help. They were sending flood refugees to Terre Haute on the railroad, and they had to be quartered and fed. Well, at that time they were just finished putting a new county home in Terre Haute—Vigo County Home. They had it finished and had the room to house, oh, a hundred people, I guess. And they had beds, but they had no mattresses and no bedding. So I put on a pitch for the bedding. And when those flood refugees arrived in Terre Haute they were fed hot food and given a warm bed. It was an activity that the whole city of Terre Haute—everybody in Terre Haute pitched in and helped. [This was in] 1937, and the newspapers didn't like it. They thought it was a grandstand play—told people that.

They had a big tournament over there [in Terre Haute] called the Wabash Valley Tournament—basketball tournament. I have seen trophies in the High School Hall of Fame from the Wabash Valley Tournament. You know, the newspaper [Terre Haute Tribune] started that—the Wabash Valley Tournament. Fella by the name of Ralph White [was] sports editor, and they, of course, wouldn't permit any broadcasting of it. We were broadcasting high school games four to five a week. People would call up and say, "Are you going?" "Why don't you?" "You going to broadcast the Wabash Valley Tournament?" "No, the Tribune won't let us." Well, they

started it, but they had a board of control that ran it—principals from all the schools in the Wabash Valley. . . . Finally, [the principals] let us broadcast the last half of the last game of the tournament. Then we got this, "How come you broadcast just that little amount? Why don't you broadcast the whole tournament?" "Well, that is all they would let us broadcast." So the pressure got on again to these principals. Finally, they decided they would let us broadcast the last game, the whole thing. So I broadcast the last game, but the pressure was still on. Then they got around to, "Yes, you can broadcast the whole tournament." So I did that for, I don't know, three to four years before I left.

[I received a] much better offer [from WISH], but I liked Terre Haute very much. I liked the people down there. They are fine people. I love them. But I didn't make any money working for that company. Eight Indianapolis men licensed a station here in Indianapolis, on 1310. That was WISH, and I knew the president of that company, Bruce McConnell. He wanted me to come over and hear something. I was the first employee at WISH. And I went out on the street and sold a quarter of million dollars worth of advertising before we had a microphone and went on the air.

Bill Behrman was the manager at Terre Haute and was [McConnell's] manager here. And I was to be a salesman. So I went out on the street and started selling. . . . Then when we went on the air, I had a couple of shows that I had sold. One was a street broadcast out in front of the Circle Theater at that time, Man on the Street. And then the war came [in 1941]. I went into the navy and was gone for four years. When the war was over I came back to WISH. When I came back from the navy they had sold the Street broadcast to Kay Jewelers and called it the Kay Reporter then.

And then I did a sports broadcast at six o'clock—a sports show. Well, Bruce [McConnell] thought that I would do better concentrating on broadcasting sports. I did a play-by-play on two to three games. Well, we did Indiana and Purdue [football] that first season. Then we did high school basketball tournaments. He thought that I could do better concentrating on broadcasting sports. So I just did a specialized sports broadcast. I also used to go out [to the 500-Mile Race] and interview drivers—do the daily reports. But that network didn't start until about 1950, and I was on that. I have been on that network, that race, ever since it started.

Luke Walton stayed at WISH until 1956, when he left to form the Luke Walton Advertising Agency.

Robert S. Sievers (ca. 1938)

Bob Sievers

(1917–)

Robert S. Sievers, "Mr. WOWO," spent his entire career at that Fort Wayne station. Shortly after graduating from high school in 1936, Sievers began working as an announcer, becoming involved with such programs as Hoosier Hop, Mail Bag, Musical Clock, *and* Back Home Hour. *He and Jay Gould performed for years on the morning show,* The Little Red Barn, *and the noon show,* Dinner on the Farm. *For twenty-five years, Sievers had a popular fifteen-minute show,* One Moment Please, *during which he would talk with folks on the street. In addition, he spun records at record hops in large and small towns across the WOWO listening area. When he retired in 1986,* USA Today *noted that he was one of only four radio personalities nationwide who had captured more than 30 percent of the available listeners in their market that year. Indeed, there are few people in the Fort Wayne listening area who are not familiar with Sievers's voice. Sievers still resides in Fort Wayne where his interview was conducted on 28 February 1995.*

Actually, this makes me sound ancient, but I first signed on WOWO December 4, 1932. I was about thirteen [and] a freshman at Southside High School, and my gosh, this is 1995. That was sixty-three years ago. So, one honor that I have is that I have said more words on that station than any other living person.

I just had the thrill of radio in my blood. What inspired me to be an announcer was the old *Majestic Hour* on the radio, a full-hour show, and their theme song was "Pomp and Circumstance." I don't know if you know the number, "Pomp and Circumstance," beautiful music. With that theme song, "Pomp and Circumstance" in the background, the announcer would come on and say, "From the boundless everywhere comes the magic name Majestic, mighty monarch of the air." Hearing that, I would imitate him. To me, that is what really thrilled me and inspired me to get into radio and to become an announcer. He said, "From the boundless everywhere comes the magic name Majestic, mighty monarch of the air." From that point on, I said, "One day, I am going to be an announcer." My mother would say, "Robert, don't count on that. I don't want you to have your heart broken. You don't have any qualifications to be an announcer." Her brother was a draftsman at GE [General Electric], and she thought that was the greatest job. The greatest thing in the world would be for me to be a draftsman at GE, and I said, "No. The heck with that, Mom. I want to be an announcer. . . ."

I used to like to go to bed early at night because I had to carry the [*Fort Wayne*] *Journal-Gazette* paper every morning and get up at three o'clock. I have done that all my life—gotten up 3:00 or 2:30. I used to like to go to bed on a winter's night when it was dark, and hear *Dragnet* and some of the mystery stories. In the dark of my bedroom, I would mentally create my own scenes—just like seeing it on television. I think that it was almost more fascinating and exciting in those days, creating your own scene than seeing it put before your eyes on television.

I can remember some of the early broadcasts of churches that were just beginning. The first church I remember broadcasting, the minister was Reverend Wambsgans from the Emmaus Lutheran Church on Broadway in Fort Wayne, because my grandparents were members of that church. Then, the Gospel Temple started broadcasting in my neighborhood, and they were on the air. That is how I really got into radio. I was a member of the First Baptist Church, but the Gospel Temple in my neighborhood was broadcasting, and I got to go there first of all, just to volume-control their loud speaking system and later on, actually to carry the microphone from the choir to the minister sitting at this table. We only had one microphone. It was the biggest thrill in the world to carry this microphone. If I said a word, people would hear me, but I never said that word.

The [big condenser] microphones were so heavy; I was in front of three thousand people one night at the Gospel Temple, announcing the *Back Home Hour.* It was my job. The floor would rise, and here would be a backdrop of the Jordan River, and the minister would be down in the water because they baptized by immersion. I would have to lower the microphone to Reverend Clifford Hollifield to get the name of the lady being baptized. One night with the organ playing softly and three thousand people in the audience, I stooped down and lowered the heavy RCA condenser microphone, and the microphone and I fell in the water with the lady about to be baptized. Here was a very serious occasion; the audience was laughing hysterically. So, this shows you how heavy the microphones were in those days.

[This was the] Gospel Temple at Clinton and Rudisill Boulevard. The choir would start out by singing "A Mighty Fortress Is Our God." I would say, "Good evening, ladies and gentlemen. From the second largest temple in America on the beautiful south side of Indiana's Summit City, it is our pleasure to bring to you in your home tonight another broadcast of the *Back Home Hour.*" And then,

Mrs. Hollifield would sing "Home Sweet Home." I said, "From the second largest temple in America . . ." (the largest at that time was the temple out in Salt Lake City). The choir would sing, and the Gospel Temple band would play, and he would give a little ten-minute sermon in the middle of it. It was mostly music. When you are getting back home from church on Sunday evening, people would tune in to the *Back Home Hour.* A lot of people [listened] because there was no television to watch on Sunday night. They had a church service at night, 7:00 or 7:30 to 9:30. Then, 10:00 until 11:00 was the *Back Home Hour.*

I had the desire to get into radio. At about every month, I would go down and [knock, knock] knock on their door [at WOWO], and they would say, "No." So, another month later, I would be knocking on their door again. Finally, they would say, "Get lost, kid. Get out of our hair." (I usually give this as a personal testimonial if I am speaking to a church group.) Finally, one morning the Reverend Paul Rader, who was the minister at the Gospel Temple, said, "Well, Bob, you do really believe that the Lord answers prayer, don't you?" I said, "Yes." But I didn't have that faith of a grain of mustard seed, you know, the miracle in my life. So, after the broadcast, he said, "Well, let's just kneel down in the carpet and pray that you get into radio." We did. He put his big hand on the back of my neck and prayed, and I almost had that goose-pimply feeling, like I could feel the power of God right there with me. And, we prayed that I would get into radio. And, after I had been knocking on the door for two years at WOWO, the announcer Claire Weidenaar called me. Just two days later, my phone rang, and he said, "Is this Bob Sievers?" I said, "Yes." "This is Claire Weidenaar of WOWO and WGL. We heard you do a commercial on the *Back Home Hour* the other Sunday night, and we need an announcer. We just want to know if you have ever thought of being an announcer?" I thought, "Had I ever thought?" you know.

The Main Auto Supply Company was a hardware store on the bottom floor. We had to walk up a long stairway to the second floor. In the front studio was our big organ. We had two famous organists in those days, Percy Robbins and Margurite Hitzeman. The front studio was Studio A, and then, we had other little studios built along the way with little announcing booths, and I remember the one studio where we did a lot of announcing had old wooden doors that you closed. The rats chewed holes under the

Jane Weston, a home economist, shares tips with a large audience of women during the "Modern Home Forum" at WOWO ca. 1938.

Well known as a result of their program on WOWO in the late 1930s, the Blackhawk Valley Boys sang modern, hillbilly, and "old time" songs. In addition to guitars, accordion, and bass fiddle, they also played horns, jugs, and washboards.

studio door where they could run in and out, you know. So, the studios weren't like they are now.

In the early days of radio . . . audience participation was the main thing. For each studio that we had when we were on Harrison Street or on Washington Street, or even the original station down on Main Street, for each program that we had, we would have a big observation room for people to sit there and watch the program. Many of our shows were audience participation. For instance, Jane Weston conducted the *Modern Home Forum* ladies' program in the morning. Ladies would sit right in the studio and watch her bake. We always had a roving microphone where we would talk to the people in the audience. We had all sorts of audience participation shows. For instance, for over twenty-five years I had a man on the street program—downtown Fort Wayne. It came from a number of different locations—originally the Roxie Grill and then the Emboyd Theater, which is now the Embassy Theater, and then from Golden's Men's Wear, then from the Boston Store, then over to Walgreens, and finally for the last twenty years from the Baber Corner. Baber was the Baber Jewelry Store at Calhoun and Berry in downtown Fort Wayne. So, it originated there, and everybody would gather around the sidewalk, and I would introduce the show by saying, "One moment, one moment, please." Then, I would go into, "Good afternoon, everyone. This is Bob Sievers," and so on. So, audience participation was a big, important aspect of broadcasting in those days.

I don't know if we ever had a "golden era." From the 1930s and 1940s would probably be classified as the golden era, as far as local talent goes. We originated so many network shows with Tommy Longsworth, Guy Fitzsimmons, Norm Carroll, Bob Shreve, Dick Galbreath, the guitar player. They were such versatile musicians not only backing up Helen Jones on *Indiana Indigo*—but all of the other shows. Some of the big names back in those days . . . local talent—Ambrose Hailey and Little Mary Lou, Joe Trim who was a country and western singer, Dorothy Moore, the Blackhawk Valley Boys, Norm and Bob, Kenny Roberts, the famous yodeler, Howard Ropa who sang songs like "Old Man River" and so on, "Happy Herb" Hayworth, the old songsmith Jay Gould, Fitz and the Fellows, Jean Brown, Sari and Elmer, and our two organists Percy Robbins and Margurite Hitzeman. Jean Brown later became our organist. That was the "golden era" as far as

local talent was concerned. Judy and Jen . . . George Arthur . . . I could go on thinking of local names like that. They were also heard on the network.

"Happy Herb," for years before I started WOWO, was on WGL, was known as the "Old Roundsman." Everybody knew him as the Old Roundsman, and he called himself that, too. As a kid, I would go up to the station—he would go on the air as the *Roundsman's Hour.* . . . He would have the *Journal-Gazette* rolled up under his left arm walking up the steps. He would sit down, and he would have a record that he would put on and just talk, but he would read from the *Journal-Gazette*. That was before we had international news service. He read from the paper and brought everybody up-to-date on the headlines, and then he always had a fictitious friend that he called "Old Joe." He would say, "I met Old Joe on the corner this morning," and he would have some funny story. He would say, "Old Joe said to me . . ." and then after he told the joke, he would have "ha, hee, hee." He would have a false laugh, but it sounded like a real laugh. So, yeah, he met Old Joe this morning, and he told him this. Then, he was "Happy Herb." In those days, though, everyone knew him as the "Old Roundsman" because that is what he had on *The Breakfast Club*. The show was actually titled *The Breakfast Club* or the *Roundsman's Hour*.

Before Jay [Gould] came there, Herb did the [farm] markets. And before Herb did, for a short time—I can barely remember it—we had a farm director, Tom Wheeler—I think was his name—from Huntington. I think he did the markets—Tom Wheeler from Huntington, but my memory isn't sharp enough to go too much into that. [These men] read the price of soybeans, corn, and wheat in the morning and oats and alfalfa and the price of hogs and cows going to market. But, everything that a farmer needed to know price wise was included in the farm markets.

I would say that [Jay Gould] came in about 1938. In those times, he was a singer, a musician. He was known as the "Old Songsmith." Oh, yeah, and then he would have boys' and girls' *Happy Club Chorus*. I never will forget; I always called him prissy-looking. He had spats that he wore over his shoes, gray spats, and his pants came clear up to his chest this way. He had little glasses that pinched on, and the thing came around and he stuffed it in his pocket here, and he would be directing this way, you know. The best way that I could explain is that he was prissy-looking. When I came back from World War II, I found that he was still directing the boys' and girls' *Happy Club Chorus,* but he was our farm director. I thought, "Farm director? He never had cow manure on his shoes in his life," you know. But he had about six college degrees. He was well-educated in biology, in botany, you name it.

It wasn't just the farm report. It was the overall picture. If you listened to *The Little Red Barn* in the morning, you not only got the latest markets or the latest news, but you would have everything going on in the sports world, and all of the activities—I call them calendar announcements, all of the organizations that were sponsoring things, and the church suppers. In other words, if you listened to that one hour of *The Little Red Barn* in the morning—the same way that it is on WOWO today. Chris Roberts does a fantastic job—if you listen to WOWO, you have all the information you need from every standpoint to start your day. And, of course, what transpires during the daytime, newswise and marketwise, you will get at night. But, it was not only all of the information that you needed, but a little humor and fun thrown in with it and good music. So, it was a complete picture.

Well, the thing is, [*Dinner on the Farm*] would be more or less a continuance of *The Little Red Barn* from this standpoint. [From] *The Little Red Barn,* the farmers would get the markets from yesterday early in the morning, and at noon, they would get all the latest activity of the markets that morning. And, Jay also had an agricultural interview, but it was news, not the markets, and we would get into greater detail because the markets would change on an hourly basis. So, at 11:30, Jay would bring everybody up-to-date on the markets at that time, and before they left the air, a reading of the markets from the late noon hour. And, Jay would have other feature articles, the latest in agricultural finds or findings, and all of the very latest farm news. I don't remember what other features that we made, but he kept the whole thing educational right up to one o'clock.

[The farmers] would work in the field in the morning, and they would come in at noon to have dinner, but the radio would go to get the latest news and markets at the noon hour before they went out to the field again in the afternoon. Jay was—one thing that I will say—he was really on top of everything. He had all of the latest releases from the colleges. He was . . . as I have said, the farmers

swore by him and at him. I would get home from working, and Jay was always putting me on with something. My mother would say, "Oh, that Jay. He made me so mad this morning." I would say, "Why, Mother?" "What he said about you, I didn't like that at all." "Oh, Mom, he was just kidding." "Well, it didn't sound like to me that he was kidding." But, that was his type of humor, you know. So, I knew Jay well. No, we just got along fine. As I said, Jay and I probably never had an argument in our life, a real argument, no.

I, here again, was working the people into the program, the audience into the program. It was only make believe. I never ate breakfast in my life—nothing but coffee, except this morning I had one pancake out with my ham buddies. But, one lady wrote to me one time and said, "Bob, next Wednesday is my birthday, and I would like to have the honor of serving you, in fancy, my favorite breakfast." (It was like blueberry pancakes or something.) So, then, all I did was use her breakfast. Then, I had ten letters the next day of people wanting to serve breakfast. So, I had them maybe stacked up for two months. But, I knew that every lady that sent me her favorite breakfast was going to be tuned in to see if she was my honorary hostess that morning. So, that was the way that I ended up having them work themselves into the program. I never will forget one morning on April Fool's Day, Jay Gould sent me this telegram from Milwaukee with double-face telegram. And, I said, "We have a real surprise; Sammy Snead, a famous golfer, and gee, I got this telegram from him this morning. He wants to be the honorary server of my breakfast this morning." So, he wanted to serve nanny berry pancakes. Of course, I had never heard of that one. I thought that it sounds delicious—you know, blueberry pancakes. So, I said, "And, Sam Snead is serving us nanny berry pancakes this morning with bacon and the works." At five minutes to ten, right before I got off the air, Jay Gould came in and said, "Sievers, that was a good breakfast this morning." I said, "Yeah, Jay, it sure was." He says, "Sievers, you know what nanny berries are, don't you?" I said, "No, but they sounded delicious." He said, "Nanny berries are what sheep leave in the pasture." Then, he said, "April Fool." And, then, here the whole station staff came in and gave me the ha-ha on the air. To this day, when I am out, in every big audience, somebody will come up to me and say, "Have you had any nanny berry pancakes lately?"

Jay Gould welcomed his listeners every morning with the phrase, "Hello, world." Gould, a partner to Sievers, began broadcasting at WOWO in 1941, performing for forty-five years on the station. Known as the "Dean of Agricultural Broadcasting," he was the farmer's companion at mealtime and in the milk house.

JACK UNDERWOOD

MID-DAY   10AM to 2PM

Handsome Jack is better known in WOWOland as "The Housewife's Hero." A real showman, Jack can always be found at any WOWO event conversing and joking with the public. Jack's smooth style and relaxing personality come across over the air every mid-day and are warmly received by WOWOland listeners. A devoted husband and father, Jack is seriously involved with the activities of his family and community.

I liked to devote my whole program to my listeners, and when anybody had any little human interest thing—or the story of one lady who had a problem of birds flying against her window and breaking their neck. Have you ever heard of that? The other day, we had a cardinal thump against our one window out there at the other place. And so, I would talk about that on the air. Then I would get eight or ten people say, "Oh, Bob, they are doing that to our windows." And then, I had a call from somebody who said, "All right. Get a picture of an owl someplace and cut it out and paste it on the window, and they will never fly against that window again." Maybe there is only one window in your house that has a certain reflection that makes the birds think that is a hole or something. Or you can just cut it out of black paper, the shape of the owl. You put that on the glass of the window, and the birds won't fly against your window any more.

With the advent of the Top 50 format, Sievers began appearing as a disc jockey at local record hops, eventually becoming one of the most popular deejays in the area. In those days, we got $35 a hop. Now, it is about $150. In fact, I think the first record hop that we did I know Cal Stewart was one of the announcers and it seems to me like, John Cigna. They did it at the Greek Orthodox church near Warsaw and Oxford on a Saturday night. That was the first record hop that we did. Down through the years, I have done as many or more than any of them. I would have about two or three record hops a week for years and years at such places as Bledsoes and Lake James, Cold Springs Resort on Hamilton Lake, Tippecanoe up by North Webster, and individual gymnasiums all over the area. I have done thousands.

The Fabulous Four [disc jockeys] were probably Jack Underwood, Don Chevillet or Doug Stevens—maybe John Cigna. But for awhile they called us "The Pussycats." I don't know why. I don't know what that meant. But for awhile Bob Chase, Marv Hunter, oh, and Joe Carr. Through the years we changed, from time to time, the four main disc jockeys on the air, but I would say Don Chevillet, John Cigna, Jack Underwood, and me for at least one time segment.

I don't think that we have given up anything with the changes in technology. We have gained a lot. But, I think what we have given up are our morals. I am shocked at what I hear on the call-in shows, these talk shows, their program content, the vulgarity and the language. Back in the days when records came out, if a record had the word "hell" or "damn" in it, we wouldn't think of putting it on the air. Now, you name it; you hear it on . . . even the talk show hosts like G. Gordon Liddy and some of these famous talk show artists. Some of their program content and the vulgar remarks that they make—to me I think this is where radio has gone down the drain. Where we have given up something, it is our moral standards. The music . . . we have the finest equipment now, the finest fidelity, but I think it is just our moral standards that have gone down the drain.

My most grueling experience on the air—I said my longest five minutes in radio was when we received the false alert from Denver, Colorado. Well, I had the Top 25 on Saturday morning. (I used to call it the Top 50, but out of the top fifty I couldn't get all the fifty records on in two hours, and I would have to skip some. So, I could just get the top twenty-five on in two hours. I called it the Top 25.) It was on Saturday morning at twenty-five minutes 'til ten in October of 1972. Normally, when we had an emergency or a news bulletin, the news machine would hit the bell ten times. When we heard ten bells, we would stop, and we would see what the news bulletin was. In those days we had three services, International News Service, United Press, and Associated Press. This particular morning all three machines were together. The bell kept ringing continuously. I went over to the machines and looked at them, and they kept ringing—"alert, alert, alert." The bells kept ringing. In those days we were worried about missiles from Russia. We had a secret word that if they ever printed the secret word, we would know that the bombs were on the way. And, in back of me on a ledge, I had a black envelope, heavy black envelope sealed, never to be opened until we had the alert. So, this Saturday morning I am on with the Top 25, and the machines are ringing continuously—"alert, alert, alert." Finally, it printed the secret code word, and the secret code word was "cauliflower." I reached behind me and opened that black [envelope]. I opened it up, and the word was "cauliflower." So, I knew one thing: the bombs had left Russia, and they were on their way. And, boy, I didn't know what to do. I thought, "Right now, I wanted to run out of the station, run home and get my wife and daughters, and drive to a lonely woods out by Ossian, Indiana, or get away from Fort

Always favorites in the WOWO listening area, Sievers (right) and Cal Stewart found themselves buried in a pile of matchbooks sent in by their listening audience. COURTESY OF INDIANA STATE MUSEUM/DALE STEDMAN, FORT WAYNE, INDIANA

Wayne where Magnavox and all of the big companies are." I thought, "What the heck do I do? We are the network control station for every radio station within a hundred miles of Fort Wayne." So, I thought, like my mother taught me, the only thing that I could do was to be honest. So, I said, "Ladies and gentlemen, we have received a special alert message. All three machines have verified it. I have just verified the secret code word, which means there is definitely some sort of an emergency, but the machines are quiet right now. I don't know what the emergency is. The only thing that I can ask you is to stay tuned to WOWO, and I will let you know as soon as I know." That particular record that I was playing on the Top 25 was a real beautiful, easygoing record—Henry Mancini's "Love Theme" from *Romeo and Juliet.* Anyway, the record ended and three minutes had gone by and the machines were still dead. I just lifted the needle up and put it back at the beginning of the record and had that easygoing music to help settle the nerves. So, I played it through twice, five minutes, and at the end of that time, everything came alive. And, all of the bells started ringing—"Cancel, cancel, cancel, cancel. Mistake, mistake, mistake, cancel, cancel,

cancel." So, then I said, "Well, it was a false alert out of Denver, Colorado. So, everything is all right." But, to receive that secret code word and to verify it and to think that the bombs were on the way—so that was the longest five minutes that I ever spent in radio.

If you really enjoy your work, enjoy your life, the years go by so fast. I said one time on the air, the years go by so fast, it seems to me that all I do is put up and take down the Christmas tree. So, here, after knocking on their door all those years, WOWO finally called me, and then the biggest surprise of all, when I was ready to retire in 1986, after fifty years on WOWO with Westinghouse—I was supposed to retire—they said, "We have something to ask you." I said, "What is that?" They said, "If we double your salary, will you work one more year?" I said, "Why?" They said, "Because we want to sell the station. We are going to sell it for—like $3 million—or more, but if our ratings go down, then we won't get that much." So, little did I realize when I was a little boy knocking on their door, and they were telling me to get lost, that fifty years later that they would be begging me and doubling my salary to work one more year. So, I thought that was quite a story there.

Eldon Campbell (1941)
HELEN CAMPBELL

Eldon Campbell

(1916–1991)

Eldon Campbell grew up in typical small-town fashion in Alert, Indiana. He delved into the world of journalism as a sports reporter while attending Hanover College. He dropped out of school briefly and went to work for J.C. Penney, developing and honing his salesmanship skills. Seeking more education, he re-enrolled at Hanover College and then at the University of Illinois where he received his first taste of broadcasting at the university's radio station, WILL. In 1938 Campbell went to WOWO in Fort Wayne, Indiana; he worked as an announcer until 1941, when he became the station's program manager. He performed on Hoosier Hop, *making the program a nationwide, Saturday-night broadcast success. When Westinghouse Broadcasting bought KEX in Portland, Oregon, he was named its sales manager. In 1950 Campbell moved to New York, where he became general sales manager for all of Westinghouse Broadcasting. Campbell came to Indianapolis in 1957, joining the staff of WFBM-TV where he was vice president and general manager until 1973. Campbell recognized the potential of cable television in the industry's early years and promoted its development in a number of markets. Highly regarded in the industry, he served as a mentor to many. The following excerpt contains segments of interviews conducted by Jack Williams on 21 April 1982 for Westinghouse and by R. Dale Ogden of the Indiana State Museum in 1986.*

I grew up in southern Indiana, more or less from a modest family, economically, and at the same time, the kind of parents who inspired me to achievements. Had they not been the kind of young people they were when I was born, I probably would still be wandering around some pigsty in Decatur County. But they inspired me, and then my dad was the kind of guy, even though he was a banker, who would get itchy feet on occasion. So while I was educated in grade school in Columbus, Indiana, my high school was in Dundee, Illinois. And from there I came back to Indiana, to Hanover College, and while at Hanover as a sophomore, I determined I wanted to go into broadcasting. Hanover offered me no opportunity for that so I transferred to the University of Illinois where I had an opportunity to be on the air on the university-owned station.

I had no contacts in broadcasting. But beginning in 1936, I had been around the university station, WILL, announcing and doing some very simplistic engineering work—on remotes primarily. I decided I would write letters to companies where I thought I might like to work. I wrote three hundred in total. And I wrote three different letters—I guess to prove a point. The first hundred letters I wrote were the most effective . . . the second hundred and third

Wayne Feed sponsored a fifteen-minute program featuring Eldon as announcer (at left). Bob Shreve (next to Eldon) provided the comedy, and the Blackhawk Valley Boys made the music.   HELEN CAMPBELL

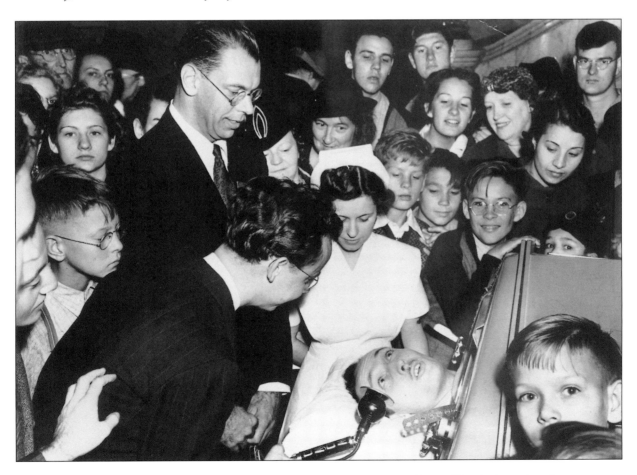

Campbell was known in the Fort Wayne area for his easy, friendly banter on the air. Here he interviewed Franklin Tooke who posed in an iron lung for this spot on polio (ca. 1939). Tooke, a graduate of DePauw University and the American Academy of Dramatic Arts in New York, brought quality programming and innovation to WOWO in his capacity as program director during the 1930s.   HELEN CAMPBELL

hundred weren't very effective at all. So I guess I wrote with believable inspiration when I wrote the first one hundred letters. And I sent along, at request, a disc audition. They were so expensive, I couldn't afford to send them to everybody. Among those who responded, somewhat interestedly, was a man by the name of Ward Dorell, who was manager of WOWO. I noted a few months later that Mr. Dorell had become sales manager. And I noted that W. C. Swartley had become the station manager. So I rewrote to Mr. Swartley, and he . . . wrote back to me very kindly and suggested if I was in the vicinity I might stop by. On my spring vacation, my senior year, I made it a point to stop by. I also, simultaneously, made a point to visit WWVA, in Wheeling, West Virginia, which, coincidentally, was on the same frequency as WOWO. We shared time at night. I did get the job in Jonesboro, Arkansas, immediately following graduation . . . and had my first experiences . . . at a little 100-watt radio station called KBTM. On the same day, in October of 1938 I received a wire from the general manager of WOWO in Fort Wayne, and the general manager of WWVA in Wheeling, West Virginia, when WOWO was owned by Westinghouse and WWVA was owned by the Storer Broadcasting Company. I had a decision to make. I chose Westinghouse because I had been impressed with Mr. W. C. Swartley and the station. And of course, the name of the company was very well known nationally and well-respected. They were both fine companies, but I had a little hankering to go home to Indiana, and so I did go there.

I started as an announcer. . . . I had spent a lot of my time in high school and college in expressive arts—dramatics, theater, and speaking and so on. But I really wanted to be on the business side of broadcasting. I used to listen in awe, as I was a kid, to radio. But I never wanted to be talent. But I couldn't get into the business any other way. I had graduated with a degree in business administration at the University of Illinois because I wanted to be in a business setting, and I wanted to be in business in broadcasting. One of the things that did intrigue me about WOWO was that they were willing to let me do part-time work in the accounting office. I thought that was neat, and so I was one of the very few announcers who did part-time work in an administrative function.

About a year-and-a-half later they put me in a job they called special events director, which was really a public affairs director in today's lingo. From there I went into production, and into program management when Frank Tooke went to KDKA. He left on December 1st of 1941, and I became program manager on December 7th. Everybody's world changed. Mine included—as program manager.

When the draft [for World War II] occurred I came out the nine thousandth-plus capsule. There were 10,000 capsules in Washington in the fishbowl. That delayed my call-up about two years. And in that two-year period, if you were a program manager of a 50,000-watt station, or a limited clear channel, at that time a 10,000-watt station, you were given a deferment for six months. And that deferment was renewed repeatedly throughout my days in Fort Wayne. I was never drafted. That was all occasioned by the Office of War Information—that program managers of clear channel stations were part of the information network of the American public.

Helen and I started out, in the process of becoming personally acquainted, as my role as an announcer and writer, and her role as a singer on various local programs. Plus we had one great advantage in Fort Wayne, which I think made WOWO the unusual station it was, and it became, and has continued to be. That is that we had an opportunity weekly to do programs, either for the NBC Red or Blue network.[22] We were given marginal times. Obviously, they were not prime hours. But we did a lot of shows on Saturday, and while we didn't care [about having to do marginal times], they were really fillers. Transcriptions and recordings as such had not become the mode, for networks certainly. So they would go to certain affiliated stations they thought could produce acceptable musical shows or talk shows or whatever. So Helen and I did a lot of both local and network shows together. I usually wrote them and announced them. Later on, I stopped announcing, and wrote and produced them.

I was the head producer at that time [prior to World War II]. I had the producers working directly for me, under Frank Tooke. I think three at that time worked for me. Carl Vandagrift became manager of WOWO and was manager of the Cleveland station, KYW, which originally was WTAM, Cleveland. And Claire Weidenaar, who was one of the producers, had an interesting experience. He was drafted and I went to work with him because of a program I was doing for Bunker Hill Naval Air Station, for Special Services in the navy. Claire was producing that show. And

The staff helped Eldon celebrate his tenth anniversary at WFBM. From left to right: Jim Mathis, Ruth Hiatt, Bob Flanders, Earl Walker, Gene Vaughn, Marthabel Geisler, Frank Sharp, Don Menke, and Hugh Kibbey.

Eldon Campbell interviewed the young Jim Armstrong, pastor of Broadway Methodist Church.

so I went to work on several people at the Naval Air Station to get Claire into Special Services. And he went to Great Lakes Naval Training Station for his boot camp. Then he came out and was immediately assigned to Hollywood, and he ultimately became the producer of *Command Performance,* for Armed Forces Radio Service. My memory is that he did that for about two-and-a-half, three years. So while he was in the navy blue, he really went rapidly out of Fort Wayne in that role, as the producer of *Command Performance.*

One week after I became program manager and the war started at Pearl Harbor, I became aware, within two hours, that the public wanted to know who was on top of the water and who was on the bottom of the water at Pearl Harbor, right away, which is normal, logical. We took about ten desks and lined them up, and off of the UP and International News Service wires the casualty lists, and we began broadcasting casualty lists by evening. Pearl Harbor occurred at around one o'clock Fort Wayne time on a Sunday afternoon, and by ten o'clock we had casualty lists for all of our territory.

We did a show based upon all the fatalities. We did it on Memorial Day, about 1943—a typical show on patriotism, the war and its impact on homes and people. And we read every name over a span of eighteen hours—those that had been killed from our listening area. And we read it as though it was rolling. It would be like a crawl in television. It was a sound crawl, behind other things that we were doing on the air—music and so on. We'd fade the music down, or we'd fade out of the narrator and this voice reading these names would come back in, throughout the entire day. We did no commercials that day. That was a kind of first for that kind of thing. I don't think it happened again until we lost a president and the war was over. When the war was over there were a couple of days when there were practically no commercials in American broadcasting. I think we were very early in the concept of giving that much to some public affair. That was the major public affair of our time.

We did farm conventions, plowing contests, implement shows. We did a poor man's version of the *National Barn Dance* and the *Grand Ole Opry* and the one down at WLW. We were one of the four in the country. We ended up on the ABC network for a couple of years on Saturday night. ABC had become an identity of its own. I say this rather ungraciously. They probably took us because we were a good filler. We were not necessarily an outstanding show. But at any rate, we did those kinds of things. I think one of the most outstanding shows of a local nature was a Christmas show we did one year with several different music groups. And in those days the great adult musical group in Fort Wayne was . . . the Lutherans—in a strong Lutheran city. And they were just tremendous. They were Fort Wayne's version of the Mormon Tabernacle Choir. We started this show with a little four year old singing "Away in a Manger." It finally ended up with going from a quartet to a high school choir to the combined high school choir and a Lutheran choir of some seventy voices, blending all into one. The soloist was a little four year old, with this tremendous crescendo of these voices. I get a big thrill out of even saying that. Again, I think it was a little early for that concept. It's been done a million times since then. It was a connective type impression of music.

We had an outstanding director of a high school group at North Side High School. I was in my last year at the station, had just about gotten myself convinced, and was getting the management and ownership convinced, that we ought to have a choir director on staff. I wanted this guy, in essence, to run a competition on an annual basis with all kinds of noninstitutional choral groups in the area—to administer and, in effect, direct it when it finally came to performance. We would pay for the expenses of running it, pay his salary. Well, I left and didn't get to do it. But I always thought it would have been a great idea.

Jay Gould was in essence the answer to that. But it didn't happen in quite the same way. Jay was former superintendent of public schools, in the general area of Kalamazoo, Michigan, in a country school system. And he grew tired of it. They didn't call it burnout in those days, but it was. Jay was an extremely talented guy. He could write music and could play it. And he had a way with young people. He wrote several different kinds of shows. We tried some of them out. Some of them weren't that good, and they disappeared. But one show that he did ultimately led to his employment by WLS, Chicago. He was there awhile, but ultimately came back to WOWO. Cocoa Wheats™ was his advertiser, and they wanted him on a Chicago station rather than the Fort Wayne station. He was there well over a year. When we hired him back, we hired him as a farm guy.

The Little Red Barn title I put on the air, but not with Jay. When Jay came back he was the head honcho of *The Little Red Barn. The Little Red Barn* originally was done for what we called "hillbilly music" in those days. It was an eye-opener when we signed on. "Happy Herb" Hayworth was the interlocutor of the show. We had weather and time, and it was live, not recorded. Then as time went on, we got out of strictly entertainment into an informational mode for the farm community we served. But it started out primarily as an eye-opener. The farm director at that time presented a pretty straightforward, head-talking kind of commentary on the markets, the other ancillary things of interest to the farm community. That was separate from *The Little Red Barn.* But as time went on, they mutated.

[At this time] Swartley had already left for Boston, so it was J. B. Conley, who was the manager of the station. And he is really the reason I was transferred to Portland. He asked that I go with him. When I went to Portland, I ceased being program manager almost at the same time the war was over. So almost all of my program management experience was in wartime.

Campbell spent the next eleven years working for the Westinghouse Broadcasting Corporation at assignments on the West and East Coasts. As he says, in 1945 he followed Conley to KEX in Portland, Oregon. The next year he was promoted to sales manager at that station. In 1950 he moved to Westinghouse's New York regional office as executive sales manager. Within two years he became general sales manager, a position he held until 1956 when he moved to Salt Lake City, Utah. Shortly thereafter Wayne Coy urged Time, Inc., to bring Campbell to Indianapolis and WFBM.

I came to work for Time [WFBM in Indianapolis], and the first thing I wanted them to do was to get into FM. The second thing I wanted them to do was speed up their timetable on color television. In Indianapolis, we were way ahead of most stations in the United States as far as colorization was concerned. In fact, one of the times I got my fingers slapped with Time was when I bought two color videotape machines. I think we got the third one off the line.

I started out just absolutely deploring the advent of cable. One day when I was making a presentation on behalf of the industry, putting down cable, about 1961 or early 1962, the thought suddenly occurred to me that I

was fighting the wrong windmill. And I wrote a letter quoting Saul Minsky. The headline was in *Film Daily,* a typical, *Variety*-type headline: "Pay TV: Future of Movie Exhibition." Minsky. I read the story and told, in this letter, that it unnerved me because Minsky knew what the hell he was talking about—the leading distributor of movies in America. I said, "At the very least Time should immediately establish a person who has the responsibility to keep current on all developments in cable. At the very best, they ought to establish a unit and get going."

Well, they did that. They put a person in, and he became the house expert. In 1963, I got a chance to go into a franchise war in Marion, Indiana, and I won it for Time, Incorporated. That was the first cable system Time ever owned, and they didn't even own all of it—only 48 percent of it. But that was the way I thought I could win the franchise. And I also felt that would be a kind of handy-dandy way for Time to find out without getting its feet too wet. We had the management contract, and we built the system.

Simultaneously, I had the chance to go into Terre Haute, and that was the second cable company they owned. I lost in Richmond, Indiana, because I didn't pick some right people. Kokomo? I walked away from it. I shouldn't have. Columbus, Indiana, I walked away from. I shouldn't have. Muncie, Indiana? They walked away from it. They shouldn't have.

The year that I left Time, Incorporated, which was 1973, they sold Terre Haute and Marion to American Cablevision of Denver, Colorado. American Cablevision by then had become the third largest cable system in America. Today it's the largest. . . . I would say to Joe Baudino when I would see him, or to other people in Westinghouse, "Why in the hell is Westinghouse dragging its feet on cable?" Well, they'd tell me about the three or four rinky-dink franchises they had.

Of course, I left Time, and within a week a friend of mine over in Illinois said, "I've got a franchise and no money." That was the beginning of my interest on a personal basis. [Now] I am a stockholder in Fort Wayne cable, called Citizen's Cable Company, which has turned out to be a very exciting personal investment. And as you may know, from some of the other people you've talked to, I'm up to my eyebrows in cable in Indianapolis, Indiana. In fact, that line out there is our company's. The little company we began with over in Illinois—we sold the assets, but we kept the corporate structure. It is the parent company of the Marion County franchise and half the city of Indianapolis. We own 50 percent and have voting control of a system in New Albany. We also have 80 percent and a management agreement of a system just west of here, in an adjoining county. So I'm deeply involved in cable today from a position of saying it ought to blow away, get lost. [But] I will always be grateful to the people and the system of Westinghouse Broadcasting Company, who I still have a great regard for. As a young man, they made me.

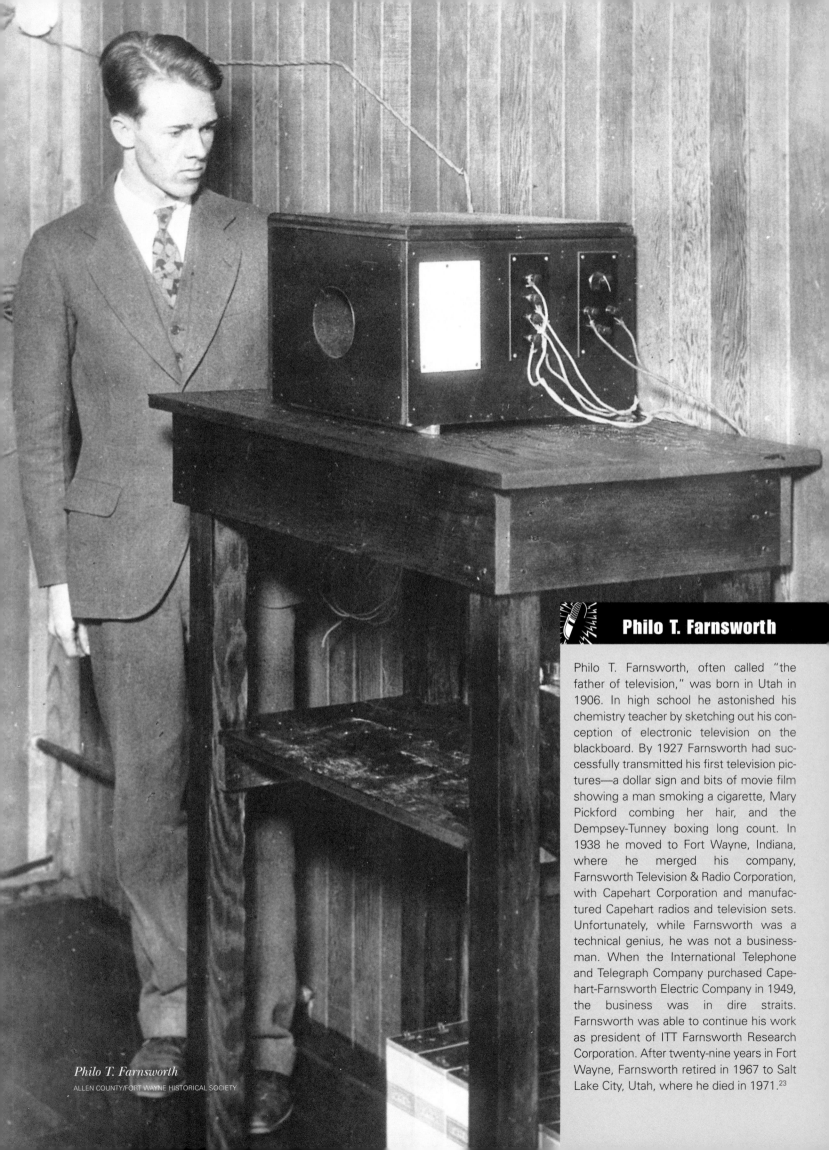

Philo T. Farnsworth

Philo T. Farnsworth

Philo T. Farnsworth, often called "the father of television," was born in Utah in 1906. In high school he astonished his chemistry teacher by sketching out his conception of electronic television on the blackboard. By 1927 Farnsworth had successfully transmitted his first television pictures—a dollar sign and bits of movie film showing a man smoking a cigarette, Mary Pickford combing her hair, and the Dempsey-Tunney boxing long count. In 1938 he moved to Fort Wayne, Indiana, where he merged his company, Farnsworth Television & Radio Corporation, with Capehart Corporation and manufactured Capehart radios and television sets. Unfortunately, while Farnsworth was a technical genius, he was not a businessman. When the International Telephone and Telegraph Company purchased Capehart-Farnsworth Electric Company in 1949, the business was in dire straits. Farnsworth was able to continue his work as president of ITT Farnsworth Research Corporation. After twenty-nine years in Fort Wayne, Farnsworth retired in 1967 to Salt Lake City, Utah, where he died in 1971.[23]

PART THREE

"Window on the Whole World"

The world came to the United States cn 7 December 1941 as the nation was thrust into a global conflict, and concomitantly the role of radio was elevated in American life. During the war radio catered to a heightened urgency to learn more about the larger world. It reached across oceans and added distant locales called Wake Island, Iwo Jima, Kasserine Pass, and Normandy to the average American's vocabulary. Broadcasters at home conveyed news of loved ones fighting overseas, worked to raise morale, rallied support for the war on the home front, and sought to create a sense of normalcy. After the war, people rushed to return to normal, but life as they had known it would never be the same. Population, consumerism, the rise of leisure-time activities, and the need for information all exploded in this era. Radio played an integral part in creating and reporting these changes, and the definition of "in the public interest" took on added meaning.

This second group of broadcasters, college-educated in the main, entered the business during the unfolding drama of World War II. For the most part they were drawn to radio, the "theater of the mind," as youths growing up in the Great Depression. Radio became a link to a wider world for the shy youngsters Harry Martin and Jack Morrow, offering them a way to perform. Tom Carnegie and Jim Phillippe found in broadcasting a creative outlet for their passion for drama. Carnegie and Hilliard Gates discovered it to be a way to remain connected with the sporting events that they so loved. Bill Fall's "nice voice" and Ann Wagner's lovely singing voice and keen intellect provided entrées for them into radio. Once the war ended, these broadcasters grabbed the opportunities afforded by the postwar boom.

The burgeoning economy opened up new venues for radio in the postwar world. Men returned to their former jobs or jammed into colleges and universities under the G.I. Bill; many women left their wartime jobs to become homemakers and start families. Thrilled to be out from under rationing, those who had saved and deferred purchases now had money to spend on a growing inventory of consumer products. They moved into new homes in planned communities in the rapidly developing suburbs of the 1950s. They drove to work in recently manufactured automobiles, listening to their favorite announcers on the radio. In an era of economic abundance, radio broadcasters advertised everything from automobiles to homes to food over the air.

Deejays and radio personalities sold middle America on consumerism as they spun records in studios and at remotes such as fairs, housing developments, and automobile showrooms. Broadcasters supplemented their incomes by playing records at sock hops. National celebrities blew into town to make appearances with local deejays, such as Ann Wagner and Jack Morrow, and to plug their records. Bobby-soxers rocked "around the clock" with Bill Haley and the Comets, and teenagers cruised the local root beer stands and drive-ins as the Top 40 tunes blared from car radios, assaulting the sensibilities of an older public. At the same time, on-air performers invited audience participation on quiz shows, variety shows, and homemaker shows, and rural Hoosiers continued to look to radio announcers such as Harry Martin for agricultural information.

Radio seized upon the intense interest in leisure pursuits of the postwar era. Since the 1930s people had

WTTV broadcast the first hour-long drama televised locally in Indiana on 23 March 1953. Shakespeare's As You Like It *starred Indiana University students David L. Smith and Lucy Emry.* WTTV/DAVID SMITH

Jerry Vance played Captain Starr on All Hands on Deck *with sidekicks Harlow Hickenlooper (Hal Fryar) and Curly Myers. The innovative children's program aired live five days a week in the 1960s.* WRTV-6/PHOTO BY RAY CONOLLY

"IN THE PUBLIC INTEREST"

tuned in to hear their local high school team games. Hilliard Gates and Tom Carnegie were among those whose names came to be associated with the broadcasts of basketball rivalries that culminated in the Indiana High School Boys Basketball Tournament in March of each year. Beyond that, radio built upon a following that had been established with intraservice and interservice sports during the war and helped popularize professional and collegiate teams. First broadcast in the 1920s, the 500-Mile Race became a radio mainstay with the establishment of the Indianapolis Motor Speedway Network in 1952, which took the race to the nation and the world.

By the 1950s television was becoming a powerful force. Philo T. Farnsworth, a television manufacturer in Fort Wayne, had developed the concept of electronic television in the 1920s. Had it not been for the depression and World War II, television might have been ready for the commercial market sooner. Once the war ended and industries retooled for peacetime, television sets became available. In the 1950s and beyond, they became a regular fixture in America's living rooms.

Established in American life as an entertainment medium from the beginning, television also became a vehicle for learning. Syndicated comedy and variety shows such as *Milton Berle*, *I Love Lucy*, and *The Ed Sullivan Show* brought people in

off the front porch to be entertained. Children laughed and learned with shows such as *Howdy Doody*, *Captain Kangaroo*, *Romper Room*, and *Captain Starr*. Other programming was clearly educational in intent. Bill Fall remembered the Ford Foundation's financing of an airborne television platform in the 1960s to educate schoolchildren. The Midwest Program on Airborne Television Instruction (MPATI), stationed on the Purdue University campus, beamed its broadcasts directly from an airplane in flight to schools in a five-state area.

Broadcasting was a means of self-expression for the narrators in this section. For those who had sought a life on the stage, it was an alternative with audience appeal. Shy individuals found it a way to gain acceptance. Unlike many of the earlier narrators, these broadcasters had been avid radio listeners as children and chose this business deliberately. The FCC had established the concept of public interest in the 1930s, but it was the war years that sharpened our narrators' understanding of their civic responsibility. Once the war ended they remolded their sense of the concept to fit the postwar world and the new medium of broadcasting, television. For these narrators as well as their listeners, broadcasting opened up new vistas. It was, indeed, their "window on the whole world."

WTTV

Bloomington, Indiana, had the distinction of being the smallest city in the world with a television station when WTTV went on the air as Channel 10 on 11 November 1949. Although the FCC had originally assigned the channel to Indianapolis, Sarkes Tarzian, WTTV's founder, wanted it closer to his home in Bloomington. Tarzian was an electronics genius who had worked his way through the University of Pennsylvania and had risen to the top at Atwater Kent Manufacturing Company. He then joined RCA and was sent to Bloomington as chief engineer. However, he soon established his own electronics company and built WTTV as an experimental station fitted with a transmitter and camera made by his own engineers. WTTV moved to Channel 4 in 1954 (freeing up Channel 10 for Anton "Tony" Hulman in Terre Haute), when the FCC approved a new tower in Cloverdale to expand the viewing audience to Terre Haute and Indianapolis. Tarzian sold WTTV in 1978 to Telco of Indiana, Inc., for $26 million, the highest price ever paid for a private station in the United States up to that time.[24] In 1997 Sinclair Broadcasting owned the station.

Sarkes Tarzian   COURTESY OF INDIANA STATE MUSEUM/WTTV

Harry Martin (Harold S. Modlin) (ca 1960s)
WRTV-6/PHOTO BY RAY CONOLLY

Harry Martin

(1917–)

In the minds of Hoosiers, genial Harry Martin is almost always associated with agriculture. Many farmers would not plant or harvest their crops until he gave them the word. Born Harold S. Modlin on a farm in Straughn, Indiana, Martin might have become a farmer if he could have made a living at it. Instead he decided to go into broadcasting, leaving Butler University before graduation for a job opportunity at Don Burton's station, WLBC, in Muncie. In 1943 Frank Sharp hired Martin for WFBM, where he spent many years as farm director. Martin was one of the first to predict that television would not last, although he spent many years on TV. His show TV Mailbag was popular, and he later shared the stage for several years with Gabby the Duck at a time when animal mascots were in vogue. While still at WFBM (WRTV), Martin and his wife Marian founded the Rural Radio Network in New Palestine. Their carefully crafted programs earned the Martins great respect among farmers in Indiana. Harry Martin was interviewed in New Palestine, Indiana, on 5 July 1996 while he was visiting from his home in Florida.

I was born in 1917 [in Straughn]. Very few people even have heard of Straughn, Indiana. It's on Highway 40, east of Knightstown and west of Richmond. We were not wealthy people by any means. But, our life centered pretty much around the little fifty-acre farm where I grew up. My father did all of the farming. My mother did all of the housework, and . . . I helped as I grew older. I was a little short kid in overalls with a dog at my heels, and I enjoyed life very much. I used to go fishing with some of our neighborhood kids. I had no living brothers or sisters, so I grew up alone except for the neighbor kids. And life was a beautiful song.

I had built some crystal sets, some little inexpensive home-built radios, and we were close enough to Cincinnati that I could pick up super power WLW, and I got a lot of enjoyment out of listening to the radio, and then a neighbor gave me his old one-tube radio that operated with batteries. It was much more powerful and more enjoyable to listen to. And yes, I soon found out that that's where my friends were. I was a lonely kid. And I felt I was a friend of these people that I heard on the radio—Don Becker of WLW and Sidney Ten Eyck, and I could name a bunch of them from the old, old days. The Mills Brothers, who got their start as a quartet in Cincinnati. And I used to listen to WLS in Chicago. But I really felt attracted to what I heard on the radio. I don't want to say it obsessed me but it interested me very, very much. And to illustrate that—this is silly, but as a kid, I took a can lid and nailed it to the post in my father's barn, and that was my microphone, my playlike microphone.

People were very much family oriented and . . . more isolated [before radio]. If they went for entertainment, they had to drive a good many miles. We did have automobiles by 1920, but it still took a long time to get to any place for meetings or for entertainment, and radio changed all of that. It brought the entertainment right into our homes. It was a great help to rural people because their life was more isolated than that of city folks. Most everybody at that time was concerned about what was going on in the world, and radio news made it possible for us to know immediately what was going on.

I would say this, if I felt I could have made a living farming, I would have wanted to farm. But not owning a lot of land, I didn't think the opportunity was there. So I went to broadcasting. [Butler University] had begun a radio broadcasting school at that time, and that was my primary interest. I think two of the professors in the radio department were very caring people who felt a great amount of empathy with me. Fred Winter was the head of the radio department, and in order to get my college education, I had to work at a night shift in a factory in New Castle, which was Chrysler at that time. I'd get off work at 6:30 in the morning, go home to the farm and have breakfast with my parents, and then drive to Indianapolis for my classes at Butler. And there were some days when I didn't have any opportunity to sleep until it was time to go back to work the next night. So Fred Winter, who had an apartment on the east side of Indianapolis, invited me to come and take my afternoon nap at his home, illustrating his willingness to help a struggling student. Maury Hendricks was another, an assistant to him, and Maury greatly encouraged me to go out and to try to find a job in radio, even if it meant quitting my college. And sure enough the opportunity came along at WLBC.

Don Burton owned [that] small station, WLBC at Muncie, and it was his station. I mean he built it himself, and he operated it himself, and he was a real broadcasting pioneer. He was the greatest play-by-play basketball announcer that I have ever heard. He didn't miss a play. He told it all as it was taking place. He had a rapid-fire delivery—and very, very accurate, remembering the names. He'd do a lot of county basketball tournaments, remembering the names of all of these different kids that he hadn't even seen playing before, but he could run down the lineup verbally and he memorized as he did it. It

was a 250-watt radio. It was a large station for that power because they had a pretty large staff of people writing commercials and a number of announcers. It was a very well-operated station and probably the best-equipped radio station at that time in the Midwest. And sure enough, the opportunity came along at WLBC, and I became a dropout and went to work in radio. Maury Hendricks told me about it. He had heard about it, and I went over and applied and got the job.

The announcer did just about everything except sweep up, and sometimes that also. The announcer had a scheduled shift on the air every day, and it usually involved about ten hours of actual air work a day. And then in his off time, in his free time, he was expected to go out and contact advertisers and find out what they wanted in their advertising copy. . . . So we had very long hours of work, and it was not a highly paid job by any means.

Broadcasting consisted of a bunch of little individually owned stations, each operated in its own way according to the local circumstances and what the needs were. In Indiana, even in the 1940s, basketball was a big item so there had to be a basketball play-by-play announcer at every station. Most of them were doing some news and a number of them, including WLBC, had their separate news director who specialized in news and who made a lot of phone calls to find out what was going on. [They'd get their news off the wire] but in addition the local news—they'd get it from the courtroom and from town-hall meetings and various meetings that were being held.

Most stations had some live entertainers. Some of them had part-time jobs at the station as bill collectors and other types of jobs. Some of the live entertainers supported themselves by playing shows out in the area and publicizing their appearance on the local radio stations. In those days, a person who had quite a bit of song writing ability, and I'm thinking of specific people like Bradley Kincaid. Does that ring a bell? Okay, he was a country singer with a guitar, and there were a number of these people who traveled around to different major stations, big cities. And they would do their program and advertise their songbook. Maybe, "Send fifty cents, and we'll send you a copy of the songbook." Well, it never had any music in it, it was just words. But these were original songs that they had written. And if they were popular entertainers, they could make a lot of money selling songbooks.

Many Hoosier broadcasters fondly recalled the Canary Cottage on Monument Circle. For years the restaurant supplied free breakfasts for the employees of WFBM as they came in to do their early morning programs. The station was located on the floors above it. The headquarters of Emmis Broadcasting Corporation stands on the same ground. IHS BASS PHOTO COMPANY COLLECTION 249915A

Gilbert Forbes, the foremost newscaster in Indianapolis for many years, ripped the news off the wire for his news broadcast at WFBM. PHOTO BY RAY CONOLLY

By 1943 I was looking for a job. . . . I wanted to better myself, make more money. We were married by then, and so I sent out letters of application. I sent one to WOWO Fort Wayne. The manager there was a fellow named Eldon Campbell. And I sent another letter of application to Frank Sharp at WFBM. Well, wouldn't you know, I got replies from both on the same day, but the salary was a little bit better at WFBM so that's where I went. Frank Sharp scheduled me for an audition, but on the day that he scheduled me, he was not there. So he called in another person to listen to me, and his name was Gilbert Forbes. Gilbert interviewed me. And I think he must have recommended me for a job because Frank hired me the next day, or the same day, I guess. I have a feeling that Frank knew all about me when he hired me. He had listened to me on WLBC Muncie. He had a habit of doing that. He'd twirl the dial around and listen to the local voices on the different stations.

Frank Sharp said, "We can't call you Modlin. It's a connotation of sentimentality and everything." And he said, "It's hard to understand, hard for people to understand." And that's true. They spelled it every way when they wrote to me at WLBC, where I used my real name. I agreed that we should call it something else, and Frank came up with Harry Martin which has the same initials as Harold Modlin. I can tell you that Harry Martin was born July 23, 1943.

Frank was—I'll use the words of Paul Roberts to describe him. Paul was a contemporary of ours at WFBM, and he described Frank Sharp as, "a dried up little old man who sits behind a big desk and pulls strings." He was a great—do you have enough time for an illustration? His management style—they had an announcer named Dave Rodgers. He was a very good announcer. And in those days, an announcer could be assigned to a certain show for a certain sponsor, and it was his show, his responsibility. Well, they sold a new Monday evening program of recorded music which Dave Rodgers was to put together each week and voice on the air live. You know, play the recordings, but go on the air live at 6:30 with his Monday evening show. That happened to be the time that Dave Rodgers always went out for his evening break, his evening meal. After he did the commercials on the Gilbert Forbes six o'clock news, ending at 6:15, then Dave would go out to lunch—evening meal. And on this first night that

Dave's new show was scheduled to air after a big intense publicity buildup—"Listen for Dave Rodgers, and so and so, Indianapolis Brewing Company at 6:30 Monday night." And after all of that buildup, Dave forgot it. He walked out just like it was any other Monday night. And airtime came, and Dave wasn't there. "What will we do? Well, where does he keep his"—he had a recorded theme on a big disk. We started looking for that. We didn't think to look under D for Dave. That's where he had filed it, under D for Dave. And so they grabbed the recording and went on the air. They had the script. The script was all written and in place so somebody else went on the air with the *Dave Rodgers Show,* and about twenty minutes later, Dave came up through the elevator door not even suspecting that he had missed his show. Frank Sharp, the big boss, was sitting on the desk at the reception area. And he said, "Dave, are you in a hurry?" "No, no, I've got plenty of time." (He still hadn't tumbled.) And Frank said, "Well, your new show went on the air twenty minutes ago." Nothing further was ever said about that. There was no recrimination, no punishment, no "Don't you ever let that happen again." None of that. Frank was that kind of a manager. He knew that Dave felt completely defeated over it. So why should he rub it in? I would say [Frank Sharp] was a great mentor, a great inspiration. I loved him; he was a great man.

I've heard Frank Sharp tell of how Dick Powell had this Hollywood opportunity, and I think Dick Powell must have considered Frank Sharp his mentor, too, a person he could go to for advice. So Dick came to Frank and said, "What do you think? Should I take this job? It's big time in Hollywood." Frank said, "By all means, take it. You'll never get anywhere as a singer and announcer here. You'll never get anywhere beyond here." Even though he was a good employee, Frank urged him to go on and seek the big time. He didn't stand in their way. He was a great person; there's no denying it.

Gilbert [Forbes] was, to me, aloof. He didn't say much. He did his own thing. And he was sometimes pretty irritable with other people who worked with him. One time he almost didn't get there in time for his Sunday noon broadcast. I was on duty as an announcer. Three minutes to airtime, and he still wasn't there. And that's very unusual for him. So I went back to the newsroom and began gathering up some things thinking, "Well, you know, I'll go on with the news. The news has to go on. If he's not here, what will I do?" So I got it together and started for the studio just as he walked in. And he scowled at me and he said, "What's the matter? Didn't you think I'd be here?"

[The station was located at] 48 Monument Circle. Now it had a history farther back than that. I think they were in the Merchants Bank at one time, but when I joined them they were at 48 Monument Circle. And that was a beautiful location because on the third floor was the Press Club and on the first floor of that same building was the Canary Cottage, a great restaurant at that time. And they had some employees who got to work early in the morning. And their greatest joy in life was seeing the radio people well fed. And they would always have breakfast—pancakes and all sorts of things—ready when I got to work and when the other early people got to work. And we never paid anybody anything. We never mentioned Canary Cottage on the air. They just were generous and wanted to feed us, I guess.

I was interested in farm broadcasting, and saw it as a way of specializing because I had a farm background. I did not have an agricultural degree, but I didn't think you needed an agricultural degree to be a farm broadcaster. You could report what the experts said. So that's what I chose to do. And I applied for the job when Henry Wood retired [in 1946]. I was already working there at the time, and in fact had worked for two or three years on Henry's *Hoosier Farm Circle* program on radio. I think Frank was involved in that too.

And at that time, it seems to me, that the farm director of a station was more of a special person than he is today due to an increased emphasis on getting away from agriculture. . . . Every farm director on the radio in those days did market reports regularly. "The hog market today is a quarter higher, top fifteen twenty-five"—well, whatever the price was, you know. And grains, the commodities that are produced in the area. Hogs, cattle, corn, soybeans would be the four principal crops. [I would do this in the] early morning, like as early as five o'clock, and midday, because farmers in those days nearly all came in from the field at noon for their dinner. . . . They wanted to get up to date on the market. I had a lot of interviews with Purdue people, agricultural specialists, and any kind of an agricultural specialist that I could find anywhere because I needed at least one interview every day for the *Hoosier Farm Circle.*

WFBM carried the early—well not early morning—eight o'clock in the morning news of America [for CBS]. And in that fifteen-minute newscast, they would switch around maybe three or four different locations and pick up a one or a one-and-a-half-minute report from different people across the country, people that they designated as their correspondents. I guess I applied for the job. And we were not employed by the network, but I discovered that they got paid twenty-five dollars for each origination, and that was big money in those days to have an extra twenty-five bucks. And in fact at one time it was a close race to say whether I was earning more of my money from CBS or more of my money from WFBM, the local station. But I wanted to do it, and I found that all I had to do was . . . to ask Marthabel [Geisler] to send TWX to the editor in New York for CBS radio, Henry [Wefing], offering a certain suggestion for a news pickup. And later that same day he would send a reply, either a yes or no. And it seemed to work out, for quite a number of times he wanted what I had to offer.

[The reports] were offbeat agriculture. Okay, for example, when they built the bypass around US 52 in Lafayette, there was a story about the fact that this was really a bypass to bypass a bypass, because things were already getting so congested. And this was long before Interstate 65 ever came on the scene. But I did a story about that on CBS, and they liked it. I did one that was nonagricultural. Firestone was developing a new blowout-proof tire, and they were having it tested at the Indianapolis Motor Speedway. So I, being the representative of CBS, was designated to ride in the stock car with Wilbur Shaw as he tested that car.[25] And there were a number of political reports, you know, like if a political convention was going on. Whenever I came up with an interesting idea that they liked and had room for, they would wire back. And this is to me an interesting sidelight.

I had to have an engineer assigned in order to feed the program live to the network. That meant calling in an extra engineer on overtime early in the morning, because the guy that was on the control board couldn't do it, couldn't handle the network feed at the same time. So I had to phone in—after Marthabel would call me at home—and say, "Henry Wefing wants you on CBS News tomorrow morning." Then, I had to call the chief engineer at WFBM and tell him that I needed an engineer for tomorrow morning's feed on CBS. And I'd always hold the telephone a long way from my ear because I knew he'd throw a string of expletives at me. "Why we can't afford to—." You know, all that stuff, but he always did it anyhow. He always scheduled an engineer. The station paid for it. I never discussed it with Frank, but I'm sure they considered it good exposure having Indianapolis—I never mentioned WFBM but they liked it anyhow. . . . So it was a good thing for me and I got intensely interesting fan mail.

[Television] really did change the role of radio. It made our lives quite different because in the station I worked for, we quickly had to learn how to do television. And nobody knew anything about how to do television so we had to go stumbling blindly along, made a lot of mistakes. It became a much bigger enterprise than radio had been in an individual station. [Television required] a lot more equipment and a lot more people, and [it was] less personal, very much subject to the whims of people in executive positions who may not know a thing about what they're talking about.

I want to say right now, I was one of the first who predicted that television would not last. I thought it was a nice idea to put pictures on it but it's not worth it. People won't pay that extra money just to have the picture. That was the one time I was wrong [laughs].

Well, this program [*TV Mailbag*] was TV brickbats and bouquets. And I sat at a desk. There was no visual impact at all. I'd pick up one letter after another and read from it, and try to make some kind of an answer. This was exactly the same thing [as *Radio Mail Bag*] only I was sitting there in front of the camera. And in fact,

people would get so they would watch the size and shape of the letter I was reading from and they could identify whether I was really reading their letter or not. [Some complaints were]: "Too much wrestling, too much wrestling on television." Then the next one would probably say, "Not enough wrestling." And it was pretty evenly divided. I had a God-given ability to look impartial, and I tried not to reveal my feelings. I tried to be very patient

Gabby the Duck
(Sidekick to Harry Martin)

Martin relates, Many people have said, "The person who can't make it on his own in show business needs an animal he can depend on. Let the animal be the star of the show." So Gabby became the star of the show. I brought him in—he lived out here with us and his six wives. For ducks, that's legal. But he lived a very pleasant rural life, except the boss would catch him every morning to take him in to work until he got smart to that, and he'd disappear when it was time to catch him—disappear into the darkness, because we went to work early in the morning. So I had to finally arrange to catch him the night before and put him in his pen and keep him in his pen until it was time to put him into the little quacker box (we carried him to the station in the car). So Gabby the Duck rode to the station with me every morning. This went on for years. And they had a special pen built for him about the size of a desk, only it was low so the camera could look down at

him inside and [we] would cover it with papers on the inside, and he would stand in there and continually quack. They had a special microphone that was Gabby's mike. And you could hear him all through the conversations that were going on. He didn't talk loud. He was a drake. In the duck world, the drake—the male—has a high-pitched "quack, quack" kind of a voice. He was in the background all the time. . . . They thought it was a good gimmick, that's all. Oh, a terrible nuisance . . . and it wasn't so easy for Gabby, either, [but] we were very kind to him, and he was regularly fed. We would end the show with him—the propman would set Gabby on the desk right in front of me. And as we were saying good-bye, he'd fly off towards the camera—papers fluttering in every direction, total chaos and confusion, and mothers with schoolchildren watching knew when the duck flew it was time to get ready for the school bus.

Gabby the Duck is shown here sampling WFBM coffee.   WRTV-6

A jovial Harry Martin interviewed guests on his long-running farm show at WFBM.   WRTV-6/PHOTO BY RAY CONOLLY

and understanding and recognize the fact that these people who wrote their comments were very serious about it, and they wanted their comments to be aired.

One of the frequently asked questions that I used to get on *TV Mailbag* was, "Does Gilbert Forbes have any legs? Is he able to walk?" Because we never saw him walking, [just] sitting at a desk. In those days, [WFBM] was the only station, the only television station in town for five or six years, I'd say. And it meant that any television set in that area would be tuned to WFBM-TV because there was no choice, no alternative. And I don't know, I think about the time that we got on the air with WFBM-TV, the FCC froze television applications. So a period of several years went by that we had the only station in town. And the rumor somehow spread that Gilbert didn't have any legs, and that's why you always saw him seated at his desk. So one night, I discussed this with him ahead of time and he said, "Let's put that rumor to rest right now." He said, "I'll walk in, and the camera will show my legs as I walk in, and then they pan up and see that it's me as I walk over to talk to you." And we did that one night live on *TV Mailbag* and that answered the question.

We started our [Rural Radio Network] in 1972. However, I did not leave WFBM. I wore two hats for several years, and they knew about it. They knew I was operating this radio network, but they didn't really like it. And I could see eventually down the road that my job was going to be threatened. So we began trying harder and harder to make ends meet and make it successful on the radio network. That was our future, and I'm thankful to them for letting me do it as many years as they did.

We started out with eleven [stations]. And then quickly we went to twenty-two when we got a new sponsor that wanted on other stations, and that went on for several years. And it grew in acceptance. We didn't try to expand with more stations because we felt we basically covered rural Indiana with the twenty-two stations. And our programs were timely, and they were very well put together, I say modestly, and very carefully timed so that we never ran over on anybody even for a second. And this made them acceptable to the stations; and then we learned another thing from Ray Wilkinson, which was not being done much with other networks.[26] And that was we shared our advertising revenue with our affiliates. We sold the advertising and like we would collect, say, ten dollars

a spot from Amiben Herbicide, we would give a couple of dollars or three dollars to each station out of that. And in some cases we had to pay whatever their going rate was. But they could see a money-making opportunity in it just by putting those tapes on and playing them.

Of course, our programming was always made up of a lot of interviews with educational people, with the Purdue specialists and anything related to farming. And of course, by then we had portable tape recorders, very much like these here. And we'd both carry recorders. Marian was able to see in those days, and she drove her car and went out and did interviews. She'd go to the Pioneer Corn sales meetings and find fifty interview guests—just line them up and interview one after another. And then those interviews would appear later in the month on our programming. They [the interviews] went out twice a week in the interest of being as current as possible. And then for the live programming, somebody had to be here all the time to feed the morning and noon market and weather reports.

John Block was the U.S. Secretary of Agriculture. In fact, I was invited several times on what he would call "trade missions." And let me stress and emphasize and please don't omit this: we never traveled at government expense. We paid our own way. And if we went in a government airplane—like we had one that we called "Ag One," we didn't have Air Force One; we had "Ag One." That was John Block's means of transportation. You paid a good price to go, but we felt it gave us a lot of prestige among broadcasters. It was a way of letting the farm listener know that we were interested in what they were doing, in helping to develop markets. And with the telephone systems that we had even then, we could file reports direct over here. We always recorded them; we never went on the air live from Russia or from Australia or anywhere else live, but we could send reports over which they would record and then insert into our program. There's a posed photograph in my book about farm exports that shows me standing in a raincoat in front of a Paris hotel on one of those reporting trips. And I carefully folded a copy of *Le Figaro* under my arm so I'd look like a real dashing foreign correspondent.

There has been over the years, a constant struggle to keep agricultural programming on the air. So many stations didn't want anything pertaining to agriculture. . . . They felt it drove away their city audiences. We were just talking last night with our son-in-law who was also involved with the Rural Radio Network, which we operated late in our lives, late in our careers. And we were laughing about a new station manager who came in—in a small town—I won't name it, 15,000 people, and he contacted us and said he didn't want to carry our farm programming any more because he was going to concentrate on his urban audience in a 15,000-population town. That was somewhat illustrative of what was happening. They didn't want to have farm programming because they thought it would automatically turn off the city people. It shouldn't, and I'm glad to see recent trends where that's been reversed. WIBC in Indianapolis is carrying a great amount of farm programming again, and they give the farm broadcaster enough time to say what he has to say. They don't cut him off with a thirty-second blurb.

I think the radio station needs to have a visible presence within the community and have people from the station attending events for community interest. I don't think they ever changed the FCC laws that said that a station was supposed "to operate in the public interest, necessity, and convenience." Sometimes they get a long way from that, but I really think that's the obligation. I think we were more concerned about that in the early days than the people that I observe in it now. Maybe not, I don't know; it seems that way to me. [With Rural Radio Network] there was no individual station, although we always tried to abide by the rules so that we didn't get our stations in trouble.

I think without any hesitation, I can say I got my greatest enjoyment out of knowing that I was a network correspondent, being heard live coast to coast. That thrilled me. That gave me a feeling of achievement, and getting, as I mentioned earlier, fan mail from people all over the country. I really enjoyed that. That was a beautiful experience, and I'm glad I had it. I enjoyed the travel that we were able to do with our own network. I probably didn't especially enjoy it at the time, but as I look back, I have happy memories of our family teamwork, working together on the Rural Radio Network. I think it was a good system.

Jack D. Morrow (mid-1940s)
WISH-TV

Jack Morrow

(1918–)

Quiet and reflective, Jack D. Morrow offers valuable insights into the nature of broadcasting. He began his fifty-year career in 1940 at a small radio station (WCMI) in Ashland, Kentucky, where young radio hopefuls went to learn the trade. Although his college degree qualified him to teach, he always had a yearning to become a radio announcer. After three months at WCMI Jack joined WIBC as an announcer, later becoming program director. In 1942 Eugene Pulliam hired him as a news commentator for WIRE, changing his name to John because it sounded more formal. Morrow stayed only a year, however; he went on to become the news manager and commentator for WISH Radio for the next five years. In 1948 he made his final career change, back to WIBC. There he had the opportunity to display the full range of his broadcasting and administrative talents. Truly a jack-of-all-trades, Morrow moved with ease from on-air salesman to disc jockey to news reporter to assistant farm director to color man for basketball games to producer of the 500-Mile Race broadcast. He also prepared license-renewal applications for Fairbanks Broadcasting Company stations. He ended his radio days in 1990 as commercial operations manager and public service director. Morrow was interviewed in February 1994 at his home in Indianapolis.

When I started out in radio, and I think a few years before that, radio was a means of entertainment for the family. It later became a vehicle for information and telling people what was going on in the world. Today, it's still a vehicle for telling what is going on in the world. In addition, it offers the public an opportunity to participate—to get their two cents in—and that's the coming of the talk radio stations. If you listen across the dial, you'll find that probably 90 percent of the radio stations have a host who is the moderator or talk host, and the other 10 percent are offering musical entertainment. Now, it's the job of the talk host to moderate the various telephone calls and personal appearances of people who come into the studios. The gamut of material runs from what's going on in the world today to politics, race relations, sex, just about anything that you want. Most of the hosts are prejudiced one way or the other. They're either conservative or liberal, and most stations have a sprinkling of both. Some stations are strictly conservative, and others are completely liberal. It's an interesting concept, but one that I personally feel is not going to last forever. It's already beginning to get a little bit old or stale, and people you talk to say they'll listen for about a half an hour, and that's about all they can take. But I'm almost positive that the swing's going to be back to entertainment, because people need that relaxation.

DIAL 1070 **WIBC** 50,000 WATTS
THE FRIENDLY VOICE OF INDIANA

Many radio stations had an announcer who read the comics to children on Sundays. "Uncle Wally" Nehrling was a favorite in the Indianapolis area.

So many teenagers sent for photos of Jack Morrow, WIBC's popular deejay on Hoosier Request Time, that the station printed postcards and sold them for a dime.

With a premise that would be difficult to sell in the 1990s, Jim Shelton's popular Pick-a-Pocket show in the 1950s invited people to pick a question from a vest especially designed for Shelton. WIBC RADIO

I think radio has also become an instrument of determining history. For instance, radio, along with television, can sway millions and millions of people to decide one way or another on a variety of subjects, particularly in politics, particularly in war-torn areas. It was strictly radio and television that probably prompted our government to go into Somalia and various other places. They can do that through word and picture. It gets the sympathy of the American people. Had you not had that, we probably would never have gone in there, because you wouldn't have gotten the word and the picture.

[The media] is not corrupt, but I think they try to sway you one way or the other. I don't know whether that's corruption or not. Depends upon what side you're on. My statement is that they do control the public. That's my own personal opinion. Can you sit through an hour of the atrocities of Bosnia or any of these countries—Africa—just sit through it watching all these pictures of kids being maimed? Can you actually sit through this and not say, "Hey, we ought to do something about this?" Now, they can control that. It may be isolated instances, but they present it as though it's going on everywhere. That's where they can control you. They can influence a president to send troops. I think they did that with [President George] Bush, and I think they do it with [President William] Clinton. They just absolutely control it.

As a child I was kind of backward and timid and was sick a great deal of the time. I wasn't really a part of any group; I had very few friends. I was an only child—very much protected—and I really think I formed the background for wanting to get into radio in those very early childhood days. I wanted to be recognized, and that's one way I thought of doing it. I was recognizing people in the radio business, because I was listening to programs. Even from the days of the crystal set, I thought, "Gee, everybody knows who these people are who do the announcing. I'd like to do that."

Of course, after I went to college, I outgrew the backward bit. In fact, it was probably the first time I had been away from home. But I never lost that little background that I'd like to get into radio, although I took a teacher's course at Miami University and got a license to teach which I never used. But I didn't like teaching.

[Miami University is in] Oxford, Ohio, not too far from home. I went home on weekends during the first year. The second year I had a job in the dormitory serving meals. That was for three years, and I also sold subscriptions to the *Oxford Press,* which was the local newspaper, and I also worked at an Oxford printing shop until my dad found out. He said, "If you're going to work in the printing business you can come home, and I'll pay you to do it" [laughs]. But I did continue the dormitory work. . . . It took about three hours. I could still eat with my friends at the regular time.

[My father] had a newspaper, and I worked on that all through high school and college during summer vacations. I not only helped write the newspaper, but I also worked back in the shop. I soon discovered I didn't want that career either. That was a family business, and I stopped the family business by going into something else, because I was the only child. It was through my father's urging that I did go out of the printing business.

After I graduated I went back and worked that summer in my father's print shop—a very hot summer by the way. I more or less decided to try to get a teaching job, but half-heartedly. I should have had my resumé out much earlier than that. But I kept thinking, "I really would like to get into radio." So I decided over a weekend that—I told my dad, "I'm going to make a stab at getting into radio. I'm going to call the radio stations and try to set up an audition and see if they'll give me a chance to talk." I got two or three auditions, oddly enough. I don't know whether they'd ever give them out now. One of the stations was WKRC in Cincinnati, and the assistant program director and staff organist was Ruth Lyons. Ruth gave me an audition, and she told me afterwards, "You've got a good voice, but you don't know how to phrase, and you don't know how to do it. I just wouldn't pursue it. I'd try something else." And so I told my dad, "I guess I'm doomed to teach, which I don't want to do, or be here." He said, "Well, you can go into partnership with me. It'll be great with me." I'd just about decided to do that when Ruth Lyons called me at home and she said, "I got to thinking about it; your voice is okay. I just heard of a station in Kentucky that'll take *anybody.*" She said they wanted an announcer just to learn—a kind of an apprentice-type thing. She said, "That's all they use down there. They've got two more down there now learning, and there's another opening; a guy just left. It only pays $13.50 a week, but if you want to try it, I'll recommend you and get you down there." My dad said, "I think

F L A S H

EISENHOWER HEADQUARTERS ANNOUNCES ALLIES LAND IN FRANCE

6   BZ334AEW

47PA

BULLETIN

LONDON--THE ALLIES HAVE LANDED IN FRANCE. THIS IS OFFICIAL.

IT'S ANNOUNCED BY GENERAL DWIGHT EISENHOWER.

ALLIED TROOPS BEGAN LANDING ON THE NORTHERN COAST OF

FRANCE THIS MORNING, STRONGLY SUPPORTED BY NAVAL AND AIR FORCES.

HERE IS THE TEXT OF GENERAL EISENHOWER'S COMMUNIQUE:
QUOTE: UNDER THE COMMAND OF GENERAL EISENHOWER ALLIED NAVAL

FORCES SUPPORTED BY STRONG AIR FORCES BEGAN LANDING ALLIED ARMIES

THIS MORNING ON THE NORTHERN COAST OF FRANCE."

THE GERMANS ASSERTED THE LANDINGS EXTENDED BETWEEN

X LE HAVRE AND CHERBRXXX CHERBOURG, ALONG THE SOUTH SIDE OF

THE BAY OF THE SEINE AND ALONG THE NORTHERN NORMANDY COAST.

BERLIN ASSERTED THAT PARACHUTE TROOPS DESCENDED IN NORMANDY.

Morrow received news of the Normandy Invasion from this Teletype in June 1944.

you'd better do it. Otherwise you're just going to mess around and be unhappy and think about whether you should have done that or not. You can always come back." And I said, "Well, okay." So, I went down there and learned how to announce. They had a pretty good program director there who later went to Boston as a main newsman. He taught me a lot of things—phrasing and that type of thing—friendliness on the air so people would think that you're one of them, you know. That's the way I approached it, and that's the way he said you should approach it.

I was so thrilled to get in it, and the other two guys were the same way. They were just thrilled to get into it. Jim Shelton had graduated from high school and had worked in a machine factory, and he was fed up with it. He always wanted to get into radio. In fact, he even went to drama school when he couldn't get a job in radio. It was the same for all three of us. We just had a good time learning and finding out things about radio that we were always interested in. I was kind of an apprentice announcer. We announced song titles, and we gave news. I wrote copy and did everything.

By the time three months rolled around, all three of us thought we were pretty good which wasn't true at all [laughs]. We knew very little. That was a whole world, and we thought everything was like that. But one evening we decided to sit down and write some letters to stations around the area. There was a station in Portsmouth, Ohio, and I know we wrote to Columbus and Cincinnati. I said, "I think I'll write to Indianapolis. I saw on the wire that one of these stations, WIBC, is going to increase their power. They might be looking for somebody." We all wrote—very few answers, of course. I did get one . . . from WIBC. "We've got an opening. Come." So I did, and I got the job. That paid twenty-five dollars a week, so I was moving up. A fellow by the name of Robert Longwell [hired me at WIBC], and the owner was H. G. Wall of Detroit. It was on the ninth floor of the Indianapolis Athletic Club. There was a ballroom at one end, and WIBC had its studios in the other end. You got a day-and-a-half off. You worked until noon on Saturday and took a bus home. Then you came back on Monday and worked the later shift. So, you actually had a full day.

I was an announcer [at WIBC] and just did about what I did at WCMI at Ashland. They had the same transcription services, but they had a few more live programs. There was a young lady who came in and did book reviews, and another lady who played the piano. I would announce those programs, or introduce them and tell what they were going to play. I did some news, and I did some sportscasts. It was a daytime station, so you were on from sunrise to sunset. The day was short, and we had a lot of announcers who really didn't work that much. I'd been there about a year, I guess, and I heard a rumor that I wasn't going to fit in too well. I had done some writing at the other station, so I went to this Miss Geiger and said, "You know I could handle that writing job." This fellow was going to leave and go to Flint, Michigan. I thought I ought to get myself a job here. If I couldn't announce, I could write. And she said, "I think you could, too." So she went to Mr. Wall, and I got the job. I kept the announcing and in addition started this deejay program, *Hoosier Request Time.* That's the one that grew so popular. That was my first deejay show and the first of its kind in town.

It was a half-hour of spinning requests, and we asked people to write in and ask for their favorite songs—popular songs. No phone calls And we invited them up to the station if they wanted to see the program. We had a studio so they could sit there, and that was every day. Then we extended it on through Saturdays from one to two o'clock. These were just popular records of the day—kind of like the Top 10 would be now. We didn't have a record library as such. We had these transcription libraries, so we had to borrow the records from Block's—the Wm. H. Block Company—and we gave them a plug on the air. "These records courtesy of the Wm. H. Block Company." When the records got old, they replaced them; we never owned them. Kids loved it. They could write in for their favorites, and we read all these stupid names and everything. In a half hour you only played about five records, because you didn't have time. So we just had flocks and flocks of high school kids every single day. We got so many, and then we'd have to turn the rest of them away. Then, they were asking for pictures, so the company made a whole bunch of pictures. They said, "Instead of giving these away, why don't you tell them that we'll send a picture to anybody who sends in a dime." Postage only cost a cent then.

After the show got popular, and I was doing continuity, the boss decided I might as well do the rest of it and run the place, because I was doing that anyway. In that particular case it wasn't too difficult, because it was just arranging announcers' schedules and seeing that people were there when they were supposed to be. Programs were pretty well set. If you had a cancellation, you had to arrange to have a filler there. And we had some religious programs, and we had to be sure that they were on time. These were just programs where a minister would come in and make a fifteen-minute talk or so and then make a pitch for money, so he could support the program. Then we carried churches, too. Those were not paid. We'd carry half-hour church services or an hour church service. Sunday was pretty well filled with church services.

We also carried Mutual Broadcasting System at a later time; that was the end of 1942 before I left. That was all of the mysteries—*The Shadow*, *The Green Hornet*, all of those. You probably don't even remember all of that stuff, but all Sunday afternoon was mysteries on Mutual, and they were very popular. I just had to keep those Mutual schedules, our own schedules, and the announcers' schedules. We made a few personal appearances, and I had to arrange those.

If they had a special news bulletin flash, they'd ring a bell that was on the machine. They'd press a button, and this thing would ring. And the engineer said, "This thing's been ringing for about two minutes. I went out there, and there's a flasher on there." He ripped it off and gave it to me. I went in and said, "I'd better interrupt this program." I did and said, "The Japanese have just bombed Pearl Harbor." I really didn't realize the significance of it at the time, you know. I wondered, "What's Pearl Harbor?" [laughs]. That was the end of radio as we knew it. It was a whole different ball game after that. We were on the Mutual Network, and we just stopped the program then and went on into network. We monitored, and they were already started. We joined them, and from then on it was the rest of the day.

Carole Lombard was one of the top movie actresses of that time, and she appeared in many top movies. Her husband was Clark Gable. She came to Indianapolis for a bond rally to sell bonds at the statehouse grounds, and that was the first remote broadcast that I'd ever done for WIBC. We went to the statehouse grounds. She made her appearance, and I got a chance to talk to her. She was a very nice person, and her job was to sell bonds. Personalities like movie stars were going all over the country then to sell

bonds, and she was the one chosen for Indianapolis. She, of course, was killed on her return flight to Hollywood. . . . I woke up the next morning and saw that headline in the paper. You can imagine the shock having just done a program with her. So, that's one memory that really lived on for a long, long time.

[WIRE] had a newsman, Dick Reed, who went to the service. I had known Dick before, just through friendship. He said, "I'm going in, and if you want to try for this news job, they're going to really need somebody who can talk and do the news and read properly." I had learned to do that by that time, believe it or not. So I went over and auditioned, and Mr. Pulliam said, "Yeah, great." I had three newscasts a day, and that's all. They were in the Claypool Hotel on the ninth floor at Illinois and Washington. [The programming] was altogether different than WIBC. They ran the soap operas, *Ma Perkins*, *Linda's First Love*, things of that type. They appealed more to the adult, the mature audience. And their newscast—everything was very formal, very formal. Wally Nehrling was the closest thing to a human being they had there [laughs]. Uncle Wally—it was a wake-up show in the morning, and he kidded around with everybody. He was the first one to do that. People really listened; he had the audience, the whole audience. He gave the time, kidded around, talked about his family; everybody knew Wally and his wife and who his kids were. He read the funnies on Sunday—the comics out of the *Indianapolis Star*. It was kind of happy-go-lucky there at WIBC, but at WIRE you got there on time; you went to your office, and you worked. There wasn't too much socializing then.

Nina, that was [Mr. Pulliam's] second wife, I think. She was a goodie; she was the operating person. She didn't like me too well. That was one of the reasons I left at the end of a year; I didn't see much future there. She'd call up—she didn't like my voice in the first place. The rest of them did. You have to watch that kind of stuff. She was still cheesed off because Gilbert Forbes was still number one [laughs]. I didn't expect to ever beat Gilbert Forbes. Dick Reed couldn't do it. [Nina] was the one that sat around all the time and monitored and called—that type of thing. When I went over to do news, he [Mr. Pulliam] said, "I believe, and Nina believes [laughs], that you would be a lot more believable if you would use 'John.' 'Jack' just doesn't sound like it's supposed to be a newsman. Too

JACK MORROW'S
WIBC HILLBILLY HIT PARADE!

FEATURING RECORDS SELECTED FROM JANES' LARGE AND COMPLETE STOCK

For the tops in HILLBILLY and WESTERN music, listen to JACK MORROW daily on MORNING NABORS from 5 a.m. to 7 a.m. and SATURDAYS on CROSSROADS PARTY from 8:15 to 10:00 a.m. and HICKORY SHINDIG from 1 p.m. to 2:30 p.m.—all on Radio Station WIBC on 1070 on your dial.

Hear These Hillbilly Hits on—
COLUMBIA RECORDS

JACK MORROW'S HILLBILLY HIT OF THE WEEK:
Mommy Can I Take My Doll to Heaven? I'm Saving Mother's Wedding Ring—Ray Smith

Hillbilly Fever—
Then I Had to Get Married
"Little" Jimmy Dickens

I've Got Five Dollars and It's
Saturday Night—I'm Gonna
Leave This Darned Old Town
Ted Daffan

Angel Mother—Luck Seven
George Morgan

The Waltz of Shawnee—
They Tell Me I'm Crazy
Lonie and Tommie Thompson

Just a Closer Walk With Thee
—Good News
Stamps Quartet

Love Song in Thirty-Two Bars
—Tennessee, Kentucky and
Alabam'
Johnny Bond

HEAR THE HITS ON
COLUMBIA 7-INCH LP RECORDS
Play automatically on new LP changers 33⅓ RPM—One Standard speed—The accented speed—Superb LP Quality—No buttons, inserts or gadgets required—"Non-slip" serrations—Complete catalog—All-time standards, latest pop hits and short classics.

JANES MUSIC

Advertisement for Hillbilly Hit Parade *(ca. 1950)*

casual—sounds like a nickname." [Jack] is on the birth certificate. I used John because he asked me to. I was John all the time I was there. Then, when I went to WISH, I was John until the time when I did the late night show. Then I used both; I was John on the news and Jack from eleven to twelve. There were a few kooks who thought there were two of us. They were the ones who sent their requests on toilet paper in crayon [laughs].

Gilbert [Forbes] had the news audience [at WFBM]. Dick Reed had been good, but Gilbert Forbes was superb. I mean, he was so authoritative. He never editorialized at all; he just really gave the news every night at ten o'clock. That was who people listened to—Gilbert Forbes.

The Byrd sisters—Dessa and Virginia Byrd . . . they had a program. They also played these organs at the Indiana [Theater] and Circle [Theatre]. There were all these staff musicians and staff bands that these radio stations had. WIRE, like I said, was very formal and sophisticated, and they had more mature programming. There was a young lady there named Madelyn Pugh who wrote commercials. She left about the same time I did and went to Hollywood. She was Lucille Ball's chief writer for I Love Lucy.

I didn't notice too much camaraderie at WIRE; it was kind of stiff at WIRE, really, and I had Nina looking over my shoulder all the time. I just didn't want to stay there any longer. But when I went over to WISH—that was a news station. They were gung ho to get moving and did. The McConnells had that station—C. Bruce McConnell and later his son, Bob. They mixed in with the employees and had parties and stuff like that—more social life. They had people like Chuckles [Reid] Chapman, and we horsed around an awful lot. They probably had fifty people working at WISH and only needed about half of them [laughs]. But, it was fun then. That was a new station; they did a lot of advertising, and my picture appeared in lots of it. I just thought it was a better opportunity.

I think we started out with the main newscast of fifteen minutes. WISH kept to that when I went over there. But then they started to expand, and we had two newscasts over the dinner hour—at five and at six. Then, somebody else had to do one of them. I think the last year I was at WISH we had about three news people to take care of things, and they asked me to do an hour of recording from eleven to twelve at night after I'd done the ten o'clock news. They knew I'd done that at the other station, and

they knew what the record was for popularity. Chuckles Chapman was on from 10:30 to 11:00, and they needed another hour after that. So, I not only did the news, but I did that as well. I came on as John with the news at 10:00 and Jack with the Barbasol Variety Hour at 11:00 [laughs]. Kind of stupid, but that's the way they wanted it.

Jim [Shelton] and I started in radio in Ashland, and I came up here [to Indianapolis] after three months. Then about a year later I got him up here [to WIBC]. He announced various programs for a few months and then went into the air force, because he was going to be drafted anyway. So he was in World War II. When he came back I was at WISH. But when he came back, he developed the Pick-a-Pocket program down on the Circle in front of the Circle Theatre, every day after the twelve o'clock news. Pick-a-Pocket was a quiz program. He had a vest, and the vest was full of pockets; he had a question in each pocket. He talked to these people and said, "Pick-a-Pocket." They'd take a question out, and if they answered it right, they got a dollar or whatever the prize was. It was a pretty popular show for a number of years. I don't know how many broadcasts he did—a couple of thousand. Luke Walton had a similar program over at Kay Jewelers. His was just a quiz show for him, and he would just interview people. There weren't any prizes involved, I don't believe. It was just a vehicle to get customers into the store. . . . I think Wally Nehrling did a street show at one time, too. I can't remember the location of that show.

Prior to moving [back] to WIBC, I went to the Pearson Music Company on North Pennsylvania, which was right next door to Wilking Music. We were working six and seven days a week at WISH. You always had to work on holidays; I guess I just got kind of tired of what I was doing, and I thought I'd try something else for a change. There was a gentleman by the name of Heberlein who was the record manager at Pearson's. He urged me, if I wanted to make a change, to go ahead, so I did. I thought this would be great. I'd have lots of people working for me, and I wouldn't have to do too much. I had four women working for me, and they were always either sick or having family problems. I tell you, I was ready to quit after about the first two months. I called a friend of mine at WIBC and said, "I'd really like to get back."

[Jim Shelton] was pretty popular as a chief announcer, so I called him and I said, "I want to get back into radio," and he said, "We've got an opening on Saturday morning, and nobody wants to do it. It's all selling stuff on the air. Can you do that?" And I said, "I think I can" [laughs]. He said, "It's all country music." And I said, "Well, I like country music," which I did. We sold trees and tulip bulbs from the Michigan Bulb Company. They still sell those by the way; I see their ads. I sold baby chicks and Rockdale gravestones. Those were seasonal; you sold those at Memorial Day specials. Rockdale Monument Company. These are companies that deal through an agency. They'd call the station and say, "We have this product, and we'll offer you so much for each order you get us.' And that's the way it worked. A Rockdale monument or gravestone sold, I think, for fourteen dollars, and the station got a couple of bucks from each order. [We sold] Bibles and pictures of Jesus that glowed in the dark and that type of thing [laughs]. . . . Oh, we sold everything—pills that made you gain weight and pills that made you lose weight. Sometimes I had a fifteen-minute program for one back to back with the one to lose weight. I worked on a salary. I had to keep up the orders. We had a girl—I shouldn't say girl anymore—we had a young lady who took care of the mail. That's all she did—kept track of orders, opened the mail, sent the money to the various companies, saw that we got ours and that type of thing.

I had worked a few [country music programs] live at the end of 1942 before I went to WIRE, and then there was a period in the 1950s of two or three years when they cut out all the records and went to live talent. We just had a whole group of them; in fact, there must have been a hundred of them—groups, different groups. There were two studios. You'd do one program, and while you were on the air with one group, there would be another group rehearsing. They just rotated all day long. And on Saturday night, they'd have a jamboree at Tomlinson Hall, [which later] burned down. We had a jamboree on Saturday nights, and all of these people would be in that show. We'd start at eight o'clock and go 'til midnight—two shows every Saturday night. [Raymond] Chickie Hopkins and Linda Lou and the Haymakers. That was Moriarity and his group—Tom Moriarity. . . . I don't think [Ann Wagner] was ever on the *Jamboree,* but she came later and was music director at WIBC. She sang with Tom Moriarity and his group. . . . [Country Cousin Chickie] played with Moriarity and his group, but he also did a single. He was a

comedian, so he had his own personal appearances. When he worked with the band, he worked as a musician not as a comedian.

A lot of those jobs came about because somebody got sick or an opening occurred. You had to make up in your own mind whether you wanted to take on additional chores. Somebody might say, "So-and-so's ill and can't make this show today or can't do this job. Do you think you can do it?" And you don't say no as a rule, or I didn't. I lucked out quite a bit because I probably could do it as well as it had been done. I followed most of the jobs and knew what to do on them anyway. I'd already had experience in news, and they needed—I think in the 1960s for a year or so—Fred Heckman needed somebody in the news department. I had done news for many, many years, and I said, "I wouldn't mind changing over for awhile and getting away from the records." Mr. [Richard] Fairbanks [owner of WIBC] went for it and thought it might be a good idea. You know, you get kind of stale after awhile; you run out.

I remember the first news assignment Fred Heckman gave me was to take a mobile car and a tape recorder and a gadget you put in the phone to relay a message back to the studio that they could record. There was a fire out in New Palestine in a nursing home [laughs]. That was the first news story he assigned me to, and this thing just burned up. They were carrying these old people out; I'll never forget that. I've laughed about it. It wasn't funny, but he got a big charge out of the idea that he really tried to discourage me in a hurry. I worked in news with Fred for a couple of years. I don't remember who took my place with the records, but Mr. Fairbanks said, "I've got to get you back on the air. I want you to go back on the air." So I said, "Okay." I went back [laughs]. I went back to deejaying again after a couple of years.

In 1963 WIFE took over WISH-Radio's 1310 spot on the AM dial. WIFE came along with its promotionals and billboards, and promotions like: "Do you know your WIFE is spending time with us every day?" [laughs]. Their ads were worded cleverly so that they used the call letters. WIFE was the first station in town to do all this promotion and then have these giant giveaways or contests—thousands of dollars in money and homes and cars. Contests and phone-ins. They gave it away by the thousands. They bought the ratings. WIBC more or less panicked and changed their broadcast day and their programming. They didn't try to duplicate, but I think Mr. Fairbanks said, "We're going to have to do something, so let's change everything around." I was off the air for awhile; they had a cowboy come in and do my program. I kept on with my other chores like continuity and promotions and stuff like that—and writing. That lasted about three or four months, and then I went back on the air again.

Bill Baker, Jim Shelton, and I all did what we called "record hops." . . . Anywhere they wanted us—out of town, in town. We had our own equipment. . . . We booked our own [hops]. They said to do whatever we wanted to as long as it didn't interfere with the hours. [The station] took no cut; it was all ours. . . . We went separately. We were all out. I was amazed at the number; I must have done two hundred one year . . . high school dances, alumni, school things, some businesses, and reunions. They would specify what type of music they wanted. We tried to entertain and joke around a little bit, and spin the records. We had group dances— I'm trying to think . . . the "bunny hop." We did all of those. Jim carried a live band with him sometimes, and paid them, and I had a live band sometimes. Bill Baker had the best equipment of anybody. He designed his own; he just had a mammoth bunch of stuff. He was out every night. I tried to hold it to weekends. It was every Friday, Saturday, and Sunday. So, it got a little old, but very profitable. We used

WIFE Good Guys, April 1965. STATE ARCHIVES, INDIANA COMMISSION ON PUBLIC RECORDS/THE INDIANAPOLIS STAR AND NEWS

WIFE Good Guys

In late 1963 and early 1964 the owner of Star Broadcasting Corporation, Don Burden (not to be confused with Munice's Don Burton), shook up the radio scene in Indianapolis with his new station, WIFE (Corinthian's former WISH). WIFE aggressively advertised its deejays, dubbed the "good guys," who played rock music for teens. The station got involved in giveaways, and other stations followed suit. These contests, however, proved to be WIFE's undoing. In 1966, when Burden applied for license renewal, the FCC held hearings to determine whether the station had rigged contests. Moreover, WIFE was accused of fraudulent billings, slanting news coverage to favor Democratic senatorial candidate Vance Hartke, and giving free time to Hartke for campaign purposes. The FCC stripped Burden of all his licenses in 1975 and gave the WIFE-AM license to a local group in 1976.[27]

that for kind of a little nest egg that we use for retirement. Turned out really well; we never spent any of it at all. About fifty dollars was our top [per show]. But then, that was good. A lot of times we'd just show up and make an introduction or a personal appearance. I worked at the Whiteland Barn, which was a teenage record hop place on Sunday night, and they'd have live bands. All I'd do is go in and spin records during the intermission. I drove down there and did about twenty-five minutes, packed up my gear, put it in the car, collected my money, and drove home. We got up to sixty dollars for that. That was great [laughs]. That doesn't sound like much today, but then, that was pretty good.

[There] was a model home area called "Imperial Hills," and that was at 9000 South Meridian. It extends west from Meridian to [Road] 135. It was quite a large subdivision. It was filled with National Homes; those were the prefab homes. Anne and Bob Clark owned all of that land there. They decided that they would take the National Homes and dress them up, decorate them, and do a lot more than National Homes did. They had three different model homes, and we set up a permanent broadcasting studio in the family room of one of those model homes. I did two hours in the morning—10:00 to 12:00—and 1:00 to 3:00 in the afternoon. Between 12:00 and 1:00, we invited people to come to see the homes and have lunch with us. So, each day, she would have a catered lunch. Then, she got the bright idea of getting a charcoal grill in the summer, and I cooked a lot. I'd start the charcoal in the morning when I was on the air for my morning show. Then, at 12:00 she'd have pork chops, wieners and hamburgers, and people would come to look through the model homes and drop off for a sandwich. Well, it got pretty tiresome after two years. Usually, the only reason for going into the station was to get my materials and to get my paycheck once a week. When the whole development was full, the people who owned that land sold their home, and they went to Hawaii. Of course, I can't complain, because they paid me also. I don't know whether I was really selling the houses or not, but they thought so [laughs].

We did all of our regular programs from the State Fair. A couple of years they had a radio building. They may still call it the Communications Building now, but they actually had studios in that radio building. And we did some of our radio programs with the live talent; Ann Wagner was there, the Haymakers, and the Dixie Four, which was a gospel quartet; Jim Shelton did his *Pick-a-Pocket* program from there. I was the announcer on a lot of those and kind of produced them—kept the thing going. Other stations used that same building for their programs as well. WLS from Chicago came down and used it to do all their farm programs from there. . . . We didn't pay to use the studios; it was a good ad for the State Fair. We gave them all kinds of publicity. "We're here at the State Fair." Of course, we had passes to get in. They wanted us to bring our people in and come out any time to do our shows. It was good publicity for us, because people got to see our personalities that they ordinarily just listened to.

Bill Dean passed away, and Mr. Fairbanks designated me as program director and also asked me if I could do the license renewal for WIBC which was due that January. Bill died in the fall. I didn't have much time. Fairbanks said, "I'll get the Washington [D.C.] attorneys here, and we'll sit down and figure it out." He said, "You write well, and you organize materials extremely well, so I think you're the guy to do it. I want somebody locally involved. I've got my Washington attorneys, but I want my hands on that."

I had to take over the administrative part plus learning the FCC. At that time, the FCC license was about that thick [a four-inch-thick book]. There were questions, and they had to be done in blue book form. That's the only example I can give you. You had to prove to the FCC that you were doing news, information, public service, entertainment,

religion, and also your EEO [Equal Employment Opportunity Commission] had to be written up in minute form—how many employees you had—whether they were women, black, white, Chinese, whatever. Those were all exhibits. And you had to keep within the percentages of the city's black working force which, I think, was around 12 percent. It was pretty complicated and took a lot of work. Then after I did WIBC, Mr. Fairbanks began buying a lot of stations. I did those also; I had to travel to do those. [His other stations were at] Boston, Philadelphia, Dallas, Titusville, Florida—later Kansas City, later West Palm Beach. I visited all of those at least two or three times a year. I did a lot of traveling. I was the one who worked with the lawyers and the FCC. I filed everything with our law firm, and they turned it in.

[The FCC] was supposed to see to it that radio stations served their main area or community. The WIBC community was seven counties, really. SMSA [Standard Metropolitan Statistical Area] was the way we abbreviated it. That was our primary listening audience. We had to prove to the FCC every three years that we were serving the community with the proper educational programs that involved city and county schools, and that we did the proper amount of public service—public affairs programs. That was a big category. We had several roundtable shows that we did once a week involving community affairs and community problems. We would discuss those. That was considered community affairs. We had to have so much time allotted to that per week. We had to promise the FCC that we would do so much news. At license time they would give you seven dates, and you would pick out those logs that you had for those seven dates during those three years. You'd go through them with a fine-tooth comb and count every single thing that you did on those logs—how much news, how many public service announcements, how much public affairs, how much time was devoted to education. You would have to graph that out and prove to them whatever you promised under your previous renewal you did.

[Licensing] didn't change until probably in the late 1980s. They agreed to allow radio stations to renew every seven years instead of every three years. Television stations still had to renew every three. And then it became a postcard affair. You didn't have to make these outlandish promises. The last one I did was in 1990, the year I retired.

Jack Morrow flipped hamburgers with Anne Clark between shows at the "Imperial Hills" housing development (September 1963). ANNE CLARK

Fans gathered around Morrow at the Indiana State Fair where broadcasts were so popular that the Fair Board built a studio for Hoosier radio stations to use during the fair. WIBC RADIO

I just finished up WIBC's renewal. The only thing you had to do was submit an exhibit for the Equal Employment Opportunity [to the FCC]. They still maintained that—still do. You have to do that every year.

You still had to do [public service announcements]. The FCC has a lottery and picks out so many stations in each city every year to come in and inspect. You have to keep your public files up to date. Now, through the lottery, we were inspected two years in a row; we just got lucky. Your call letters are picked out of a hat, so there's nothing you can do about it. I think we were picked the years 1988 and 1989. It's just a chance thing. Some never get picked. It's just a lottery. Fortunately, I had all the public files in good order. But they go through those with a fine-tooth comb; they want to know what you've done and what you haven't done. EEO is the big thing.

I'll frankly say that WIBC probably took their community responsibilities seriously—more so than other stations. I think some of them just threw them off and just got by on what they could. But we were always very careful to serve the community, keep records on it, and Mr. Fairbanks was a stickler on that. I was in charge of that, but he would always remind me, "Now are we keeping up with everything? Are we doing our job?" That was his theme, and he was very up on that.

We worked pretty hard; we really did. People think that people in radio have it made. It was enjoyable. It beat working for a living.

Hilliard Gates (Gudelsky) (ca. 1940s)

NBC 33/RAE GATES

Hilliard Gates

(1916–1996)

Hilliard Gates, one of Indiana's most popular and beloved broadcasters, was interviewed in his home in Fort Wayne, Indiana, in November 1994. Although his health was failing, he happily recalled his long career. Gates got his start at WKBZ in 1937 in his hometown of Muskegon, Michigan. After three years of on-the-job training, Hilliard answered an ad for a play-by-play sportscaster in a trade magazine and was hired by WOWO in Fort Wayne, where he expanded the sports department. William Kunkel, publisher of the Fort Wayne Journal-Gazette, *brought him to radio station WKJG in 1947 to help manage the operation and act as sports director. For the next forty-five years, Gates juggled his roles as administrator and sportscaster with aplomb. While deeply involved with sports, Gates continually advanced his station's status, going on the air in 1953 with WKJG-TV, the first television station in Fort Wayne. He broadcast almost all the Fort Wayne Pistons basketball games, as well as the first NBA All-Star Game play-by-play. He became a close friend of the Indiana, Purdue, and Notre Dame football and basketball coaches, gaining an inside track that enabled him to enhance his reports of their games. Being asked to cover the Rose Bowl for Purdue in 1967 and for Indiana in 1968 were highlights of his career and testimony to the widespread confidence in his ability. He also became a fixture in the statewide broadcasts of the boys Indiana State High School Basketball finals. When recounting the high points of his career, Hilliard Gates rarely took credit for his accomplishments; he almost always attributed his successes to his many supporters.*

I was one of four boys in one family, and it was just ordained that I would gravitate into sports with three brothers. . . . My last name was Gudelsky. That was a family name in Muskegon that went back to my grandfather who came over from Europe to Muskegon. My dad was the oldest of seven children in that family. I went to Muskegon Junior High School, which was about seven or eight blocks from our house, but it was just across the street from my grandmother's house. So, I could run over there at noon. Then, after I graduated from Muskegon High School, I went to Muskegon Junior College for two years. I played some sports in junior high and high school, but I played my most successful sports in Muskegon Junior College—tennis and basketball.

I was interested in sports all my life, and when the radio went on the air in Muskegon, Michigan, I could hear the Muskegon Reds playing the Grand Rapids Central Bulldogs in football; I could hear [the broadcast]. And then, the next morning or afternoon you could get the papers. Oh, sure, it was a different ballgame. Not that it took away from what the newspapers did, but they had to structure their stories differently. By the time the newspaper, the *Muskegon Chronicle,* would hit the sidewalk or porch, most of the people knew who made the long run, what the score was, who got hurt, and that kind of thing. . . . And the newspapers didn't want to be cooperative, because they were losing something. But then, it didn't take long before they knew that even though it was on radio, then the people wanted to read it. They wanted the longer version of what was going on or what an outstanding writer thought about the ball game. It's the same with a news story.

I got into it pretty early. I started in 1936 at the end of my second year of junior college. [WKBZ] was my first paying job—1937, I think. I may still have been in junior college, but I still did the games. My first broadcast was a football game at Hackley Field, and we played Muskegon Heights. . . . I was nervous. I didn't think I did a very good job. I didn't take it seriously enough. Since I had done the P.A. system for a couple of years I thought it would be easier, and I wasn't smart enough to "chart the game."

I started to work full time at KBZ at twenty-five dollars a week. . . . I had to work eight hours a day on the board. Do you know what I mean when I say I worked on the board? It meant reading the news and running the phonograph records, and everything like that. I didn't have sports all the time. I had a fifteen-minute sports show every night at 5:45, but I had to write that too, and I wrote that between records. . . . We never called ourselves deejays; we [just] played the records in those days—eight hours a day. All the basketball, football, and hockey games were after that. I did that for twenty-five hours a week at the beginning.

I loved to write. I really loved to write, and I still do. And I think that was the strongest part of my broadcasting in radio. I felt I could feel the impact and write the words that would pass the impact along to the readers. . . . In broadcasting, I wrote everything myself. When I would go on the air, every word that I read I had typed myself. Some of that could be AP [Associated Press] material. . . . I reworked everything that I did on the radio unless it was a breaking story that happened just before I went on the air or too late to rewrite. Then I would take the UP [United Press International] or AP story. I wrote a tremendous amount of material. . . . The newscasters don't write their own stuff—the big guys on the major networks. They're handed the mate-rial; they may have time to go over it and substitute a word or two. The big newscasters have a bevy of writers.

[My career with WOWO started when] I read an ad in *Broadcasting* when I was in Muskegon—my third year, I think—and it was a blind ad. *Broadcasting* was the "bible" in those days. It came out every month. . . . I saw an ad that said "Sportscaster Midwest." It was looking for a play-by-play broadcaster with three years experience or something like that. I answered the ad. Now, I had already worked for WKBZ in Muskegon for about three years or so. The letter came back from WOWO-WGL in Fort Wayne. They called me down, and I came down on a Sunday. We had a meeting on a Monday morning, and Mr. [W. C.] Swartley, who was the general manager for the Westing-house station, was there and the program manager, whose name escapes me. Eldon [Campbell] was in on the meet-ing, too. Franklin Tooke was the program manager, and he took my audition. We sat down for several hours and talked. He gave the audition to Eldon. Eldon heard it, and I was hired. I came in 1939, and I was awed by it. I had been to Chicago to see WGN, the NBC studios there, and they were large and nice. But Westinghouse put quite an arrangement into the building—that was on the second floor of an office building, and they took a large part of the entire area. They built modern studios in those days. The station is not there any longer, but it was big league. That was one of the things I noticed about WO the minute I came in. It was much better equipped than Muskegon. It should have been as a Westinghouse station. They were electronic to begin with. The equipment was better; they had writers to write the news and commercials. They had several engineers on the premises all the time.

When I first came to Fort Wayne in the radio business, I had the greatest mentor that history ever knew, and that was Eldon Campbell. We lived together. When I came to Fort Wayne from Muskegon, Michigan, Eldon was not married, and I was not married, and he was living in a little room somewhere. Within a couple of weeks after I was at the YMCA, he said to me, "Why don't you and I take a room?" We found a house—a beautiful old house with a bedroom in the front of the building. It had double beds, and we lived together. The only time we broke up was when he got married first, and I got married second. Our wives, as you know, became fast friends. [Eldon] was assistant program manager, and then he was elevated to program manager. But he was one of the people who listened to my audition when I sent it from Muskegon. . . . I sent them a play-by-play on an old acetate disc that was cut right in the control room of WKBZ in Muskegon.

We were part of the NBC network, and this was—I don't think it was the first day, but it was in the first three days. The staff had a picnic at a resort north of Fort Wayne out on a lake. . . . The managers and the department head people were all invited, along with the announcers and the engineers and everybody and their families. This was July 4th; the family picnic day was that day. I had just come to WOWO; I had been on the air a couple of days. Now, this is July 4th. And two days before the program manager came in and said, "Hilliard, I'd like to have all the people we can get to come to that family picnic. And we've got to feed to the Red network of NBC with the 'Inkspots.'" (Do you remember the Inkspots? Great singers.) And I said, "Oh boy, I want to hear that." He said, "Well, you're not only going to hear it; you're going to announce it." And that was one of the first things I did on WOWO. The NBC people had given me the script. The [Inkspots] had been at the Embassy Theater—the Emboyd Theater in those days—and they did fifteen minutes on July 4th on the NBC network. And when I finished the fifteen minutes, I absolutely dropped the script and fell on the floor. I was so nervous. That was the first time.

I would say that we [at WOWO] were closer than anything else I've been around to being a family. The people were terribly interested in each other; they were interested in each other's families. We would have picnics together. On certain special days they would call us together, and we would have coffee. That came completely from the managers. The managers were like that. It was a family, and that's why they were so successful. And they were successful. I couldn't get that esprit de corps from my people [at WKJG]. But we weren't as big, and television—there's no way. You do your own thing and the heck with the others. You do your own thing. There's very little spirit of camaraderie in the television studios . . . because I think they're all personalities. They all have their own thing. [But] the greatest group of people that I worked with in my radio career was the staff that Westinghouse assembled at WOWO in Fort Wayne.

WO and WGL—we were together in those days and came out of the same studios, but not the same program-

ming. We were a Blue network NBC station[28]—Red network on WGL. They were both owned by Westinghouse, and they were broadcasting simultaneously. We didn't duplicate very often. We might on a July 4th parade or something like that—put it on both stations. We had sales people for WGL and sales people for WOWO. Once in awhile we would put something together. I would say the staffs were not duplicated, but there were some that would be both. The announcers did both stations. In fact, it was a practical joke when I first came there and asked, "How do you know if you're on WO or WGL?" And the answer I got from the program manager was, "You'll know." We had a guy by the name of Bob Sievers, who is still living here and is a wonderful guy and a very happy-go-lucky guy. Bob was the kind of kid you could joke [with]. You could come up to him while he was doing newscasts and tickle the back of his neck and things like that. But he would go along with it; he was a great kid and still is. Bob Sievers had to make a station break, and he was in the booth where you say, "This is WOWO Fort Wayne." You know, NBC had the chimes, and then you came in and said, "This is WOWO Fort Wayne." And one noon, it was time for the station break, and Bob said, "This is ah, ah, WOWO—no, this is WGL—no, it's WOWO." Finally, he said, "What the hell station is this anyway?" [laughs]. And that went along for a long time. Every time I see him I kid him about that.

There were two stations, so we alternated on both stations. . . . We would do the high school games on WGL and the college games on WOWO. I'd do a high school game on Friday night and jump in the car and drive to South Bend for the Notre Dame game, or drive to Lafayette for Purdue, or to Bloomington for Indiana, or Northwestern at Evanston, or Columbus for Ohio State. Then, we would come back after the games. But anyway, I got that job. Eldon was already on the staff; he had just come from Illinois—University of Illinois. Eldon was at one station in Illinois; I can't recall the call letters. He was sports oriented—didn't play sports—but he was terribly interested. That was a marvelous thing for him when he became program director. The question has been asked about how we got into sports so drastically at WOWO-WGL. When I came to WO and GL, they were doing some of the high school games on WGL—not football, basketball. I went to Muskegon every Saturday night after I finished

Hilliard Gates listened carefully in the control booth. NBC 33/RAE GATES

After Gates became an executive at WKJG, he continued to broadcast many sports events.
Here he called a high school basketball game ca. 1960. NBC 33/RAE GATES

my announcing because I was seeing Rae, my future wife. I would come back around six o'clock Sunday night.

One day after I came back from Muskegon, I took out my road map—just sitting at my desk. We were doing the high school games and the high school tournaments, not on WO; we were using WGL. . . . And I kept saying, "We're not doing college sports." With WO's power we could get a tremendous audience, and our expenses were not great, because the mileage was brief—what I would call brief. So, first of all I went to Eldon, and, of course, Eldon was a sports guy to the heels. I said, "Eldon, we can get Notre Dame football; we can get Indiana, Purdue, Ohio State, Ann Arbor, Michigan. We can make a lot of money on football." And he went into [Steve] Conley, and Conley called me in. He said, "Convince me." And I did, and that's how we got into doing major sports. Then the Pistons came along at that time. The Pistons started to play professional basketball in Fort Wayne in 1941, and here we are right in the middle of that. We did all the Piston games all the time they stayed in Fort Wayne. It was fun, but it was money for Westinghouse.

Bringing a game from Bloomington was reasonably expensive, but, boy, look at the audience you had. And usually, when Purdue was home, Indiana was on the road. We couldn't do a complete Notre Dame schedule because they were national in scope, but we did an awful lot of Notre Dame games. I remember meeting the athletic directors at these universities, and they could hardly wait until we would get down there and do their ball games.

First of all, I got all the releases of all the Big Ten teams and Notre Dame every week in and out of the season. I was aware of who was inching up on John Jones as the starting quarterback at Notre Dame. I would know who was hurt. I would be at Notre Dame and Indiana and Purdue or any major college game—well, a Saturday game—on Friday. That was an absolute must for me. And I told the manager at WOWO that I would not give up the college Friday night to do a high school game here. That was a little later in the program. Then we would have my assistant do the high school game on Friday night, and I would go to the scene of the Big Ten or Notre Dame game.

Preparation was my middle name. If I couldn't prepare, I didn't want to do the game. I wouldn't do the game. In football, I memorized the first offensive team, the second offensive team of the home team, the team I was following. I memorized sixteen or eighteen players on the opposing team, and I would know that by the time the kickoff came. I also had an individual who would go to the locker room, watch the guys get dressed, and see if the kid who was injured the week before was in uniform. If he was in uniform he probably would play, but it wasn't positive. But I got it positively from the coach eventually, you see. I didn't have enough talent that I didn't have to prepare. I had to prepare. Some guys were glib and just kind of rambled on and on and on. You know that. I never went to a ball game—basketball, football, or hockey, where I wasn't on the premises two hours in advance. . . . They had a press conference ahead of time; they had a dinner ahead of time. I knew the coaches well enough that I could take them over in the corner and say, "Now, I know Jones is hurt. Is he going to play tomorrow?" They would say, "Don't you tell anybody, because Jones is my best back, and they think he's hurt. He's not hurt. He's going to play in the game." And I had all that. I would never go on the air and say that I knew last night that Jones was going to play. That would be breaking a trust—something I wouldn't want to do. And I got to know all those people. I would call them during the week and say, "Are you going to be at the game? If you are, would you come out at halftime with me?" That was simple. I never would go up to anybody and say, "I'd like to know if Jones is good enough to play Saturday." I would first say, "Are you busy? I have a question that you may not want to answer, but is John Jones going to play Saturday?" It got so he would say to me, "The papers say he's going to play, Hilliard, but he's not going to play. I can't take a chance with him this week. We'll play him next week."

I traveled with the Pistons. I did every home game, and I traveled with them in the airplane . . . 'til they moved to Detroit, which was about 1978. That's a guess. Fred Zollner [owner of the Pistons] was quite a guy, and also Carl Bennett, who to this day is as close a friend [as] anybody could have. The Pistons basketball team started as an industrial YMCA team in Fort Wayne, Indiana, in 1941 and . . . it was professional [even] in those days. They had the National Basketball League—Sheboygan, Wisconsin, the Chicago Stags, Indianapolis Kautskys, Cleveland something. Gradually Minneapolis came in, and various other cities expanded. . . . It started as the NBL and later became the NBA. I did the first game played in Fort

Wayne as the Pistons opened their season in 1941. I did their first game. For awhile Fred Zollner wanted us to do all the road games but not the home games, because he thought it would hurt the attendance. Fred Zollner was never terribly comfortable broadcasting home games, but the cost of a home game was minimal compared to going on a trip to New York—going into the [Madison Square] Garden and buying facilities. You had to buy their engineers; you had to buy their photographers, camera people. I didn't have to pay to go to New York, because all of my travel expenses were absorbed by Fred Zollner, which was a great thing, and Westinghouse liked that.

[During WW II] I was not one of the early ones selected for the draft; it was January or February of 1942. When I came to Fort Wayne, I had terrible asthma attacks during the hay fever season. My doctor diagnosed it immediately, because I couldn't get rid of a cold that summer. . . . I went to Dr. Chambers, the biggest sports fan in Fort Wayne; he was our station's doctor. He worked with me, and I ended up at the hospital the first year with a special pump arrangement. At the end of the hay fever season, I was better. Then I began to tolerate it. I got it the next year at the same time. Then I was called by the draft. It was winter, and I went down to the recruiting station. When they asked me if there was any reason why I shouldn't go in the army, and I said, "I owe it to my country to do what I can for the army." And then I kicked myself. They asked if I had any problems from a health standpoint, and I told then that I had tremendous asthma and hay fever. The guy said, "Well, we need recruits. Ordinarily, we wouldn't take you, but we'll put you in a special category so you won't have to go overseas." . . . The next morning I found out I was to go to Camp Croft in South Carolina, which was an infantry base. But on all my sheets it said "limited duty." It was a huge camp. I got into barracks with all the guys—terrific. I did my early training with my rifle; I shot and did everything like that. Pretty soon a guy said to me, "I understand you used to be in radio." And I said, "Yeah." And he said, "We do a radio thing every Friday night. Why don't you go over and see what you can do." I told him I was an announcer, not an entertainer. He asked me to come over anyway, so I went over. They had guys who were the best singers and dancers and musicians and everything. Marvelous people were at Camp Croft, South Carolina. . . . Then at the end of thir-

teen weeks, the commander called me in and said, "I don't know what to do with you. You're a nice guy, and you work hard, and you have a lot of skills, but there's not much like that that you can do here at Camp Croft." I said, "Well, then send me home" [laughs]. He said he couldn't do that. So, I filled out shoe coupons for the guys who needed new shoes. I had a desk, and I typed shoe coupons, and I did that for about three months. Finally, I said, "There ought to be something better than this." So, I called home and told Rae that I had to get ahold of somebody at Baer Field [in Fort Wayne], because I went on recruiting drives with the people from Baer Field. I had put on war bond drives and emceed a dance band show every Wednesday night for the servicemen's center in downtown Fort Wayne; so, I was very close to the people at Baer Field. I finally had enough guts to call Colonel Copsey, who was the commander, but I knew him. I told him where I was, that I was typing shoe coupons, and that I couldn't be shipped overseas. I told him I could come back to Fort Wayne at Baer Field and run all the war bond drives and go all over Indiana and Ohio, selling war bonds. He said he'd think about it. About a month later, I was called into headquarters, and this sergeant said, "You're the luckiest guy in the world. . . . You're assigned to the special services division at Baer Field in Fort Wayne" [laughs]. I came back here to Baer Field, and I worked. We were out of town a lot in the area. We had the best dance band you ever heard, and we had good people who could dance and sing who came through Baer Field. It was a staging area for one of the air corps divisions, but I didn't know that. So, we had wonderful people to put on the stage radio show on WOWO that I emceed.

There was a white paper that the FCC distributed after the war, and I think they wanted the stations to get more involved in community service. You know, you had your license renewed every three years, I think. You put everything you did all in those three years on a free basis, aiding the community somehow, and you documented it. We never used to do it before that. We felt it was necessary to a degree, but it wasn't priority number one. They scared the radio station licensees around the nation, and so the manager of the station decided that I could have the time for that. I could certainly work that in—maybe come in an hour or two earlier in the morning. I was getting paid by the salary, not by the hour. You wouldn't get a license if

Always a favorite with collegiate fans, Gates proudly broadcast the Rose Bowl games for Purdue in 1967 and Indiana in 1968.

Well known for his preparation, Gates set up his spotting board in his office before a football game. He placed cards with both offensive and defensive players' names and positions on a board facing him so that he could easily refer to them during a game.

you didn't have a package that shows what you've done for your community or in your licensed area—what good you have done for those people over the last four years. You would never be given another license. You've got to operate for the public and the people. I think anybody who lives in a community for any length of time knows what the community needs and what they're not getting. Since the rock and roll craze, would you have any idea how many more music minutes are on a radio station as against news prior to that? Well, the time on most rock and roll stations was and is devoted to music. That's not public service. Why, in my management days at the stations I encouraged everybody I could to get into an organization—not the Ku Klux Klan or something like that. I wanted our people to be in organizations that would lend public good, not necessarily to the station, but it would come back. If you were on the YMCA board of directors and they had a big problem and they didn't quite know what to do, there was nothing wrong with getting up in the meeting and saying, "Well, we'll give you a half an hour of time to spell it out and see what we can do with it." That's your obligation, and we did that. We did that at KJG when we got it going. I defy anybody today to go into a market and get a radio and start going over the dial to see if they're doing anything within 2 percent of what we did fifteen or twenty years ago on the radio. It ain't there; it just isn't.

Gates recalls how William Kunkel convinced him to move to WKJG in 1947. It's quite a story. Do you want it nail by nail? [laughs]. Okay. William Kunkel was publisher of the *Journal-Gazette.* I knew him well; I would see him frequently and thank him for all the things that [his writers Park Williams and Cliff Miller] did for me. . . . One day Park Williams called me up and said, "Hilliard, would you like to have lunch this noon?" And I said, "Park, you're too busy to have lunch." Park said, "No, I've got to have lunch today." I met him at the [Berghoff] Gardens. We talked about everything else, and pretty soon I said, "What did you call me about?" And he said, "You know, Bill Kunkel's going to build a radio station in Fort Wayne?" I said, "He's going to have a tough road, because he owns a newspaper in town, and they don't like duplication of things like that." And Park said, "Well, he's the head of the Democratic Central Committee in Allen County, and I think we've got enough political clout." I asked why he was telling me. Did he want me to go back and put it on

WOWO? He said, "I just wondered if you might be interested in joining a radio station that Bill Kunkel would own?" I thought there were a lot of advantages to owning a newspaper and a radio station. He said he thought it would increase my salary and give me another echelon up or so. I said, "I don't know how to answer this." And he said, "I just asked if you would be interested." I said that I would be interested, but I didn't know what I should do. I asked if he had hired anybody to be on the station yet or whether he was just talking about it. He said that I was the first one and that Bill Kunkel liked me and knew more about me than I thought. Bill Kunkel had a hell of a lot of money; he owned the paper, you know. Anyway, I said to Park again, "Nobody's been hired?" Park said they hadn't gotten that far; they didn't even have a license yet. "Why do you want to know if anybody's been hired? That's an unusual question." I said, "Well, if nobody's been hired, I want to be the manager" [laughs]. He said he'd go back and talk to his boss and call in the morning. He called me in the morning and confirmed that nobody had been hired.

We went on the air as WKJG which is William Kunkel Journal Gazette. It went marvelously for awhile. Bill Kunkel had a restaurant in his *Journal-Gazette* offices, and the head people of his newspaper ate lunch together in this dining room—real nice—small but nice. As soon as I went to work for him, one of the things Bill Kunkel said, "Even though you're not in the *Journal-Gazette* building, I want you to have lunch with us every noon that you want to or can. I won't hold you to it; if you can't do it or don't want to do it some days, you don't do it. It's just there for you." I told him I would love to be there, because I was such a fan of the two guys I palled around with. Occasionally, I would go. I decided I was too busy to go often. I was out getting a staff together and buying equipment, but I would occasionally drop in. In October 1948, we'd been on the air for awhile. We'd even built a building down south on Rudisill Boulevard—beautiful studios. It was World Series time. I called Bill and said I was coming down for lunch but couldn't stay because I wanted to hear the World Series. He said, "I've got a World Series radio for you." So I went into the room, and Kunkel is there seated at the end of the table with the little radio on the ledge beside his seat. I heard the ball game for awhile, and then I jumped in the car and got back out to the studio, which was ten or fifteen minutes away. As I came in, the receptionist asked

Revered by coaches for his broadcasting ability, Gates met his good friend Bobby Knight, basketball coach at Indiana University, on the floor at a game.

The past presidents of the IBA were photographed in 1972. From left to right: Bazil O'Hagan, Jack Douglas, Eugene Strack, William "Tom" Hamilton, E. Berry Smith, Lester Spencer, Hilliard Gates, William Fowler, Ben Falber, Jr., Eldon Campbell, Reid Chapman, Ed Thoms, and Joe Higgins.

me to call Park Williams. I called Park to ask what was the matter. He said, "Bill Kunkel died." And that was that; so I didn't work for him for very long—nine months or so.

The next phase is that [Fort Wayne] had another radio station that came on right near the time we came on the air. A former United Telephone guy who lived in Lafayette, Indiana, Ed Thoms—a big, tall, good looking man—got a license to build another radio station in Fort Wayne. Nine months later he goes on the air. We're still on KJG; we're not doing very well. We had sports coming out of our ears; that's what kept us alive. I can't tell you how much later he went on the air after we went on the air, but it was close. He got on the air fast. And, he had three of the strongest businessmen in Fort Wayne moneywise behind him, and he was an excellent engineer. I met him, had lunch with him, liked him, and I know he liked me. One day he called me and said, "Meet me at the Keenan Hotel dining room." I met him, and he said, "You know, we're not doing very well with that station that we put on the air." And I said, "Well, we're not either." He said, "How'd you like to have our company buy your company, and we'll take our license and send it back to the FCC?" I said, "I'm not going to give up KJG's call letters, that's for sure. It's got *Journal-Gazette* background even though it's not owned by the *Journal* anymore.[29] It's known as the *Journal-Gazette* station." And he said, "What if we use your call letters, and put our station off the air?" I said, "What about studios?" . . . We put FFT off the air; we built some modest studios and moved everything into the new studios. But they were not like our studios out on Calhoun Street.

Ed [Thoms] and I were sitting at lunch one time and I said, "Ed, you know it's time to look at television." This is about 1949 or 1950. He said, "That's right." I asked if he was in a position economically to consider going after a television license. He said, "I think so. Let's talk about it some more." So, we got the other two guys in a meeting, and we talked about it. Next, we hired a consultant, and before too long we filed with the FCC for a television license. It takes a year or two to get it. We're going along pretty good with the radio station. I'm happy; Ed's happy; the owners are happy. Then, we get a call from the FCC. They want us to appear before the FCC and tell them— there were other people who wanted licenses in Fort Wayne—why we should have the license, what we did for the community, our experience. We appeared before the

FCC. I've got to be honest with you, it was nerve wracking for me, but they asked questions that I could answer. Ed Thoms hadn't been in the business that long.

In 1953 the FCC granted WKJG a television license, the first in Fort Wayne. Ed Thoms was vice president and general manager of the station; Gates was assistant general manager. From a makeshift studio in the Purdue Extension Center, Gates signed WKJG-TV on the air on 21 November with the words "Ladies and gentlemen, you are watching history being made." In an interview by Dave Nichols for Fort Wayne Magazine, *Gates described how he felt that night: "I knew it was momentous. I knew it was the beginning of a new era in Fort Wayne. And I was awed by it. I was proud to be a part of it. I wasn't nervous—once I got started."[30] Although Gates went on to become general manager of the station in 1962, his first love was sports. For almost forty years he was a fixture on television with his play-by-play broadcasts of sporting events. He may be remembered most for his statewide broadcasts of the High School Boys Basketball Tournaments, including the famous championship game in 1954 in which tiny Milan defeated the Muncie Central Bearcats. At retirement, Gates estimated that since 1936 he had broadcast more than five thousand sports events on radio and television.*

One of the highlights of Gates's career was the opportunity to broadcast the Rose Bowl games. He recounted every detail of the story. Anyway, one Sunday night the doorbell rings in this house [and it's] Walter Walb, the president of the Purdue Alumni Association. I brought him in and sat him down. He said, "Ever think of doing the Rose Bowl game?" I said, "Are you kidding?" And he said, "Well, I'm president of the Purdue Alumni Association, and the athletic department has asked me to come here and ask if you want to do the ball game." And I said, "Well, that's probably the nicest thing I've ever had thrown at me. Of course, I want to do it." He said, "I'm not worried about your doing it; I just wanted to know if you want to do it. I know you could handle it." I said, "I think I can, but it's going to be a big gulp when I say 'This is Hilliard Gates from the Rose Bowl,' I'll tell you that." I was assigned to the game with an announcer who used to be in Milwaukee, but he was out in Los Angeles doing Southern California sports. I knew him well because Wisconsin would come to Indiana or Purdue and I'd go up there. That's a terrible coincidence. I'm sitting next to a guy that I know and like. We got into the pregame meeting, and the Tournament of Roses had a guy that took us around. And then they had this meeting to get the format of the show. Finally, somebody said, "Well, how should we divide the game up?" I said, "Well, this is a home game for Southern California; I think he should do it." He looked at me and said, "No, I think you ought to do it." I told him he should lead it off, because it was his home game and that I wasn't going to do it. That was it. He opened it, and I took the second and fourth periods. Now, we got a heck of a game going in the fourth period. Well, the next year, Indiana gets invited to the Rose Bowl—1967, and I know everybody at Indiana, too. The athletic director called me on the phone and said, "Would you like to do the Rose Bowl game again?" And I said, "Are you kidding?" He said, "No, we've got to make an assignment." I said, "You've got announcers in Indianapolis; you've got WIBC that's done sports for a long time." He said, "Yeah, but we liked the way you handled it. I wouldn't ask you if you hadn't done it last year, because I wouldn't know you could do it for sure." I said, "I'd love to." So I traipse out with my wife Rae again, and we spend about twelve or fourteen days there. I did the second game with the same guy from Southern California.

I would tell anybody who wants to do television sports: "Do it on radio first." All the bugs can be erased on radio, and the public hearing you would never know there were any bugs. My voice presentations on radio and television, other than leaving quite a bit off the television narration, are the same. I do the essentials for television. On radio, you have to put them all on, because the person listening has to know what's going on—who's got the ball; who made the basket?

[I'd like to be remembered] as trying to be fair—a guy who got more out of this than he deserved probably. By that statement I meant that so many things came my way that I never could possibly have done on my own—even in the business. And I had the friendships outside of the sixty people at WO and the football staff at Indiana or Notre Dame—the National Basketball Association guy. Maurice Podoloff was the first commissioner of that, and he gave me everything that you could hope. I'm not talking about money, but putting me in situations for the games in the play-offs and the NBA All-Star Game. I mean that's heavy stuff for me, and it's competitive. I always felt I got my share; I never felt if I wasn't chosen that I was better than the guy who was chosen.

Tom Carnegie (Carl Kenegy) (1953)
INDIANAPOLIS MOTOR SPEEDWAY

Tom Carnegie

(1919–)

For Thomas Carnegie, broadcasting is "theater" and was a way to combine his love of sports with his passion for drama. Born Carl L. Kenegy, he was an outstanding football and baseball player until he contracted polio in his senior year of high school. He graduated from William Jewell College in 1942 and began broadcasting on WOWO that same year. It was there that he took the name Tom Carnegie. He soon was covering all kinds of sports for the Fort Wayne station, as well as announcing and doing comedy. He left WOWO in 1945, having been lured to WIRE by its owner, Eugene Pulliam. The next year he became chief announcer for the public address system for the Indianapolis 500-Mile Race; this position, which he has held for more than fifty years, earned him the title "Voice of the Indianapolis 500." In 1949 Carnegie began to teach part-time at Butler University, chairing the radio department and directing the university's radio station, WAJC. He relinquished that role in 1953 when he became sports director for television station WFBM, a title that he held until 1985. Also in 1953 he became the television voice for the Indiana High School Boys Basketball Tournament. He covered the Olympic Games for Channel 6, announced for the United States Auto Club, and produced two documentaries, The Flying Scot *and* With a Name Like Unser, *and a motion picture,* Race to the Sun. *In addition, he is the author of* Indy 500: More than a Race. *Carnegie was interviewed in the spring of 1994 at the Patrick H. Sullivan Museum in Zionsville, Indiana.*

I think the immediacy of radio became apparent in my early days. I remember as a youngster, growing up and listening to newspaper carriers hawking extras. All of a sudden when radio began to be popular, began to be universal, news was immediate. There were no longer extras put out by the newspapers. To me that indicated that people took radio as their source of immediate information. Perhaps in-depth information came later, and with that came a realization that sports events and news events could be made so exciting and so dramatic on radio, and I think that realization led to the proliferation of radio so that it became a part of every person's life.

My parents, who were both college-educated (and that was somewhat rare in that era), impressed upon me the importance of classroom work and the importance of being a friend to the teacher and being a student. I was an only child, and at times I wished that I had somebody else around in the family, because my parents were very strict. I felt that maybe they would not have been quite as strict if maybe there were some others around to look after. I was always trying to do the right thing morally and in the classroom. As my dad used to say, "The rules are clear, and the penalties severe." And that is the way that I grew up. They were very interested in my athletic playing days. While that was going on, they attended games and wanted me to participate in athletics. And I had a year off for illness [polio] and was unable to compete in the games that I really wanted to play, and that would be football and baseball. And so, I spent more time in speech-related activities and trying to learn how to describe sports events. My father was a good speaker. He was a Baptist minister—American Baptist Convention in Pontiac, Michigan, and Waterloo, Iowa, and Kansas City, Missouri. He was a good speaker, and he encouraged me to study oratory. With that and debate came the very valuable lesson of being able to think on your feet. I think that is what is lacking today in so many of our newscasts where all of the material is scripted beforehand, and there is no opportunity to deviate or you throw the timing of the entire show off. Then, you put those same people that look so good in a structured situation out in the field where they have to ad-lib, and there you see the lack of training, the lack of background. I have noticed that throughout; it is the individual who is trained in thinking on his feet and talking to an audience, a live audience, that did best in radio and then later on television.

My very first job [was] in Kansas City. I made fifteen dollars a week for a sixty-hour week at a minimum. And I got my early training while I was still in college. I worked there at KITE in Kansas City six days a week, sixty hours a week—minimum of sixty—fifteen dollars a week, but that was good money. It helped me get through college, believe it or not.

I was a "mail pull" announcer. In the early days, the stations that had a good frequency that were able to get out, their broadcast signal would be heard in quite a few states. Kansas City had such a station in KITE. Plug Kendrick owned it, and it was a mail pull station—and Colorback and Diamond Iron, and pills for alcoholism, and things like that. We had dog-eared scripts that we tried to read, to put it in our own words. By dog-eared scripts, I mean all the announcers in the station used it. We were judged by how much mail we pulled; that was how our success as an announcer was rated. And I remember in our mail room, we had a slot for each state of the union,

for pulling mail. By "mail pull" that is how the station got paid. They got paid per inquiry. In other words, a spot did not cost Diamond Iron "X" number of dollars. The cost of it depended on how much mail we pulled for them. So you learned to be friendly. You learned to talk to those folks out there, and you learned to encourage them out there to send their order to Diamond Iron. Then, you would spell it out: D-I-A-M-O-N-D, Diamond Iron. So, I had a little background before I wound up in Fort Wayne, Indiana, for my first full-time job after I graduated from college.

I felt once I got into radio, that was where I intended to stay. I enjoyed it, you see; it wasn't work to me. I enjoyed the minutes I was on the air; I enjoyed the preparation; I enjoyed the hours in the studio; I enjoyed the people who were involved in it. They were very creative people, and they all had warm and wonderful hearts. I felt that the people in the industry were exciting and fascinating, and I wanted to be in it, and I just knew that I was going to be in that field forever, if the field would have me. It was up to me to hone my skills, to hone my abilities, and see that I was able to stay in it.

I did not want to do mail pull all my life, and I knew that I wanted to get into sports with a good station. I tried to pick out some stations with some power and stations that I had heard of as being where you had an opportunity on the staff to do things. So I wrote to Indianapolis. I wrote to WIRE in Indianapolis and got no reply. I wrote to several others. These letters that I sent out were longhand, because we did not type letters and that sort of thing then. I got a reply from WOWO that they were interested.

I was nervous for quite awhile, you know, to where my voice would crack. Have you ever been that nervous? Well, I was very nervous. The first interview was one in which they asked me to ad-lib, to re-create a football game. This was a severe test of your ability to describe play-by-play. That was one that I did. I had no idea what was going to be in the interview. I think that is what got me the job more than anything else, because I had done some of the walking up and down the sidelines, doing the P.A. [public address] at ball games for William Jewell College. You don't often realize how those little simple things that you do along the way will teach you and help you later on. I am sure that simple thing[s] helped me in the interview. I don't remember much else about it, except that I was very, very nervous. And, I was nervous for a good year and a half on the station. I was always worried about my voice cracking. And, I remember that E don Campbell said, "Chew gum. That will help." So, I chewed a lot of gum for the first couple of years.

I was staff announcer [at WOWO], and that meant everything. I started off doing the news at 6:30 [in the morning], which was one of my best schedules ever. I would do the news and then whatever came along later in the day, and I remember doing sports events on the weekend or Friday night or something. But it was an ideal schedule because you got down at the station at six o'clock and you were on the air at 6:30. You ripped the news off the wire, and you went in and read it. And you know, you just organized it yourself. Then, you were through by 1:30, and so that gave you a lot of time. I always enjoyed that. I was never fortunate enough to have that kind of schedule later on, but then one of the popular shows of that era was *Jane Weston* on WOWO. (The Jane Westons would change, but the name was always the same.) It was a half-hour show around one o'clock in the afternoon, a homemaker show. I was finally selected to work that with the current Jane Weston—you know, recipes, things like that. Again, it was the ability to ad-lib, to express yourself, to put yourself in a family situation. I made an extra three dollars a week out of that show. I took my first three dollar talent fee and bought a coffee table. I will always remember that, and I still have that coffee table.

I did a crazy show called *The Nut House Neighbors*. This was sponsored by Morrow's Nut House. Can you believe that? Every day. And worked with Norm Widenhofer, and Norm was quite an organist and very talented and had a lot of fun. And, he and I would get in there and start to laughing and doing this crazy . . . we would just do various skits every day—the stuff that I would dream up. *The Lonely Women* was a story, soap opera, at that time on national radio. So, we had a *Lonely Men* story that we would do every day. You talk about corny, but we liked it. [Norm] would play [the] soap opera music. He would later play the organ at theaters there and everything. He was exceptionally good. It was a big, beautiful organ in our studio. He would do this organ music as part of it. They always played the organ on these soap operas, but he would go one step farther . . . and it was so dramatic, his organ playing.

Tom Weaver was the farm expert at WOWO. See, we had farm editors, all kinds of things that other stations did

later on. I remember Tom Weaver was our farm editor, and we would do a takeoff on Tom Weaver, and we would have our own farm report, you know. And, we would tell how many carloads of wheat were on track eleven in Chicago and we would say, "What in tarnation's difference does the track number make?" You know, dumb stuff like that. People listened to that. You would go down the street . . . my wife would tell me—that was before air conditioning—and stores would have their windows and doors open, and people would be listening to that crazy *The Nut House Neighbors* sponsored by Morrow's Nut House, every day, five days a week. We had a lot of fun doing that for a while.

One thing that I did early on—Fort Wayne in that era was a major league city in one regard, and that was the Fort Wayne Pistons, which today is the Detroit Pistons. Fred Zollner owned them, and he had a piston manufacturing company, and that is the reason for the Detroit Pistons. It was then the Fort Wayne Zollner Pistons. He later moved them to Detroit because of the growth of pro basketball and the league felt that Fort Wayne was too small a city. I am not so sure that was a great move, and we regretted it in Fort Wayne when it was done. After all, there is a Green Bay in pro football, and Green Bay is not the biggest in the world. But at any rate, Jerry Bush, Carlisle Towery, Bobby McDermott, Ralph Hamilton— these are some of the names that I remember. The team was outstanding, and it played at Northside High School Gym. I went to all of the games; we broadcast a lot of the games . . . all of the games, I guess we did . . . come to think of it. They did not play as many games in a season as they do now, but it was the National Basketball League which later became part of the National Basketball Association, the NBA. And there were teams like Sheboygan, Oshkosh, Tri-Cities, and the old Northside Gym would be filled every home game. That is where I learned to do a basketball game, which is not a contemplative game, by Western Union ticker. It is hard to conceive that you would actually do that—but in order to save money and that sort of thing, I would not go with the Pistons to Oshkosh—but I broadcast the game because we would have a Western Union operator sit in and a Western Union operator at the other end. They would send back dot-dash-dash, what was going on, and so I made up a game. If you ever heard a game that was more confused, more time-outs called, I had it, trying to figure out what that guy was telling me. We didn't do that too many times, but that was the early days of radio, you know.

I did the [high school basketball] games in Fort Wayne starting in 1943 when Fort Wayne Central won the tournament, and Murray Mendenhall was the coach. And then, of course, we were pulling for Fort Wayne Central, and I think that is one of the reasons that I got so heavily involved in it. It was a school within three or four blocks of the station that was going through the sectionals, regionals, semifinals, and finals and finally won it. I got very heavily involved with it and thoroughly enjoyed high school basketball, eventually. And then, when I got the job in Indianapolis, I did the tournament for WIRE, so it was continuous. Eventually did it on television starting in 1953, and that is when I worked with Tony Hinkle on television. And we did it for, I guess, twenty-five years or so.

I came from Missouri, where high school basketball did not amount to much. I got here, and I could not believe the religious fervor with which the fans attacked high school basketball. I remember all of a sudden, I am doing a tournament, sectional tournament in the old Northside High School Gym, and, my gosh, they are playing nine games in one day. Here is Monrovia coming in and all these other towns that I can't think of their names right now. I knew nothing about them. I got a lineup out of the program or something. All of a sudden, all of these names, and that game is over, and here comes another one—nine games in a day. Well, that was unbelievable. These kids were screaming and yelling all day, and the field house was full. What is going on here? In that era, there were about seven hundred high schools, and so in four weeks, they trimmed that down to the final four. The term "final four" originated in Indiana. All our games are played in one classification which I think is the secret of high school basketball. No A, Bs, Cs or 1-2-3-4s, and I think that is the delight of the game.

So, the station, again, because it was powerful—WOWO felt that we should do collegiate football, do collegiate games. So every year, we would pick up a schedule of ten, eleven games involving Indiana, Purdue, Notre Dame, because we were close to Notre Dame, also. So then, that began to amount to some travel, going to the games. That is what I thoroughly enjoyed, being on the scene of the action of a major event like that. I will always

remember that my very first game was at Ohio State stadium. You can imagine that my previous experience was of being at tiny William Jewell College at Liberty, Missouri, walking up and down the sideline doing work on the P.A. All of a sudden I was at Ohio State stadium that seats 100,000 people. I was clear up at the top where it was so far that I almost could not see the action. They looked like toy soldiers down on the field. I was so far away. I prepared a lengthy opening during the first fifteen minutes and gave a very prepared story of each and every ball player. When you multiply that eleven on each team by two and you have got twenty-two, and all of a sudden the game is under way, and I am still giving the lineup, you know. I soon learned that I better hustle along, but that I enjoyed.

It is interesting how your paths cross—later on, I mean. One game that I remember was Notre Dame at the Great Lakes Naval Training Academy. I will say this is around 1943, along in there. During that time because of the war, Great Lakes had an exciting, major football team and basketball team. Notre Dame in that year was undefeated going into the final game. This was the last game of the year, and it was played at Great Lakes. And, we were doing the game from Great Lakes. Art Lewis was the announcer working with me. I remember Art. Prior to the game, we had an opportunity to meet the coach of Great Lakes, and that was Tony Hinkle, Paul D. "Tony" Hinkle of Butler University. In the service, he coached basketball and football at Great Lakes. And I am from Fort Wayne doing the game, and very few broadcasters were there— maybe two or three, believe it or not, but again our interest in Notre Dame. And, Notre Dame was defeated in the last fifty seconds by Great Lakes. It was the only game that they lost. Steve Lach was involved in that last touchdown; I can't remember any of the other names. And, I got an opportunity to meet Tony Hinkle afterwards. Then afterward, I am working with Tony when I moved to Indianapolis, and there he was at Butler University as a football and basketball coach and baseball coach. I worked with him a lot, and I always did remember that game as a great, great game down to the last minute and the victory. "Undefeated Notre Dame loses their first, and Great Lakes with Tony Hinkle wins it."

I was doing a football game one day, and Wally Nehrling, who was a WIRE employee, came up to me and said that they were looking for a broadcaster, I mean a

Eldon Campbell hired twenty-four-year-old Carl Kenegy as an announcer on WOWO in 1943 and changed his name to Tom Carnegie. He counseled the young Carnegie to "chew gum" to ease nervousness.

Carnegie and Tony Hinkle became regulars who broadcast the Boys Indiana High School Basketball Tournament from Butler Fieldhouse for Channel 6 for many years.

sports broadcaster, at WIRE. "Mr. Pulliam has heard of you and wants you to come down and see him." So that is how it happened. I went down and talked to Mr. Pulliam.

[Mr. Pulliam] was very visionary—I thought very fair. He was again one of those individuals that because of the newspaper business was that involved in the community and politics and government. He had through the editorial page a way to speak to the reader. So, he was a controversial man as a result. When you own the two major newspapers in town—the *Indianapolis Times* was the third, but it was owned by Scripps-Howard outside—you own the two newspapers and you have a radio station and you are as powerful as he was, you are subject to criticism. Anybody who gets involved in politics is, and he was definitely involved in politics. He let his opinions be known through the newspaper. So, he was rigid.

Looking back at my experiences at WGL and WOWO, I feel I was most fortunate in getting a job there. That was a rare opportunity to learn some very, very important lessons in broadcasting—that broadcasting can be exciting, that the programs you do—no matter what they are—can be entertaining, and that you as a broadcaster should get involved in community affairs, become a part of the community in which you are living and in that way, you make your station more valuable. And, it all has a commercial connotation in the end; you know, you want to pick up that paycheck on the weekend. If you work for a successful station, that is much easier to do. So, I was just most fortunate. And then, to move to WIRE—bigger market, more money—and you think things are going to be the same, but they weren't.

WIRE was a money machine. They just ran network and a few local programs and just ground out the money. And doing things that were different . . . took a lot of time to get that philosophy onto that station . . . going out and doing football, basketball, and studio shows. By the way, I had the most popular show in Indianapolis for several years. It was called *Dinner Winner*. This sounds silly to you, fifteen minutes every night, Monday through Friday. If I call you on the phone, you tell me what you are having for dinner. If you tell me pork and beans, why you win a dinner for six, and Kingan was the sponsor of it, the meat company [chuckles]. Oh, gosh, everyone listened to *Dinner Winner*. I got more fame over that program than anything. Weird, huh?

I felt that WIRE communitywise never lived up to its potential. We got some things done, but you know, we eventually began to do things at the State Fair and other areas. I don't remember people leaving, because, you know, it was a pretty good market and a big market. We never had the number of personnel that I was used to at WOWO.

I thought the atmosphere at WIRE was rather cold. You see, again because when I went there—maybe this was Mr. Pulliam's idea in trying to change it . . . and that is when we began to get sports going at WIRE, but it was a network-oriented station. If it was on the network, we carried it. The network was running twenty-four hours a day; so, there was no time to be involved in local community. And besides that, it costs money, and it is just easier to take the network. We have a newsroom, and your news was at five o'clock or six o'clock. You have the noon news and some early morning, and that was just about it—very structured—very, very structured.

[WIRE] had gotten me established to the point where I was able to move to another station that was really doing things. That is how it helped my career, just as a transition, really. It allowed me to get my feet on the ground in a bigger market and to make some friends. And there must have been some reason I was contacted by Frank Sharp of Channel 6 and asked to come there. I remember meeting him in his car on Pennsylvania Street somewhere. He was talking about going to work there. And I was certainly ready, because I knew that we weren't going to get television. So I really treated that as—very disappointing. I was very disappointed when I first went there—bigger market, bigger possibilities, but they weren't doing anything, you know. And gradually, it was like pulling teeth to get things done.

I hated to leave [Mr. Pulliam], really, and go over to the WFBM stations, but I could see that he was not getting television, and that was the only time that I felt that he had been poorly advised by his people. He had a construction permit for television, and he began to let us know that we were going to be in television. He even built studios over at the Star/News Building. He had a couple of cameras that we rehearsed in front of, but the Federal Communications Commission controlled the licensing of television. So, he had a construction permit; the William H. Block Company, the department store, had a construction permit. Mr. Harry Bitner, who was the owner of WFBM, had a construction permit Mr. Bitner, to his credit, went ahead and spent the money necessary to put a station on the air. Who was Mr. Pulliam going to get advice from? It was his chief engineer; it was the people at his radio station. And, they saw this new station going on the air in black and white, and they heard about color. Gene Alden, the chief engineer, advised Mr. Pulliam, "Why hurry? You know, they are going to have color real soon." Well, as it turned out, we didn't for fifteen years or more. "Why go to all that expense of buying that equipment? When we go on, we will go on with color, see." They just were hesitant and didn't make the move. Well, as a result, the construction permit was taken away from them because they had not shown progress toward getting it on. You had to show progress. So then they began, "Oh, maybe we made a mistake." So, they tried to buy the William H. Block Company's permit. The deal was made. They argued about whether it was going to be for ten thousand or fifteen thousand, whatever. Finally, got it advertised in the newspaper which you had to do for legal reasons. Just as they started to advertise, the FCC took away Block's construction permit. So, it was a new ball game. Channel 6 was on the air; they are going, but all these other channels went into hearings. He spent hundreds of thousands of dollars—by he, I mean Mr. Pulliam—later on, trying to get television and he had it in his hand at one time. And he never did get it. Never did get it. And so that is the reason that I left when the opportunity came to go on television, because I knew that I wanted to be into television. That was new. That was the wonderful new part of our business, and I wanted to get into pictures [chuckles].

[WFBM] had pretty much the same philosophy as WIRE. But now, all of a sudden, they had TV, and there weren't TV programs available. If you were going to be on the air, you had to have local programming. So, all of the sudden we had boxing shows, studio wrestling, *Meet the Press* with Gilbert Forbes. We got a five-minute show here, a five-minute show here, another five-minute show. Lots of things going on in the studio, because that was the way you filled up your time.

We had one camera man . . . who had just an old Bell & Howell motion picture camera, hand held, no sound on it or anything—go out and take some black and white pic-

tures for us. And, we did not have, even as late as 1953 and 1954 and 1955, did not have a developer for film. We took it to a local film lab where they could develop black and white film. It was called "Filmcraft" out at Forty-sixth Street. Everything he took, he had to take out there, and then they would bring it down to the station. I don't know . . . it was just so slow getting started. I always hated to work with film, because it was always so tedious to edit, just so tedious to edit . . . you know, the splicing and the gluing. Golly, people who work in television today with the ease of videotape just have no idea of the time that it took to put together even a short story in the old film days. And eventually, we had color film, but you see, I never felt film was really compatible with television, engineeringwise. And, it wasn't until we got into videotape—and now you get beautiful pictures from videotape, because videotape was made for television. Motion pictures were made for theater, not for television. Electronically, it is a much better picture than what we started off with.

I remember about the first time that we ever used color film on a remote—I mean, out in the field—was at the 1964 Olympic games in Japan. So, it was a lot of years, you see, for color to come in, even color in the state basketball tournament. In the early days you had to have a lot of light for color—cameras are better now—so, we had to augment the lights at Hinkle Fieldhouse. That is where the tournament was held. We started that year in the sectionals and put lights, additional lighting over the field house floor. Well, we turned the lights on in the sectional, like on a Wednesday night before we would go on the air on Saturday. Charley Dagwell, Tech High School, looked at those lights—and it was so much different; it was like the difference between the outdoors and a cave, you know—and he made us turn them off, because he said that there was just too much light in the eyes of the players. Well, I tell you that was a big blow. We had spent so much effort and promotion and telling everybody that we were going to have television in color.

I remember NBC and their doing the 500-Mile Race, and I just, as a youngster, listened to it, but Graham McNamee was the announcer of that, of the 500, and he was one of the premier, national network announcers at that time. At that time, the radio broadcast was originated by WIBC, and I don't remember when they took control of that in association with the 500, organized the network

Carnegie began broadcasting his popular daily Trackside *shows from the Indianapolis 500 in the mid-1950s. He remembered, "We did a half-hour every day from the Indianapolis Motor Speedway. That was before we really had the film crew. That was before videotape, and we were out there rain or shine for a good many years."* PHOTO BY RAY CONOLLY

and eventually, the Indianapolis Motor Speedway assumed total control of the network; so, WIBC doesn't have anything to do with it at all now or it hasn't had for a while. I had nothing to do with that because I got involved in running the P.A. system almost immediately—in fact immediately—when the race resumed after World War II.

I was thrown into something that was bigger than I anticipated by far. And, when I looked down and saw that some of the newspapermen like Blondy Patton, sports editor of the *Indianapolis Star*, didn't get there until so-called halftime. The race was halfway over by the time that he got there, for example. It was a horrendous traffic jam. I had worked some qualifying on the P.A., and George Hoster, an Indianapolis Ford dealer, was the man in charge of the public address system, and that was a holdover from the prewar years. Now the year was 1946, and we doing the P.A. from top of the old pagoda, the Chinese- or Japanese-style pagoda which is right at the starting line.

Without warning here comes the start of the race, and George turned the P.A. over to me, and I did it the rest of the way. I had never seen the 500; I had listened to it, and I didn't know much more about it than names and numbers. Looking back on it, I had a good number of years—I was appointed chief of the P.A. the next year. So, evidently Wilbur Shaw, who was a three-time winner, figured that I did all right as a starter because I have been there ever since—but I felt as I look back on it that it took me ten years or so to feel comfortable in that environment, about a sport that was new to me that involved mechanical terms from carburetors to spark plugs to tires. It was more complicated than just man and the story of his involvement. Still today, to me the most interesting part of the Indianapolis Motor Speedway is not the width of the tires or how much the

car weighs or what it is made of or what the skin is made of; it's the people involved. That has been my philosophy all through: they're the heroes; they're *all* winners if they are in the 500. There are no losers there, and I think that attitude has helped me. But again, it was ten years before I felt that I knew enough about it so that if I said something, I wouldn't make a mistake.

We [at Channel 6] were the first to be out there in doing a daily *Trackside* broadcast. We started in conjunction with the Indianapolis 500 the very first venture that they had in regards to television, a one-hour telecast on each of the four qualifying days. So, we had originated that for them, and I did the announcing on that. And, that went on for years before the ESPNs of the world began to get interested and to send it nationally. And, that went on before there was a national telecast of the race, although ABC has been out there a lot of years now, but there was no television of the event. The Indianapolis Motor Speedway was—really Tony Hulman—was very concerned about live television.

You have to remember that you don't have that philosophy now, but in those days, everybody felt that if the thing was on live, it would affect the ticket sales greatly—not just a little bit, but greatly. And, you have got to remember that you can see the race on television better than the best ticket at Speedway, and that worried them, you see. And so, Channel 6 was permitted by Tony Hulman to go on the air in 1949 with the very first television of the race. That was 1949, the live telecast—three cameras, one in the first turn and two on the main stretch. They did it again in 1950. You know that there weren't probably a thousand television sets in the area then in 1949. There were more in 1950. But then a couple, maybe two dozen people called up and canceled their ticket orders, and that caused the

Eugene C. Pulliam

Many people associate Eugene C. Pulliam exclusively with the newspaper industry, particularly with Central Newspapers, Inc. (CNI). But he also owned radio stations for twenty-three years. With the rise of radio, Pulliam recognized the importance of broadcasting as a disseminator of news, and at the same time, as a potential threat to his newspaper interests. He subsequently purchased WIRE in Indianapolis in 1936, and WAOV in Vincennes in 1941. At WIRE, Pulliam's interest in news resulted in the station expanding its coverage. After he was unable to obtain a television license, Pulliam became disenchanted with FCC regulations. He sold his radio interests in 1960 and concentrated on the newspaper business until he died in 1975.[31]

shutoff. That was the way it was for a good many years. I don't know when it was started, but I was not involved. I didn't go to Channel 6 until 1953. You got to remember that Channel 6 started—the very first broadcast was live at the 500-Mile Race. John Townsend, a local attorney, was one of the announcers on that. Paul Roberts, who I worked with at WOWO also, was with WFBM. He was staff announcer, and he worked it. And, Dick Pittinger was the other one. He was doing sports for Channel 6. So, the background on Channel 6 to answer your question as to the Speedway: how can we cover an event and also make some money, give an opportunity for local programming? That is what we did, and that is what we did for a lot of years out at the track.

I used to think that [to be a good announcer] it was totally voice, but it isn't. It is the richness of the delivery. It doesn't have to be particularly resonant or anything, but it's the richness, and it is so that your delivery is recognizable. You know, people can put a name to you. You don't sound like every other person. You have a technique or way of saying things or a different voice quality that brings attention to yourself. It is the personality in the voice, and you develop personality in your voice through voice lessons, through learning how to express yourself, learning the value of highs and lows in your conversation. All of these little techniques that help you develop a richness of character in your voice. And then, you get into television—I always look at our business as theater, theater business. You go sit in an audience in a theater production, and that is what we are doing every day. And so, those people on the stage are using all of their talents toward entertaining you or informing you, and that is what we are doing except that we can't see our audience. The same techniques that are available to the theater . . . and that is why I think theater should play an important part in the background of anyone in our business in the broadcasting end of it—I mean in the actual voice end of it. It is theater. That is what I work at the 500-Mile Race in the public address system. I am on the P.A. to inform, but to create an aura of excitement. And, your voice can do that so much better than an automobile, sometimes. They don't know whether an automobile is going 200 miles per hour or 225. Who is the one that tells them? Well, I am, you see. So, I am excited. I am putting on the show; that's theater. That is what it is.

James R. Phillippe (ca. 1950)

Jim Phillippe

(1919–)

In April and July 1995 James R. Phillippe was interviewed in the relaxed atmosphere of his north side Indianapolis home. A Hoosier by birth, Phillippe grew up in southern Indiana, in the small town of Dugger. He received an undergraduate degree from Indiana University and a master's degree in drama from Cornell University. After graduation in 1943 he tried his hand at various positions in radio and theater. However, it was as an instructor at Marshall University that he discovered his love of teaching. Returning to Indiana, he took a job as head of the drama department at Butler University in 1946, later becoming the head of its radio and television department and manager of WAJC, the student-run radio station. During his tenure, he established an internship program and saw the number of students in radio and television grow from 25 to 175. While teaching, Phillippe also announced at WIRE in Indianapolis, and for ten years he produced television shows part-time at WFBM. While he retired from Butler in 1986, he continued to broadcast on the public address system at the Indianapolis Motor Speedway. Although he has had a varied career, he says that it is his activities associated with teaching of which he is most proud.

In the town of Dugger, I think the highest population was close to 1,400. I don't know exactly what it was when I was born. It isn't that today. My father had a grocery store, and of course, we knew a lot of people. In those days you didn't declare your affiliation as far as your political party was concerned, simply because you wanted business both from the Democrats and Republicans. So, my father would never let us talk about anything like that. Our school was small. We had a grade school that was separated from the high school. I think to some degree, I was somewhat reticent or timid in many ways and yet bold in some other ways. I never was big enough to participate in sports, which I loved. (I think when I went away to college, I weighed 110 pounds. So, you know how big I was.) I was a yell leader for four years, so I served as a yell leader for the teams in Dugger. I was in trouble a lot of times, simply because I had a lot of energy—wanted to do a lot of things, and people just didn't move fast enough for me. Teachers didn't move fast enough [laughs], and I just simply was in mischief. I would do a lot of things—didn't harm anybody, but we had three or four of us that were playful, and we had a lot of fun. We'd tease a lot. We would tease the teachers even to the point that we'd get kicked out of class, to be honest about it [laughs]. Our parents would have to turn around and take us back to the school, which was embarrassing. We didn't have too much in our school, it being a small school like that. The facilities were limited. Our activities were limited. Actually, the number of different courses we had were limited, and I think that

"Gentlemen, start your engines!" The words of Tony Hulman, owner of the Indianapolis Motor Speedway, thrilled spectators and the radio audience alike. Here Hulman is seen with Phillippe and Luke Walton.

This studio set at WFBM was typical of those used in television in the 1950s.

had a big effect on me. When I finally went to college, I then felt very—insecure, I guess is a pretty good word for it. I didn't feel that I had the background to compete with people that came out [of] Tech High School [Arsenal Technical], or Shortridge [High School in Indianapolis] and some of those places. So, I developed an inferiority complex for part of that time, until I realized that I could keep up with them, and in some cases, could pass them.

I majored in speech and drama. There were no radio courses in those days. There were no radio departments, so anything that was being taught in radio was made a class in the speech and drama department. But you see, when I went away to IU [Indiana University] in 1937, broadcasting was just a baby, not started until the 1920s or something like that. I did a lot of comedy at IU, and I think it's more difficult to do comedy than it is to do tragic acting. But I was willing to do anything.

When I graduated from Cornell [University], I got a radio job announcing in Binghamton, New York. I think I lasted there two or three weeks. I didn't like it. I was stuck in a place that I didn't know anybody, number one. Number two, I was in what I called a "padded cell"—that was the announce booth [laughs]. You didn't see daylight or anything else. I just didn't like the routine of a booth announcer. And so, I left there, and I was still gung ho about drama, and so then I went into New York City. I got a job at the Waldorf Astoria Hotel chasing mail at night time and made the casting rounds during the day. I did this for a couple or three months, and I saw the same kids every day at the same casting offices as we moved from one to the other. I got to know several of them and found out that some of them had been there two or three years and had never gotten a part, never had been cast in anything. I thought, "Boy, this isn't for me. It's too long to wait," and I didn't enjoy working at the Waldorf Astoria that much either.

From 1943 to 1946 Phillippe worked in theater and radio stations in Charleston, West Virginia (WGKV), Huntington, West Virginia (WSAZ), and Evansville, Indiana (WGBF and WEOA) before going to Indianapolis. I didn't have a job. So [my wife and I] went back to Dugger with my parents there. We lived with them for about six weeks or so, and I joined a teachers' placement [service] in Chicago. I could not believe it. It was right after the war. Everybody was looking for help. So, it wasn't just me. I had

thirty-some offers at different universities and colleges throughout the United States. I just couldn't believe it. And, of course, they were willing to take anybody, I guess, that had a master's degree or better. But, a job offer was at Butler, and it was in the state of Indiana, and it was close to people. A lot of our fraternity brothers and all we knew were here in Indianapolis. They didn't have a drama department at Butler, and I was hired to start one, and that I did. And we came to Butler in 1946. [I put together a four-year degree in drama but] I didn't teach; I just set the classes up, got the professors, and I got it all lined up for them. . . . They had a radio department here at Butler, and, of course, they found out that I had been in radio and all. So, they asked me to teach a class in radio, which I did, as well as [later] teaching in the drama department.

We didn't have anything but a tiny little old stage, but [I directed and] we put some big plays on there. We had this little FM station at Butler, and I was helping do things there. We had trouble with Channel 6. They were on TV then, and the frequency that we were on, being WAJC-Butler University, was interfering with their TV signal. So, they came to us and said, "If we find another frequency for you to be on, would you get off this one?" And we said, "Certainly. No problem." They found 104.5, which was a commercial frequency and was not limited in power at that time. Nobody wanted FM in those days; FM was not popular. There were no FM sets for people to receive the signal, very few. And those that did have them, they were individual sets—you didn't have a combination of AM and FM radio. You had an FM set, and you had an AM set. Sure, we traded, not really knowing what was going to take place down the line, how popular FM was going to become.

To begin with, [we were] 360 watts, or something like that. It was very small, but it was enough to interfere with their signal. So that trade was made, and then probably 1953, or 1954, Butler hired a full-time chairman of the department of radio and TV, and I still taught a class, but I didn't have anything to do with the management or anything else, or programming. I served as chairman of the department of drama, but still taught in radio and TV.

I wanted to learn something about television. Shortly thereafter I approached Channel 6, and they were hiring people like me that had a theatrical background for producers and directors. This still was a part-time job. My main job was still at Butler, and I worked weekends; I worked vacations. I filled in all summer long for vacations. I got to a point where I signed the TV station on in the morning. Got up and went at five o'clock in the morning to get down there and sign the station on and worked 'til eight or nine o'clock in the morning, and then go to Butler. So, I could take what I had learned there; I could take it into a classroom. That's important, because people like myself, we had no classroom to go to. We just flew by the seat of our pants, and a producer and director was the boss of any live show that went on. Announcers, cameramen, and everybody had to do what he told them to do.

We were always experimenting when we were doing live shows. You learn the term "terminate" real quick. "Terminate" meant just shut it all down; go to black. You're sitting at home watching the TV, and it all goes black for awhile. That's 'cause we were all confused on our live show, and things weren't working out right, and we weren't getting the right shots or something, or we lost ourselves in the script. We weren't all on the same line on the same page. And, boy, as a producer and director, you just say "terminate." And everything shuts down. Then you're on the intercom system; you talk to the cameraman, and you say, "Now, I want you to get this shot set up on camera one, and we want to take this shot on camera two. You get over here. Announcer, you get ready, this is where we're picking it up. Talent, you're going to do this. Okay, everybody ready?" Sometimes it just went to black, depending how big the problem was, and sometimes we would just throw out the call letters—you know Channel 6, or whatever it was. Have that there briefly, or if it really was a problem, why then the announcer would come on and say, "The problem is beyond our control. This is [a technical problem]; we'll be back in just a minute."

The hour of around 4:00 to 4:30 to around 7:00 in the evenings were live shows on Channel 6, and you just lined these sets up along the wall, one right after another in a U-shaped studio. Our production booth had all plate glass, and we could look out onto all of this. We had three producers at a time—like I'd take this first show, and as soon as it was over with, I'd get out of the seat and the next guy would move in for the next show; and the next guy would come in for the next show. Then, I'd come around again and go back into the third or fourth show, getting it ready. A lot of them were live. Some of them were cartoons. We did a tremendous amount of live commercials

that we had to have sets for; they'd have a set with a background and everything else. And they'd be tearing down this set after it was over with and be putting up another one in its place for the next time around. So we had three producers on duty at that time. When you got through at seven o'clock, you were tired. Mentally, you were bushed. But we didn't have any videotape in those days, and so you did live—did a lot of live stuff.

Now, when it came to a newscast, what we had were photos that came over the wire machine. And the newscaster would determine what stories he was going to use and the pictures that would go with those stories that came in. It was a photograph, and sometimes we had some film, but these were photographs. Well, we had a blackboard, a big long blackboard, and we'd put the number one picture up in the left corner of that blackboard—the number two, three, four, five and six all the way across the top of the blackboard. Then, we would drop down and reverse it, and go the opposite way—six, seven, and eight would come back across and then down again and across again. Now, this was done simply because you didn't want to take a camera and go all the way from the right side to the left side and pan it—you know real fast or flip it around. So, you could follow it and kind of turn, just drop it down slowly. Pick up the next one, and then you'd go like that, because you didn't have that many cameras to work with. Many times they only used two cameras . . . very seldom using three. So, that was the way you did the news. And then if he was through with that particular picture, then you'd come back and focus on the newscaster until he was ready to go with another picture or insert some film that he had from stories that may have happened two days ago or something, but was able to get film and show it.

As far as I know, we were the first ones to do wrestling. Came right into the studio and set up the wrestling ring and had the pros in there, and they wrestled. . . . You couldn't get too wild in the studio because we didn't have that much room for people. The audience and the crowd was small. Those women that we invited (I don't know how they determined who was going to be in there). The first group [that] got there lined up, why they got in. They would hit people with their purses, the women would. It was wild. They put on a good show [laughs]. They'd come right up to the ring, and they were deeply involved. They [the matches] weren't put on either. I mean, we didn't stage it; we didn't have time to stage it. We'd just get the ring up in time, and away we'd go.

For years we did the high school basketball tournament out at Hinkle Fieldhouse, and I must have produced and directed those five, six, seven years. I don't remember exactly. But we always took the remote bus, and in those days could drive the remote bus into the Hinkle Fieldhouse. We got the remote truck into the Hinkle Fieldhouse and parked it under the bleachers. There was space to park it in there. We had three cameras for the basketball games. We were the only ones, that's WFBM in those days, Channel 6. We originated the broadcast, the televising of the game. There were roughly eight, nine, ten TV stations in the state of Indiana at that time. Evansville had one. Elkhart had one. I think South Bend did, Bloomington. Indianapolis may have had two at that time. Muncie had one. So we fed those stations the basketball game. Now, some of those stations would have their own announcer. As an example, Hilliard Gates did his play-by-play. Tom Carnegie was the announcer for our station. If they wanted to take Tom's voice, they could do that. Some chose to use their own sports announcers as I said, and I remember Hilliard being there with his own monitor and Carnegie being down from him with his monitor. And the gentleman who owned the station in Muncie, [Don Burton], he did his own play-by-play too.

You talk to your cameramen, and you give them a certain responsibility, or area or things you want them to be responsible for. And when they're not on the air, they're my eyes. They're the producer's eyes. They're looking the floor over or telling me on the mike, saying, "Hey, Jim, I think we've got something over here." And they'd show it to me, and I'd say, "Yeah, fine. Stand by." And they could talk to me. See, we had that intercom system. And then, too, you had what was called a "zoom lens" that you could zoom in and you could zoom out. It was difficult to keep it in focus when you did that, but some of those cameramen were very, very good cameramen, and they could handle that. If a tight shot was not going to be staying there very long, we could come back and enlarge that floor, or enlarge that picture, and get everything that was going on. But, we'd talk it all over. They had a script, and we'd go through the script, but we could never call a ball game. You'd never know what's going to take place. So

that's where you fly by the seat of your pants, you know. But you always knew what the cue would be for cutaways, when time-outs came. You knew the opening, how you were going to get into it. For the most part, you knew the closing, but in between was—well, at halftime you had everything set up for halftime too. But the game itself, it was just go as you can.

We used to do the [beer commercials] on Saturday night. A lot of them were done around the wrestling and the boxing and things and late night shows and theme movies, and would cut in with live commercials. Yes, live TV commercials. And of course, we always got the beer cold, and at that time they weren't permitted to drink it. Well, I think in the beginning, they were able to take a sip or so. But then it got to the point where when you brought it up to your lips, or to your mouth, then the camera left it, and so you didn't drink on TV. But we drank it after the commercial was over with. We didn't let it go to waste. And sometimes things wouldn't go right, and we'd have to open three or four bottles before we got it just right [laughs].

I go back to about 1947, 1948, 1949—someplace in there—that I met Tom [Carnegie]. That was before Channel 6. I was teaching at Butler, and I was chairman of the department of drama, and I was teaching in the radio department because I had been in broadcasting for two or three years in the commercial field, and so I was teaching there as well as in the drama department. Carnegie came in, and they needed a chairperson for the radio department. I don't know how this occurred, but Tom showed up and he would be there about three days a week because of his other job. The rest of the time if a problem arose I took care of it. Anyway, we got to be good friends. And so one day, he said, "You know, I need some help out at the Speedway." He said, "Would you like to help me?" I said, "Tom, I don't know the front end from the rear end of a car." He said, "Well, I didn't either when I started." And I said, "Yeah, okay." So that's the way it started. Forty-six or forty-seven years later, here we are. But that's how it happened.

Phillippe recalled the changing role of women at the Speedway. Betty Sullivan was a camera gal with WTHI in Terre Haute. She came over here to the track, and they weren't going to let her in. And she fought the battle for a long time. To my knowledge (and I think this is accurate)

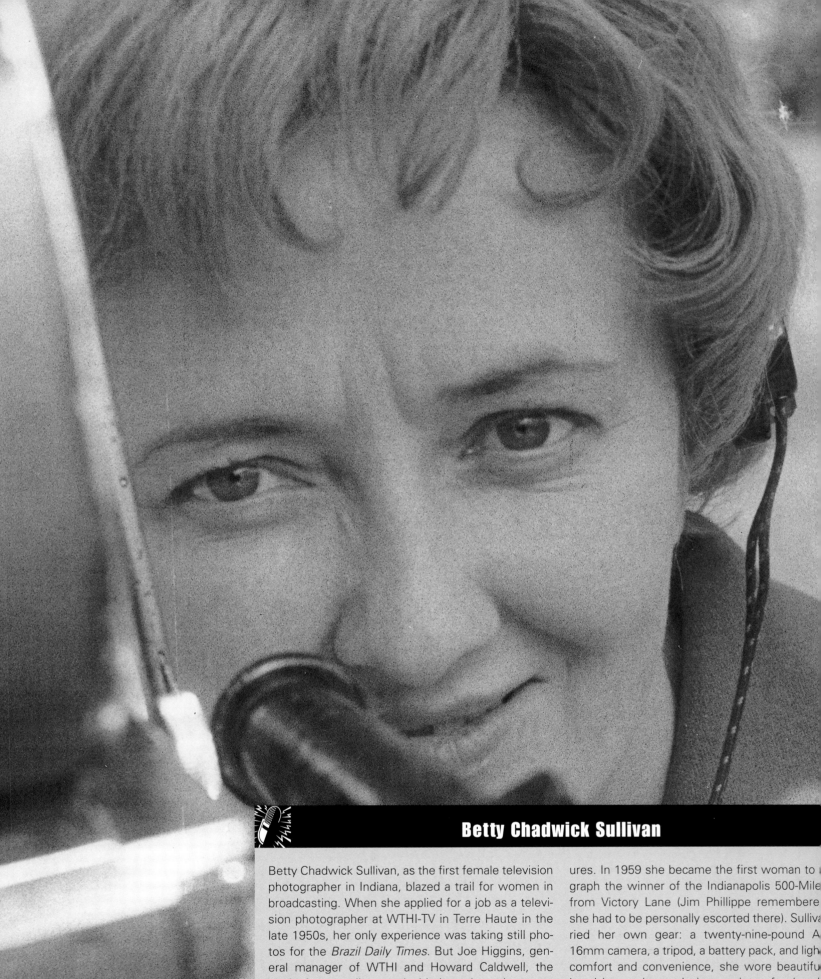

Betty Chadwick Sullivan, an early female photojournalist in Indiana, is a member of the Hall of Fame.

Betty Chadwick Sullivan

Betty Chadwick Sullivan, as the first female television photographer in Indiana, blazed a trail for women in broadcasting. When she applied for a job as a television photographer at WTHI-TV in Terre Haute in the late 1950s, her only experience was taking still photos for the *Brazil Daily Times*. But Joe Higgins, general manager of WTHI and Howard Caldwell, the station's news director, decided to take a chance on her, and within a short time they realized that she was "something special." An energetic self-starter, she could be found at the scene of any newsworthy story, and within a short time she was promoted to chief photographer for the station. She never hesitated to seek out interviews with celebrities and political fig-ures. In 1959 she became the first woman to graph the winner of the Indianapolis 500-Mile from Victory Lane (Jim Phillippe remembere she had to be personally escorted there). Sulliva ried her own gear: a twenty-nine-pound A 16mm camera, a tripod, a battery pack, and ligh comfort and convenience, she wore beautifu lored jumpsuits made in a variety of colors seamstress mother. With her name, the station letters, the word "News," and the familiar "eye" on the back, they became her trademar lowing her example and through her encourage many young people found a career in televisio tography.[32]

she was the first lady cameraman to ever be in the pit area, to take pictures. See, women didn't used to be in the pits at all. Oh, no. Women couldn't even go in the pits. I can't go back to the year that was changed, but it was changed many years ago. So you can go strolling through there now, if you have a badge, and, of course, women [are] working on crews. Women are up there timing and keeping stats and everything else. But at one time it was strictly a man's area; no women allowed.

[At the station, there were] no women producers, no women directors. No, strictly men. Women served as talent. There were a lot of women on TV. As a regular announcer, I don't think we had any women, but we had some women that did special shows and commercials. Ann Harper was one of those. But she worked basically over in radio as an announcer and disc jockey, and then would do occasional things over on [the] TV side. But, women were mostly used in offices and writers and that type of things, but no producer or directors. And as far as that is concerned, as a permanent staff announcer, no—women in homemakers shows, women narrating a movie, you know, where they cut in and out, that type of thing, but no permanent staff announcer.

[From 1954 to 1956] there was a group that was formed here in Indianapolis to try to obtain Channel 13. We were called Midwest Broadcasting, if I recall correctly. A fellow by the name of Frank Parrish was to be manager of the station. They had a board of directors that was putting the money up. Frank came to me and asked me if I would be interested in that particular job as a program director. And at that time, I thought, "Well, that might not be too bad. I might be interested in doing that." So I joined them. We had to put everything together. We had to show how our studios were built, how they were laid out—floor plans, and everything else. We had to program it from five or six o'clock in the morning until 1:00 or 2:00 the next morning. You had to come up with what talent was going to be involved. You had to come up with how many cameramen you would use. I did all of that. I put all of the programs together, the people that we would hire, the orchestras and everything else that would be used, and the talent and worked days and days and days on that. When we had the hearing, there were three or four other stations that were trying to get that same channel. WIRE was one, WLW in Cincinnati was one, WIBC was one, and

Midwest. We, the board of directors, went into Washington, D.C.—oh, before the hearing date was established, Frank Parrish died with a heart attack. He had a heart attack and died. That moved me as the main person—not that I was going to be manager of the station, but that moved me in the position of where I was going to be the main witness, I guess, or the main person to carry before the FCC and all the rest of them. It threw me into a position I certainly didn't want to be in, but I didn't have any choice. We brought on a new manager, but it was too late. He knew very little. We showed his credentials and they understood what happened. So we go to Washington, D.C., for the hearing. It's just like a courtroom. There's a hearing judge, and there's a lawyer advising the hearing judge. They put you up on a stand, and out there in front are all the lawyers from WIRE, the lawyers from WIBC, the lawyers from our company, and the lawyers from WLW. I mean they're after you hot and heavy.

Any lawyer could pop up and throw a question at you, and you had to answer it. They had your outline; they had your programming; they had your station; they knew what you were going to do. And they'd tear into that, and try to tear it apart, you know. As an example, someplace in the line they caught a fact that WIRE or some studio didn't have a ceiling higher than five feet in one of the studios. And one smart lawyer got up and said, "Are you going to hire midgets?" Well, we sat back and WLW and WIRE just tore each other up, because they had past experience from broadcasting radio. These lawyers had gone in and dug up all the mistakes and things that had happened on these stations and were trying to prove that they weren't qualified or capable of having a TV station. We sat there pure; we had no past experience. They couldn't get us for anything like that. The only thing they could do was to turn to our book. But anyhow, you know, we were just in clover, and we were flying our stockholders in each day, and then the new manager and I were staying up all night with them, coaching, telling them what they were going to be hit with the next day and what to say and what not to say. . . . They'd fly back home, and we'd bring in another one. Anyhow, one of the lawyers jumped up and said, "Well, obviously you people are very well-coached," knowing that we were coaching them of course, but that didn't make any difference. They asked you ungodly questions, questions that you don't think could ever be

Betty Chadwick Sullivan, in one of her signature jumpsuits, filmed Ken Beckley interviewing Harry Reasoner in the mid-1960s.

Phillippe posed with race car driver Roger Ward, fellow broadcaster Ann Wagner, and students John Hargrove and Tom Elrod as Butler University's radio station WAJC raised more than $1,400 during the Cancer Fund Radiothon in April 1969.

important to whether you got the channel or not. They'd come at you from all sides. And so, I guess I was on the stand for almost four hours. That's a long time. We were given the initial decision. In the meantime, they found out that one of our stockholders [had been involved with] tax evasion. So the next thing I know, we have sold out to Cincinnati. They went around and instead of trying to fight it, which I think we would have lost with that tax evasion penalty, they sold it. And I don't know how much money WLW paid to get them to drop out, but they dropped out, and WLW eventually got it.

When I became chairman of the [radio] department in 1965, I believed in an adjunct faculty. I believed in bringing people in to teach a class who were involved in that particular aspect of broadcasting every day. I had Tom Carnegie teach sportscasting. We had people like Howard Caldwell teaching newscasting. I had station managers; Eldon Campbell was one that taught station management. I had the head of sales departments in the TV and radio come in and teach sales. These people brought a world of experiences into the classroom that you would never, never find in a textbook. We had textbooks which they used religiously, but they could apply their daily activities to whatever that book had to offer, what chapters they were involved in, and what the subject was. Now, I believe strongly in that, and I think the results that we got from that philosophy were—excellent broadcasters graduated from Butler. We have them all over the United States, and they'll come back and tell you that they got a lot from dealing with those that were in it every day. For me to try to teach that when I wasn't in the commercial field, I would have to rely on past experience and what's in the textbook, and wasn't happening. Things change almost every day in the broadcasting industry. So, I just felt that was a strong, strong part of our curriculum.

[When] you're talking about ethics, one of the things you didn't do—we weren't even allowed to say "hell," or you were fired. If you swore on the air, you were done. We've come a long way, haven't we? There is nothing sacred anymore in broadcasting. The other thing [was] that you did not knock the opponent, the opposition—I'm thinking commercialwise. If an Oldsmobile versus a Ford commercial—the Oldsmobile never mentioned Ford. Ford never mentioned Oldsmobile. You just talked about the qualities of your car. You didn't rub one against the other

as they do today. You were forbidden to mention in that commercial any other name of a competitor. It just wasn't done like it is done today. So, Ford's spot was strictly about the Ford. It wasn't about [how] it outlasts this other car, or whatever. That was the way it was done then. You always tried to be honest about all the programming that you did. You wouldn't try to be biased; you'd try to stay away from any opinion, unless it was so labeled. That's about all I can think of.

Things change so rapidly as far as news reporting is concerned. The amount of leeway that you have today as compared to even ten or twelve years ago almost permits you to do about anything you want to do. There seem to be very few rules and regulations as to what words are used and how you describe something, how vivid it is. To me, you still try. We always tried to tell them to be honest and not to give their opinion, but to try to look at the facts and go from there. And I think you follow the same thing in journalism in print, although again there is so much freedom that I really don't like all of that freedom. I think it's a little difficult to teach ethics from the standpoint that we all come from a different background. We've all been under different codes that parents set for us and what might be right for one is not right for the other, or at least there's not the concern for the other. But to go back to your question fully, yes, we worked on ethics all the way through. We tried to tell them that, if they were going to give an opinion or anything like that, it had to be stated as such—that this was a commentary or that this was their belief, and not to try to force their belief on other people. A newscast can come over the wire, or stories can come over the wire or come through audio, and if I don't particularly like that myself, I can just discard it. And who knows? But that wouldn't be fair. If I didn't believe in that particular thing—and I know people have done that. I was in broadcasting, and I know some newscasters would say, "Well, I'm not going to give that story," because it did not go with the way he felt. That's not constant; I think that's an exception, but there are some that will do that and we try not to. We tried to teach our kids to be honest all the way down the line and above all make sure they had the facts before they started jumping to any conclusions—make sure they knew what they were talking about. We worked privately with these kids. I turned out some great broadcasters.

And I'd say the most satisfying thing that happened to me is that we took that department, and we went from a seven- and eight-hour broadcast day, we went to a twenty-four-hour day [completely student-operated. And we increased WAJC's power to 48,500 watts]. We went to 175 majors when I retired. Seeing the department grow, seeing the kids mature, seeing them develop as broadcasters, and then having them to return, or send me notes or call me and thank me for what we did—that's a great reward.

Ann Wagner (Harper) (ca. 1951)
WRTV-6

Ann Wagner

(1924–)

When Ann Wagner Harper was growing up in Vincennes, Indiana, she realized that "radio was just like a window on the whole world out there." As a very young girl, she decided that she was going to be a part of it. A charming and articulate woman, Harper had to have considerable determination to achieve her dream in an industry that was almost entirely populated by men. Fortunately she was blessed with a lovely singing voice, which provided her with an entrée into broadcasting. She got her early radio training at WAOV Radio in Vincennes, where many young broadcasters learned the business. When an opportunity arose in Indianapolis, she landed a job singing at the Columbia Club at night; during the day she was a vocalist on PM Party *at WIBC. Soon she was also singing country music on* Circle B *at WFBM-TV with Tom Moriarity and his group. After several years of working three jobs, Harper opted to stay at WFBM, where owner Harry Bitner cast her as a disc jockey—the first female disc jockey in Indiana—in* Make Mine Music. Party Line, *Harper's last on-air program, appealed especially to women. In 1961, at the age of thirty-seven, she went back to Butler University to earn her undergraduate and master's degrees. After teaching high school for five years, she became an assistant professor in the radio and television department at Butler. For twenty years, Harper taught and mentored a new generation of broadcasters. She retired in 1988 as head of the department and a full professor. After more than forty years in Indianapolis, Harper moved back to Vincennes where her interview was conducted in May 1995.*

Well, I was born in 1924 in Louisville, Kentucky, and I think radio came in about that same time. Then we came to Vincennes, and from that time on, I was a Hoosier, and I still am a Hoosier. I grew up in Vincennes. Those were kind of hard times, but we didn't know it. I grew up with the ability to go to grade school where I had elocution; I had piano lessons, violin lessons, some voice lessons; and this is in grade school. And then when I went to high school at Saint Rose Academy, I continued to study voice. . . . My uncle, Joe Wagner—he's still alive—said he would pay for one voice lesson, and Sister Maurelia said, "I'll give her one on my own," so I had two voice lessons [a week] for four years at Saint Rose. And of course, radio was everywhere at that time, but on a much smaller scale.

[Radio] was the most wonderful entertainment that had happened to us, you know. It was where the action was. It came into our homes. The newspaper did, but in a different way. When radio came in it was just like a window on the whole world out there, although it wasn't

Wagner broadcast Annie's Almanac, *a daily program for WIBC. Left to right: Paul Burton,
Ann Wagner, Tom Moriarity, Jack Simpson, and announcer Barry Lake. Easy Gwynn, host of*
Easy Does It, *joined the program as emcee.*

Wagner loved dressing in her cowgirl costume with the fringe on the shirt and the culottes. Here she posed with the
Circle B Ranch *gang at WFBM with foreman Dick Pittinger. From left to right: Country Cousin Chickie (Hopkins),
Paul Burton, Tom Moriarity, Wagner, Pittinger, and Dick Green.*

worldwide at that time like it is today. It gave us a whole new dimension in our way of life. It meant, "Shhh, we're listening." It meant opening our ears to music we hadn't heard to that time and to people we didn't really feel like we knew. It meant afternoon and evening entertainment. It occupied a very prominent place in the living room, just as the television does sometimes now. We didn't have as many radios as we do now, but the one we had was large and very, very important. And it brought sports. I remember as a little girl, being in the country where my grandmother and grandfather lived, on a Saturday afternoon, drying my hair and listening to a Notre Dame ball game. And, of course, it told us what was for sale, what was new, and all of this. And it gave me a dream. I said, "I'm going to be there maybe some day," and I was.

[Radio] focused on everything at that time. It had to be everything to please everybody. There wasn't just one format, you see. The radio had all sorts of programs from religious programs to farm programs to news programs to helpful hint programs to kitchen-on-the-air kind of things, which I did for a little while. It had music, lots of music—full orchestras. I sang with a full orchestra on WHAS. Live. Live. Studio audiences—live studio audiences as we had at WIBC with *PM Party.* There was a lot of drama through the soap operas. I might add that those soap operas came on transcription. I remember soap operas when I was a little girl that first came on radio—the family sitting around in the afternoon—my grandmother listening to those—Ma Perkins and other people. They were just a part of your lifestyle—the Amos and Andys, the Jack Bennys, the Fred Warings—all of these things that just became your way of living.

I guess I looked at [radio] as a means to an end. It gave me an opportunity to use my talent and have a job that I liked, but I don't think that at twenty years old I realized all the importance of it. I just knew that it was where I wanted to be. I left a scholarship [at the University of Louisville] to stay in there, and I left a 50,000-watt station to go back to one in Vincennes that was much smaller so I could learn radio. I saw all of this big world, and I wanted to be a bigger part of it, but I wanted to know how to do it. My singing always allowed me to do that. You see my talent—that allowed a woman in a place of importance too.

I came back to Vincennes in late fall of 1945, not immediately to WAOV. I think that was very important, because

that was my first attempt at disc jockeying [spinning records over the P.A. system during the holidays at H. Brokkage & Sons]. I did talk to Vic Lund, who was the station manager at WAOV, and . . . he said, "Why don't you plan to go to work for us?" I went over there, and I was hired: number one to answer the telephone, be receptionist, do the program log, program the music, take the corrections over, and if you're a real good girl, we'll let you sing on the radio. So, I got my own show, and they did plan that because they knew I could sing. I had what was called *Silver Lining Time.*

The staff was all male, but they were wonderful young men who were there only until they could move into big markets, because they were all very good. Of course, the newspaper, the [Vincennes] *Sun Commercial,* was owned by the Pulliams, so stations sent talent into the Indiana State Fair in August. I represented WAOV at the State Fair. That's when I met Frank Parrish, and Frank said, "Ann, there's an opening at the station. Why don't you come over and audition." But I didn't do anything about it.

[Gene Stocker] came on as my accompanist, and at that time everything changed. He extended my reach into the music world. I remember saying to him, "You know, I had this invitation to audition in Indianapolis." And he said, "You?" putting me down. And I thought, "I think I'll go; I just think I will." [By the time I applied] Frank [Parrish] laughed, "Well, you know, Ann, the job's been filled." But he said, "There is a job I think you might be interested in. Art Berry at the Columbia Club is looking for a vocalist." I went over to the Columbia Club to the Cascade Room. I guess I impressed him because, as he said, "You look pretty good, you knew the key you sang in, and you didn't sing too bad a song." He said, "I am going to have an opening. We work here six nights a week, Tuesday through Sunday, and it's formal." And I said, "And what does this pay?" He said, "Thirty-five dollars a week." I said, "Well, I'm making that much at home, but I'll tell you what I'll do. You get me a job at a radio station during the day, and I'll sing for you at night." Well, you know, he did—sight unseen, voice unheard. [Richard Fairbanks at] WIBC said they'd take me, and I made seventy-five dollars a week.

There were very few women in broadcasting when I started out. I think sometimes I can best explain things when I say where they were not. They were not a.m.

announcers; they were not in sales to any great degree at all; they didn't manage the station; they weren't the engineers at the stations; they very seldom held a license to a station; they weren't the program directors. Of course, no one required them to be. A woman's place was more or less in the home when I started out, so it was very unusual. Now, women were secretaries; women were continuity writers; women were in traffic and in the music library; they were receptionists; they did keep the books.

I worked from about 8:30 in the morning 'til about 5:00 at WIBC Monday through Friday. Then I raced home and changed into my formal attire to get back to the Columbia Club by shortly after 6:00, and I worked 'til 11:00 and then midnight on Friday and Saturdays. On Sundays I sang at the dinner hour which was maybe 5:00 to 7:00. And I slept about five hours a night. That's all I had for three years. I had Monday night to date.

My job [at WIBC] was to sing on *PM Party,* and Sid Collins was the announcer. Sid and I were very good friends. We always had trouble working together when it was just a one-on-one kind of thing, because we'd always break up and I don't know why. And I remember that Frank Edwards was there. He was in the news department and always interesting. He was the flying saucers man, you know. There was a Gene Kelly who was a tall six-foot-eight or nine sportscaster, a full orchestra—Walter Reuleaux's orchestra. Bill Jolly did the arrangements for me. Dave Hamilton was the male vocalist at that time. The Dixie Four were there; they were recording artists and big in spiritual kind of singing. Jack Morrow was there, and he did some of the country shows with some of the country performers. Tom Moriarity, Paul Burton, Jack Simpson, Country Cousin Chickie, and there was a female vocalist, a big gal who was very good at country. I think her name was Emmy Lou. They decided they would try to make the best use they could for the money they were paying me, you know, so they [gave me my own fifteen-minute show, Monday through Friday, *Annie's Almanac,* and I also could work in the music library].

When you're very young, being a vocalist is very good, and since I chose to stay in Indianapolis, little by little they realized that my speaking voice was outstanding. That's what they said. You can always get a vocalist; you can always get a cute little gal to sing a song, but you can't get someone to speak well. What happened to me was I was doing television for WFBM and still working at WIBC, because I did both of them for a little while.

The Columbia Club was just about to end the idea of a live orchestra in the Cascade Room. Television had come with the race in May [of 1949]. In September . . . Hugh Kibbey sent me a letter and said, "I know you're on vacation now, but when you get back we have an idea for a show."[33] And I thought, "Oh my. This is marvelous. This is television." So, I did, and his idea of a show just nearly blew my mind. He said, "Now I hate to tell you this but it's a country show. It's going to be called *Circle B.* Bavarian Beer wants to sponsor it, and it's going to be on once a week," with me as a singer of country music. I said, "Well, I've come from classical to hymns to bands, why not?" I said, "Well, Hugh, who's going to play that music?" And he said, "You know them well. Tom Moriarity, Paul Burton, Country Cousin Chickie, and Jack Simpson, and Dick Pittenger will be the announcer." And I said, "Well, my goodness, if they can play it, I can sing it." It was just like that. So, we went over to a western attire place; my culottes with the fringe, my cowboy boots, my shirt with all its decoration, my tie, and my hat, and I still have all of those in mint condition. And, you know, that was the most fun I ever had, because I felt like I was at a costume party. I just came out of myself and probably did as good a job as I had ever done, because I felt so at ease with these good friends and this opportunity.

That's when WFBM decided that they absolutely had to have more facilities. We were in a little room—I remember they hit my head with the boom microphone and I almost wasn't able to perform. They were growing, and that's when 1330 North Meridian came into the picture. And, that's when I really had problems, because that was a distance from where WIBC was. At that time, I was going back and forth there, and I was ending up doing thirteen television shows a week—thirteen television shows a week. I had to give up something. So, I talked to Mr. Fairbanks and I said, "I think the time has come that I'm going to have to do something." They offered me a staff position—staff announcer—at WFBM, which I don't know that any woman had had, so that I could come and feel secure and leave WIBC. So I did. I just went strictly to WFBM at that time as staff announcer.

Paul Roberts [of WFBM] had passed away, very early in life. Their main disc jockey for radio died, and they had been bringing in some very fine men to do the show, but the public just couldn't handle it. They couldn't quite get over Paul. If it had been Easy [Gwynn] it would have been the same way. So, Mr. Bitner, kind of a shy, introverted sort of person—I didn't know him well—had been in California. He had heard out there that someone thought it might be a really good idea if a girl, if a woman became a disc jockey. So, he came back and he said, "Nothing else has worked where Paul is concerned. She speaks very well. Tell her to come in there and learn the control board, and let's put her on the afternoon show." And, the afternoon show was called *Make Mine Music*. Durward Kirby had been the disc jockey there before he went on to join Garry Moore, and Paul had just been tremendous. I thought, "Oh, this is marvelous."

I was the first female disc jockey in Indiana. That is for sure. When you go to Miami in 1958 and you're the only female disc jockey among sixteen hundred, that's pretty unique. A lot of them who were on the air had an engineer running all the turntables and doing things of this nature. I did it just complete, myself, from programming the music to everything that went on. I did it; it was mine. I had two weeks to learn how to do it.

It went very, very well, and I loved it. I had some mighty big shoes to fill, but people accepted it. I was on three hours in the afternoon during drive time opposite Easy Gwynn. Here's my friend, who used to write the introductions to all my songs that I was going to sing that night. . . . Here I was doing this disc jockey stint. And, of course, when I started in 1950 or 1951 the music was very mellow—the Perry Comos, the Dinah Shores, and the Patti Pages and the Doris Days and the Frank Sinatras and all of this was easy to do. I loved the music. Then, in 1955 when rock came in—Elvis, Bill Doggett. I went to that. In fact, they think that Elvis introduced it, but Bill Doggett was the one who really introduced it, and I had him on the show. He came in, and I have a picture of him introducing rock. So, we just went from the easy, me low to rock, and then the easy, because those artists stayed. I saw all of that. I operated four turntables, two tape decks, the microphone, everything—did all the cuing, all the live commercials and all the recorded commercials.

I read my own; I programmed my own; I wrote every introduction or had every introduction. I did a lot of homework on that. I would have files on all the artists. The rules

about my show, my *Make Mine Music* show, were that I never say "I," that I never sound like I'm preaching or teaching and that everything I say someone can say, "Ann said that today." I learned that on that show. It was supposed to be entertaining and educational and all of that, so it took a lot, a lot of work to prepare and to do it. Then they would bring in these artists. Oh, my goodness.

I interviewed a lot of people who were through a department store—anything that could tie in with a commercial or an ad, you would give them a little time on the show, because they thought that show was terribly important to get to the people. Along with all those things that I would do, I also had to appear at all of the high schools in town and give lectures beginning with Crispus Attucks. They thought I stood for things that women should stand for, and maybe I could come out and talk with them about etiquette, and just let them meet me. I went into almost all the schools. One heard about it, and then I had to go into all of them.

WFBM, with both the radio and television going on, there was a lot of camaraderie with the announcers. I know where I was concerned, they all respected my position, respected my success, allowed me to work just as hard or harder than they did. If I had something to carry, I carried it. It was not one of those let's baby Annie kind of things. But, there was a wholesome attitude. WFBM from beginning to end was a very wonderful place to work. It was really dedicated to the community, dedicated to do right. When another station came on television, they welcomed Channel 8. They felt that then they could even do a better job. There was this openness about it. [WFBM] stayed so much the same when I was there. It didn't even change too many personalities at that time. Very little [turnover]. That staff of announcers—some of them are still at that station. Dick Lingle. Frank Forrest was there. Of course, it changed licensees. Harry Bitner sold to Time-Life, and that's when Eldon Campbell came on the scene.

Eldon—he was an outgoing person compared to Harry, who was the behind-the-scenes kind of wonderful man. Eldon was gracious, involved in everything—with announcers, with other radio stations, with talent. He was just such a strong personality in his own right. A good boss, a really good boss. He was there. He was around you; he knew what was happening. A lot of changes took place in the program directors and a few areas like that, and maybe those were good.

I didn't do anything on radio or television that wasn't live. Everything was live. As WFBM-TV bragged, they devoted over twelve hundred minutes a week to programming live. . . . I think, in the early days this was wonderful. It was the way to do it, although some of the networks I would imagine had taped shows that surrounded it, but our shows were live. The people accepted that; they loved it. You just came into their home, and you were a part of their family. They made you a star. When you were going to appear, they were there. When you asked them to do something, they did it. They were overwhelmingly eager to become a part. This was fascinating. Radio had been fascinating, but television was absolutely captivating.

Little by little [women] came into play. They weren't there when the station was originally on the Circle in Indianapolis, but they came into being as WFBM increased its broadcast day and had the facilities that they had built at 1330 North Meridian, where they still are housed. At that time, when they had built the studios at 1330 North Meridian, they had two duplex studios, one forty by sixty, another thirty by forty, furnished with the most modern cameras and sound and lighting equipment that was on the market. There was a permanent kitchen set complete with refrigerator, range, sink and all the latest in homemaking devices. And, of course, they had news programs. Gilbert Forbes had *News Highlights*. He would walk from the radio station studio over to the television studio. Harry Martin, who not only did weather but also did news, did farm reports, news for the farmer. This was on each weekday afternoon. Bill Crawford was a weather expert. He had been such in the U.S. Air Force, and he didn't just predict the weather, he explained it.

I remember the weather show that I did with Harry Martin on Sunday afternoon was sponsored for nine years, with the same weather man and the same lady, by the same sponsors, Stewart-Carey Glass Company. And I remember on one Sunday afternoon, Harry mentioned that we had a little weather book that we would be happy to send. During the next two weeks they had over five thousand requests. That will give you a little idea about audience participation and reaction.

Now, the biggest audience response that I can document would be the audience participation from the *Party*

Line program. When we did *Party Line,* it was a whole new idea that came out of New York. It was a program where we exchanged household hints. We offered outgrown clothing, no longer needed household items. We requested information on household problems, and believe me, we got it. And then, there were special needs. We had projects. This program often organized committees for action. These conversations were held to as brief as we could keep them. We paced the program so it would stay entertaining; we offered membership cards, and as of September 15, 1958, some 7,136 housewives and a few men had become card-carrying members of *Party Line.*

We went beyond service to each other. We gave our time, the hour to them, to do whatever was needed in the community. The March of Dimes—we had a kick-off coffee at the governor's mansion—Governor [Harold] Handley at the time—and I was chairman of that March of Dimes. They helped the Little Red Door. Riley Hospital—that's where we collected nylon hosiery for a handicapped woman who used them to stuff dolls for the Riley Hospital children. We had a complete file of volunteer blood donors for "Operation Blood Bank." We helped in an answer to an appeal for the Marion County Health Association's halfway house. We got clothing, appliances, furniture. I even gave my nylons. Party Liners also made over three thousand bibs for children including those at Riley. We aided families in need. One family of nine whose house had been destroyed by fire—we collected clothing, furniture, toys, food supplies—this kind of thing. We had an "Operation Toy Lift" that the station put on, and we airlifted all sorts of things to flood disaster victims. One of the great things we did was for the Muscatatuck School for the Retarded. We went down to see what they needed, and then we came back and we collected pianos, furniture, dishes, just everything that might be needed. We had to get an entire moving van to take all this down. We helped churches. The Franklin Volunteer Fire Department—we collected toys for children. And then, of course, we ended up having a lot of fun as we did on our busload from Indianapolis—at 2:30 a.m.—to get to *Don McNeill's Breakfast Club.* That was a big publicity feature. Then, we had picnics. Seven thousand were eligible to come, because they were members. We had that at Riverside Park, all the food donated by our sponsors and all the fun and games for everyone, young and old.

Wagner announced Harry Martin's Stewart-Carey TV Weather *program for nine years on Sunday afternoons (November 1954).*

Dr. Bill Crawford doubled as a dentist and WFBM's first weatherman for several years in the 1950s and 1960s. The popular weather expert died in 1968.

Wagner and Ozzie Osborne, hosts of Party Line *over WFBM, prepared to board the lead bus in a three-bus caravan from Indianapolis to Chicago in April 1955. It left at 2:00* A.M. *in order to get to Chicago in time for an appearance on* Don McNeill's Breakfast Club.

WRTV-6

Well, that tells you a little bit about what we did in the way of helping people. The station was completely behind it until it just became overwhelming. This thing grew and grew. I think it reached its peak; I reached my peak, and you just know if you don't want to start down, you'd better stop at the top. And too few people today do. I felt when it was time for me to go—and I say that because it was time for me to either leave town, go to a different market, or get out. My philosophy was always, "Leave at the right time. Quit while you're ahead. Retire a champ. Don't be a has-been in show business." These things worried me. I didn't want to have that happen. I had married at that time, and I had a husband who was all for what I did, but also pushed me in a direction that I'm glad I went. He said, "Leave the station, and go to Butler and finish your degree."

I resigned from Channel 6 and WFBM radio with the blessing of everybody there and went to Butler University. I was thirty-seven years old, and I had been out of the classroom for a long time. So in 1960, I decided, "All right, I'll look into that career change." It was at that time that Jim Phillippe came into my life again, because he heard that I was thinking about coming to Butler. He called at the station. Jim and I had worked together at the station, you know, and were just good friends. He said, "Ann, I just thought I would make a suggestion to you. You're going to make quite a career change, and I think it's a wonderful idea, but I think you should consider speech as a career, because it

WAOV

Both Reid Chapman and Ann Wagner Harper remembered their first jobs in the broadcasting business at WAOV in Vincennes, Indiana. In the days before more formal training programs, it was one of many small stations where young hopefuls, such as Gene Allison, Robert Petronoff, Neil Van Ells, and Emmett Jackson, got some experience on the air before moving on to positions in larger markets. Vic Lund, station manager, sports commentator, and able mentor, hired Chapman and Wagner because he was looking for youthful talent. Named for the "courageous, golden-haired maid, whose bravery created the saga of *Alice of Old Vincennes*," WAOV was welcomed to Vincennes in 1941. Indeed, it was immediately and enthusiastically embraced by the community, as radio reception had been unreliable even from the highest-powered stations. Eugene C. Pulliam, owner of the *Vincennes Sun-Commercial*, WIRE in Indianapolis, and numerous other media venues, stressed the need for radio service in Vincennes—because there were so many floods in the area—when he applied to the FCC for the license. The only station between Evansville and Terre Haute serving west-central Indiana,[34] the new full-service station boasted state-of-the-art design and equipment.

Vic Lund at his desk at WAOV.

would fit in so well. I would like to set up a meeting with the chairman of the speech department and let him counsel you and see what you think about it."

I graduated in 1963 with my undergraduate. I started immediately to work on a master's and completed it by 1968. In the interim, I did teach speech at Lawrence Central High School and coached debate. It was when I was nearing graduation in 1968 that Jim Phillippe called me. At that time, Jim had left the drama department chair and had gone to the radio and television department, because it had moved out on [the Butler] campus from the Pennsylvania Street area, and he thought it had great potential. And, of course, they had the license to WAJC, and he said, "I need help. I really need somebody to help me. I'm out here with about thirty-seven to forty majors, and I just need someone." So, I had an interview, and I went to Butler and I was with Jim in the department until 1988. He retired in 1987. That's when I took over the chairmanship and the management of the station at Butler University. And, of course, the people we taught had all sorts of respect for us. They knew we had been there; we had done it. We weren't teaching them just from a textbook. We were teaching them from experience plus degrees and the textbook and contacts that we had.

This [teaching] was as unique as some of the other things that I had done. The students we turned out were all over the United States and famous. You see, this was the only completely student-operated station in the country. I don't know that any [other stations] have become that. I think they still have some professional help—some of the faculty are part of the station. [The students] were the program director; they were the staff; they were preparing; they were the staff on air; they were the engineering staff. [Jim Phillippe] was the manager. I was the assistant manager, and we had an engineer who was on faculty teaching. But those students ran that station. They prepared the log; we just supervised, and we stayed away. It was by the field house, Hinkle Field House, and we seldom went over. They ran it.

I taught speaking—we called it announcing. I taught radio production. I taught them how to do it. I had done it, and now, of course, I was back there teaching others how to do it. I had labs where we covered all sorts of problems and all sorts of ideas. I created two courses that I was very proud of. One of those was "Broadcast Law." That was extremely difficult. I was not a lawyer, and I had to learn before I could teach the students all those things, which I did. [I taught] broadcasting as it originated with the FRC [Federal Radio Commission] which preceded the FCC. I taught them [to be] up to date and having to stay up to date with the rules and regulations, because they had to operate that way on the station. They were going into stations where they had to become a part of that. So, that course I was very proud of. It was a required course for all seniors, and it was also a graduate course. I also created a course called "Music in Broadcasting," and there I felt very much at home. I had to do a lot of selling, because people said, you know, "Is that really academic?" I said, "It's really academic to broadcasting." So, I created that program, and that's when I used a text called *The Dee Jays.*

We always had it as a part of our philosophy that we had to operate "in the public interest." The public interest was always something you could define many, many ways. A lot of times you'd ask them to define it for the sake of letting them think a little bit and have them realize that there were many ways to say it. I always tried to teach them that they had to be prepared; they had to work; they had to realize it was twenty-four hours. Radio/television didn't end at five o'clock Friday afternoon. I tried to teach them that the first impression was so terribly important. They had to look good; they had to sound good, and I just cringe today when I hear how some people sound—big names—how they sound. I told them that they should never stop learning the business; they should be willing to start where the job was. Go. Don't feel that Indianapolis is the only place to work and start at the top. You don't have to start at the bottom, because, you know, you've had all this experience, but be willing to pay your dues. And I tried to teach the women that even though the door was open because of the laws and all of the things that said you have to hire, you'd better have something to offer. That was probably the hardest thing.

I just kind of fell into [broadcasting] and had enough people interested to push me. I don't remember myself having that kind of drive, and yet, I guess I did. I knew I had to be on my own, and I had to get someplace, and this was just kind of where I landed. But I didn't want to go beyond Indianapolis. Now, this is an interesting thing. When I was there, I had several opportunities. I could have gone on the road with Jimmy Dorsey's orchestra to sing. But, you know, I really didn't want to. I just kind of liked the feeling of being a part of the community. And with television coming in at the right time that was a whole new experience. That just opened a big wonderful door to me, so it was the right time to be there and to be in the right place. I know that sounds kind of corny, [but] I don't think I've had very many disappointments. I just feel that I have been just about the most fortunate person there ever was in my careers.

William R. Fall (ca. 1950s)

Bill Fall

(1917–)

William R. Fall started in broadcasting purely by accident. Enrolled at Purdue University as a speech pathology major, he learned about WBAA, the university radio station, from a fraternity brother who suggested that he audition because he had "a nice voice." After graduation, Fall went to work at WEOA, Evansville, until World War II intervened. He spent four years as an officer in the navy, then left the service and returned to WEOA as program director. In 1950 he was recalled to active duty. When he came back, he went to WFBM-TV in Indianapolis. In 1960 Fall moved to West Lafayette, where he went to work as an operations officer for the Midwest Program on Airborne Television Instruction (MPATI), which would achieve some recognition in experimental education. Established on the Purdue campus and sponsored by the Ford Foundation, the program experimented with and proved the feasibility of televising programs from two converted DC-6 aircraft flying over Montpelier, Indiana. On the air from 1960 until 1968, MPATI served close to eleven million students in a five-state area. After MPATI flew its last mission, Fall stayed at Purdue as a professional staff person, retiring 1 March 1982. John Warner, a historian working with Weintraut & Nolan, interviewed Fall at his home in West Lafayette in 1997.

It was sort of an interesting circumstance that got me attracted to WBAA. I don't think I was even aware that there was a radio station owned and operated by the university, manned by students. I was in summer school, and I talked with a fraternity brother of mine who made a telephone call—Harry Snyder. And Harry said after—not at that telephone conversation, but subsequently—he said, "You've got a nice voice. Why don't you audition for an announcer's job at WBAA?" Harry was working there as a student announcer. So, through that suggestion I went over and auditioned and got involved in the radio station and was taken on as a student announcer. And that was my introduction to the world of broadcasting.

It was a good training for those of us who were wanting to go into broadcasting, and there were quite a number of us. Really, we did go on from that experience into careers in—well, we did interview programs. My wife [Joyce] did a—well, she wasn't my wife then, but I married her—she did a woman-on-the-street program called *Woman on Main Street,* in downtown Lafayette. And she did that out in front of Rosenthal's, and through that experience, Henry Rosenthal got interested in broadcasting. (Henry eventually owned WASK and Channel 18 here.) I was Joyce's announcer for this in terms of [giving] her an opportunity to catch her breath. I think it was a half-hour program. But she would ask questions, and Jessie Fein, who owned the theaters in town, would give her complimentary tickets that she would give away. That was one of the things we did.

She did a storybook hour. I ran across something not too long ago—I don't remember where it is now—but she had done a story-time thing and sent out things for kids to call her, and she had gotten some of them back from the kids. We did just about any kind of programming that you could think of for kids. We were responsible for the writing of it and producing it and the doing of it on the air.

There were sport programs of every description. We had fishing, hunting, and those things. And we did *Radio Stage,* used radio drama material. Some of us even adapted stuff, short stories for use on *Radio Stage.* [At Purdue] there was no liberal arts, so there was no school of drama. There was a speech department where you could learn how to make a presentation, but there was no department of dramatics. They had *Play Shop.* A lot of students expressed themselves through that medium.

They had direction from a professional, or the station manager, or program manager, or whatever. I don't remember precisely what he was called, but there was a man by the name of Gilbert Dunbar Williams, Gibbs Williams. He was the paid staff person, and Ralph [Townsley] was the paid engineer, and Marie Davis was the secretarial type that I remember. There were about four of them, maybe several of them. Three of them constituted the staff. They had some student engineers, and as I remember it, some of them got a stipend for working the transmitter. Basically, everything that went on at the station was student-oriented. The students did everything. Gibbs Williams, to my knowledge, was never on the air. I know we would make propositions to him on things that we'd like to do, on assignments we would like to be given.

We would do quite a few remotes and a surprising number for that day and age. We had no recording facilities outside of the transcription, nothing that we could carry around like the reporters do today. Dick Shively did sports broadcasts prior to Johnny Decamp. Interestingly enough, Dick went on into a career in broadcasting—owned Channel 18 here at one time and also a station in Grand Rapids, Michigan. And I think he still has broadcast properties down in Alabama or Georgia. He is still involved in broadcasting. We did play-by-play of football and basketball when Johnny Decamp was brand new. (In my

senior year in 1941, Johnny was a freshman. He gravitated to sports, and . . . remember he worked with Shively.) Those were basically the remotes. One that I remember that I was responsible for was the dedication of the Hall of Music. I had a stack of three-by-five cards about three inches thick. (And I wish I had them and all that personal data.) All of the dimensions, all of the oddities of the building were all on little cards, and I shuffled through and found out anything you wanted to know, and sat there and was the announcer at the dedicatory program. We also did a Mother's Day program, which . . . we broadcast over, I want to say WLS. It featured a glee club [which came] from all of the fraternities and sororities. . . . Never in my life 'til that time had I done any kind of a setting where my voice, amplified, came back to me when I was talking.

We were limited in space in the station there in the engineering [double E] building, because it had just been carved out, and the intention was to get larger studios. We moved from there and got into the Hall of Music. (Those studios had plenty of room. Those big studios are no longer used and haven't been used for years as I understand it.) We had an audience show called *Campus Variety.* That was fun because several of us wrote it—all student written and produced. It had a student band, and it was a variety show with a lot of cornball. Oh, it was cornball. We had a lot of fun, and always had people in the audience from all over. A good time was had by all.

Basically in those days WBAA's signal covered a good part of the state of Indiana. It didn't have any [directional] restrictions that the FCC put on it later. I can remember it went all the way to Evansville, because in the early years it was still possible to listen to WBAA radio for a football game, a basketball game in Evansville. You can't do that today. But we had a pretty broad coverage—it was around the state, slopped over into Illinois, of course. I don't know how far east we went. To my knowledge, there were never any real surveys that were taken. There may have been, but I'm not aware of them.

Beyond WBAA, from a chronological point of view of my own life, I went to Evansville and worked in Evansville until I got called to active duty in the naval air arm. I got washed out of that because of eye problems. Reenlisted in the V-7 program,[35] served during World War II in the navy. Then went back to Evansville, and worked there at an FCC duopoly, which is sort of interesting now

MPATI's two DC-6 aircraft were parked awaiting maintenance at Purdue University's airport in West Lafayette, Indiana.

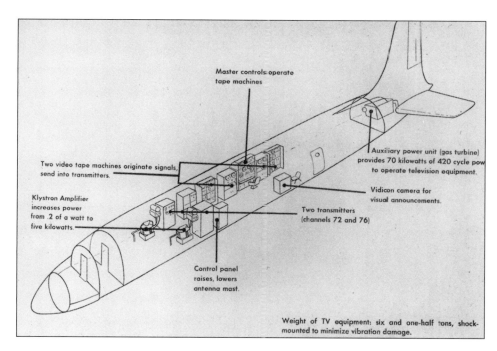

Master controls operate tape machines

Two video tape machines originate signals, send into transmitters.

Klystron Amplifier increases power from .2 of a watt to five kilowatts.

Control panel raises, lowers antenna mast.

Auxiliary power unit (gas turbine) provides 70 kilowatts of 420 cycle power to operate television equipment.

Vidicon camera for visual announcements.

Two transmitters (channels 72 and 76)

Weight of TV equipment: six and one-half tons, shock-mounted to minimize vibration damage.

Onboard equipment served two functions: to transmit educational programming and to further research by Westinghouse engineers.

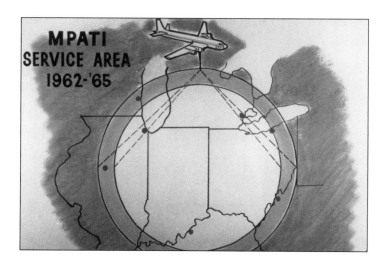

MPATI SERVICE AREA 1962-'65

Circling Montpelier, Indiana, MPATI aircraft broadcast educational material daily to as many as 2,500 subscribing schools.

because you can own as many [stations] as you want, wherever you want to own them, but back then they were concerned about the monopolies. Evansville-on-the-Air [WEOA] had a monopoly. They had WEOA, which was an affiliate, and they had WGBF, which at that time was handling NBC Red and NBC Blue. They were in the process of dividing up NBC. They also had an experimental FM station (W45V) and we, as announcers, worked them all. When I came back from the service, the FCC duopoly rule was in effect. They had to sell one of the AM stations, and they elected to sell WEOA, which was the lower power one. WEOA was sold off to the Bitners, [who also] had a newspaper in Pittsburgh, and they owned WFBM. . . . So, they bought WEOA and sent a man named Don Menke down there as general manager. Don asked me if I would be the program director of WEOA. Again, I was not an expert in math but it didn't take me long to figure out I could make more money being program director than being an announcer, so I said, "Yes." I served as program director until 1950, I guess it was, and then I was recalled to active duty in the navy during the Korean affair and returned from that to a position as program manager at Channel 6 in Indianapolis. I was no more qualified to do that, I guess, than to be program manager at WEOA. But, that's where I wound up and spent about seven years at Channel 6 and then came back to Purdue. My wife was a town girl, and we had always said when the opportunity to return [came], we would. The opportunity presented itself. Quite frankly, I was fired as program manager at Channel 6 when we lost a ratings war, I think, two years in a row. The ax fell, and then, like the baseball manager or the football coach, I was fired.

Anyway, I had an opportunity to return to Purdue. We were to be a part of the very exciting, innovative, educational experiment called Midwest Program on Airborne Television Instruction [MPATI]. The university hired me for that MPATI position, and after MPATI was wrapped up, they hired me back to the television unit so my twenty-two years of broadcasting involved instruction time. So I've seen both sides.

The MPATI program was given a home here by [Purdue president] Fred Hovde, when he started to realize that we had an airport here and this would be a logical place to house such a thing. He offered the services of the univer-

sity to be a home for the project. It was funded largely by the Ford Foundation, consisting of almost $16 million, which even today would be a sizable wad of money. It was a very innovative program for its time. What we did, in essence, was to take two DC-6 aircraft, put two UHF-TV transmitters in each one of them (Channel 72 and 76), design a retractable antenna that would hang down from the belly of the plane and would be lowered when the plane was on station. [We] put a couple of Ampex VCR two-inch machines in each aircraft and sent them to fly over Montpelier, Indiana, and broadcast instructional material. We did that for about eight years. It started broadcasting in the spring of 1960 and broadcast through the spring semester of 1968. And that's that. The basic problem of that program was spectrum. The FCC did not want to permit us to broadcast on those frequencies. We needed more, and they said they'd grant us spectrum space in [the Instructional Television Fixed Service, or ITFS], ultra high frequency, only 2,500 megahertz, but we had done no experimentation [at those frequencies]. We didn't think a thing about it and had to learn quite a bit about UHF. . . . So that was one of the things that shot us down, and an awful lot of antagonism on the part of some of the land-based educational stations. This [MPATI] was set up as a separate organization—it was just housed at Purdue. In the early stages of it, while it got off the ground, it was housed in the Purdue [Research] Foundation. R. B. Stewart had a big hand doing all the maneuvering, but once the project got started and got under way, it was an entity unto itself. We did separate it, really, from the university. Our offices were in the basement of the Stewart Center.[36] We had a big hanger at Purdue built to house our aircraft. The long runway was built to handle the DC-6. . . . And we had production centers at various and sundry TV stations around, and Cincinnati did some work for us. Detroit did some more and Chicago. The television unit at Purdue produced some material for us. We had a good lineup of topflight instructional materials that really sustained the MPATI project beyond the cessation of broadcasting because of the popularity of the materials. We became a resource for television stations wanting to be an MPATI channel.

Some of those materials were really way ahead of their time, a lot of instruction. They were specific. For instance, we did a Spanish series, and a school up in Monticello, thirty miles north of here, used that because they didn't

WBAA equipment. COURTESY OF INDIANA STATE MUSEUM

WBAA

WBAA, established in the basement of the old Electrical Engineering Building at Purdue University, received its license on 4 April 1922. WBAA was the first educational station in the state. Purdue was a logical spot for such a pioneering enterprise; its students had conducted experiments in wireless radio as early as 1910, and by 1919 nearly 150 students were enrolled in radio courses. From the beginning the station focused on public service with programs geared toward agriculture, entertainment, and education. WBAA aired farm market reports, tips from agricultural experts, live drama, and classroom broadcasts from "The Purdue University School of the Air."[37]

have anybody in the school system that would qualify as a Spanish teacher—nobody. They used this material on the air, and they did so so effectively that they actually organized a trip to Mexico with the kids. I don't remember all of the details of that, but we did something similar with French, with math, with science and literature and some priceless footage of a thing done by the University of Michigan called "From Franklin to Frost." It was priceless footage of Robert Frost, the noted poet. And they had a humongous library. We went out of business when MPATI wiped out. It was a not-for-profit organization so it had to dispose of its materials to another not-for-profit organization, and it chose to give its assets to the Great Plains Instructional [Television] Library. Great Plains continued to use the MPATI material. When the MPATI project folded, the only thing that we really needed to dispose of as the aircraft. And that was another interesting assignment. I had to help broker that, get that job done so that we could maximize the amount of money that we got out of it.

The commercial folk didn't have any interest in it one way or the other except for the news value of it, but I suppose if they had a serious accident someplace, they'd have been interested in it. But it was the land-based ETV [Educational TV] stations that felt we were encroaching on their domain, not so much from the broadcasting of instructional materials as from the competition for money. See, ETV from its very outset didn't have any commercials, and that was where a lot of our opposition came from. It wasn't total, but there was enough of it from important places that we had a constant sniping from the NAEB [National Association of Educational Broadcasters] folk. I remember one of the fellows that worked for MPATI here was a member of the NAEB, and he related an exchange he had in Washington, D.C., some years after the MPATI thing where NAEB was making their position in favor of satellites. This guy was there at the time, and he heard this impassioned plea from the head of the NAEB for satellites, one of the things that could be done by educational programs. I said, "Bill, 23,000 miles is okay but 23,000 feet is no damn good [laughs]." I don't know how much of that impacted the ultimate decision of the FCC. I know that higher-ups at the NAEB had to hear people. I know that. What really was the beast that shot us down, I don't know. I do know that the technology itself and the idea of doing what we did, using the UHF frequencies, really made the difference for UHF broadcasting. Just our very existence and the demand of the schools for antennas so that they could receive, forced the Blonder Tongues [a manufacturing firm] to concentrate their efforts on [improving the quality of the service]. We wanted them to pay a lot more attention to that because of what we had to use. Now, we would be flying on a day like today, for example, and be checking antennas on school roofs in this part of the country and in this kind of weather—two hundred-mile radius. We covered parts of five states. We covered all of Indiana, parts of Ohio, Kentucky, Illinois, Wisconsin, [and] Michigan.

FRANCES FARMER

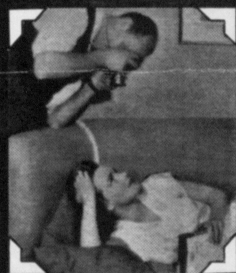

The later years at Channel 6

Photo session at Paramount

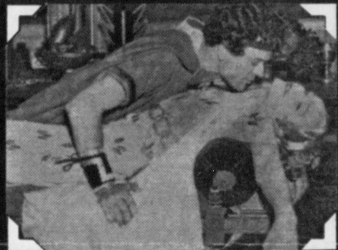

In the film "Come and Get It"

In "The Twelve Temptations"

"Everything in Radio (and Television) Is Local"

Reid Chapman remembered wondering whether anyone was listening to him as he broadcast on the radio in the 1950s. He knew for certain that at home his family was glued to the little screen. The sale of television sets had jumped dramatically in the 1950s; they were becoming a staple in American homes and were changing the way people viewed their world. During the next thirty years, syndicated programming helped to promote a heightened sense of national community and culture. However, it was on the local level that television operators began to develop an intimate relationship with their communities.

The narrators in this section are a diverse group, some associated with radio, some with television, others with both. Each oral history tells one part of the larger story of how local broadcasters came to be a vital part of their communities through their association with community programming and news coverage. From the standpoint of management, Reid Chapman, E. Berry Smith, and Bazil O'Hagan talk about the role of television in an era in which television and radio were vying for dominance of the market. Howard Caldwell and Barbara Boyd discuss the newscasters' expanding sense of civic responsibility as people came to rely on television for their primary source of news. Amos Brown recounts the fate of one minority-owned radio station as television eclipsed radio in the coverage of community issues. These narrators provide insight into the ongoing relationship between radio and television and into the evolving concept of public interest.

In the postwar era, national television reporting underwent a metamorphosis in style and content. In the 1950s the networks televised the staid, plodding sessions of the

Kefauver Crime Commission and the Army-McCarthy hearings. By the 1960s the evening news had evolved from talking heads with still photos to vivid moving images. Chapman and Smith remembered how the death of John F. Kennedy brought the country together in communal mourning. The networks stayed with the coverage from the hospital where Kennedy died, to Lee Harvey Oswald's anguished expression as Jack Ruby shot him on live TV, to the burial of the president, demonstrating the power of television to freeze images in collective memory. Live coverage of civil rights activists, peace marchers and political dissidents, the Vietnam War, the Chicago Seven, and Kent State riveted audiences with impressions of a society in turmoil. After the Watergate scandal, investigative reporting assumed a significant role in the world of newscasters. National news coverage was etching its message into the public consciousness and exposing audiences to a wide range of issues and diverse points of view.

On the community level, public service became inextricably linked with public interest. In the late 1950s and 1960s, as part of their FCC mandate for local programming, stations aired old movies, emceed by local personalities or by faded movie stars, and entertained with talk sessions devoted to the latest trends and issues. Once the popularity of these shows waned and syndicated programs replaced them, evening newscasters began to raise the issues and concerns that once had been afternoon fare. Local commentators began focusing more attention on health matters, informative, soft series on consumer issues, and program segments highlighting the needs of special groups. Taking their cue from national newscasters, some stations committed more resources to investigative reporting, but it was a minor part of the total newscast. People grew to depend on their local newscast for information about the high school ball scores, the school board meeting, and the weather—things that were not carried on the national news. This was news that affected them directly.

Television's rise brought trying times to radio. In the 1950s radio stations had begun to expand their own news departments.[38] However, as television carried more local news, radio stations were forced to reduce and in some cases eliminate their news departments in order to remain economically viable. Amos Brown speaks to some of those issues, although his situation at WTLC was more complex. Radio stations began to cater to specific musical tastes and encouraged listener participation with talk shows, heeding the desires of its audience and adapting programming accordingly.

The narrators in this section illustrate a generational shift from a sense of the public interest associated with the code and the FCC to a more internalized one. Their excerpts demonstrate how individual radio and TV stations adapted to a changing marketplace as television grew into the primary means of reporting community news. Television became a less creative and more serious business as local newscasters began to feel a personal and professional commitment to raising the awareness of their audiences. In a pluralistic environment, women and minorities assumed a more prominent role. This group of narrators shows the varying forces that affected the transition of the broadcasting industry as television came to alter the perception of community and explore new meanings of "in the public interest."

Bruce Saunders, weatherman on WSBT for thirty years, checked the weather before his broadcast. WSBT STATIONS

Jim Gerard interviewed presidential candidate Hubert Humphrey on the set at WFBM in 1968. The Jim Gerard Show *premiered on Channel 6 in September 1966 with George Nicoloff and his orchestra. Gerard's show became an all-talk format that won national awards for outstanding programming from 1967 to 1970. Two years after the show went off the air in 1975, Gerard moved to Channel 4 where his show remained on the air until 1986.* WRTV-6/HELEN CAMPBELL

In 1987 WSBT broadcast Minority Forum *with Rod Johnson and guests.* WSBT STATIONS

In the 1980s deejays such as Gene Kuntz on radio station WITZ in Jasper, Indiana, continued to be active members of the community. Kuntz received numerous awards for community involvement and for innovative programming in the small-radio market. WITZ

Reid G. Chapman (ca. 1948)

CHAPTER FIFTEEN

Reid "Chuckles" Chapman

(1920–)

Reid G. Chapman, a man with a twinkle in his eye and a ready chuckle, became actively involved in broadcasting in 1943 while growing up in Indianapolis. Having been intrigued by radio as a child, he endeavored to get into the business after his discharge from the navy. He announced briefly at WAOV in Vincennes before returning to Indianapolis as music librarian for WISH-Radio. Working hard and taking on extra assignments as they became available, Chapman advanced to staff announcer and deejay, acquiring the name "Chuckles" from the sponsor of one of his shows, Chuckles candy. The name stuck. By the time he left WISH in 1956, he had worked in every department. This variety of experience prepared him for his move into management at WANE Radio and Television in Fort Wayne. In 1958 he became vice president and general manager of WANE-TV, and over the next twenty-five years, he brought the station to prominence in the community. He left to become corporate vice president for Indiana Broadcasting Corporation, the parent organization of WANE, a position that he held until his retirement in 1982. Chapman came out of retirement periodically to help friends in broadcasting and to serve as executive director of the Northeast Indiana Radio Reading Service, Inc. Captivating and energetic, he has made a lasting impression upon broadcasting in Indiana. His interviews took place in April 1995 at his home in New Haven, Indiana.

I think that broadcasting down through the years has been one of the most remarkable inventions of communication that the world has ever known up to this point in time. I think the way broadcasting started out in the United States following World War I, it was all positive. It brought communities together. It was a great era of excitement in the early days of radio when the family would sit around and listen to a little speaker that would identify a town several hundred miles away with call letters, and the family was all excited. The family entered into a log what the call letters were, what station it was, and what point it was on the dial. That was all positive. Good things came out of the golden days of radio—the coverage of sporting events and so forth. The thing in the most recent years that has been the most disappointing has happened since 1982 when the broadcasting code of good practices was thrown out by the federal courts in Washington as being, in effect, unconstitutional, because a portion of the code governed the amount of commercial time that was allowed in an hour. The courts threw it out as being restraint of trade. Since 1982—and that hasn't been very long ago—when the code was thrown out, the caliber of quality, the responsibility of broadcasting has gone downhill rapidly. What I hear today on the air and what I see on television is very offensive and very disappointing. I'm almost at a point of being ashamed of the industry that I spent most of my life in and was so proud of.

I liked sports, but early in my young life in the late 1920s I began to be excited about this new thing "radio" that had first come into being. My first exposure to it was on about, oh, I would say, 1928, 1929 when I visited my cousin in Cincinnati, Ohio. His father, my uncle, had gotten my cousin a crystal set, which was the very early stages of radio. They would hook up the antenna to the old bed springs, and then you would have earphones and with a little thing kind of like . . . oh, it's hard to describe—they called it "a cat whisker." You would twist that around—that cat whisker—on a crystal and it would pick up signals. And, Cincinnati had one of the early broadcast stations in the country, WLW. When I visited down there, we'd go to bed, and he would get this crystal set out, and we'd listen to WLW. I can remember my mother coming upstairs, maybe about eleven-thirty or midnight, and saying, "Aren't you boys asleep? Turn that off, and go to sleep!" Well, I came home, and I was fascinated by that.

I became really intrigued with WLW Cincinnati and its great staff of announcers and quality programming, and I began imitating some of these announcers. When I went to grade school—I started out at School No. 80 in Broad Ripple and went through the first and second grade. When School 84 was built at Fifty-seventh and Central, I started there in the third grade. I began to take part in any kind of an activity that would allow me to either stand up on a stage and recite something, or to be part of a singing group. I soon rigged up a make-believe microphone stand, and on the top of it I put—as I remember—put an old tin can and punched holes in it to make it look like a microphone. I would go around in the schoolrooms, and they would allow me to go around and promote paper sales and cookie sales, and I would imitate the voices of some of these radio announcers that I had become infatuated with on radio. So, that's how I really got the bug.

My father was a CPA with George S. Olive and had been with them since 1920. Then, in 1937, he broke away and set up his own office in Vincennes, Indiana, and he chose not to move the family down there because we were all deeply involved in high school and educational activities in Indianapolis. He called me one day early in 1943 from Vincennes where his office was and said, "Reid, there's an opening at the radio station here in Vin-

cennes at WAOV, and the manager is a Rotarian friend of mine. If you want to come down for an audition, I would recommend that you do so." That's how I got my first job.

It was a little 250-watt radio station that covered Knox County, and probably had maybe fifteen or sixteen employees, something like that. Very small. It was located in downtown Vincennes in the old Grand Hotel, which was one of those unique old-type hotels with the iron cage elevator. I think it had three stories, and it had been there for many years. The radio station was located in the hotel. I had been there when I was younger when my dad would bring the family down, and we'd stay there. We thought that was, boy, that was super—to be able to go to Vincennes and stay in the Grand Hotel.

Most of it was records and transcriptions, but they did have some live programs. Every day at 11:30 they had a program that was live called the *Happy Meek Family*, and this was *real* country music. I mean, this was mountain music. They would come in with their guitars and their banjos and their harmonicas and mouth harps. They were sponsored by a patent medicine company. I didn't have to do the commercials for the patent medicine company—thank goodness—but once in awhile I would be called to substitute and have to do it. And, that's when you really had to put your heart into it as to what this medicine could cure . . . everything, you know [laughs]. But they were a big account. Then, on Sundays, and sometimes during the week at night, some of the small churches would come in and would buy fifteen minutes or a half hour and do church programs.

The program manager was Emmett Jackson, and Emmett came, I think, out of Indianapolis originally and then came to Vincennes. Emmett probably didn't make very much money. I know I was hired at twenty-two dollars a week in 1943; so, maybe Emmett may have made five dollars more a week than I did. But, he was very, very patient in taking the young new fledglings, such as myself, and teaching. The manager of the station, Vic Lund, had been a sports announcer at Indianapolis and had worked for the publisher, Eugene Pulliam. The station in Vincennes at that time was owned by Eugene Pulliam who also owned the newspaper, the *Vincennes Sun-Commercial*. So, there was that kind of connection.

We were there mainly to be an entertainment vehicle. We had a twelve o'clock newscast that was fifteen minutes, which the manager of the station did himself. It was sponsored by Saiter-Morgan, which was a big hardware wholesaler in the Vincennes-Knox County area, but you always knew that you did not endeavor to scoop the newspaper. If there was ever going to be anybody that got an important story first, the *Vincennes Sun-Commercial*, the newspaper was to get it first. Then, it was okay for the radio station to talk about it after the newspaper had the first story. That was kind of an unwritten rule.

But I started on February 13, 1943, in Vincennes at WAOV, and about six weeks after I started, there was a tremendous flood that took place along the shores and along the banks of the Wabash. The levy did break and the water rushed toward George Field, which was an air force training base there in the Vincennes area. The manager of the station made arrangements to borrow a portable short-wave transmitter, and I went out in a motor boat with the operator of the motor boat into the Wabash. We headed over toward Lawrenceville—nothing but water—and at a certain time we knew that we were to begin broadcasting. That was my first experience of doing an ad-lib type of report, and I was petrified. I could see the tops of the telephone poles that ran along the Baltimore and Ohio Railroad that went between Vincennes and St. Louis. As far as I could see, it was just water and the tops of those telephone poles. So, it was really an excellent bit of experience. I don't happen to have the vaguest idea how I sounded, but the manager was happy; so, I guess I managed to make some kind of sense out of what I was trying to describe.

In August of 1943, I got a letter from Felix Adams the program manager saying, "We have an opening for a music librarian at WISH. If you'd like to come up and you'd be interested in it, we'd be glad to put you on." . . . Bruce McConnell was the president [of WISH] and, I think, majority stockholder. Bruce McConnell was born in Scipio, Indiana, a little crossroad down in southern Indiana, and he became a salesman for Hamilton-Harris Tobacco and Candy Warehouse. Mr. Harris was one of the really early pioneers of radio because I think he had probably the first station in Indianapolis that went on the air along about 1921 on North Alabama Street. It was in his garage. If it wasn't Ed Harris, it would have been his father maybe. But, Bruce McConnell began working for Hamilton-Harris Tobacco and Candy Warehouse as a salesman and trav-

eled to these little filling stations from town to town selling Hamilton-Harris cigars. I think it was called Homemade, HM, Hamilton-Harris cigar. Then, he rose in the ranks to become sales manager, and he then became one of the officers, and I think that's when he got himself started as a leader among some friends to put another radio station on the air in Indianapolis. Remarkable man, truly. Bruce McConnell had this very unique ability as a businessman, number one . . . and very soft-spoken, rather quiet, but he had a unique way of surrounding himself with people and involving himself with the right people to enter into a business venture. He had a good eye and a good ear for what is a good potential business, and he did very well with the early start of that little radio station, WISH.

Felix Adams, who was the program manager, knew that I wanted to eventually get on the air. I took the job as music librarian as kind of a stepping-stone, and that was the way to get in the front door. My first responsibility at WISH was as the announcer on Saturday afternoon during the opera program. Then, shortly after that, Felix Adams came to me, and he said, "The boss (meaning Bruce McConnell) has a new account. It's the Fred W. Amend Company of Danville, Illinois, makers of Chuckles candy. They have purchased a half hour, six nights a week, from 10:30 to 11:00, and we need somebody that will do the show." I said, "Well, what's the show?" Felix said, "Well, the show is: play popular records and read short commercials about Chuckles candy. That's all there is to it. Are you interested?" "Yes." Well, it meant that I had to come back every night because my job as music librarian was 9:00 to 5:00, and I'd go home by bus. I'd have to go home for supper, and then come back about 9:30 and get records ready for the program. I would be off at eleven o'clock; catch a bus; probably not get home until midnight. I said to my wife, "This is the way it is, and it doesn't pay anything extra, and you pay your own bus fare going back and forth, but it's an opportunity." She said, "Go for it." So, I went for it. I started out—without asking anybody, just on my own—started out by telling little jokes or little two-liners, and then I would chuckle. That was the beginning of a career that has hung with me to this day: "Chuckles" Chapman [chuckles]. I weighed probably 120 pounds and had this deep voice. To the listener I sounded like I must have been a pretty heavy guy, and I called myself

"250-pound, ton-of-fun 'Chuckles Chapman.'" I'd read these dumb jokes, chuckle a little bit and then play records and sell Chuckles candy. The sponsor loved it; McConnell was happy—so, that was the beginning.

The night show was on for about six years. Chuckles candy dropped their sponsorship of it, and we had a few local people who picked it up, but eventually it was dropped, and I came to them with an idea. I said, "I'd like to do a take-off on the Tom Breneman's *Breakfast in Hollywood* program," which used to be on the [NBC] Blue network in the mornings. It was a program that originated from Sardi's Restaurant in Hollywood; the women would come and have breakfast with Tom Breneman. He would try on their hats, and they would laugh and carry on. It became very popular. So, I said, "I'd like to take off on it and call it *Breakfast with Chuckles.*" I got one of the salesmen who went out and sold it to Polk Milk Company. It originated from the old Guaranty Cafeteria, which was just off of the Circle there on North Meridian Street. It was every Saturday morning. For a number of years, we had *Breakfast with Chuckles.*

Audience participation was kind of big in the early days of programs like *Ladies, Be Seated*, and *The Breakfast Club* in Chicago. *Don McNeill's Breakfast Club* was on for so many years, and they'd have little gimmicks and little things that they'd get women to do or people out of the audience to do. When we finally got this *Breakfast with Chuckles* show put together and it originated in the Guaranty Cafeteria, we had to come up with some things to fill up a half hour. You just couldn't do it by modeling goofy hats. So, we had the eldest lady . . . we'd give away an orchid. And, we had to have some kind of a contest or gimmick that would get not only the women interested in it, those who attended the show, but we had to make it exciting and entertaining for the people sitting at home who would wonder what's all this laughter about, see. So, my brother, Bob, and a brother-in-law, Bill Kaiser, and a neighbor who lived across the driveway from me, we'd meet on a Friday night—the show was the next morning—we'd meet on a Friday night at my house and create these goofy things that we were going to do the next day. I think I got paid a certain fee for doing the show, and then if I wanted anybody else to work with me, I had to pay them out of my own pocket. I'd maybe pay them five bucks for participating on that program. It was unbelievable to think

that they would do these things for five dollars. But, my brother could tell you that that five dollars coming in every week was extra money that he couldn't get, because when he handed over the grocery money, he didn't have anything left. That was his spending money.

[Eventually, the show] moved from the radio into television, and it became known as *Chuckles Open House*. It was on Sunday afternoon, and it was on for an hour. It was sponsored by Sutton Sales, Johnny Sutton, who used to be a television distributor. He had a place at Thirty-eighth and College. John did his own commercials in front of the camera; so, he was a good one to ask to be the sponsor because he liked to be on television himself. And so, the radio show moved to television. The WISH studios at that time were located at Fifteenth and Meridian, and they occupied the second floor. They were built primarily at that time to accommodate television, and they had an auditorium. So, it was ideal. You had an auditorium that seated about two hundred people. We had a stage, and so it was ideal for that kind of a show.

It was pretty much the same, although, we didn't do as much of the goofy stuff that we did on the radio, because we used to send people out from the cafeteria around the Circle to create excitement, you know. We didn't do that when we were on television down on North Meridian Street. So, it was more along the lines of regular type of audience participation programs that had become popular on television.

I was in the station [on 12 April 1945 when Franklin Roosevelt died]. Jack Morrow was, I think, in the newsroom preparing to do his six o'clock newscast, if I'm not mistaken. I was probably going to do commercials around it, and the word came through that—I think we were on the network at the time. In the meantime, Jack's news machine bell was ringing like crazy, and we knew something was wrong. The network broke in to say that President Roosevelt had died at Warm Springs, Georgia. I think Jack got his announcement on, but then the network immediately took over. We joined the network and then just stayed with them because they knew how to handle that kind of a situation. You know, you almost just stop and say, "What do you do? Golly, we don't read commercials; we don't play what we normally would play in the way of music." The network seemed to know just how to handle it. So, that went on for several days, because it was a

Chuckles candy sponsored a take-off on Breakfast in Hollywood *called* Breakfast with Chuckles *that featured Reid "Chuckles" Chapman. Here Chapman expressed surprise at the antics of the two men in the horse costume, one of whom was his brother, Robert Chapman.* COURTESY OF INDIANA STATE MUSEUM/WISH-TV

The "Goofy Hat Contest" proved to be a very popular event that enticed all sorts of respectable ladies to don outlandish hats in the hopes of winning a prize. From left to right: Mrs. Gertrude Davenport, Mrs. Margaret Catterson, and Mrs. Kathryn E. Weaver (1946). COURTESY OF INDIANA STATE MUSEUM/WISH-TV

period of mourning from that point on until he was finally buried. They had all kinds of commentators and verbal reports, but a tremendous amount of symphonic music, appropriate music for that kind of an occurrence. I can remember the coverage of the [funeral] procession in Washington. Arthur Godfrey was really big on radio at that time. (That's before he made his transition to television.) He had actually been a radio personality in Washington, D.C., and I can remember him describing the procession as it went down Pennsylvania Avenue and hearing his voice break. He wept on the air. It was a very, very impressive—very effective report. Since then, you've had FDR who died while in office; you had John Kennedy who died while in office. The impact on the broadcaster, in both cases, was just something you will never forget.

In the larger markets, television began to become a factor as soon as World War II was over and the development of television was allowed to take place. The larger markets were the ones that got the first television stations on the air. And the big interest, on the part of the public, began to swing over immediately from radio over to television. The networks began to feel that right away. They were the ones that really began to feel it first. But even the local radio stations—I was on the air [on radio] following the first telecast in Indianapolis, when Channel 6 went on the air. It was what—1948, 1949, somewhere around there, and you'd have that funny feeling sitting there in the afternoon, doing your radio show, wondering if anybody was listening. I knew what my family was doing at home. They were sitting around watching that little circle that didn't have anything but a test pattern on it, or if there was anything on there, maybe it was just barely visible, but it was just exciting to have something on there.

When I was transferred to Fort Wayne, I came up with the primary responsibility of managing [the McConnells'] radio station WANE. However, I knew that they had applied for and had gotten permission from the Federal Communications Commission to build a television station in Fort Wayne. My job was to help build that station, put it on the air. It would become the third television station in the Fort Wayne market.

The day I arrived [at WANE] was a January morning. I think it was January 3, 1956. The staff knew that this new manager was coming up from Indianapolis, and they also knew that his name was "Chuckles." So, they had never

seen this individual, but they were convinced that he must be a very jolly type of person. I drove up with Mr. McConnell and Bob [McConnell], and the chief engineer, Stokes Gresham. The station was located on the thirteenth floor of the Fort Wayne National Bank Building. (That building today is called the Commerce Building.) There were actually twelve floors to that building, but by going up a stairway there was an enclosure on the rooftop that probably had been put up there as a warehouse or to store some of the mechanical equipment. When McConnell had put that station on the air, they had done some remodeling up on the roof and put up this enclosure, which became the studios for WANE-Radio. When you got off the elevator at the twelfth floor, you had to walk up this extra flight to get to the studios. I think that when they furnished it, they probably must have gone to the Salvation Army or the Goodwill store or something and picked up all kinds of odd pieces of furniture and so forth to fit it. We did have [a] fairly decent reception area down on the twelfth floor, before you went up the stairway. So, they weren't the most exciting surroundings. I'd gone from very nice facilities in Indianapolis up to this thirteenth-floor setup. Then, when they bought the television station five months after I arrived there (Channel 15), they also purchased a rather unusual situation because the television station was actually licensed to Waterloo, Indiana. Waterloo is right next to Angola, and Angola is right at the very northeast corner of the state in Steuben County. That's where the FCC had assigned Channel 15 for a future television station. So, when the station was put on the air in 1954, they had to accept the fact that the license was assigned to Waterloo. Then, they erected the transmitter tower as close to Fort Wayne as they could get it, and that was in Auburn, Indiana. So, the transmitter and tower are located in Auburn; then, they rented facilities on the top floor of the Lincoln National Bank Building for their offices. So, they were spread out all over northeast Indiana— offices in Fort Wayne, tower in Auburn, and studios in a two-car garage in Waterloo, Indiana. Well, you can imagine, what a start. To make it worse, this was a UHF station, and that is very much different from the television stations in the larger markets which were VHF. None of the television sets that were sold and manufactured in those days were equipped to pick up UHF. You had to have a special adapter, a little box that you attached to the back

Tom Berry sang to the ladies on **Breakfast with Chuckles** *in the early 1950s.* WISH-TV

In the 1950s Chapman spun records at remotes such as this one that aired from the grand opening of an A&P grocery at 38th and College Avenue in Indianapolis. COURTESY OF INDIANA STATE MUSEUM/WISH-TV

of your television set, and then put the box up on top of your set. Then, when you wanted to move from a VHF station, which the television set was equipped to do, you had to turn a switch on the top of the television in order to get the UHF channel. However, to complicate it even more, the antenna that was on top of the house of the individual's home was designed to pick up the VHF signal. So, you had to get a special type that they called a "bow tie" and attach that to your antenna. Then, you had to turn it in the direction of the UHF station in order to pick up the UHF signal. So, it was very, very "Rube Goldberg"—to give it a description.

The first television station on the air in Fort Wayne was Channel 33. It went on in 1954, and it was a UHF station. They located themselves out on West State Street in Fort Wayne. So, for over a year while that station was being constructed and when they first went on the air, the people in Fort Wayne were very excited that they were going to have their first television station. They got their antennas up on top on the roof; they had their UHF bow tie on it, and they didn't worry about anything else because all they did was just flip that antenna in the direction of West State Street. When that station went on the air, they received that station without any problems. When Channel 15 went on the air in 1955, their transmitter and tower was located in Auburn which is about a forty-five degree angle the other way. When it went on the air, hardly anybody could pick it up because their antennas weren't directed that way. So, they had to go out and buy another piece of equipment, which was called a "roto-tenner." It was a little gadget that would automatically turn that antenna up on the roof in the direction of the other station that you wanted to get. Some people bought the roto-tenner, and some people didn't. Channel 15 had two strikes against it from the very beginning, and I think that's probably what made it such a good deal for McConnell to come in and make a bargain with them and buy that station. Then, he sold the whole ball of wax in Indianapolis and Fort Wayne to Jock Whitney. When they came out to inspect what they had purchased in Fort Wayne, they couldn't believe it. Luckily for us and for the community, the man representing the John Hay Whitney Company in New York was a man by the name of C. Wrede Petersmeyer and he spells his name W-R-E-D-E, which is an interesting way to spell Reid. Wrede Petersmeyer was

probably one of the most delightful men that ever came into my life. I always looked up to him as being a real gentleman and a very outstanding broadcaster. The first thing he said was, "Well, we're going to change that. We'll go out and buy land on West State Street. We'll build a new station out there, and we'll move the radio and the television station from Waterloo and Auburn and the Lincoln Tower and consolidate the whole thing out on West State. Then, people won't have to have a roto-tenner, and all these antennas that are already in the direction of West State will be able to pick up Channel 15." So, between 1956 and 1958, they built that station, and Channel 15 began to make a solid niche in the marketplace.

In the early days of WANE, as at other television stations, everything was live. I don't know if we had complaints about it, but the faux pas were numerous. From a historical standpoint it's too bad that somebody didn't keep a record of all those bloopers, those goofs that . . . everybody made them in the days of live television. One of the complaints that became rather prevalent in the early days of television was the fact that you did your commercials live. The commercials for the most part were done live, because in local markets they didn't have advertising agencies that were equipped to produce commercials and when you did, it was not the best quality. So, it was easier to do a commercial live than it was to have it on film. One of the problems in the early days of television was the fact that the beer companies were among the big sponsors, and so you had them doing these live beer commercials with your talent sitting there pouring this glass of beer and taking a swig of it and telling how good it tastes and so forth. Well, this got to be a problem—an internal problem. It became evident and the audience began to think, "Well, I wonder how much beer those guys consume in the course of a day?" So, that became a quick problem.

It was kind of an industrywide problem. In fact, it became part of the "code." You could hold the glass up, pour it and show the foam and the sparkle, but you didn't imbibe. We had a fast food restaurant in Fort Wayne—Azars. They were one of the real early sponsors on television. They had a big sandwich called the "Big Boy," and it probably was a triple-decker. And, they delivered these sandwiches over to the television set; maybe the commercial was going to be on the late news, and they would deliver the sandwich over to the station about a half hour before the show was to go on the air. When the commercial came on, you'd see the announcer opening his mouth very wide and chomping down on that sandwich. We had a few announcers that gained weight doing the Azar commercials [chuckles]. Or the live cooking show—there are oodles of cooking shows on the air today, and if they'd ever show the crew they probably are a very plump crew because to do a cooking show on television is no easy matter. You have to prepare two meals, and invariably the leftovers go to the crew. Some of those dishes are pretty exotic.

Regarding his tenure on the IBA Board, Chapman recalled . . . I can remember when JFK [was assassinated]. I was on my way back to the television station in Fort Wayne, and it was about twenty minutes of two. I had attended a luncheon, and I had my radio on, and the report came through. It was Walter Cronkite who gave the report, and immediately I went back to the station. At that particular point in time, I was the president of the Indiana Broadcasters Association. I'd just gone in at the meeting which was held in French Lick in October, and this was November 22, 1963. I hadn't any more than hit my office than the phone started ringing, and I was getting calls from little radio stations across the state saying, "What do I do? I don't have a network. I'm not part of a network. What do I do?" This was their first experience of going through that kind of a tragedy, and the only thing I could say to them was, "Well, if I were in your position, I would cancel all regular programming, all commercials, and I would get out everything you can find in your library in the way of appropriate music and play it until this whole period of mourning is over. Come in at your regular times; make your station breaks. That's the way I'd handle it. You just have to ride with it." I've often thought that if that were to happen today, with the tremendous proliferation of channels that exist, how would the broadcasting cable industry handle that kind of an emergency? Would you still be running MTV? Would you still be running, you know, this thing and that thing? I don't know whether the broadcasters of today have really faced up to that.

I can tell you an incident that will be a piece of history. When I was president of the Indiana Broadcasters Association—this was shortly after I'd gone into that office (and I'd already gone through the John F. Kennedy incident)—we were having a board meeting at the Indianapolis Ath-

letic Club. In the midst of the board meeting, I got a call from Governor Welsh, Matt Welsh, and said, "Oh gee, the governor is calling me. I better stop the board meeting." So, I went to take the phone call. And Eldon Campbell, who was running WFBM Radio and Television at the time, was in the governor's office. They were discussing a record that was being played all over the state, which was creating a real furor, "Louie Louie." The words of the song were, depending upon your frame of mind, quite suggestive. The governor was upset, and Eldon was upset. The governor was saying, "Reid, is there anything that you can do as an association to alert the broadcasters to this terrible song. It should not be allowed on the air. I know we get into the censorship thing there, but is there any way? Do you have any suggestions?" I said, "Right off the top of my head, no, but I'm holding a board meeting. I'll go back and deliver your message." So I did. The governor never knew this, but the board kind of laughed and said, "My God, what are we going to do to handle this one?" Supposedly, there were two sets of lyrics, and I never did prove this. There was one set of lyrics which was bad, but there was another one that was more explicit. We decided to send a telegram to all of the members of the IBA alerting them to this song and the fact that there might be lyrics that they might want to check, and Governor Welsh is not wanting to impose his authority on us in any way, but wants us to know that he's concerned—something like that. Well, we did that. The newspapers got hold of it and really gave him a kind of a hard time—that he was trying to control the music being played on radio. I never did know whether there were two sets of lyrics. I remember that I drove home that night after the board meeting and stopped off at a record shop in Marion, Indiana. I stopped off to get a copy of this record, arrived home, and said, "Can we listen to this?" My kids wanted to know why, and I told them. They laughed, and they said, "Oh Dad, there's nothing wrong with that song" [laughs]. Even to this day, when I hear it, I have to think about that whole incident.

All in the Family. I remember when it came on and we had previewed it. CBS had notified us that they were going to allow us to see it before the show was aired. That was not uncommon for the network to give us the opportunity to see something before it went on the air. And so, I remember sitting in the client's room watching the show.

It was sent down on the network line at a time when we weren't carrying anything from the network so we were able to watch. And it was exciting; it was fantastic. It was so revolutionary. It was at a time when I have to admit I was probably alone among the liberals that were endeavoring to understand the changes that were taking place. I thought it was neat that they were bringing "out of the closet" attitudes and characteristics that had been kind of held back or that were not particularly important to display. I thought it was neat. You've got this redneck who is saying things openly on the air, and poor Edith is playing that role so beautifully and Archie is, you know, just so typical of many people that you can visualize and say, "Oh, I know somebody that's just exactly like that." If you get these things out in the open and have them on national television, it just has to make some changes for the better of society. I think I felt that way for a long time. Then, as I got a little older and I looked back on it, I think it also ushered in an era of television that maybe has gone too far. With the lack of the "code" in existence anymore, now it seems like anything is open—do your thing, say what you want to think, and say it anyway you want to do it. Use street language if you want to; that is the way life is. So, television says, "Let's mirror life. Because street language is part of life, you use it on television." I think *All in the Family* was probably the start of that. It got out of control, particularly when the "code" went out of existence. I think it's been

Ann Colone

"Women's programs" provided one of the few on-air opportunities for women in the early days of television. In 1958 WANE-TV hired Ann Colone, a former secretary at WGL, to host the station's *Women's Page* program, which eventually became *The Ann Colone Show*. Determined to cover more than the usual tips on fashion, cooking, and traditional issues, Colone didn't hesitate to discuss controversial issues or taboo subjects such as drug abuse, abortion, rape, divorce, homosexuality, and teen pregnancy.[39] In his interview Reid Chapman remembered that "Ann Colone had a lot more talent than to just saddle her with a homemaker show. She included that in her format, but she was almost a comedienne. She was open to anything, and the wilder the better. That's the way she really made her name. She did a lot of unusual things— the more unusual, the more it attracted. We had an audience—not at the outset, but eventually we had an audience. We served a lunch and women would write in for tickets. There was a similar program on WLW-TV in Cincinnati for many years, *The Ruth Lyons Show*, that was broadcast from a hotel, and we patterned our show after that. That was another one of those ways we could reach out into the community and have people come in and be a part of the station. Ann did a great job in helping us in that area. [She] was on a long time. Like all things, however, it went through a cycle, and ratings began to drop." In 1975, Ann gave up her program to become publicity director at WANE.

Ann Colone (center) in 1952.
PHOTO BY STEPHEN PERFECT

unfortunate. *All in the Family* was to television what Bill Haley and the Comets was to the music of radio.

I think that Hollywood particularly established this idea that they could pretty much portray what society was like—or should be like— through the movie industry. Since Hollywood went from making predominately movies for theaters to programming for television, that whole concept of allowing them to picture what society is like, or what society should be like, began to creep into the story line and then into the plot line of the programming that television was showing. In doing so, they watched to see what the acceptance was on the East Coast, which they figured was more sophisticated and more ready for this kind of change. It was just as though they shot their pictures all the way from Los Angeles into New York and bypassed us, because they figured that was where they were going to get their support. And so, the Midwest said, "Wait a minute. We're really not ready for that." I think what we have today is a terrific example, because I think it's just been crammed down everybody's throat that this is what the public wants. I'm not sure they do.

As station manager, Chapman oversaw the news department at WANE, including the station's editorial staff. I remember the first [local issue] that we did, which raised a big rumpus right off the bat. We did an editorial on Little League baseball and took the stand that it was entirely too controlled by adults and parents who wanted to impart to their young players that winning

Colone interviewed the Rolling Stones in 1964 for her show.

C. Bruce McConnell sent Chapman to WANE Radio in 1956. Shortly thereafter the station was sold to J. H. Whitney & Co. from New York.

was the most important thing. We took a stand that baseball should still be promoted in the vacant lots by kids who want to get together and just play ball. Oh, boy. We really caught it for that one [chuckles]. We got their attention.

The investigative reporting came later. This was probably ten years later. It began to be a thing that stations in larger markets began to do in order to show more participation in the community. In other words, rather than just do a one-minute editorial and you wanted to really prove a point, then spend some time. Go out and take your camera crew and your reporters and really dig in and find out the answers to some of these problems, or expose some of the problems. In the case of an investigative report, really, the management of the station keeps out of it entirely. You keep hands off. You turn it over to your investigative reporter and your news department with instructions that they have to be pure and objective. They cannot instill into those investigative reports personal opinion or slant in any way. Before it goes on it has to be reviewed in the presence of your attorney to make sure that you're free of any libel and that sort of thing.

You really put your faith in your news director and hoped that he had that kind of training and knew how to be objective. Investigative reporting is a very responsible job. CBS has done them where they have caught all kinds of hell. I think *The Guns of Autumn* is one of those that CBS will always remember, because they endeavored to expose the amount of hunting that is done on private land as kind of an entertainment for customers who rent an area of private land for their favorite customers to go down and shoot. They bring in animals, and it was a sport. I had probably the most letters I ever received, mostly postcards, from members of the National Rifle Association objecting to CBS and *The Guns of Autumn.* I don't think CBS will ever forget that investigative report. It didn't stop them, but it was really a very important program.

Vietnam was the first—I think I'm right on this—the first on-the-scene reporting of a war that this country had been involved in. When I say "on-the-scene," I mean actually having reporters there making live reports with the sound of guns in the background and planes and giving an actual description of what's taking place. The reporting of the Vietnam War by television really tore this country apart—torn between the realization that they were getting firsthand on-the-scene reports from the correspondents assigned to that area of the world, plus a reaction among the public saying, "This is terrible. Why do you feel it's necessary to bring this kind of horror into our living room," which was a way of saying underneath maybe they were ashamed to think that this country was involved in this kind of activity. And yet, the news people I think were right, and I'm glad they did it, because I think it's helped bring out in the open the real truth as to what really existed. We're just now beginning to get a lot of that truth. But at the time that it happened, that was one of those incidents where reporting the truth as it was taking place was difficult for the American public.

The reason I was involved in Fort Wayne was because I saw that as one way that we could bring the station into the community and have the community know the people that were working for the station. And so, I purposely made it a point whenever I was invited to become a member of a club or an organization, and it wasn't difficult. It wasn't difficult to find yourself as president of one of the groups because if they looked around and said, "Do we have a volunteer?" and you raised your hand, well, that's all you needed. I also feel that a good broadcaster ought to do that. In fact, I used to encourage it for all of my staff, too. Other department heads—I encouraged them to become members of civic groups and to be involved in the community, because I just think it's just part of your responsibility.

Television is an amazing invention, and I think more so than just radio. Radio allowed you to use your imagination, to visualize in your mind, to think more about what came out of the speaker. Television kind of takes that away from you, and everything is so explicit and so much in front of you that you don't need to think; you just look at it and react to it.

E. Berry Smith (1977)

CHAPTER SIXTEEN

E. Berry Smith

(1926–)

E. Berry Smith, easily one of the most charming broadcasters in all of Indiana, is an astute manager, skilled at running stations. Upon graduating from Butler University in 1949, Smith secured a job in sales at WIRE. From 1954 to 1956 he worked at Franklin Securities, before moving to CBS, Inc., in Detroit, Michigan, for a year. For the next seven years he moved around quite a bit, working as the general manager of television stations WFIE-TV in Evansville (1957–60), WFRV-TV in Green Bay (1960–62), and WLKY-TV in Louisville (1962–64). In 1964 Smith landed in Evansville at WTVW-TV as president and general manager, a position that he held for seventeen years. When WTVW-TV was sold, he relocated to South Bend to work for Schurz Communications as president and general manager of WSBT-TV. He became senior vice president of Schurz Communications in 1989. In his early years, he was known for his ability to turn stations around, to make them profitable by instituting good business practices. As he has said, "If you run the station right, everybody should be happy." Smith's interview took place in his downtown South Bend office at Schurz Communications in January and March of 1996.

The next major change, the advent of digital television, will be dramatic, and it's coming. That's the problem we're dealing with right now with this telecommunications bill, which has not been resolved. There's no equipment yet designed to receive digital except some experimental equipment. I'd say probably in less than five years—but anywhere from two to five years—we'll see receivers that can receive it or converters that will make it work. . . . The FCC arranged that over a fifteen-year period we would phase out the analog signal and our only distribution would be on high-definition digital television. Then we would turn the analog frequency back to the government, and they could do with it as they see fit. And now they're talking about: "We'll auction it right now." If they auction it right now, no broadcaster could afford it. It's going to cost eight to ten million dollars for every station to put in the equipment for digital broadcasting, and digital broadcasting is not going to charge one dollar more in advertising. . . . Auctioning will destroy free over-the-air television. There's no way we could go to auction for these frequencies. We couldn't afford it, so we'd be out of the broadcast business, and this thing [Schurz Communications] would be a shell. We'd go along doing analog, but all of a sudden people would say, "That's old fashioned now. I'm not going to watch that anymore." It's just a mess

Roughly 60 percent of people have cable. Forty percent don't have cable today—someplace between 35 and 40 [percent] don't have cable. And then homes that do have cable, only

29 percent of their sets are attached to cable—only one set as a rule. So, you have a tremendous number of people out there whose only access to programming is free over-the-air television and radio. It was designed that way to provide a universal service available to everybody, regardless of means. And with this [digital television], you create a true have and have-not society, unfortunately. Some people are elite enough to feel that not everyone is entitled to all of this. Now, that's true elitism. But this is the price of progress. So, maybe not everybody is really entitled to live in this computer age? I'm concerned with the access in broadcasting because 80 percent of the people say that's their primary source of news—broadcast television. If they can't afford to buy this new system—it's not free over-the-air—then they're not going to be exposed to it.

I was born in Daytona Beach, Florida. I lived there until I was six weeks old. My parents weren't very bright. They came back to Indiana. . . . So, I grew up in Indiana from six weeks. And so I was reared here—Indianapolis. I went to grade school at Our Lady of Lourdes. I went to high school at Tech because I couldn't afford the twenty-five dollars it cost to go to Cathedral [High School]. I didn't have twenty-five dollars. My old man bailed out when I was about ten years old.

I was interested in broadcasting to the extent that I listened to the radio and enjoyed the radio and . . . I probably thought I could be Jack Armstrong, the all American boy, if I really put my effort into it. At least I could play the guy on the radio—be Jack Armstrong. No, I was a premed student when I went into the army. I got out of high school kind of early. I had taken a West Point exam because that really intrigued me, but then I flunked the physical. The following year another congressman nominated me, so I said, "This is silly." I took the physical. I could not go into the army, though, until that class was sworn in, even though I flunked the physical. The theory was that if everybody else got run over by a truck then you'd go anyway. [Instead], I got out of high school early and went out to Butler.

I was a bum when I went to Butler—I mean a real bum—my mother was working. I had an eight o'clock class, so I'd say, "I'm up, Mom." She'd go to the factory at seven o'clock, and I'd go right back to bed. And so, my first semester at Butler, I had fifteen hours of unofficial with-

drawal—failure. So to get back in the following September, I had to do all kinds of cockamamy untruths as to why it happened and how it would never happen again. So then, I started with a minus grade point average and got through that first year with not much better, but enough to count. Then, I went into the army and learned how to behave myself, and be a decent citizen—or try to be a decent citizen. When I came back I had the highest grade point average in the school of business at Butler, but I'd learned how to be a halfway decent citizen. Then, I did not go to med school. I had some professor say, "I'll never recommend you. You'll never get by it because of the grade point you've got." I said, "Well, screw you. I'll figure this one out" [laughs]. So I went into the school of business.

I had to work someplace, so [after graduation] I thought, "Where do I want to work?" I got out the yellow pages, and started going down—like this, you know abstract—a, a, a, b, b, b—and I came to a radio station. Hey, that sounds pretty good. Somebody has to go out and find sponsors. My mother was involved in politics, and she knew [C. Walter] Mickey McCarty (who was the editor of the [Indianapolis] News or something) enough to call him—they owned WIBC—that I could get an appointment. So I went to see Mickey McCarty. He said, "Hell, we don't have anything to do with a radio station, but I know the guy who manages it." So I go to WIBC, and I'm starting to walk in, and the guys are coming out going to lunch saying, "There's nothing here but I know where they are hiring. WIRE is hiring. The guy's name is Dan Park." I was standing in the lobby. So I go by the Claypool Hotel. Up I go and there is a young lady, and I said, "I'm here to talk about employment. There must be some kind of a job where people go out and find sponsors." She said, "Yeah, we call them salespeople here." It was Helen Huber I was talking to, and so they gave me an application and I filled it out. Somebody left, and Dan Park hired two guys.

Dan Park was one of the founders of the IBA. Dan Park, Bruce McConnell, D. Coe, those are the three major people. Dan had been active, I guess, in Pennsylvania where he'd been before the war (I think that's true). In fact that's how he got involved in the IBA, because Dan had slave labor. They kept moving the presidency among those three guys. Helen [Huber] was his secretary and was active in the association, as acting secretary—not getting paid for it or anything. They were going to meet at the

Claypool or some place and they needed somebody to haul stuff—well, "Hey, come on." So by default [I was] going to the meetings in 1949, by, you know, hauling chairs or whatever it was for the goofy meeting. They were the ones that organized it. That's how I got interested in it, at that time.

I think 1948 was their year of organization. This was 1949 when I went to work there. There were other state associations, so it was not unique, but it was the first time it had been done in Indiana. One of the major undertakings—there's always a problem with the Indiana basketball finals: the IHSAA allocation of [broadcasters] seats. So, the broadcasters took it upon themselves to take that chore (there were more broadcasters carrying the game than there were seats for this broadcast) and come up with some kind of a plan that would allocate these fairly. Of course, no one thought it ever was done fairly, but I saw Helen do it often. It was done in an extremely fair manner. In those days, probably a third, maybe not even a half of the general managers for radio stations were also doing the play-by-play of the basketball games. There would always be a spring [IBA] meeting that took place at the time of the state finals. The finals were on Saturday, and the broadcasters would meet on Thursday, I guess, because Friday there was a luncheon of the coaches and all of that. Then, they hang around and do their play-by-play of the game. They used to use the Athletic Club as a place to hold drawings for the seating arrangement. That was a great deal of concern to be fair in the allocation of seats. Everybody had their arguments why they had to have three seats or two seats. Dan always got three seats because he had union in there, and he claimed he had to have an announcer, a color guy, and a union engineer. (He stretched it.)

Smith worked at WIRE for five years, then Franklin Securities, and CBS, Inc., in Detroit, before moving into management at a television station. I'm in Detroit, and I get a call (or a letter; I don't recall which) from the people at WAVE, and they said, "We just bought a station in Evansville, Indiana—a television station. Why didn't you tell us you were not happy at Franklin [Securities]? Why didn't you tell us you were leaving?" I said, "None of your business." (That's what I thought; I didn't say it, but I thought it.) I said, "Why do you ask?" They said, "Well, we bought this television station, and we've got to get

someone to run it, and we'd like to talk to you about it." I said, "Okay, I'll talk about anything if it's something like that." (There were only about five hundred stations in the country at that time.) So, the guy who was doing the hiring was out of the country on vacation. They said, "When he gets back, we'll give you a call." Okay, so they do, and they offer me a job. . . . And I talked to [my wife] Mary, and I said, "You know, there's only five hundred jobs like this in the country—in the world, and I don't care whether it's a UHF or a VHF." And I said, "When am I going to ever get a chance like that?" (I'd never even been in a television station except to walk through one once [laughs].) I spent two weeks in Louisville at the home office reading orders and stuff—you know, taking a crash course in FCC rules and regulations.

[It was so much fun] because I didn't know a damn thing about it, so everything I did was new and interesting. I didn't know enough to know when I was doing it wrong, but we tried. It turned out to be quite successful. In retrospect, I was really young, and I know it. I think the only thing I did right was that I admitted that it was my first time [running a station]. And, "It ain't going to get done unless you help me get it done." And I said, "I don't know beans." I knew the sales end of it because it was not that much different. They all helped me, and they helped me a lot. And for that, I was grateful, and we had a good relationship to the extent that the chief engineer wanted me to be godparents for his youngsters. And later I left; two or three of them called me and said they'd come to work for me, and so it worked out. They were good for me; they were good to me. And I appreciate that.

Smith worked two years in Evansville and two more in Green Bay, Wisconsin. I left because this company was organizing a media company to buy the broadcast radio, television, and outdoor [advertising companies]. Wow, and I want to be part of this thing. So to Milwaukee, and it turns out this company had a problem they thought they could resolve and they didn't. This company was a small business and not a corporation—it was organized by a bank. Had six directors, but these six directors also had interests in other broadcast properties. Well, it took us over the legal limit, and the directors resigned, and I'm sitting there king of nothing [but] an outdoor company. About that time an associate of the bank had an interest in a station in Louisville that was having all kinds of problems and fights between groups of owners. They asked if I'd go down there. At the same time one of the other groups of owners [in Louisville] asked if I'd come down. So, I went down as a neutral party to run that—a turn-around situation. It was losing its shirt. We got it into the black. At the same time, one of the principals in the Louisville station was having a fight in Evansville with the same people in Milwaukee that I'd been with before. They wanted a neutral party. So, I came back to Evansville as a neutral party between these two fighting factions. I came with the other station, a competing station [WTVW] in 1964, and that's the one I stayed at until 1981.

My interest was in running the station, running a *good* station. That sounds kind of Pollyannish, but it's not meant to be. I would be honest, and I would not do something that would favor one guy over the other, because there's no reason to. If you run the station right, everybody should be happy. Both [competing parties] knew me and both trusted me, so they worked it out. I stayed on with them [WTVW-TV, Evansville] until they sold the station [in 1981]. When they sold the station I lasted about twenty minutes. The new owner—I picked him up at the hotel and went to the office—and he said, "We don't need you anymore. Thank you very much. Sayonara." They asked me to fire the general manager, but I said, "No, I don't work here any more. You have to do that."

When I left . . . I had a company car. I brought it back two days later and turned it back in. And when I walked in the lobby, everybody that was on duty in the whole building came to the lobby to say, you know, "I'm sorry. Goodbye and all," which was, I think, an indication that there was a good working relationship in the station. The philosophy was: "You're big kids, and you know how to work, and we'll train you as much as we can but then you do your own thing and just do it right." We just had people, I think, that respected each other. I had a rule that if you don't like each other, that's fine. But don't take it out in here; take it outside. While you're here, you have to live with these people. And they did. And I am sure there were antagonisms, but we would not let them bring those kind of fights into the building, and they knew it. And, they didn't really dislike each other that much anyway. This was before "harassment" became a buzz word and all. But we had no problems with things like that—no romance. There wasn't that much loving going on.

We may have [had some investigative journalism], but we never called it that. We had two or three stories that probably would qualify, but we didn't have an "I-Team" [Investigative Team] or anything like that. But, we had a couple of young guys who liked to poke around and find stuff, but we just did it in the normal course of their reporting work but no projects as such. Of course, they were getting more involved in improved technologies (which were extremely rapid in their arrival), and then expanding the hours on the air with news, and finding out that after the initial investment, the news can be a pretty profitable operation for the station. At first blush you'd say, "No," because it's so god-awful expensive, but advertisers want to be in and around newscasts. It lends credibility to their commercials, and so far stations have been able to support their expansions. Our station in South Bend, when I first came here, had an hour early newscast. Since then they've gone to news at noon, thirty minutes in the morning, and now sixty minutes in the morning early, and seven days a week a newscast at six o'clock at night, and ten or eleven o'clock at night. So, it's happening all over the country. The news is expanding, and it's for the good. But, news takes a lot of bodies.

I felt, and still do feel, that editorials are fine but that an editorial ought to be so [well] researched, whatever the topic is, that by the time you finish the research you find, wow, the opinion I had going into this, my predetermined opinion, is a hundred and eighty degrees wrong. You had really turned it around. That's an editorial. You turn it around. Anything else is commentary, and I think ought to be labeled as such—as opposed to the editorial. If I am in broadcasting, the editorial is the voice of the licensee. You cannot have your personal thing. It's got to be that of the licensee. Commentary—if the station allows it—can be your personal thing. Editorial is that opinion of the licensee. And that, I think, puts a severe responsibility on the general manager, although I don't think a lot of folks have ever accepted that. They get on and raise hell about the chuckholes and things like that. Big deal. Nobody likes chuckholes; that's a safe thing. And just talking about the war in Afghanistan when you can't think about anything else to talk about. We did not do it there [in Evansville]. Now, here in South Bend we did. When I came here it was in place, and the news director had always been the voice, so it continued.

Smith sold a commercial remote for WIRE to Charlie Stuart Studebaker in 1950. Studebaker, one of Indiana's premier automobile companies of the day, boasted "self-adjusting" brakes. Tom Peden (left) announced, and Jim Lowe (center) spun records.

Several strong leaders founded the Indiana Broadcasters Association (IBA) including Donald A. Burton of WLBC in Muncie, John Carl Jeffrey of WIOU in Kokomo, and C. Bruce McConnell of WISH in Indianapolis. Initially the IBA was established to promote cooperation among Indiana broadcasters, to promote practices that would serve the public interest, to protect members from unjust actions, and to establish links with other associations around the country. Some of the staff at WISH were actively involved with the IBA in the early 1950s. Seated left to right: Dan Park, Helen Huber, William J. Schull. Standing left to right: Frank Parrish and E. Berry Smith.

Then you had your own ground [rules] on how you handled certain types of stories, how you handled the tragedy when there was a death, an accident or something—and the timing of that and the notification. Even though you had film, things like that don't go on the air. You deal with a labor dispute so that it doesn't become a propaganda tool for either side, the company or the strikers. You don't let anybody use it as a platform. . . . Don't let somebody get that microphone and turn it into a shouting, screaming [match], which sometimes happens. And then, we felt that you handle it fairly. It's just good common sense. And if your people can't do it, you've got the wrong people. But how do you treat stories like children who've been harmed or things that affect children? We had a situation where Santa Claus was killed in a helicopter crash, and it was the Saturday before Christmas. He was landing and hit the wires. You don't go on the air and say, "Santa Claus was killed today," although one of our competitors did say that. If your people don't have that common sense, you've got problems with your people and how they deal with it. That's why you hope that the people that you have in those situations have a background that can compare with the audience. They either have kids, or they have nieces or nephews, or they still remember from their own childhood enough to be sensitive to what children need—that they've seen enough tragedy in their neighborhoods and their lives, and that they're concerned. Also, that somebody doesn't learn from their radio or their television that their husband or dad has been killed or something like that. Those kind of things. And then politics—politics are politics.

The Kennedy [assassination] was probably a local broadcast lesson on what you could do and what you should do. There was just no question in anybody's mind. One advertiser called and said, "I want my spot taken off." I said, "It's already off." I only recall one that even said that. As far as I know, probably every station stayed on the air overnight with nothing, just to see if something might come along. There's not been a situation comparable to that, but I think that it's terrible when the death of the president becomes a training for what broadcasters could do. I had forgotten about that.

Then, the next time I had something like that was in Evansville. The outgoing mayor, in 1974, left office in January and was killed by some woman in early 1974 who mistook him for the current mayor. He lived about three days. He hung on by a thread for those two or three days. Oh, all the locals were doing the same thing, covering the situation and maintaining a level of taste that was not offensive to the family—but at the same time answering all the questions people were asking. She was just whacko, had some complaint about something, some silly governmental thing that had not been done. She didn't know that he hadn't run for reelection. He left office in January (it was like March or April). One morning about eight o'clock at the back door, there she is, "Bang." We had learned from Kennedy what was expected of us. Although on a smaller scale, we put that to practice. We covered the funeral Mass pretty much the same way as the Kennedy Mass. I was on the board of the Catholic newspaper there. Father Joe Niblack was our commentator, and in the meantime those other [stations] were calling somebody else; everybody had their own priest. But we were equipped then, and we went live for four or five hours and covered the funeral and the processional. But like I say, we learned it from watching the Kennedy thing, which had only been ten years before, so it was still kind of fresh in most people's minds.

The "golden era" is probably whatever you feel best about. When people refer to the "golden era" as live television—it was awful—black and white. There were goofs on the air. The writing was no better than it is today. There was no videotape. Videotape wasn't around until the early 1960s. So, there were mistakes on the air. It was like in the good old days, "Oh, I was a kid in the good old days." The guys who maintain the 1940s were the "good old days"; to me it means the outhouse. That to me is not the "good old days." Same thing with this. Television was golden because it was all new. The only thing that would be golden about it would be the fact that it was new. But in comparison to the programming that's on today, or that has been on in the last ten years—no. There were one or two good shows, but the fact that they did live drama, didn't make it good drama. Some writers gave it the name the "golden age of television," and it stuck, but not as far as I am concerned. It was like the outhouse of television compared with today. They have flush toilets now.

We consider ourselves [Schurz Communications] a medium size—the markets in which we operate are medium-size markets. In broadcasting, we have four television stations: South Bend, Indiana; Roanoke, Virginia; Springfield, Missouri; and Augusta, Georgia—two NBC affiliates and two CBS affiliates. We're in radio here in South Bend and in Lafayette, Indiana, where we have three stations. In the cable business in Hagerstown, Maryland, and in Coral Springs, Florida. We have eight newspapers, including the *South Bend Tribune*, which is the largest. The others are smaller: Bloomington, Indiana; Bedford, Indiana; Danville, Kentucky; Hagerstown, Maryland; a small town in California I can't remember, near the Mexican border. I would add that we're small to medium from a corporate standpoint, from a news company standpoint. Our markets are all medium-size markets, and we're comfortable in those size markets.

The Schurz family has been in this business since 1872 with the founding of the *South Bend Tribune*. Two men started the *South Bend Tribune*. A man named Miller and a man—I believe the fellow was named Crockett. The next generation—Mr. Miller had no kith nor kin, but his nephew was Franklin Schurz, Sr., and he asked him to come help on it. Then the other family continued to be a minority owner. About 23 or 24 percent of the stock is owned by the Crockett and Ray families, but the rest [is owned by] the Schurz people. When Mr. Miller passed away sometime in the 1930s or so, the Schurz family controlled the business. All of the children are active in the business. The eldest, Frank Schurz, is the president of the company. His brother, Jim, is the senior vice president for newspapers. He's next door. Then, the next son is the publisher of the Bloomington and Bedford newspapers. The daughter, Mary, is publisher of the Danville, Kentucky, newspaper. So, they are all active in the business.

We think the niche is there. We are not one of those people who say, "If you can't become gigantic, you're not going to survive," because we think there is a niche in the service we can provide and do it successfully. Nothing wrong with big. We are always looking for acquisitions. But we don't move quickly, and by the time we've made up our minds, somebody else has come along and bought it. Also, we buy in with the idea to make money with it. We operate as if we were borrowing a 100 percent of the money, and we have to pay this money back. Even if we have it in our pocket, we still want that thing to pay for itself. Otherwise, we say, "Why do it?" So, this limits some of the things we might be involved in for acquisi-

tions because the prices have gone so high. But we are always looking, and have made some acquisitions slowly. Since I've been with the company we've acquired the Lafayette stations—Springfield, Missouri, a television station there. So, we don't just rush out and buy everything that's available because this is a long-haul business.

I do think the broadcast media has had an impact on our national identity. I do indeed, and it has not necessarily all been good. But I could use the assassination of the president as an example. I think there it certainly had—I felt at least—a healing effect, a bringing together which was positive in that everyone could share in it and share immediately. When Lincoln was assassinated—at least there was telegraph, and people were aware that something was going on—but they were not really a part of it as they were for the Kennedy assassination. But by the same token, it seems to me also that it can lead to trivializing some things in our society. In that, I would say the O. J. Simpson trial led us to a cynicism toward the legal system. We trivialized, I think, the event which was a murder and exchanged that for excitement over the individual who was charged with the murder and totally lost sight of the fact that it was a real murder trial. Television did not cause that. Television was the messenger, but it brought a bad message, I think. Had we not been there to be the messenger, it wouldn't have happened. So, maybe we are to blame. But I think as much as anything, television—more so than radio—has created a desire for information and a desire for knowledge. I guess ten years ago, library usage records paralleled the increase in television receivers. [Television] stimulated people to find out something else. The "couch potato" is the exception, I think, in terms of the normal home. So, I think television has opened a whole lot of areas of interest to people who would not have had that opportunity before. That does not mean that all that's been on the air has been good, because I think some of it has been trash.

I would never have agreed that operating "in the public interest" as a necessity and operating at a profit were necessarily opposed to each other. Eldon Campbell used to say something, "The station that serves best, sells best," which I always thought was a pretty neat line, because it was true. So, you can operate in the public interest and be profitable. If someone is defining the public interest and quantifying it and saying you must have

Shortly after his arrival at WSBT, Smith waited on the set of the Job Telethon for a call from President Ronald Reagan.

WSBT, a station with a long involvement in the South Bend community, was abuzz as reporters and staff waited for election night returns in 1968. Franklin D. Schurz, Sr. (center with hand on hip), a member of the Hall of Fame, guided WSBT for many years.

Schurz enjoyed a lighthearted moment. He began his association with the South Bend Tribune *in 1925, just a few years after WSBT signed on the air.*

"X" number of hours of this type programming and so many hours of that type programming, then you do start having an effect on profitability. When you quantify what public interest and service is, a lot of it is in the eye of the beholder. What is important in South Bend, Indiana, might not play well at all in Augusta, Georgia, or vice versa. I think that so long as some governmental agency is not defining what the public interest is and you have the choice to say, "This, I believe, is my responsibility to define the public interest for this community," you can make money. [Schurz Communications has] done it; we've done it for years. We've had that obligation since we've had that first license—in our case in 1921. That was the first [license] in Indiana. We've operated in the public interest ever since. [Public interest] was a lot easier when it was defined. I can live with the definition quantifying; it is when you quantify it and qualify it and say you're supposed to have three hours of let's say chil-dren's programming. And, then they say, "Here's what we think ought to be on that children's program." Then, you're in big trouble. I can even live with quantification, but not qualification.

I think, by and large, the great bulk of local broadcasters have a great sense of their responsibility. They want to be good citizens. I go to affiliate meetings, and they're quite vocal in addressing their television networks about program content because of their concern about how the people in their community will react to such program language and stuff. I think the local broadcaster is a different person than the national network broadcaster is or the producers in Hollywood. They're a different breed and have a different set of values. I think they have a far better set of values than those in New York or Los Angeles. And they have a far greater respect for the community than those people in New York or Los Angeles. My opinion.

Bazil J. O'Hagan (ca. 1960s)
PHOTO BY CHARLES LINSTER

Baz O'Hagan

(1928–)

The interview with Bazil J. O'Hagan, affectionately known as "Baz" (with a short ǎ), took place in his home on a cold, blustery November afternoon in 1996, with snow clouds filling the sky. He began his career in engineering at WBBC-Radio in Flint, Michigan, in 1950, but he did not stay there long. The next year he moved to WJIM in Lansing, and a year later, at age twenty-four, he directed the construction of WBKZ-TV in Battle Creek, Michigan, one of the nation's first UHF television stations. For three years he worked at WICS in Springfield, Illinois, where he also taught. In 1956 WNDU in South Bend hired him as chief engineer for their radio and television stations, with the understanding that when a job opened in management, he could have it. He rose through the ranks, becoming president and general manager of Michiana Telecasting Corporation, the parent company of WNDU, in 1980. He retired in 1993. An engineer by training, O'Hagan is first and foremost a people person, and he is proud of his skills in that area.

can remember making a crystal set one time, using a bare core of toilet paper for the core. I wound the wire around that and made a coil out of that. I was interested in that. I was always interested in things very mechanical, and being raised on the lake, during the summer, most of the time I worked all summer long, and in the winter, it was kind of dead, so I played a lot of ice hockey during the winter. Those were the things that interested me most.

When I finished high school, out of a class of—I think there were forty-two in my high school class. Incidentally, all twelve grades were in the same building. Only about two of the students went on to college, because this was in the Pontiac-automobile area . . . Pontiac, General Motors and they made buses and trucks and cars. It seemed everyone expected that that would be their career. I started that way, and I worked for a couple of years in the factories, and then realized that I really wanted to do something better than that. But college, regular college, didn't seem all that attractive to me, but trade school did. I got in touch with a school in Chicago called DeForest which had a three-year program in design and electronic engineering. I graduated from that school and became licensed by the FCC as an engineer and began the process of engineering.

My first experience was in radio [in Flint, Michigan, in 1950]. In those days the transmitter had to be attended, and it was kind of a lonely job, out in the country in a little building all alone. There was not much to do except write down numbers every half hour. I did that just one summer. Then, I was hoping to get into a television station, but at that time there really weren't very many, and my expectation was that one day I would get into a TV station in

Detroit. I made myself kind of a polite pest by being at the station about once a month, looking for a position. During that period of time I did television servicing and made more money at doing that than I did for many, many years following that. But I did finally get the chance to go to work for WJIM radio and television in Lansing, Michigan. When I told my father what I was doing, he thought I was crazy, giving up all that big money. I think I went to work for $250 a month or something like that. It was really not very much money.

The TV station in Lansing at that time had the offices in the downtown building, and all the equipment and the transmitters, both AM and television, were in the Quonset hut which was just on the outskirts of town. And when I worked there, I worked totally alone; ran everything completely alone—including the film projectors, slide projectors, network services, and both transmitters. The typical operation would have at least one, maybe even two technical people at the transmitting plant and then all of the program origination, film and slides or whatever, occurring at some spot where there would also be technical people. But here we did the entire operation by one person. So, I learned a lot. I had to learn.

I stayed in Lansing for close to three years, and I met my wife there. That's her home. Then from there, I got a very nice promotion and became chief engineer of this UHF station in Battle Creek, which was technically a good facility but it was a business failure. It was pretty evident to many of us who were working there that it probably would not make it. And sure enough, it was off the air in about six months. Well, word got around that here was this guy, O'Hagan, who knows how to build UHF stations. So I was contacted by several other companies, and one of them was the H & E Valement Corporation out of Chicago. They had a franchise, or license, I should say, to build a station in Springfield, Illinois. In Springfield then, I went there as chief engineer and stayed for another three years.

Then I came to Notre Dame here, as chief engineer [in 1956], with the expectation that I would be transferred to the management as soon as an opening occurred. Engineering tends to produce introverts, putting it kindly. My wife says that I'm a normal person; I'm not a typical engineer. I really wanted the people end of the business, and I wanted to make some more money too, and I saw more money there [in management].

[WNDU is] owned by a coordinate commercial tax-paying corporation called Michiana Telecasting Corporation, and the stock of that is owned by the university. . . . As far as I know, we are the only for-profit, tax-paying institution or corporation owned by a not-for-profit. There were a couple of others in past years. There was one, WBAY in [Green Bay], Wisconsin, and there's another one [WWL] in New Orleans. Both of those are now gone; they have been sold to regular commercial owners.

There were some mistakes made in staffing the station [WNDU] by the original general manager. He was a real nice guy, but he came from a VHF station in a major city and somewhat copied staffing. And we just had too many people. So, we had to downsize, and I became the one who did all the calculating and planning. But as I said, when I came here I came here with the understanding that when a management position would open, I would get it. Well, unfortunately, this first general manager died at the age of forty of leukemia—left a big family behind—wonderful man, just snuffed out. It was like about six months. Well, then the man who had been sales manager was promoted to general manager, and he immediately made me his assistant. That's how I got into [management].

Actually, the general manager chose to keep himself mostly involved in the sales end of business—because he had been sales manager—and really tried to move the balance of operations over to me. And so, I gained a lot of experience in a hurry. And as a station manager, my duties didn't change. I was already doing that, but as you know, as your career progresses, you like to have little stair steps, and that was one of them.

Actually when it became my responsibility to establish policies, I made it very clear that we were not editorializing, and today the station still does not. My reason for that was that regardless of how we could try to disclaim it, the public perceived an editorial on our station as coming from Notre Dame. And I did not want to be in a position to try to speak for the university; so we chose not to editorialize. I think it was a good choice.

The Vietnam War was the first time the American people saw a war, really saw it. They saw the battlefield action. They saw troop movements; they saw smoke; they saw burning children. It was a real, real eye-opener to the American public. I don't know of any other event that television covered that had the impact that it had on public

Dancers whirled around the set of Jan's Polka Party. *Jan Griswold and her partner Frank Baker were favorites of WNDU's northern Indiana audience (ca. 1965).*

O'Hagan presented roses to Susie Sharpf, Miss Susie, who was host of Romper Room, *a popular children's show in South Bend (ca. 1965).*

opinion. The Kennedy assassination, and all, the funeral was a very, very good use of television. The whole sequence of events there, with stations taking off their regular programming for three days. I think it was three days—was very, very unusual for an industry to do that. And I thought it was very responsible of the three networks to kill all the programming, all the revenue for three days just to have that on.

At that time Notre Dame had a journalism department, and we would get some students working as interns (maybe for a half a year or something like that) then as employees, cub reporters when they had gotten out of school. So we kind of had the pick of the litter when it came to that, but we hired people who were not Notre Dame people also. What did I look for? I looked for journalism skills, and if we expected a person to be an anchor, then we looked very carefully at their appearance, how they presented themselves. Are they good clean people? By that I mean, did they have an abuse or a bad record of any kind, and are they stable? Because you invest so much money when you hire a person—by stable I mean job related—being steady. If they had a history of bumping around every year or two years, we wouldn't make the investment in them. And we had great success with keeping our people.

We established the [teaching] programs ourselves. The department heads were expected to teach a class, and typically you had just one class which would meet, perhaps, three times a week. And we always conducted it right in our building. Tended to be more production oriented, where the students would have a final exam by producing something, either a commercial or whatever, some kind of programming. The station now has either one or two full-time people who are professors. The station pays them, and the classes are conducted in our building. One of the courses was kind of a survey course, covering the industry. And a second one—I don't know which order they progress now—but the second one is more production oriented.

One of the fun programs that we had on here was called *The Professors*, and we had a group of three or four or five professors, and typically two or three of them would be here and just sit around the table and talk on whatever subject they wanted. And they always tried to outdo each other. It was done live, and it was really, really kind of a fun

program to watch. It was on late at night after midnight. That was one thing that we did. . . . I don't think we told them what to talk about. It was kind of a fun show to watch. Let's see, what else did we do? We did live children's programs with characters. What else did we do? Those are the only things to come to mind. Of course, we did a lot of news from the very beginning, and public affairs programs, which typically, unfortunately, are talking heads. They're not rated very well. There was a time when the FCC required that stations find out what the needs of the community were and then program for those needs.

However, because most of the [syndicated] entertainment programming was done on film and done in Hollywood . . . you had the West Coast influence. The news and information kind of programming on the networks originated either in New York or Washington or both. And by sharp contrast between these two styles, it's true that the Midwest was kind of left out. The programming that the midwesterners had preferred just wasn't there. . . . Probably over a period of time, we have adopted the tastes of both coasts. I don't think people today even recognize that the West Coast influences entertainment and the East Coast influences the news of the nation.

In the 1970s, [cable] came about because of John Dille's father, Jack, who at that time (I think it was just about at that time) was the chairman of the board of the National Association of Broadcasters. Very active in the industry, and they owned a newspaper and two radio stations and a TV station all in Elkhart. He got together with Father [Edmund Patrick] Joyce [president of Notre Dame] who was the man I reported to at WNDU, and with Franklin Schurz, who is deceased now, who owned WSBT and the *South Bend Tribune*. And the three of them decided that it might be a good idea to get into the cable television business. So, they appointed an executive committee, each of them appointing one person. I was appointed from our company, and we, the executive committee, put this whole thing together. We applied for fourteen franchises and got every one of them. Both are deceased—a man by the name of Arthur O'Neal of the *South Bend Tribune*, and Paul Brines. He was the—what did he do? He was the number two man in the newspaper in Elkhart that Dille owned. And we kept it for a short [time]; really not very long. What happened was, both Arthur O'Neal and Paul Brines died. They both died. Paul was probably in his sixties or maybe even seventies, and O'Neal was in his fifties. And they both died at the same time. And I was trying to run the thing alone and still running the TV station and radio station, and it just got to be too much. So I went to the three owners and suggested that—maybe we ought to sell it and they all agreed. So we sold it to a family by the name of Buford from Tyler, Texas.

It was a real eye-opener to me to have to deal with politicians. Because in order to get a [cable] franchise, typically if it was from a city, we had to be approved by the board of public works and then the city council, and committees of both of these groups we'd have to go through. And you can go to a council meeting, as an example, knowing which councilmen are going to vote for you or against you. You get there and find it's turned around. That was a real eye-opener, and I was disappointed in that. Another disappointment to me was: this was very early on in the cable industry, and many of the equipment suppliers were charlatans. For example, we signed a contract to construct some miles of cable and with a complete set of specifications. When the project was finished, it didn't come anywhere near meeting the specifications. And the salesman told me, "Well, you should have known we couldn't meet those specifications."

You could run a television station without ever having a piece of paper with clients. They all paid their bills. They were very honest people. Our write-off for bad debts was less than 1 percent regularly—less than a ½ percent most of the time. Television is really a clean business and radio, too. I don't think cable is that way today. It's a mature industry now. And I think it's run in a very honest fashion. I'd like to see more competition. Anytime you don't have competition, there's too many things that can go wrong.

I always felt that being a university-owned station—particularly a private and I'll even add Catholic institution—that we had to out perform our competitors in the good things the stations do. So, we kind of bent over backwards to cover local events, such as elections and providing time for debates between candidates, and various other things. We had a policy that we would not carry paid religion, by that I mean programs that are purchased for presentation of religious programming. We did put on a Catholic Mass, which still goes on Sunday morning, and typically we would have at least one other nondenominational religious

program on Sunday, also, for which time was donated. We donated the time.

I would say the creation of Golden Dome Productions [is what] I'm more proud of than anything else. And I didn't do it alone. . . . First of all, it's a television production company that used the same people and same equipment as the station. We did have a separate staff of producers and creative people, but everything else was shared between the two. And we put that together primarily to produce programs for the university of two or three different kinds. One would be, when they wanted to have a nationwide television hookup with the alumni groups; we would produce that for them. That would be one classification of programs. Another would be, programs that would be educational. We have not done a lot with that. And the third—actually I guess there were four—the third would be a distance-learning process. . . . Distance learning means that the professor is in a classroom in South Bend, and it's hooked up with two-way communications with groups in other cities around the country. That is being very successfully done right now in the executive MBA program at the university. We never really got very far with that. The thing that we really did the best, and continue to do the best, was producing a half-hour program for a week on international public affairs issues. And we really, really do this well. We have been all over the world shooting stuff for this. We've been to Rome; we've been in Africa and all over the United States, and it's amazing the number of people you can get. Chief Justice [Warren] Burger, as an example, we caught up with him in Rome and got something out of him for one particular program we were doing. It is a very, very effective tool. It's on PBS stations around the country, and it's called *Today's Life Choices*. You may have encountered it. And it's a half hour per week. That's very ambitious, and so those are the types of things we do with Golden Dome. . . . And they're doing a lot of interactive videos. Another thing that they do is commercial production, too. Example, Warsaw, Indiana—I don't know if you're familiar with this—but Warsaw is the world capital for the making of prostheses, artificial hips and joints, and knees and that sort of thing. And there are quite a few companies there. Well, they have a continuing need to educate doctors about their new products; so we did a lot of work for them. And also, you're familiar with the product Kitty Litter? That was originated by a man who

Golden Dome
Productions

A technician readied a camera for WNDU's telecast of a Notre Dame football game (ca. 1965).

O'Hagan enjoyed a laugh with Tom Hamilton, vice president and general manager of WNDU, in 1981 as Hamilton retired and O'Hagan became president and general manager of the station.

lived up here in Michigan. He died a year ago. This man used video instead of letters. After he sold Kitty Litter and had all of this money, he wanted an entrepreneurial supporter and we did a lot of video work for him, very successful stuff.

The biggest change [in broadcasting] is that it's now a mature industry. During the years that I was in it, all except maybe the last five years, the industry was just growing. Revenues were up every year. The size of the staffs were up, newer equipment, new buildings and so on and so forth. Then all of a sudden they reached maturity, business maturity. And that's a term I'm sure you understand. Then you had to begin to watch your bottom line much more carefully, because you couldn't depend upon continuing increases of revenue. That's the biggest change, I would say, and that occurred about the last five years of my career.

I used a phrase—and I used it over, over again—and that is that it was my responsibility to create an environment which would foster creativity. And if you think that through, there's a lot of importance just in that statement, because you're dealing in television with people with very big egos. If you can keep them all focused and going in the same direction, allowing them to be creative—which is really the thing that separates the management style of many men I know. They try to dominate people within their stations, and it doesn't work. It doesn't work. They either perform poorly and they become stilted—that's not a good word—they became afraid to do anything *creative* for fear that they're going to be criticized. Well, we never criticized creativity even if it was bad. So, that was my biggest philosophy.

Howard C. Caldwell, Jr. (mid-1950s)
PHOTO COURTESY OF WTHI-TV

Howard Caldwell

(1925–)

Howard C. Caldwell, Jr.'s easygoing, boyish charm is well known in the Indianapolis area, where he spent much of his career as a newscaster and anchor at WFBM-TV (WRTV). He had come a long way from the enthusiastic young radio fan who worried that his shyness might keep him from becoming a broadcaster. An Irvington native, Caldwell received his degree in journalism at Butler University. He worked as a reporter on the Hagerstown Exponent *before moving to his first radio job at station WTHI in Terre Haute in 1952. When WTHI acquired a television station in 1954, Caldwell made the transition to the new medium, working for a time in both radio and television. Soon he was anchoring the late television news. In 1959 he went to WFBM-TV in Indianapolis as news editor and produced the newscasts that he anchored for the early and late evening news shows. Caldwell's well-honed journalistic skills came to the fore in the 1980s with his award-winning commentaries and* Howard's Indiana, *a twelve-year film series that took him all over the state. Highly regarded for his involvement in the community during his career, Caldwell has continued in that role since his retirement from WRTV in 1994. Caldwell's home was decorated for the Christmas holidays when he was interviewed in December 1996.*

I think of radio growing up in Indianapolis as sort of a rare thing because there were only two stations operating—AM stations—plus Cincinnati moving in here in the 1930s. As a kid I was awed by this, and I suppose it made my mental processes come alive, but I didn't know it at the time. I was caught up in a lot of the kid shows and all of that. When radio came along in the 1920s, it was pretty much entertainment. . . . Although I started out in it as a communicator, [by the mid-1950s] I guess I thought of [radio] more as background music and something you turned on in the car. Maybe I was just too preoccupied by television [when] that came along. I'm sure radio brought us all closer in some ways. But for me, it was just sort of a background thing for music mainly. Now, if I'm in the car and I want to know [something], I go to the [radio] news and see what's happening, quickly.

I guess the one [change in broadcasting] that's the most startling to me, and affected me the most, is the growth of the news. When I started out in the business, news was just a little thing in television. And while it was accepted in radio, in television it was more of a novelty. And in the 1950s in Terre Haute, I can remember our general manager saying, "Well, we have the news because it's a prestige thing. We're not going to make any money on it. We're going to lose money on it, but we want to do this." Because at the time, there was more entertainment programming locally, and news was just a small chunk of that. So that's the thing that has been most dramatic to me. Now, we have hours of news—twenty-four hours of news.

[Broadcasting] was something I wanted to do, and my dad always said, "Be sure that whatever you end up doing, you enjoy it. It's fun to earn money, but it's worse not to enjoy what you're doing." He enjoyed what he was doing all of his life. My dad [had] seen experiences where people who owned businesses hired sons, and it was more of a negative than a positive. (In the advertising agency business, as you may well know, segments of that agency could walk away and form another agency and take their clients, because it is such a fragmented kind of a thing. Each account executive has their little turf.) In fact, there was a turning point, because, when I got out of the navy along with the radio thing and we were casting about, Dad came up there to Great Lakes. He was on a business trip to Chicago. He'd been in the navy himself, and he loved seeing Great Lakes. I gave him a little tour, and we had dinner, and I said, "Dad, maybe it's time for me to give this [advertising] agency thing a try."[40] He looked at me and said, "I don't think it's the right time. You went over to Waukegan, and you auditioned for somebody, and they encouraged you. I think you ought to try that first." That was the best advice I ever had.

Of course, a social consciousness comes along as you deliver news, and you're aware of the plight of an awful lot of people in not very desirable circumstances. And I think you do become [more aware], unless you are just completely able to mouth things and not think about them, and I couldn't do that. I think you end up caring. You're aware of things more than you would be otherwise.

Through the years, particularly on the network level now, we've had these accusations that it's all a liberal establishment, or some sort of conspiracy to influence the way things go in this world and this country. I've never bought that because I've seen how news works. It's a fragmented thing. There are so many people involved; reporters are out on their own seeing things, and there are many different backgrounds and different thoughts and ideas. So maybe there is somebody who comes back to the shop that wants to shape that story a little bit, but I've never felt any overall conspiracy of any kind. There are just too many people [with differing views] in the business.

But I also would say that the viewers have become so perceptive that they challenge [news reporters], and stations can only live by their ratings and their sponsors, really.

[As a boy] I was an avid radio listener. I kept logs on the programs that I would hear, and when the time changed in the summers, I would always revise all of that. But I would listen definitely to certain broadcasts. I was fascinated by the play-by-play in baseball. I was fascinated by the soap operas, and by the kid shows, and then by all those wonderful evening shows of *Jack Benny* and the *Lux Radio Theater*. My dad loved *Lum and Abner*. (They were Sigma Chis.) That was a regular in our household, and that was only fifteen minutes every night. But the other thing—Dad was a friend of Weir Cook who was a World War I ace hero who flew for Eddie Rickenbacker.[41] Dad and Weir Cook worked up a kids' show and sold it to WLW-Cincinnati, and it was re-creations of things that happened to Weir Cook. (He flew with Quentin Roosevelt, who was killed in the war, and all these other interesting people.) They had professional actors doing that. But Weir Cook also was on the program and actually mixed in with the actors, and I thought it was great at the time, of course. They got a sponsor for it which was Pennant Syrup. And that was [in] Columbus, Indiana. Pennant Syrup was the product—maple. So they called it *Weir Cook and His Pennant Flying Corps*. I went down there one day [to WLW] on a spring break to see all this in action; it was presented live—fifteen minutes, twice a week. I know that contributed to my awe and my fascination with radio and broadcasting.

I've always had this attraction—as I think I said earlier, when I was a kid, I was a big radio listener. I was fascinated by the idea of radio, [but] I never thought in terms of news and radio, because I wasn't exposed to much news on radio, I guess, until the war when I was older. But as a kid, I had these double interests. I was fascinated by the idea of working for a newspaper someday or maybe being in the broadcast business some way. I didn't quite know how or where, but just the idea. When I got into high school and got with a speech teacher who was innovative, he came up with a radio announcing course. Of course, I just rushed into that and everybody said, "Oh, you have a pretty nice voice. You ought to do something." All I was thinking of was being an announcer, because that was the most visible thing about radio of the day. The local personalities were announcers, and they introduced some music.

Howard Caldwell enlisted the aid of glamorous actress Vivian Blaine to raise money during a telethon at WTHI.

A youthful Howard Caldwell delivered the news from a solitary desk in the mid-1950s. WRTV-6

Caldwell and Ken Beckley broadcast together as the team approach to news gained popularity. Beckley began his career as a reporter/anchor at WTHI-TV in Terre Haute in 1963. He left for WLOS-TV in Asheville, North Carolina, in 1965 and moved to WRTV in Indianapolis in 1967 where he continued as a newscaster until 1976.   WRTV-6

Caldwell and Les Walden visited the Taj Mahal in India while waiting for an opportunity to interview Indira Gandhi in 1964.   WRTV-6

They weren't called deejays or anything, but they read commercials and they made station breaks, and they did things like that. Well, I remember my dad one time sitting looking at me at the dinner table, and somebody was there who I had taken a course with at Northwestern [University]. This was after the war, and we were all talking—this fellow had just joined WIRE—and Dad says, "Well, I guess that's what Howard wants to do; he just wants to be an announcer" [laughs], which didn't seem very challenging to my father.

I went to school after the war in the late 1940s. At the time there were a few broadcast courses coming along, but most of them were geared to production and programming and not the news. If you wanted to be in news, you were in journalism. Since then that's changed, and they've got a merging of journalism and broadcasting. They have broadcast journalism classes and so forth. But I always was glad, because when I ended up in broadcasting in 1952, I had this background of a lot of journalism courses. I thought in terms of what the writing was about, and what to look for. . . . I was farther ahead than I would have been if I'd just had the broadcast courses.

I was hired at WTHI-Radio in Terre Haute [in 1952], because I had a journalism degree. It took me a long time to find somebody who was willing to let that be enough to hire me because the first question was usually, "How many hours have you been on the air?" I'd say, "Well, not really any professionally." But I found a man who was looking for somebody that knew something about news, and he decided a degree from Butler University was okay. So I was hired to cover news, to cover beats and write, and they did audition me. And they said, "Well, we think maybe you could end up on the air."

[Shyness] was a concern. That's why I never thought seriously I would be in television, and I'm not sure I would have been, if it hadn't walked in the door. That's what happened in Terre Haute. After eighteen months, it walked in the door. I had a general manager there, [Joe Higgins], who was very encouraging, a good motivator. He liked to challenge me and encourage me, and I think that helped. In my [first] eighteen months of being on the air, he was the kind of boss that said, "If you want to make more money, why not do more things?" So when the sportscaster walked out, the two of us who were in the news department divided up his sports obligations. I started in play-by-play

basketball, which lasted for two seasons, and there was ad-libbing there, which was wonderful, and that was eighty games a season. Two seasons of that really loosened me up, too. By the time TV was there, I felt ready. I really felt ready. When I think back, [without that] eighteen months, I never would have figured what I could do.

I'm pretty sure that when we started out, [the title] was just "newscaster." And at some point the "anchor" came. I'm not sure that we even called them "anchors" when I came to Channel 6 news. I was hired there to be an anchor, to be the assistant news director, and then to be a reporter as needed. That all went for awhile until the late schedule came, and I was put on the late news as well as the early news. In fact, we were producers too, so it got to be pretty much an inside job, as we would say, until the mid-1970s when we could split off and producers became a separate job.

[Eventually, television news went to] dual anchors, and Channel 8 was doing that first. I remember that Mike Ahern was doing it with Rolland Smith and somebody before that in the early 1970s and maybe late 1960s. No, I guess it goes back before that, because we actually started doing it in 1970. I anchored that hour alone for four years, and then in 1970, Ken Beckley joined me on the early evening news. I can remember thinking, "Hmm," you know. But, that made it better because, still being the producer, I could get a chance to check something while the other guys were reading. When we went to the hour in 1966, we began to introduce the sports guy. At first, the weather guy was at the weather set rather than sitting with us, but the sports guy was always sitting with us. That's when that interplay began. In 1973 I joined Ken on the late news. I had been taken off the late news when we went to the hour, because they said, "You are managing editor now."

I think the [importance of the] personality [of the newscaster] came with the length of the added time, certainly. We didn't have time to fool around there when we only had ten or fifteen minutes to do a newscast, and we were trying to get everything in. But as the time got greater, I think it was encouraged by management to warm up a little. But the philosophy when I came to Channel 6 was "We are a news team; nobody is above anybody else here; we're all together in this." We always felt that if we did the best job of news coverage, then we'd get the viewers. Well, that's okay up to a point, but there are an awful lot of viewers that go with the personality.

This market kind of has a reputation [that] the longer you stay, the more likely you are to be accepted—and if you're a native it helps. Channel 13 went through all of these changes. They were always bringing somebody in who was going to shake up the market. Paul Udell was promoted as "the man with the legs that would cover the news; he won't just sit behind the anchor desk." He lasted about a year and a half. Finally, Channel 13 settled in with Tom Cochrun who had gone to Warren Central High School and Anne Ryder who had grown up in Indianapolis. At Channel 8, Mike Ahern grew up in Indianapolis. I grew up in Indianapolis; it was just funny. I don't know if that's unique to this market or not, but it might be.

Now, Bob Gamble was the boss of the news department. There's no question about that. It was different than it had been in Terre Haute, where I worked with the general manager. Now, I had a good relationship with the general manager. I could always go up there and talk to him about things if I wanted to, but I had to be careful, because Bob Gamble was my immediate boss. We were about the same age; I had to be careful about that. We had, I figured, about eleven full-time people and a couple of part-timers. This was the spring of 1959, and they were servicing AM radio as well as television then.

Then Time-Life [the owners in 1957] said, "We want to build a better [news] department, a stronger [news] department." Eldon [Campbell] found Bob and said, "You do it." And so all sorts of things happened during the 1960s, for which I think we all look back with considerable pride. We set up a "beat system," and they weren't doing that in Indianapolis in broadcasting. It was just sort of a hit-and-miss kind of a situation—at least that's the way it seemed to be to me. And we added reporters, experienced reporters, people who could get out and cover beats. Bob was far more knowledgeable about the photographic aspects than I was. He knew what he wanted. He wanted good news people who could get the film, get these things, and he was very demanding about what we did. This film had to be carefully edited, and it had to be carefully scripted (which I had done in Terre Haute) scene by scene, and this was his specialty. He was constantly critiquing and constantly demanding that it be done better. So it became a very professional organization. Then we were

early into editorials. Bob did them with an editorial board, and he got into some areas that had not been dealt with much here. One was civil rights and the racial problems here in Indianapolis, and we had some criticism and some controversy going there. He [Bob] got some national awards for those things. He also wanted documentaries, and the station cleared network time. We aired them on prime time, and one of them was called *The Negro in Indianapolis*. (You wouldn't say "Negro" today, but that's what we said then.) It was a three-part series. There was also one done on the lack of public housing in this city, because there were all of those years when the leadership said, "No, we don't want any of that federal money." And we got into the segregation problems in the school system. I was not directly involved in these things. I was on the day-to-day operation of getting the newscast, but Jim Hetherington was brought in, and he was the author of a number of these things. He also got into the editorial area. Allen Jeffries was brought in. He also worked in the editorial area. So, there were some very prestigious awards that came to WFBM in those years based on subject areas and based on the photography. There were national awards involved there.[42] That was a new level for Indianapolis at that time for television. Right in the midst of it, in the middle 1960s, we went to the hour, early evening, local news, which was a first. Channel 8 came on with it two years later. Then years later in 1987, we were the first to go ninety minutes on the early evening news. I can't claim that for early morning, because Channel 8 and Channel 13 were ahead of us on all of that in the 1980s. I guess if you want to talk about a glory era, the 1960s for Channel 6 would be that, and the ratings reflected it.

But the 1960s forced us [to discover our strengths] because of the Vietnam War and the civil rights uprising and the presidential assassination and the assassination of other prominent people. And so, we had to make a decision there [on controversial issues]. We were either going to get into the thing or stand off. And we jumped in. The public didn't quite know what to make of it either. The public felt that many things we talked about, because we talked about them, it was going to make [things] worse, particularly in the matter of racial relations. We got some nasty phone calls, and I was proud that we held our ground on it. Maybe there were times when we went too far. As I said, the audience out there is always a test.

WFBM-TV newsmen Allen Jeffries and Jim Green (seated) broadcast from the City Room of the Indianapolis Star *during the station's coverage of a presidential election in the 1960s.* THE INDIANAPOLIS STAR AND NEWS

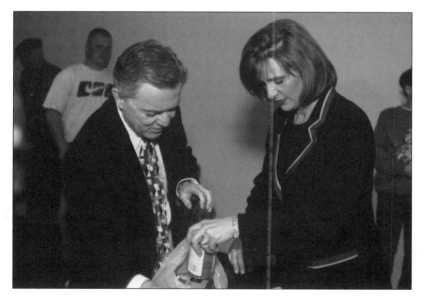

As a part of community outreach, Mike Ahern and Debby Knox helped at WISH-TV's annual holiday can and toy drive. Ahern, who joined WISH in 1967, does commentary on current events besides anchoring the 24-hour News-8. Knox began her career in northern Indiana and came to WISH in 1980, joining Ahern at the news desk soon after her arrival.

JOHN REKIS, WISH-TV

Tom Cochrun and Kim Hood coanchored the news at WTHR. After nine years as an anchor, Cochrun's work in documentaries led him to leave broadcasting to start his own production company in 1995.

ROD PORTER, WTHR

After the jobs of news director and producer became separate positions, Caldwell had more time to develop personalized stories. Somebody finally said, "Why don't you do a little [reflective series on life in Indiana]. I mean you've grown up here, and you're interested in history." That was just great; that put a lot of things together, so I began searching out some things in my head, "Oh, why don't I do this or that?" So I did a story about the Scottish Rite [Cathedral], and I got interesting reactions. People would say, "I've driven by that building for years, and I didn't really—I just moved to Indianapolis a few years ago, and I wondered just what [it was]." And so, that was fun. I did a little tour around to see what's there and what's that all about—Booth Tarkington's home up on North Meridian . . . and then Meredith Nicholson's home over on Delaware, some of those things—authors, people of the past who had done things in Indiana. Then we began to go on trips, and we could just go a lot of directions—a little old funny general store or someplace in a town. I began to get letters from people, "Why don't you do such and such about such a thing?" We had a helicopter at the time; that was fun. Sometimes the days were long because we had to get going early in the morning, and I was still doing the late news. But it was a fun thing to do. One of the things that resulted from that was a little series on the Wabash River; we flew clear over into Ohio where it started. We did a five-part series and did different segments, and went all the way until it went into the Ohio—got in boats, talked to people. So it was just a conglomeration of things that usually had a historic aspect to them. Sometimes it was built on an individual, like a Herman B Wells, or somebody that I thought was just very special that I wanted to talk to.[43]

[*Howard's Indiana*] started in 1980, and then about the mid-1980s, they kind of said, "Well, we don't know." I said, "Well, maybe it's run its course." I sort of got away from it; then a couple of years later, they came back to me and said, "We've decided we had some faulty information in our ratings, and we'd like you to reinstitute it." So I went back to it again. By this time I was doing the *Perspectives,* too. Now, *Howard's Indiana* took a lot of time because there was a day of traveling, and then there was a day of just looking at all of the stuff that was shot, logging it, writing it, recording it, and then doing it on the air.

[My interview with Indira Gandhi] was part of a series that the Time-Life ownership initiated so that several of us had an opportunity to do something in another part of the world. It was a great opportunity. Gamble had done one—went to the Berlin Wall. And Gene Slaymaker, the radio news editor at the time, had done one in South America regarding the hunger and some of the deplorable conditions down in the South American countries. [Dave McGhee and photographer Dick Baldwin went behind the Iron Curtain in Europe for a documentary.] When my turn came along, we talked about Vietnam and India. Just before we left, the prime minister of India, Shastri, had a heart attack and died while in a meeting with Russians at Tashkent, and that's when Indira Gandhi ultimately became the prime minister. So we revised all of our trip at the last minute and headed right for New Delhi and spent a week doing things—stories about India, but all of the time trying to get an appointment with Mrs. Gandhi. Time-Life had a bureau there of two men, which didn't hurt us, and there also was a cover story about her in *Time* magazine, which came out rather favorably, but they never really had a personal interview. So all of this fell together finally after one week. We went to her modest home. (She was like director of information or something in India.) We spent about a half an hour of interview time with her, and that's how that came about.

[This was in] New Delhi. She hadn't moved into her new quarters, and she, of course, was the daughter of Nehru. (There was always confusion about that because her [married] name was Gandhi. [No direct link to Mahatma Gandhi.]) The taxicab driver—it was dark when we got to her home. He took us to the former home of Mahatma Gandhi, so then we had to get that clarified, partly because of our English, I suppose. But we were not given any restrictions; we were not asked to submit the questions in advance or anything. She just came in, sat down and we talked. I was very pleased because Chester Bowles, who was our ambassador to India at the time, wanted to know his questions in advance. And I never wanted to do that. A portion of that interview was aired on the *Today Show*. We were NBC at the time, and really we were the first to interview her after she became prime minister. I had thought about this for so long—but by the time the interview occurred, I don't think I used [my prepared questions]. I mean, things sort of came together, and she was a very charming person and very easy to talk to.

It seems to me that radio, particularly here in Indianapolis, was pretty timid about covering local news. They weren't very aggressive about it. Maybe because it didn't produce enough dollars at the time, but it was the 1950s before they even started doing local things But I guess we always point to the JFK days in which it was sort of hands-off the president's personal life, and I think that applied to most major candidates at the time. It was just not considered part of the deal. But that has changed. And I think it's changed a lot because of the competitiveness of the business. [There] just wasn't that competitive attitude at the time.

I'd like to think that television's absorption into news and public affairs has enhanced the mind of the typical American, as far as information is concerned. All of this information is bubbling forth—culturally, politically, and entertainment, and in all sorts of things. You don't have to be wealthy; everybody has access to this [news and information] for the most part. I mean if you can come up with fifty or sixty dollars for a little television set, you're there;

you're tuned in. And if you want to make the most of it, you can. I'm sure that along the way, there's an awful lot of negatives. There's bound to be, because every aspect of life almost is thrown at you. You have to be selective, and you have to think about this. You can just let [yourself] be carried away with all of the nastiness, all the violence, all the sexual activities that are offered to you. But I guess if you want to, if you really want to make the most of it, you can become much better educated in the process. And I think television has done that.

Every once in awhile I think, "Well, it was sort of a miracle that all of this came together, because it doesn't come together for everybody"—the timing and some of the things that just happened to me. Television walked in the door. I didn't have to go out and scrounge and look for that (I'm not sure I would even have had the nerve to do that.) The whole thing just adds up to a great deal of happiness.

Barbara A. Boyd (ca. 1990)

WRTV-6

Barbara Boyd

(1929–)

Barbara A. Boyd, with her outgoing personality and cheery smile, became a local celebrity during her twenty-five-year career as a consumer reporter at WRTV (WFBM-TV). Born and raised in Evanston, Illinois, she had dreamed of becoming an actress and had studied radio and television, but it was not until she was forty years old that she auditioned for a job on TV. When Boyd joined WFBM in 1969, not only was she one of the few women in television, she also is credited with being the first African-American woman on television in Indiana. She handled general news assignments and feature stories until Bob Gamble made her one of the first local consumer reporters. Still, she describes her stint as anchor on the noon news from 1981 to 1984 as a highlight of her career. Never one to be shy, Boyd dared to address subjects such as breast cancer and discrimination practices like redlining in her consumer segments. With her unusual warmth and humor, she was able to strike a chord with her audience that few reporters could match. Boyd's interview took place in her home on the north side of Indianapolis in November 1996.

Barbara Boyd is definitely known as "the consumer reporter." However, I think I was on TV for about two or three years before anybody really knew who I was. Plus, it takes time to get established. I mean, you heard a lot of [my] voice, because I did a lot of voice-over. But I think doing the story on my own mastectomy from my hospital bed sorta launched me. And I think that every reporter has that kind of story. You know, something that puts a stamp on you says, "Hey, I wanna listen to that person again," 'cause of what they did. Anything after that was, "That's a Barbara Boyd kind of piece." And that's when people began to call and say, "Hey Barb, I'm doin' so and so and so. You're into that consumer stuff and"—you become identified with your beat. . . . And you'll find that people will call you because they find that you are credible.

On the part of myself, I'm pretty sure I was hired as a dual token—female and as an African American. I don't think I would still remain there all those years because of that—because I think I did a good job. And I don't think, given the kind of bosses that I had, you couldn't stay there if you weren't doing your share.

When I first started, there were a couple of years that I was the only female in the newsroom. Not that it was all bad you understand [laughs], but it just seems like all of a sudden you saw a woman producer, another one director—you know, outside of the secretary—then the reporters were slowly added. Then, I think, the other changes were the way we did stories—

the involvement of the reporter to become identified with stand-ups—stand-up opens and closes. And then came the franchise pieces: I was the consumer reporter; [Reid] Duffy had *Duffy's Diner,* and Jack Rinehart did *City-County.* Everybody [operated in] a beat kind of system, because you are definitely responsible for something in that area each and every day—well, franchise meaning that there was Jack, Duffy, Barbara, and Ben Morriston—Ben Morriston with his *Call for Help.* Those were franchise pieces. And the attitude towards women in the business—there used to be a big joke about "get the broads out of broadcasting." You know, joke, joke, joke, joke [laughs]. But all of a sudden, you know—not all of a sudden; it was gradual, and it was so subtle. You know, it just sorta oozed in, and the old guard just sorta oozed out. And all of a sudden you looked up, and it was a whole new kind of young and, you know, women.

We started doing consumer reports back in the 1970s. Community awareness. I mean, we started that consumerism. I was the only one doing it for several years, you see. We started it about 1972, maybe 1971, 1972; just getting the good news out; making sure everybody was up to date on consumer things. What's new, what's old, what to look out for, blah blah blah. The other reporters—because that was their area—had the expertise, and they were able to maybe be the first ones out there with what was happening in their particular area. So, I think it was positive in a way that you knew that you would always get the first and the best, the most comprehensive, complete [coverage] from a franchise reporter. However, there is a down side. You get in a niche, and that's where people expect you to stay.

I just thought [television] was something that I'd always wanted to do, because I was in theater and speech and I wanted to be in movies. This is the next best thing to it, you know, to be on *television.* But it never dawned on me that I was breaking ground, that I was gonna be held up as a role model, that people would be watching what you do and watching your progress. I just went on and did what I had to do and enjoyed. For an example, some woman [might stop me and say], "Hi, Barbara Boyd." "Oh, hi, how's church?" I couldn't figure out how she knew me other than that maybe she was in my church. It just didn't dawn on me that people recognized me from TV. Then it started to sink in, and I had to start blocking off

time when I'd go out, 'cause people would stop and talk to you. People would often say, "Hi, Barbara, and I hope you don't mind that I call you Barbara, because I've been listening to you for so long, it just feels like you're a member of the family." And you do just wanna stop and talk to people because without them [laughs], you wouldn't be anywhere. You know what I'm sayin'?

I always used to say to interns or students, journalism students, "You have to be very careful what you say and how you say it because people listen and hang on to every—if you are a credible person—*every word you say.*" It dawned on me one day after a story . . . how powerful our words are, how careful we have to be about what we say and how we say it, because it affects young ones who are watching and old ones who are taking advice from me.

I think that [reporters] *do* have to be responsible. But you see, what happens is, it starts with the hiring of a person, and how much the boss or the person hiring trusts the judgment of that reporter. In a sense, nobody ever checks your work, really. You're sent out to do a story, and it's assumed that you will have good judgment. It's assumed that if you feel that you're going to have something that's controversial, you'll go to management or to the lawyers and say, "Hey, if I say *this,* is it gonna get us into trouble?" If you go out there and you blow it, then there are consequences. Then you've been irresponsible. You know, Bob Gamble knew what his standards were. He knew that you don't bring no, in his own words, "You don't bring no crap." You check it. You recheck it, and then if you find that it's not right come to me and we'll talk about it. He knew when he hired people, he knew he passed on his standards. And everybody knew that. They knew Bob didn't take any crap and that he was a pure journalist, and he wanted the best every reporter had to offer. And if you didn't do that—everybody'd shiver when he said, "You got a minute?"—'cause you came in and you knew you were gonna get reamed.

I think television really tells a lot, you know, facial expressions. They say that people can look at you on TV and tell whether you're an honest kind of person, whether you're credible and that kind of thing. Aside from the educational requirements—I don't even think all that's really necessary—I think that personality, honesty, and a sense of knowing right from wrong, knowing how to write well, all those skills—thinking, judgment, sincerity, loyalty—all those things [are the most important]. I think that the one thing people always said about Barbara is "You know, she's for real. She's Barbara." And I think people sense when you're sincere. And with the kind of things that I did, what was not to be sincere about?

I remember when we got a TV and a black person came on TV, everybody ran to the living room. "Ooh!" Of course, they were mainly entertainers. "Look at [Nat] King Cole, and look at, oh, so-and-so!" And you'd just sorta stand around—I mean it was just the greatest thing since apple pie! And as it went on, and you saw the Max Robinsons and—it's just like me. I never thought that I would be in television, because there just wasn't that opportunity. I never even thought about being—of course, when I was comin' up there wasn't any television, you know. [Now], you see Bernard Shaw; you see Carole Simpson. And when I go out to speak now to African-American students I tell 'em, "Hey, your shot is just as great now. I mean, the opportunities, the doors are [open]. The industry is there." Whether or not you can get in is something else. But I think it gives them hope. And I have kids come up to me say, "Hey, you're my role model, and I figured if you could do it at forty." . . . And it gives them that kind of hope that they too can do it. And I'm not gonna say it's gonna be easy. Nobody will get in television the way I did it. I mean, that kind of day is gone. "Well, shall we try her?" Now it's—gotta have all the qualifications, gotta tow the rope, and even still, you may not make it. It's hard for blacks *or* whites to get on TV. You know, when I was getting in, every station had two—two African Americans. That seems to have been it—two, everybody. Now, even here locally everybody has about five or six—on air. That doesn't include the ones behind the scenes.

I was born and reared in Evanston, Illinois, home of Northwestern University. Went to Evanston Township High School—graduated from there. I always wanted to be a movie star. I went to the theater every single Saturday. In Evanston, we lived about a block from the post office. I'd go down there at night. I'd be Ginger Rogers, and I had my tap dancing shoes [laughs]. And I had this full skirt, and I'd go down, and nobody'd be in there, you see. The floors were marble, and I'd tap dance, you know [makes tapping sound]. Doin' my Ginger Rogers bit. . . . I went to University of Illinois, went to Roosevelt and [Indiana University], and then went to Columbia School of Tele-

vision and Radio in Chicago. Moved here to Indianapolis in 1962 with my husband Ted Boyd, who came to Evanston in 1951 as Boys' Work Secretary of Emerson YMCA. Then he became the executive director there.

When 1969 rolled around, Channel 6 was doing a documentary on Indianapolis. And within the documentary they included a Head Start classroom. So they went to a Head Start classroom to do the filming. I told Ted, I can just see this in the big boardroom. "Ah, do we have any—you know I think it's time we had some 'colored' women on TV. Let's go interview that lady in that classroom." And so sure enough they called; they wanted to interview the woman in the classroom where they had filmed for the documentary. But when they phoned, I got the phone call. So before we put any calls through to the classroom you sorta screened it. So I asked the guy, I said, "What do you want? May I ask the nature of your call?" So he said, "Well, we're in the process of auditioning African-American women." (Naw, it wasn't "African-American;" it was "black" then. It might even have been "Negro" [laughs].) So anyway, I was joking and I said, "Well honey, if you're lookin' for a star, here I are" [laughs]. So he said, "Would you be interested?" I said, "Well, sure. What do I have to do?" So he said, "Just a little five- or six-minute vignette on anything you'd like." So anyway, I did something on the office since I was the office manager. Did a little stand-up—a little walk here, a little walk there—went to each of the girls, you know, several girls' desks and talked about their role in Head Start. And then I did a stand-up close about what my role was, to pull it all together. "We're a little cog in the big wheel." Then I had to go to the station to read a script, a new script—an audition. That's exactly what it was. [In all, eight women were auditioned including the classroom teacher.] So one day Ted and I are driving [and I said], "I'll probably be working there one day." So he said, "Yeah, right." But sure enough, February 10, 1969 rolled around, and I was the one that got the spot. So I got the job. I walked into this room. (You know I really didn't care whether I got this job or not, right? 'Cause I got me a big job. I mean, I'm makin' seven thousand dollars a year. You know, I'm the executive secretary!) So I go off into the room and, honey, there are seven white men sittin' up in the room. Well, [there was] Jerry Chapman, Warren Wright, Earl Johnson, Bob Gamble, Casey Strange, and Steve Scott, who was black. He was the public affairs director. He used to be on radio—Steve Larue, on radio. And it was Steve that sort of encouraged me to really try out. So, honey, they're in there interviewin' me and, huh, I don't remember whether Eldon was there or not. I don't remember. So we were getting ready to leave, and Bob Gamble and I come to the door at the same time. (And I used to see Bob doin' the editorials all the time. I know now that I used to watch Channel 6.) So I looked up at Bob, always so bald. (I used to comment, you know, "Why don't you put some powder on his head?" 'Cause it always just *shined*, you know.) So I looked up at him and said, "Hmm, you do have hair!" [laughs] "Gosh!" And finally he ends up bein' my boss. But he turned out to be a good buddy. He gave a lot of help—suggestions and so forth.

Jerry Chapman [hired me]. That's who I finally went in and had the final talk with. It was Jerry Chapman who at that time was on the radio and was the right-hand man on the left-hand side of Eldon Campbell. I think that somebody made a conscious effort and said, "Hey, it's time for some breakthroughs." And Channel 6 made that step, which I think was sort of cool and sort of brave, 'cause—I think it was initiated by Eldon Campbell. It just took somebody with courage to do that. I mean, it takes courage on every level—to do something where no man's gone before. Just like when they wanted to put me on as anchor. "Will the white community accept her?" Or, just like when they didn't want two females to anchor, "Nobody will accept that." That's what I was told when [I was trying for] the noon show. By the way, I was the first [female] anchor of the *noon* show—not the newscast, the noon show, not prime time. Tina Cosby was the first to do prime time. Let me see, when Ben Morriston was taken off the noon show, I had always filled in for anybody that was absent on that show—always had been told I did a great job. And then when it came time to fill in, I didn't get the spot. (This was in the early 1980s.) Well, I didn't get that spot. I went in and talked to Bob about it—says, "Some reason I wasn't considered for the noon anchor spot?" He says, "Well, you already have a segment." You know, I produced a five-minute segment every day on the noon show. So I said, "No, you're not hearin' what I'm sayin'. I want to know why I wasn't considered for the anchor position." So he says to me, "Two women at noon?" And I said, "Four white males at six?" There just wasn't that kind of thinking then to have two women. It

still is pretty much that way. You don't very often see two women. It used to be, I think, [Channel] 13 used to do it for a while. Once in a while it'll be that way but not very often.

I loved [doing the noon news]. Oh, I thought it was the best of all worlds. I got a chance to anchor as well as continue [the consumer reports]—have something on the five o'clock, and go home at 6:00. It was just—it was wonderful! That's why I never understood the premise about most people consider you to be the consumer reporter so we don't want you to anchor. See I was doing both. I mean, just like Clyde [Lee] anchors and does medical reports, just like Debby [Knox] anchors and does medical reports.

Eldon Campbell was a real mentor for Boyd and set the tone for the station. Honey, [he was] fantastic, for real, brilliant. I don't care where you were, or who he was with. I mean, it could've been the president of the United States, or president of the broadcast division, Eldon Campbell's gonna say, "Hi there, Barbara! Hi, John! Hi, Jack!," or, "Hi, Clyde!"—the janitor, anybody. Everybody. That man made you feel like you were the most important person at that station. He was the kind of guy, even though he was the GM [general manager], you could just go in, sit down and talk to him. I've found that a lot of people are uncomfortable around their boss. I don't know, it's probably because I was open. But I felt like, hey, he's a guy—puts on his pants like my daddy. I could just go in and talk to him. . . . Of course, now, there were times you talked to Eldon and you didn't quite know what he was talking about [laughs]. He assumed that you knew what he was talking about. And you just said, "Uh, well, okay." That's right. "And of course, you know so-and-so," and you never knew who "so-and-so" was. "He was the one that did such and such." Yeah boy! And you'd go, "Yeah, okay Eldon." He was a great man. And I never give a speech without mentioning him and what he gave me. 'Cause he'd always say to me—and he'd see me in the hall and he'd say, "Hey Barbara! You havin' fun?" And I'd say, "*Yes.*" Hell, I was happy to be there. And then I finally asked him, "Why d'you ask me that all the time?" And he said, "Well, you know when people finally get an opportunity to do something they always wanted to do, or something they thought they'd like to do, and now that you're here I ask you, 'Are you having fun?'" And the answer was the same first day as the day I left. I had fun from the first day I got there.

Viewers came to know consumer reporter Barbara Boyd by her signature line, "Have a great day and stay on top of the world." She always liked to end her reports on a pleasant note.

When WFBM hired Carl Stubblefield, he was the first African American on television in Indianapolis. WRTV-6

Bob Gamble brought a high standard to the news department at WFBM when he arrived there in 1959. Here he broadcast election returns ca. 1960 with Howard Caldwell at the desk. PHOTO BY RAY CONOLLY

At age sixteen Barbara Boyd appeared on Rubins's Stars of Tomorrow *on WGN in Chicago.*

I gotta say guys gave me a lot of help. I didn't know beans about how to write a script; I didn't know how to stand. Had it not been for Allen Jeffries and Jim Hetherington to tell me about all the little ins and outs of the business—I had no idea how to write a script when I started there. I didn't even know what I was gonna do. I'm tellin' you, that Allen Jeffries was the brightest man in the world. He was assistant editorial writer. Jim Hetherington did editorials and Allen Jeffries was his assistant—had the greatest voice in the world. He was a big announcer on radio. I don't care what you would ask Jeff, he knew the answer. I mean, if he didn't know it, he knew where to go get it. And, of course, Jim Hetherington was just plain bright. I'm sittin' back there with the mental giants of the world—little pea-pod me [laughs]. Guys like that helped me along the way. Bob Gamble in his own way helped. Bob was a pure news person. He didn't think I'd last, because when I started doing consumer stuff and features like that, that wasn't his shot. His shot was hard news. Of course, that's when TV sorta began to change. Features were being brought in, something to soften the hard news angle at the end of the day, [to leave you] with a smooth taste in your mouth. And television was beginning to change into happy-talk kind of stuff. I don't think he cared for that too much. As a matter of fact he told me, "I really don't think you'll last around here too long."

Nobody likes to say it, but they'll still always want to opt to give the *guy* the hard story, the big story. I mean, you really gotta fight for it. Of course, I didn't care. I didn't particularly care for hard stories so it wasn't a problem for me. But there are some women who don't like to do features, because they do not want to be considered as a "fluff reporter." That didn't bother me. I always felt that there had to be something pleasant in a newscast. . . . Some people get very upset, sayin' they don't have the hard news story. They're not number one or number two. But I always looked at it this way. Hey, I'm endin' up on a happy note. I'm the last one they hear, and they're gonna remember me [laughs].

It began to get hard toward the end, because you'd done it all. You've done it from every angle. But it's the twist *you* give the stories, the twist the *reporter* gives that story, the angle that they take that can make the difference. It's what you put into it. You know, being a reporter is sorta like being a priest. Your story has to be as mean-

ingful and as fresh as the first time you take communion. Like the first time the priest gives communion has to be as meaningful . . . as the last time. And that's the way it has to be with a story. Nobody cares that you had a fight with your husband the night before or things didn't go right. They want the news—they want it on time, and they want it to be quality. And that's up to you, and they want you to be credible. That's up to you to deliver that, and schlepp all that other stuff aside.

What happens when you're in television is that you're exposed to so many more things than you would be if you were just a lay person. Everywhere, you're exposed to different kinds of charities. I did stories on the Salvation Army and so became a board member. And I had a breast cancer [operation]—somebody from Reach to Recovery came to see me, so I'm on the cancer board. What you find out is that there's so many needs when you go out and you're able to see so much. And I was always taught [that] when you can, or if you're able to, to share and to give something back to the community that has been so good to you. (And this community has been *very* good to me.) If being on a board or doing a fund-raiser for Oasis or Dayspring—whatever helps raise money to help somebody else. But you interact with people socially who help you get stories down the line.

See, I used to work in the English Foundation Building. We were seeing a film that was being presented by the American Cancer Society on how you should always do the self breast exam. And so I practiced that. When I found this lump, I pointed it out to my doctor, and he couldn't find it. I said, "Honey, it's there." Sure enough, he found it. I went to the station doctor. And I went to my gyn man [gynecologist], and then he sent me to a specialist. So the specialist said, "Well, let's plan on doing something Wednesday." I said, "Oh no, we can't do Wednesday. I'm going out of town on assignment. And on the weekend we're going up to Chicago for a party. I'll get with you when I get back" [laughs]. If I knew then what I know now [finger snap], I'd get in there just like that, 'cause it can spread, you know.

So while I was in the hospital, I was doing the story on Reach to Recovery, [a] support group for mastectomies. I figured, what better person to do it on than me? See, because in a lot of stories that I did, it involved me. When I did a story on Reach to Recovery, I never thought about the impact it would have on people. It just never dawned on me. But honey, we did that story on breast cancer. So I'm in there talkin' about how I practice self breast exam. (I'd had the surgery [but was] still in the hospital.) So I called Tom Read who was the assignment editor. I said, "You know Tom, I think I'd like to do a story on Reach to Recovery. You think that's possible?" He said, "Yeah, we can send a guy over." I said, "Okay, I'll write the script." . . . I finished the script and got it pretty well polished up. Jim Hoffman came the next day and the chick from Reach to Recovery came in. But prior to that, doing the stand-up—doing the sit-up in bed—I talked about how I practiced self breast examination [and about how] there was always the support afterwards. The woman from Reach to Recovery was there. And so we were going on. She was showin' me this prosthesis—I mean it was a *huge* prosthesis! So I punched it, you know. I said, "This is obviously for a larger lady, you know, bigger lady" [laughs]. And I learned then that a prosthesis is weighted for you against your other breast so you won't be lopsided! And we talked about things like that. And so honey, after that, oh the switchboard lit up. Lit up! Men were talkin' about—since this was on air, they felt free about talkin' to their wives about it. Wives felt they could talk to their husbands about it, and girlfriends could talk to their boyfriends. Now that it was on television, it was all right to talk about it. One man called up—said, "I know that Barbara Boyd does a lot, but this sittin' up in hospital sayin' she had this mastectomy—I think that's carryin' things too far. She just went too far." He thought I was just—I don't know what he thought. But then, people were saying what a great thing that was. From that, I traveled around the country going to different television stations talking about breast cancer. We did a half-hour show on it. We really enlightened. It was so funny. When I went in to Bob [Gamble], I said, "Bob, I'd like to do a half-hour show on breast cancer." He scratched his head, and he looked at me and said, "Well, do we have to use a *breast*?" [laughs]. I said, "Well Bob, I think if we're gonna talk about breast

cancer we do." We had oncologists on and other cancer specialists and did panel shows on it. It was really enlightening to go around the country and to talk about it. When Betty Ford came to town, I interviewed her. My entry to her was, "Say, bosom buddy" [laughs]. She laughed and said, "Oh, you too?" I said, "Oh yeah."

[During my career at Channel 6, I] didn't find [being an African American] a problem. I mean, nobody ever turned me down for a story because of it. Even in southern Indiana, where you'd think it would be the worst, I was always warmly greeted. There was always something in common we could talk about. You were a mother—we could talk about that. You're a grandmother—we could talk about that. I remember we went down there, we're doing a story [on a] woman who worked at Head Start. Oh, of course, I had worked at Head Start. We could talk about that. And of course, if you're a man, if you like to fish, we could talk about that. If you like to golf, we could talk about that. You always find something that you have in common with the person, sorta talk about that. That helps to relax them, you know. But, no, I've never had a problem.

I didn't realize the impact that [being an African-American woman on television] had. I didn't realize the importance of it. But then it dawned on me. I don't know—maybe it was my mother or my mother-in-law who was saying, "What a great responsibility. Young men and women, African-American men and women will be looking." And then I got to thinking, "Yeah, I do have quite a responsibility." But then, being a reporter, period, is a responsibility—doing the right thing, researching what you have; presenting a balanced report—you know, being credible. Because I am African American, they see that. They see the credibility. They see, "God, if she could do it, we can do it too." I have spoken to many high schools and universities and colleges, and I say to African Americans, "The doors are open. Get ready. There aren't gonna be any excuses any more." You know, "I didn't get a chance to do so-and-so." The doors are open. Get ready so when your opportunity comes, you can blow it all in.

Amos C. Brown III

Amos Brown

(1950–)

The interview of Amos C. Brown III took place in June 1996 in the fast-paced offices of Hoosier Radio and TV, where he is currently employed. Brown attended Northwestern University, and while there began his broadcasting career at WNUR-FM, a student-run radio station. After graduation in 1972, he worked for the National 4-H Services Committee before moving to WTLC in Indianapolis, where he quickly rose through the ranks. During his tenure as station manager, WTLC was known for its involvement in the African-American community through programming such as Like It Is, Operation Breadbasket, *and* Morning with the Mayor *and community drives such as* Baby Love for Healthy Babies *and* Just Tell It, *aimed at stopping violence. In an effort to correct misconceptions about black audiences, Brown conducted demographic studies of the African-American community, presenting his findings in a variety of forums in Indianapolis. In the 1980s WTLC won numerous awards and was known for its investigative journalism, especially in regard to the police department and its relationship with the African-American community. Yet when WTLC found itself in financial difficulties, the news department was eliminated, an announcement that did not go unnoticed; the* Indianapolis News *reported on 2 August 1992 that "the voice of the black community in Indianapolis got a little softer Friday." Changes in management followed, and Brown left two years later for Hoosier. Today he continues to be involved in broadcasting and also is contributing editor for the* Indianapolis Recorder.*

I was educated that the broadcaster—yeah you're in a business to make money, but you're also in a business to serve. I think today the stress is on business, and service to the community has really been taken over more by television than radio. Traditionally, it was the radio station that did the radio-thons, or led the way for the Community Chest, or [got] the community to go down and put tons of food in a truck to feed hungry people, and what have you. Today, it's television. I think that radio has become a jukebox with lip service to serving the community, as opposed to—it was different. It was almost like my first radio teacher at Northwestern. His standard stock phrase was, "Radio is a business." He drummed that in. He was the introductory course, and he drummed that in to everyone. And then we had an older professor (who was the chair of the department) that nobody liked, and nobody understood where he was coming from. He kept stressing the rules and the ethics. He would give a test. Every time he would give a test, he would somehow sneak in the rules and regulations of what constituted a legal lottery on the air: prize, consideration, and chance. If I remember nothing that has burned into my consciousness, those three elements were. We kind of joked about it when we were young, but looking back at it, you know we were being taught a certain ethic. And the ethic was, "Yes, it's a business, but it's also ethics, and it's also giving back in [kind]."

Brown recounts the story of WTLC's beginning as he learned it from the station's staff. [Before] WTLC started, [its] frequency was the classical music station, WAIV. That went on the air in 1961. A group of people who worked at Eli Lilly and Company somehow got the license. They played classical music. One of the people who was one of the owners of this WAIV was Norbert Neuss, who is the big who's-it at the Fine Arts Society. They were not making money with WAIV, and we're talking in the days of six- to three-, five-, six-, eight-dollar commercials—classical music—they weren't making anything. So they sold the station to a group of black and white investors locally that included Jim Beatty, Frank Lloyd, Pat Chavis, Jr., Paul Cantwell, I think [John] Hesseldenz.[44] I mean it was all of these folk in the local Democratic establishment at the time. Evidently, it was their goal to put on the first radio station to serve the Negro community full time. Up until that time there were stations that were doing part-time black on AM. WTLC goes on the air January 22, 1968, and supposedly within six to eight months, all of the other people who were doing part-time black got out of the format. They said, "Let's get the hell out of that." Just took the community by storm. Finally, something of our own, and a whole community that didn't have anything to hold of its own, had something. Now, it may not have been the greatest thing in the world.

Well, the owners started fussing. [The station] started at the Dearborn Hotel; moved from the Dearborn Hotel down to 1700 block of South Delaware—a business slum on a dead-end street next to a railroad track, next to a pickle factory—now, we're talking gutbucket neighborhood—slum industry. The first general manager was supposedly a white guy who I never met, but he is evidently a legend. He knew enough to hire good people and knew enough to keep it going, but he was torn. The owners were fighting among themselves. A lot of the fight had to do with—would WTLC be just a jukebox, or was it going to make some positive statements in the community? Within a year—either a year or around the start of the year 1970 (it was a license renewal year) Dr. [Frank] Lloyd and a

faction opposed the license renewal of his partners. With Frank was the attorney, Bob Davies, who at the time was a big wheel in Baker & Daniels, and Judy Barrett who was with Doctor Lloyd a long time, a nurse, administrative assistant in his practice and what have you. I don't know whether anybody else was with him at the time, but those were the major players. So it was basically Doctor Lloyd against everybody else. He went to the [Federal Communications] Commission and said, "They are not doing it right; I can do it better." These were in the days when anybody could walk in off the street and basically say, "I can operate this station better, and this is what I am going to do." This was in the days of quotas in terms of how much programming you were going to devote to news and public affairs. So you basically were outpromising the other guy. Well, this was a big fight and yelling and screaming and hollering and brouhaha and what have you. So finally before it got completely out of hand, the partners settled, and the other owners sold to Frank. So in the early part of 1973, Frank buys them out. The station became black owned, and that's when the Lloyd era began. Frank yet believed he was supposed to be in business, but he believed that WTLC existed to try to make a positive difference in the lives of the black community and in the community as a whole. He wanted to make a positive difference with the radio station. It was just a question of, okay, how the hell do you do that, and how do you make some money?

When I moved here, which was in 1975, obviously WIBC at that time was one of the dominant stations. WIFE (the old WIFE-FM) was the WLS of Indianapolis. But on virtually every station, you got news, at least somebody ripping and reading, and maybe a reporter who actually went out and covered the news. WIBC had this staff of four and they would not only do reports, they would do three-part, or four-part, or multi-part series, and kind of minidocumentaries, and they kind of set the tone. You had WIFE doing their thing. You had WIRE; it was a major force in country music, and they weren't just playing music; they had personalities who went out into the community. It was just like each station had its niche, but it was like, "Yes, we're going to entertain you, but we're also going to be a civic part of this community." You had two, at the time, general managers: Jim Hilliard, who was on WIBC, and then Don Nelson, who was the general manager of

Delores "Sugar" Poindexter, longtime host of gospel programs on WTLC, finds herself caught up in the music. THE INDIANAPOLIS STAR AND NEWS

Brown, one of the most visible personalities on WTLC, hosted numerous radiothons during his tenure there, including this one for Martin University. Here Brown interviews Rev. Boniface Hardin, president of the school. THE INDIANAPOLIS STAR AND NEWS

WIRE in its heyday. Don was running WIRE when I got here, so that's at least the mid-1970s to at least the early 1980s. These two people were like on civic boards, and I think one of them, probably Jim Hilliard, was on GIPC, if my memory serves me right.[45] And so these guys were plugged into the "good-old-boy network" that ran Indianapolis so that the power structure and local media had their hooks into each other.

I think the first use of [WTLC] radio as a weapon for good was because we cared, and I think that was the campaign that put WTLC on the map. "Hey, wait a minute. They're crazy. They're getting ready to do something." This was 1974 or 1975—really more late 1975. At the time there was no law in the state of Indiana that mandated vaccinations prior to entering school. Frank [Lloyd] and Andy Johnson, who was more of a health professional than he was a broadcaster, felt something had to be done. "What can we do to get immunizations?" So I don't know who invented the promotion, but it was a multilayered promotion, and it started at the classroom level. This all started around the permission slip. "Okay kids, take this permission slip home to get a shot. Have your parents sign it." The classroom with the highest percentage of returned slips by a certain date would get something. The school with the highest percentage of slips returned by a certain date—the school would get, like, a sock hop. The teacher with the classroom with the highest whatever, we put your name in a hat of the other good teachers, and you're going on an island—so we're going to send you on an airplane. One permission slip would go on, and the parent was going to go somewhere. And somehow there was an incentive for the principal. So all along the line, kids would get a T-shirt or something; the school would get a party. There were incentivized levels bankrolled by the radio station, really out of Frank Lloyd's pocket. I think there were some real minor sponsors, but the station basically carried this message and took immunization levels that they're telling me were 20 to 30 percent of the school level (I think that's how bad the problem was) into the 90 percent like that. It was backed up by radio spots every hour—every hour plus deejay chatter. So it was the full weight of the property behind the problem. The attitude was, "Beat them over the head until they're sick of hearing it, so they'll fill out the permission slip and be in, [because] they don't want you to talk about it anymore." So it's saturation

coverage. There was a follow up the following year just to reinforce that. It helped the success because we carried it. It earned a National Headlines Club Award; it earned the station's first CASPER Award, and it helped the legislature finally pass the law that bugs parents to death now, that requires immunization. So that was the first time. "Wait a minute. What is this WTLC doing?"

And then [we] came behind that with a little bit more sophisticated "Get Out the Vote." Then came behind that with a three-year campaign—1977, 1978, 1979 called "Writers' Fair." This was in seventh and eighth grade, and you write an essay in your language arts class. And again this is backed up on the radio, "Participate in the Writers' Fair." The first and then the final best essays would— "We're going to put them on display in the lobby of the grand Hyatt Regency Hotel." And of course everybody thought, "Oh, my God, that lobby. Oh, well this is Indianapolis. We're hot shit now." And the prize was the top forty or fifty kids—we were going to put on the bus, and they would get to spend the day in Chicago, and they were going to go to the museum. I think one year before the announcement of who got to go to Chicago, Ossie Davis and Ruby Dee came to town to talk reading and the importance of reading.

Doctor Lloyd had this feeling that just about everything we did, news and information, he wanted the station to have control over—that it should be the station's thing. So in other words, different groups didn't have their own talk show. The only exception was *Operation Breadbasket* which came out of St. John's Church. Basically that was an hour-long, one-part, would-be church service—one-part spiritual, one-part throwing stones at the establishment, one-part raising trial balloons. It was almost like if you were white and you wanted to know what was on the black community's agenda, turn on the radio Saturday morning at eleven o'clock. It served the same function as *Meet the Press* or *Face the Nation* serves on Sundays for the country. You're raising trial balloons; you're throwing stuff out there; you're threatening; you're laying your agenda out to see will it fly or to warn somebody, "Hey, we're getting ready to come kick your behind. You better be. . . ."

By that time, they needed somebody to volunteer to do some work on Sunday when the church was on the air. So I said, "I'm not doing anything on Sunday. I can sit over here, get a little extra money, and read the Sunday paper."

So I started doing that. I can't remember how I started doing voice work on the air, but by the summer of 1976, some friends of mine I had gone to college with (we'd worked on WNUR together), one of them worked for the Democratic National Committee [DNC] and was setting up an audio service with the DNC. He calls me up, and he said, "How would you like to come and help us out with this audio service at the convention? We have no money to pay you. We have no money to put you up, but you get a floor pass." At that point, I'm twenty-five. What do I know—New York. I had another college friend of mine who worked for a newspaper in New Jersey; he lived in New Jersey. I stayed with him and, you know, paid the plane ticket. Covered the convention, and then before going, I said, "What if I could sell reports from the convention?" The station said, "Sure." So I called a few of my clients, and I said, "Hey, I'm going to do this, and it's going to cost you this. Would you like to do that?" And they said, "Sure." So that got my voice on—doing reports. I'd do the reports and plug in the audio that we already did from other stuff and go out—bingo. And that kind of started the audience. Somehow right after maybe a few of these *Mornings with the Mayor,* somebody said, "Why don't you do the show?"

So it then transformed from the mayor coming on with the morning deejay and taking calls to a full-hour production number. WIBC wouldn't take any calls on controversy; Gary Todd wanted to keep it light, *Opportunities for Service.* And all the time [Mayor William] Hudnut and Gary Todd were on the air, it was all that very lighthearted.[46] "Mayor, fix my street." Our thing was that there were *no* restrictions. You know, I think in the years we did that show, we may have censored three calls, and these were people that wanted to get some really personal stuff against Hudnut that just was totally out of bounds. But it was whatever the callers wanted. And that quickly started controversy, because some of the black elected officials (Democrats on the city-county council) started bitching, "You must screen these calls, because all these people are doing is calling up and asking Hudnut to fix my street or get rid of rats or take a traffic sign down and collect the garbage. Why aren't you asking this man about these substantive or these inside—?" Doctor Lloyd's attitude was, "It's what the people want to ask. They're calling the mayor, the chief executive officer. Now, if they want to call

the chief executive officer of the city and ask a dumb-ass question, that's their business. It's not our job to ask this guy a question. Our people see him every day. It's the job of the caller." So the whole thing created this practice, and people lived for that show. They would call, "When's he coming on again?" Because, in their mind, they had a problem that they wanted to solve. As the years went on, the show got elaborate. Now, [Hudnut] would go to Gary Todd by himself. He had to come to TLC, [and] would bring deputy mayors, bring assistants, as well as do follow up. "Well, last month we had Miss Jones on South Lynhurst who had this problem. Well, I am proud to say today we put up a new street sign—ta-da!" It became an institution, and as we checked around the country, very few if any big-city mayors would go every month on radio into their minority communities and take on all comers on the telephone. So in terms of what the call-in show was, that was the only one. We may have done some—once or twice, some emergency safety valve after a shooting, and tried to use it as a safety valve. "Hey, what's your comment?" But in terms of the regular one—that was it in those days. The call-in show was Hudnut. You know Bill Hudnut was the call-in man. Call-in radio really didn't start in this town until they changed IBC, and I think, you know, because people weren't used to it; it was just a totally different thing.

We did a thing at the end of the year that Al Hobbs started.[47] Al decided that, you know, we need to do something, because we'd get all of these letters, "We need help for Christmas." So he organized something in which we tried to raise money and tried to give a basket of food stuff at Christmas figuring that: the toy pieces are covered; the stray cash piece is covered; the kids' clothing piece is covered; where's the food? And we would always be amazed. How come WIBC isn't raising some money at Christmas? You know, how come WIRE isn't raising money at Christmas? Why is it? You go to other cities and the big radio stations are raising money for the holidays to help hungry families, whether it's KDKA [Pittsburgh] having a radio-thon for this. How come we don't do this here? So, for all the good they had done, there was some human side in this business that we kind of filled. Part of that was WTLC (that's "Tender Loving Care"). The heart was always a part of the logo, and there was a sense of people.

One of the legendary things was after I got there—I think I'd been there a year—Doctor Lloyd still was dissatisfied with the news operation. We had a female news director and a couple of reporters. He still didn't like what the news department was doing. It was not doing what he wanted it to do. . . . Frank just didn't like the news programming so he eliminated the news department. This was like in 1976, the first part of the year; just eliminated it. At that time Gene Slaymaker had been working with the people in this department. (Gene had been with the old WFBM-Radio, had [earned] lots of awards. Evidently, he'd had a falling out with the people at McGraw-Hill, so he's out playing consultant.) He and Doctor Lloyd hook up, and Lloyd hires him as a consultant to look at the news operations. So, Gene came in as news director. We hired two kids fresh out of Butler, one white and one black. (And after R. K. Shull in the *Indianapolis News* yells, "How dare you get rid of the news department?" Again, this is an environment where WIBC has Fred [Heckman] and his huge news department, and WIFE has got a news department; WNDE's got a news department. Everybody that's any kind of AM has got a news department. So we're like fifth, sixth news department in town.) Gene comes to rebuild a news department. And really what Frank wanted was a *news* department. When Gene put it on [Frank Lloyd] wanted a news department that would report the news of the day as well as report the regular news— report news of particular interest to African Americans, whether they were things that they either wanted to hear, or things that were important, and if it became necessary, speak out, but only speak out if speaking out would make a difference. The converse was, by asking the questions, then it forces newsmakers or government to deal with the issues. In terms of TLC's golden age, that was the golden age of news and information. We would do seven-minute newscasts; the programmers to the jocks went crazy. I mean this was a seven-minute newscast with five minutes of content, which was unheard of on a music station, but that's what we did.

Some broadcasters have the feeling, "Okay, I've got to do public service. Now, we're going to run a few spots and be done with it—just to say I ran a few spots." If you got results, fine, if you didn't, tough. Others would say, "Fine. You want me to help you publicize your event or activity or some worthwhile thing? I'll put you on our talk show at five o'clock on Sunday morning. You've got a thirty-minute talk show." And groups are satisfied. "I've got a thirty-minute

talk show." And so they think they've done something. They get ten spots. [These groups] think they've done something. The station writes them a check for two hundred and fifty dollars. They think they've done something. And they still wonder why people don't know what they're doing. . . . [Doctor Lloyd] created the environment of freedom, creative freedom, and gave—whether you were in programming, whether you were in sales, or whether you were in management—the creative freedom to do well.

[WTLC] was a very big family—but it was community. It was not sophisticated. There were no mentors; there were no role models. There were no other stations that were doing what we were doing. So with everything we were doing, we were writing a new page. We were doing things that our own brand of radio—black or urban radio— was not doing. The attitude was, "People don't want to hear a lot of talk. Play the hits and shut up." Being a monopoly did provide some insulation, because you had the freedom to experiment and do some different things and go out of the norm on the grounds that: okay, if [the competition is] going to come after me, either come after me duplicating what I'm doing, or do better than what I'm doing. And nobody wanted to take that piece. And then as we felt more comfortable, and the awards started coming in, we felt that pride. We thought here, "The only difference between us and WIBC is they have a lot more expense, and they have a lot more revenue. That's the only difference. We're just as good as they are."

WTLC represented the basic value structure of Indianapolis's black community, and that was a conservative value structure. In addition, the orientation of the announcers was, "If you couldn't say anything positive, don't say anything." So all the time—through Al Hobbs as general manager and to some degree while I was there—you never heard the announcer say "hell" or "damn" or anything worse. You never heard the announcer talk about, "Well, we were hung over last night," or "They had a party," or any kind of any derogatory references to the black community—talk about welfare moms, or the welfare check or anything like that. It was that kind of a *positive orientation*. We would censor language in the records. When rap started which was 1979 or 1980, we played it. When rap first started, it was not rap as it is—it was not hard-edge. It was kind of fun and playful and rhythmic. And we played it. When it got too cumbersome, and we heard a backlash from adults, we said, "Okay, we've got market dominance, we can afford . . ." Teens weren't a moneymaker necessarily for us, and so we said, "Okay, let's try to be more adult-oriented." We were trying to grow older with the audience or the community. Yeah, but I would say—and make no apologies—it reflected the value structure, and we reflected the establishment.

In my memory, I don't think WTLC made an official profit until maybe 1976, definitely by 1977. So those early years, we were really trying to establish economic credibility and credibility in the advertising marketplace. It is a fact that a black-format station will do 80 percent of its twelve plus share of revenue. (So if a black station has a six share, they may do a four share of revenue.) There is a format bias. So WTLC's first step was to crack the format bias, to crack all of those "old wives' tales" and shibboleths and lies about what an African American will and will not buy. It was to the point of getting a list of the twenty accounts we really wanted and just systematically attacking them. Now, let's attack this category and attack that category. When WTLC started out in the early years, the sales philosophy was, "We're black, and buy us because we're black." Doc [Lloyd] wanted a philosophy really more sophisticated than that. Educate—give the people solid reasons why, not just, "Hi, buy me because I'm black." And that kind of led to being a little more scientific, a little bit more knowledgeable. We knew that you had to pick up the copy faster, service the client better and harder. Bend over backwards to do things that the other stations would give lip service because of the stigma. You had to try to recruit better talent, and with four people, we were out performing and out producing stations that had five, six, seven, eight or nine folks. And the revenues for the station grew. I think the late 1970s were a good time for radio. I think going into the 1980s when the ownership changed from Doctor Lloyd to Ragan Henry, that just moved the station to another level. That's in terms of revenue. The revenue jumped substantially, as did the profit margin.

Ragan Henry came as owner [in 1981], and Ragan liked the art of the deal. Ragan, being African American, understood where Doc was trying to position the station and felt that it was a positioning that he was comfortable with—comfortable with the news service and the whole box of wax. His operating officer was this white guy named Chuck [Charles D.] Schwartz. Chuck had worked at CBS

Radio and had been a sales manager at CBS—had run the CBS, WCAB-Radio at CBS—somehow got frozen out in some kind of a network power play, and so he started working with Ragan as chief operating officer. Schwartz came in, and it was like going [from being] owned by doctors six blocks away, to being owned by a lawyer eight hundred miles away. And it had a different financial footing. I mean it was profit margin. It was getting revenues up to support the expenses necessary to achieve the profit margin. It was reverse budgeting. And within two years the profit had gone from maybe $800,000 to $1,000,000.

[Ragan was] another gregarious guy—Harvard Law. He was with one of the prestigious law firms in Philadelphia. He liked to do the deal. He was the kind of a guy whose deals are legendary. He'd do a deal, and he'd cash the investors in after their six or seven years. He liked to deal. He didn't stay with a property long. All the properties he had at the time he bought us, he no longer owns. I mean he's just gone—in and out. But again, this was the 1980s. This was high-flying moneys available—don't worry about it; borrow from Peter to rob from Paul to pay John. And you know, we're looking at sales just going up, up, up, up. You get your confidence up. Schwartz says, "Why can't you charge a hundred dollars a spot? Hey, you're a monopoly; you're worth it; you've got a great. . . ." So, we charged whatever we could get.

Ragan had promised the company he had set up, which was called Broadcast Enterprises National—he had promised some of the investors that after a certain number of years after forming this company, they'd cash out. So, he was looking to cash out the company and some of the profits. So it was a question [of which station] would he sell. Well, Schwartz decided this was the time for him to make his move, and instead of working for someone, he'd become the owner. So Schwartz starts to maneuver to buy TLC [AM and FM], an FM urban station [WBLZ] in Cincinnati, and then a station that Ragan had bought the year previous in Philadelphia, an old-line talk FM called WWDB. There were four stations involved. At the time, Al Hobbs was on the board. At the meeting where everybody was deciding how these properties should spin off, there were people who really didn't want Schwartz to have anything. Al is there pushing. "Hey, you know, Schwartz has got some money up front." Anyway, Chuck gets it. He

As a measure of the African American community, people protested WTLC's "Miss Brickhouse" beauty contest. Eventually WTLC ran a "Mr. Brickhouse" contest as well before both were dropped.

Gene Slaymaker, director of news and public affairs at WTLC-FM (1976–92), began his career at WFBM-AM-FM-TV in 1960. While at these stations, Slaymaker's tenacious pursuit of news stories resulted in numerous award-winning editorials and documentaries including "War on Drugs" and "Who Killed Richard Fisher?" Slaymaker left WTLC when the news department was eliminated. PHOTO BY JULIE SLAYMAKER

Amos Brown found an increased voice in the community through his column in the Indianapolis Recorder. IHS INDIANAPOLIS RECORDER COLLECTION C7871

was supposed to buy four stations for $29 million. Now this was 1986, going into 1987, just before the bottom was getting ready to fall out. Well, the story of how Chuck financed his purchase is a proven fact that just because you are white and/or Jewish in America does not mean that you have automatic access to money or credit. He caught hell trying to get financing. The deal kept going up and down, up and down. Would it close? Would it close? Okay, finally it closed. We didn't know what the structure of the deal was. And so the first couple of years things were going along great. Then there was one recession, and the sales dropped off. There was a small competitor that was siphoning off audience, but not siphoning off money, but the net effect was it caused the revenues to drop. So about—I can't remember the years, 1988 or 1989—he sells Cincinnati. And I think that gave him like eight or nine million dollars. That gave him some relief. (The call letters were WBLZ.)

And it was somewhere in there that the first news department squinch occurred. At the same time, right about 1985, Ragan buys the old WIFE. It was one of those things where a venture guy calls and says, "Ragan, I got this dog. Help me out." Ragan buys it, keeps the format, which is big band, and figures this is like an insurance policy. TLC never needed an AM to block somebody else. The big band worked for awhile. Then when Chuck bought everything, he decided, "Well, I don't need two general managers. I don't need two staffs. We'll combine them." He still had a separate staff for the big band, but the same management as TLC, same sales department. So we were going out trying to sell a combo [WTLC and WTUX], "the old and the soul—big band music and urban."[48] What it really did was it brought to the big band advertisers what they never would have gotten on their own. If we went to them direct and said, "Do you want to be on a radio station that reaches people over fifty?" they would have said, "Go stick it." So on one level those listeners got the benefit, and we were able to do some things and had some nice numbers, even though they were all old as hell.

And we tried to do some news and the whole ball of wax, but by the time of the Gulf War—that hit at the same time that Hoosier [WHHH] started. That started to siphon off audiences and revenues, so there was a slow revenue decline year after year. That started to squeeze the profit. [William Shirk] had wanted to own an FM, and he con-

vinced the Commission [FCC] that they could put a Class A drop-in in Indianapolis. He convinced the Commission. It had not allocated a new FM for Indianapolis. When they invented [Docket] 80-90 drop-ins, they bypassed Indianapolis. They did not think it could be done. Shirk proved it could be done. He started the application process. They accepted the allocation, and then he outlasted umpteen groups, many of whom were African or women—minority fronts for majority players, because the preferences were minority-race, minority-female. So he outlasted them all and put on Hoosier 96 as a drop-in October of 1991.

[Chuck Schwartz] had been at WBBM [Chicago] and WCAU [Philadelphia]. He's thinking, "Well, this is a music station. What the hell do we need with news?" And he's got a talk station in Philadelphia. "We'll have one person doing news." So all of a sudden, here comes the pressure to cut and scrimp, and scrimp and scrimp. Finally, we get to 1992, and the sales are not growing. They're getting stagnant, so there's increased pressure. And so, okay, the decision comes out (this is like in June) and he said, "I think it's time to exercise the insurance policy," which was to change the format of the AM to do something, and obviously [the] enemy was Hoosier. What the hell do we do? So, we came to a consensus that we would take and create something for black adults on the AM which would allow us to go younger, maybe even change the no-rap [policy] on the FM and try to battle that way. Everybody signed off on it. They went to a secret project, just me, Schwartz, and Al Hobbs. We devised a format for the AM, trying to keep it where we didn't have to add extra expense, using existing personnel. The other thing, we not only had to cut all of the people from the AM, we had to cut out the whole news department—just cut it. It was like, okay, we're going to go this far, we might as well go all the way. This is survival. That's how it was billed to us, as survival.

So to make that long story short, at the end of August 1992, [Schwartz] shut the big band [on the AM]. We just killed it; we just pulled the plug. We felt bad about doing it. We thought it was cruel to go from Frank Sinatra to Motown. We thought that was cruel and unusual punishment, but the best way is to put one out of its misery. Take it off for a week, take all the hell, and then turn something new on. And we got a lot of publicity and a lot of, "What the hell are they doing?" And we went on TLC, and we would always—if you're going to market something, market it. One of the secrets of success of TLC was, "If you're going to do it, tell folks. If you don't tell folks, you're not doing it." So we said, "We're going to make an announcement and make the most important announcement we've ever made in twentysome-odd years. Be ready." People thought it was like life and death. We said, "Well, Sunday morning we're going to do this." And on Sunday morning at nine o'clock, "Yes, it's Sunday morning at nine o'clock. It's the dawn of the new era." We explained, "This is what we're going to do." Boom, and this new station took off like a skyrocket. Now, the revenue didn't come in. The advertisers were all sitting back and saying, "What the hell are you all doing?" But we felt we were going in the right direction. So all that fall of 1992, here comes this new station, which was basically a gospel in the morning, light jazz in the late morning, [and] oldies in the afternoon and the rest of the day.

So Schwartz comes here. On like the coldest day in twenty years, he comes in. This is January 9th. Well, after all of this then a couple of dustups—there had been a couple of negative articles, and there had been some real tension. They had moved *Breadbasket* that had been on the FM for twentysome-odd years, the longest running program on any station. [Paul Major] just finally said, "I don't want it here any longer. It loses ratings."[49] I said, "No, it doesn't." I ran in graphs and charts and ran the numbers to show the audience did listen. I didn't want to move it. And finally he said, "I'm going to move it." At that point, there was a nasty article in the paper—probably got leaked—and he knew who leaked it, but he couldn't prove it. At that point, things they were doing to me, I could take. But [blaming] that move for the *Breadbasket* to me showed at least Schwartz's colors and Paul's colors that they were going to eviscerate the station.

You've asked a couple of questions about the role of broadcasters. I think where it is now, you can tell someone's commitment from their track record. Paul Major, who runs TLC—here is someone who owned a black AM in Tampa—really did not have a stellar record in the community. It did all of the standard stuff, all the boilerplate stuff and nothing cutting edge, nothing out-of-the-way. He is from what I call "the old school of broadcasting," the two-martini lunch, the two-hour lunch-type situation, and coming into an operation where they had people who

rarely drank and didn't lunch, it just did not hit the right way. It was the wrong mesh. It was the wrong person for the property.

A lot of times what a station does is reflective of top leadership. If top leadership wants it to be actively involved and backs it up with effort, it's going to be active and involved. If the top leadership is going to give it lip service, it will get lip service. And what TLC is now is lip service. They screw up *little* things. The best example is just from this week. For the last two years, ever since that first year where they had those services at St. John's on Martin Luther King's Birthday, WTLC broadcast it. When we went to the two WTLCs that first January, we broadcast the services on both stations. [Paul Major] came in and moved it to the AM. I said, "Okay, that's fine. That's fine, if you want to play that game." Last year they didn't have it, and he blamed the telephone company. He said, "Well, we were moving the studios from one location to another one." But this past Monday, it wasn't on at all, and I've yet to hear an excuse. They used to broadcast on New Year's morning a religious service—you know, religious interfaith service. It had been on the air for maybe—I'd say every January first—maybe every year I've been here. That's twenty years plus. It wasn't on this year for the first time. Nobody even knows why. It's those *little* things.

At one point in those last months at TLC, people kept saying, "Well, we know they're trying to freeze you out. We know you're not happy, but you can go on and be a talk show host." And I said, "I'm not ready to do that, to be a talk show, to do a Liddy.[50] I'm not ready." I said, "I know I can do that if I want to. I may wait until I'm fifty. Is that okay? I want to retire then." I'm not ready to do this yet. There are some other things I want to do. And I think the column in the [*Indianapolis*] *Recorder* allows me to be more of a commentator on community issues.[51] Community service—this is what Tom Binford [a community leader], told me a long time ago. He said, "In this town it's not who you are, it's who you represent that gives you your clout." And I knew in making the switch [from TLC to Hoosier 96] that I just had to have patience and wait for folk to sink in and then the requests would come. That has now happened for the most part. So, you know, I'm still active. I'm still involved. Television visibility was all very small and low power. I think that also helps. It's not diminished; it's just become another role. It's just become a different role. And at forty-six I ought to be something different. You can't do the same thing you did when you were twenty-six.

I think major, big-city radio [stations have become formulas and jukeboxes and to some degree cookie cutters. They all sound the same; they all sound alke. To some degree, small-town radio is the same with their own satellite. Radio is an industry and maybe has allowed television to capture the immediacy, the on the spot, the live on the spot and the something bad is going on. "We're going to give you information to get you past it." Now, maybe I'm reacting a little bit more because of Indianapolis, but it is criminal that radio has now allowed television to be the on the spot. You know, it's even to the point that they are more on-the-spot news than WIBC, because if something bad happens between 1:00 and 4:00 they're not interrupting Rush Limbaugh for nobody. Television now has taken away radio's claim to fame on school closings. There is now no reason for you to listen to the radio in the morning for school closings. Turn the damn TV on. WIBC has invested years in creating this image of school closings and [Channel] 6, 8, and 13 have just killed, just knocked the underpinning out of them. And we as an industry have allowed that to happen.

"A Unique Compact"

Jeff Smulyan has said that broadcasters have "a unique compact" with the public because they use the public airwaves. Licenses are granted by the government. Unlike cable service for which a fee is charged, over-the-air broadcasts are free for those who have the equipment to receive them. These circumstances suggest singular responsibilities for broadcasters. The federal government and the broadcasters themselves have recognized this. Yet they have questioned: to what degree should broadcast stations be regulated or the industry be self-regulated in order for the public interest to be served? What does public interest entail? How does a station's definition of this concept affect its profitability? Owners and managers, from the mom-and-pop stations represented by Don Martin to the far-flung empires operated by John Dille and Jeff Smulyan, have wrestled with these issues.

The narrators in this section come from very different enterprises. Don Martin describes his market in rural Salem, Indiana, as one in which listeners expect to hear sports, news, agricultural reports, weather, and local happenings, which for some includes obituaries Mom-and-pop stations such as Don Martin's remain, as John Dille has noted, "'the daily diary of American life'" and a reminder of the genesis of the broadcasting industry. In the midsized market of Evansville, Bettie Engelbrecht speaks of such a close community involvement that people stop her at church to comment on her station's fare, and Charlie Blake tells of the community support that WIKY has given each year to the Westside Fall Festival sponsored by the Westside Nut Club. Bob McConnell and Dick Fairbanks talk about operations striving to remain profitable in complex urban environments. As contemporary presidents of media companies, John Dille (Federated Media) and Jeff Smulyan (Emmis Broadcasting Corporation) provide insight into the concept of format radio in the volatile environment of the 1990s.

As narrators in earlier sections have indicated, the FCC tried to quantify the concept of public interest, leading some owners and managers to question whether public interest and profitability were mutually exclusive. Most of the broadcasters in this section felt that they were not. With the easing of FCC regulations on ownership in the "Marketplace Approach," competition for market share became fierce. In the environment of the 1980s and 1990s, owners and managers of radio stations in urban markets relied heavily on acquiring knowledge of their audience and analyzing demographics. With the proliferation of radio stations in large urban markets, stations could no longer be all things to all people; they had to identify the listening tastes of different racial, ethnic, social, and economic groups. Only by keeping a close watch on their particular audience could they serve the public interest while still making a profit.

In a capitalistic society, success and longevity are measured by the bottom line. Yet many stations continued to broadcast "in the public interest" despite the lifting of restrictions; they recognized that it was just good business. In small markets especially, the audience had expectations that programming would reflect the values of the community. Many broadcasters expressed the feeling that public interest was no longer connected with ethics but had become more a matter of taste. Some of our narrators indicated that airing programs of questionable content was acceptable if there was a large enough audience;

they felt that the market should regulate itself and that the twist of a dial was the best censor.

The following oral interviews suggest some of the changes in philosophy of owner/managers from the 1940s until the present. In one way or another, all of these narrators recognized the importance of public interest to the continuation of their enterprises. Some regarded community involvement as integral to their being. Others felt that to be successful, they had to keep their finger on the pulse of the community. Still others concurred with Eldon Campbell, mentor and role model for many Hoosier broadcasters, "The station that serves best, sells best." As these narrators describe the relationship between civic responsibility and profitability, they reveal broadcasters' evolving sense of public interest within the cultural transformations of American society.

Robert B. McConnell (ca. 1946)
WISH-TV/PHOTO BY RAY CONOLLY

Bob McConnell

(1921–)

Robert B. McConnell, like his father C. Bruce McConnell before him, made an impact on broadcasting in Indiana. McConnell attended Indiana University, but in 1942 he left to join WISH, which was owned by his father and some other Indianapolis businessmen. Shortly thereafter he went into the navy, where he was involved in recruiting and patriotic programming for the war's duration. After his discharge in 1945, McConnell returned to WISH. In 1950 he became vice president and general manager of Universal Broadcasting Company, the parent company of WISH, WHBU, and WANE, and the next year he was named president and general manager of WISH Radio and Television, a position that he held for the next twenty-nine years. From 1975 to 1986, he was president of Anderson Broadcasting Corporation. He retired from WISH in 1980, but came out of retirement to become chairman, CEO, and director of the IWC Resources Corporation (the Indianapolis Water Company) for five years. Since his second retirement McConnell has remained active in civic affairs. Throughout his career, he sought to be open and accessible both to the people who worked for him and to his audiences. This was part of his legacy in broadcasting, and part of what he saw as his responsibility as president of WISH and later at IWC. McConnell was interviewed at his home on the north side of Indianapolis in August 1996.

One of the big changes, particularly in radio, is that we went from a mass media to a specialized media. Radio started out like television has become—the only thing that counted was how big your audiences were. Radio today doesn't do that. Radio stations are very specialized. They get a target audience, and they go after it. I see television going in that direction. With the advent of cable, you have the weather channel, and you have specialized channels that just show certain kinds of programming. Your networks still haven't done that. That's a specialization which I see in radio. Still, I believe there's too much generalization. To me, there are too many rock and roll stations and too few other specialties, because they find out there is maybe not a limited audience—but a somewhat limited audience just for that one thing. So, that's one of the big changes I've seen, the trend for specialized audiences.

My first job in radio was a very menial job. I was just taken with the glamour of it because at that time if you told anyone that you worked for a radio station, it was pretty much like saying you're working for a television station today. You were somewhat of a minor celebrity. I think it's only after you're there for awhile, and then as you begin to age yourself, [that] you look back and see things happening, and you begin to realize you're in a changing world and changing business.

Of course, [radio] broadcasting was a glamorous business at that time. It was probably like television is today—and maybe even more than television is today because television is sharing with cable and a lot of other things—but at that time that was the new means of communication. There was a certain amount of glamour attached to it. Big stars were on the radio; newscasters were prominent people, and it was a good time. It was one of the fields that carried a lot of prestige for one thing. I mean when people found out you worked for, "Oh, you work for a radio station?" The first question they always asked you, "Are you an announcer?" I'd say no, and I really disappointed them. The announcers on the air were the ones that people identified with. Those were the people they probably knew. And if you did some behind the scenes job, which most of the time I did, it wasn't nearly as glamorous as being on the air. But, it was a fascinating business. The good things that we had in those days in communications came through radio, and people stopped waiting overnight to find out who won the election. They would find out at night on the radio. Prior to that time, they waited for maybe two days for a newspaper to tell them. So, it was part of the fabric of our lives.

My father was the head of a company called Hamilton-Harris & Company, which was a tobacco wholesaler. They called on small merchants. (That's before you had the big food and drug chains.) Many of the retail outlets all over Indiana—and all over the country for that matter—were ma and pa operated. These were individual operators, and Hamilton-Harris sold to these people. My father was a good salesman. Prior to that time he'd been a salesman in the 1930s on the road. [His territory was] central Indiana and southern Indiana. He'd call on the small filling stations and the small grocery stores, and they bought candy, cigarettes, and sundry items. When he became sales manager of the company in the late 1930s, all of a sudden, he found people from the radio stations in Indianapolis coming in and wanting his recommendation for tobacco [advertising]—probably because the two biggest categories in advertising on radio at that time were the soaps and the tobaccos. (Procter and Gamble, Liggett & Meyers, and American Tobacco and what not. Those were the backbone of radio.) He finally said to himself one day, "If this is that good, I

ought to get into it." He met some individuals in Terre Haute, who wanted to start a station. He got with them and some other local businessmen, and he decided to invest in it and filed for a radio station license. They filed and got a radio station [WISH]; he got a grant. And the grant came along right before World War II.[52]

When I came home that summer—I was in college—I went to work at the radio station. The radio station went on the air in the summer. I was so fascinated with it that I decided I would defer going back to school and stay at the radio station. Then the war broke out in December—that's when they attacked Pearl Harbor. I was working for the radio station at that time. Then, it became obvious that I, like all young men, was going to get drafted. I had been handling a lot of public service stuff for the station. There was an ensign out at the naval armory who came over one day, and . . . he said, "Bob, I would like to talk to you about joining the navy." I said, "Well, I'm going to get drafted one of these days anyway. I think it's going to be all right." Well, the final deal was to become the public relations guy in the recruiting station in Indianapolis. He said that it would last six months, and I would go someplace else. And I finally signed up. The fact of the matter is I stayed in Indiana through the war in public relations. Not at the station—I was in the navy—but I saw a lot of guys come and go, and I finally ended up running a recruiting station in Muncie, Indiana (of all places), right at the end of the war. And the only time I was ever at Great Lakes, where they inducted everybody, was when I went up there to get discharged. At the end of the war, I'd spent four years in the navy.

One of the assignments I got which I always will remember, there was a navy captain [who] had an experimental television station in Chicago, WRKB. This was when radar was a brand-new thing. Nobody knew much about radar, and the navy set up a radar school. Somehow, I don't know how, I was selected to go and live in Chicago for six weeks or something like that. We put out a printed circular—I used to have it someplace, but I don't know where it is now—on radar in Chicago. I lived up there and did that and then came back to Indiana. I remember that because it was fascinating to me. Radar was something we didn't know much about, and they were looking for people to train for radar. I got the privilege of writing up that brochure that they put out all over the country.

The owners of WISH in 1948 included Franck McHale, Herbert Krimendahl, Frank McKinney, and C. Bruce McConnell, Bob's father.

In my younger days, I was a fairly good musician; I played the piano and organ. And I was a little embarrassed when I would go into the bars at night, and between my uniform and my playing, I would get a lot of free drinks. But I did some shows in the navy; we had recruiting shows. I would go in. We had a guy from Cincinnati, Charlie Dameron. He was an entertainer on WLW. Charlie would sing. He was a bit older than I was. We'd produce these programs for the navy, and we'd ship them all over the state—that's one of the reasons I guess that I stayed here—I was doing these recruiting programs, trying to keep up morale.

We gave them news. We had one program—we went over and would talk to the people that we recruited that week to join the navy and talk to them on the air, interviewing and letting people know [who was] joining the navy. We had a program on the steps of the Federal Building downtown called *Hi, Sailor*. We'd stand out there with all of these guys who were getting sworn in and just joined the navy. We'd go around "What's your name, sir?" and that kind of thing—like the old *Man on the Street* program. People really liked that because it showed who was joining the navy. Here's a guy from Merrillville, you know. Here's a guy from Anderson. These shows had a pretty good audience for what they were; we didn't compete with Bing Crosby.

After the war, I came back, and my father insisted that I had to go into the sales department. He wanted me in the sales department, and . . . he had a manager running the station. I came in scared to death, and he said, "Well, don't worry about it." He gave me a briefing on how I should do this, and they put me in the sales department. I did better than I thought I would. I didn't have real confidence back then. I guess I have always been a little bit of a con artist, and that is what it takes. I remember one of the statements that the guy who was the manager of the station told me when I came back. He said, "I want to tell you something. The guy that brings it in, always makes more money than the guy that puts it out." I'm not sure that's true, but that was it. The salesman was going to make more dough than the announcer, was what he really meant. I remember the first time I sold an ad. I sold this small spot, and I was kind of apologetic about the size of it. He said, "Look we throw that money in the barrel, and we don't know the big money from the little money." He was a very clever guy.

[My father] sold the station in 1947. We had some small radio stations around the state at that time. We had Anderson, South Bend, and Fort Wayne. He put me in the job of running around and seeing that those stations were performing right and that nothing was happening bad at those stations. That's how I got involved in Fort Wayne.

He sold it to a guy named Frank McKinney in town.[53] I am sure that you know the name. He was head of Fidelity Bank at that time. He was a politician, a big Democrat; he had formed an alliance with a senator from Utah, and filed for a radio station in Indianapolis. My dad was absolutely sure he was going to get one in Indianapolis [and was afraid that WISH would lose its network affiliation to them].

I just think that broadcasting at that time was considered a damn good business. There were a lot of people getting rich off of it. I think like every other businessman, you know, you get into the business materially. The business was somewhat controlled by the government and politics, and [McKinney] probably thought he had the political connections to get the grant. He got the grant . . . , and they were affiliated with the network and other people. You've got to remember McKinney was a big man. He was Democratic National Chairman under Truman. As a consequence, he was a big man nationally. He and my dad became very good friends, as a matter of fact. I think he wasn't trying to take something from somebody else; he was trying to get a radio station and he was going to do what he could with it. And, I have to say that we took CBS away from WFBM [in 1955].

Now, when we bought Fort Wayne, I went up there and lived there. I drove up on Monday morning and came back on Friday night. I wasn't very happy, nor was my wife. That's when my daughter was born, and I just had gotten her home from the hospital, and my dad said to get up there. I said, "Dad, I just brought the baby home from the hospital." He said, "Well, do you want to stay with the baby, or do you want to work?" And that's the way it was. I went up there, and that's when finally we sent [Reid] Chapman there. We had to get the management that we had up there—they had three guys go together at that station. The biggest thing they did—they all bought the same size desks; they had equal offices. One guy was manager, one was chief engineer, and one was in sales. The brother-in-law, our attorney in Washington, called my dad about investing some money in the station. We did once, and they ran through that and still wanted more. That's when I was asked to go up there. It was either straighten it out or else. We didn't want any fights, and we finally bought them out. We just bought out their interest. Then we sent Chapman up there. Chapman was a good guy, and we always liked him a lot. We thought he'd listen, and he did. He went up there, and he was popular in the community and knew everybody, and he did a good job. We had to have somebody that was honest and willing to work.

I remember in 1950 [a prominent] Democratic attorney suggested that [my father] and McKinney ought to pool their interests and that's how they got back together; they formed a merger. Dad put the three stations in the corporation and took the station [WISH] back. When he took it back, I was [named] as vice president.

Mr. [John H. "Jock"] Whitney . . . had decided that television was a good investment, and he wanted to buy stations in major markets, and he would only buy CBS.[54] Tulsa was the first one, [then Houston], and finally bought [one in] Sacramento. They had a broker working for them, and the broker came out here [to Indianapolis] once and called on my dad and said he had a customer that wanted to buy the station. He said, "Everything has its price. What kind of an offer would you consider?" Dad pulled this out of no place and said, "Ten million dollars." He came back about two weeks later and offered $10 million. That's exactly what happened. That's no money today. I mean a lot of stations sell for a $110 million or something like that. Back then in 1956, that was big.

[Whitney] was a good friend of [President] Eisenhower's, and Eisenhower said, "Jock, you've got a lot of money. You ought to save the *Herald Tribune*." (That was one of the big ones.) The *New York Herald Tribune* was in trouble. He said, "We need a Republican newspaper." That's how Corinthian got formed because they then put us in the same company as the *Herald Tribune* and put the profits from the television stations to support the *Herald Tribune* which was losing money.[55]

So he kept the paper alive because Eisenhower asked him. His philosophy after the war was that he would take part of his personal fortune and set up this company with his own money to loan money to companies the banks wouldn't touch. And, broadcasting was one of them. When he first got in broadcasting in Tulsa, Oklahoma, in

cable, cable was just in its infancy. Wrede Petersmeyer went out there and ran that thing. And all of a sudden they decided that the television station is better, and he bought that station. It came up for sale and they bought that. It was their first station. Then they started buying, but they would only buy CBS stations because of Whitney's relationship with Paley.

I'd have to be honest and say I'd probably never have had that job or had been in broadcasting if it hadn't been for [my father]. I'd never have been as involved. I earned my place, you know. I think time shows that. He sold out of the television station in 1956. He didn't want me working for the new owners. . . . They came in, and we had been looking—[my father] had high blood pressure, and we didn't know how long he was going to live. He lived a lot longer after that. He just assumed that I'd always work for him. Whitney bought the station and one guy, Wrede Petersmeyer, moved here, and he was about my age. He got it up and running, and he offered me a job. He offered me a contract, and I turned it down. I said, "No, I think I'll tell you what I'll do; I'll stay and work for you." I said, "We'll just have a gentleman's agreement that if you don't like the way I'm doing it, you can fire me." I said, "I don't want you to be obligated, and I don't want to be obligated. I like broadcasting, and I'd like to stay in it." When they were going to close the deal, Dad came to me and said, "What are you going to do, son?" And I said, "Well, I'm going to stay here." He said, "You are crazy. They will find out what you know and kiss you off." (That is true of a lot of big corporations.) And I said, "Dad, you know I wanted to work at the station, and you know that it surprised a lot of people at the time. They think that I have this job because I'm your son. And they don't think I've got a bird brain. But I'm going to find out if they are right or if you are right." He didn't like it. He stomped out of the room. He admitted many years later that I did the right thing to work for Corinthian. Obviously, I was able to do it. And I was a young man—thirty-five years at the time.

[J. H. Whitney & Co.] came in and established control over everything. It was an entirely new experience for me. Many times I thought maybe my dad was right and I should not have stayed there. There's the budget. They established rates and charges. We had to fight for how many people you had on the staff and whether you would need them. Chapman would remember that. Number one, they came in, and I won't say they paid too much—it was an investment—but they paid a price above and beyond what the market thought the station was worth. The first question after the deal was closed and everything was: how much can you boys raise the rates? Now, we had always operated here on a philosophy that we're doing okay; we don't have to jack the rates up. Stockholders were making a profit, and we're paying good salaries, and what more do you want? Their whole deal was: we paid too much for this station. How are we going to get the money back? They didn't say it in so many words, but that's really the bottom line of it. We had meetings every time the ratings book came out, and we'd go through and individually price the spots. This was a new experience for me, I must say. But that's typical of big companies. I had never worked for a big company. That was a forerunner of how big companies operate. Everybody has a budget. It all of a sudden became not how are you doing overall, but how are you doing compared to the budget we set for you which may have been unrealistic. Are you making as much money as we predicted you ought to make? That's the difference. They exercised every control in the book, and it's typical Harvard Business School management. I went to Harvard one summer; [the company] thought that would be good for me. The broadcasting industry had set up a summer school up there for four or five years at Harvard. I took the time off, and I went up there, and after going through that experience I could see where they were coming from. I still don't particularly think that that's the only way to run a business, but that's the way big business operates.

Oh, broadcasting was highly speculative. You see, when you talk about a broadcasting station, its assets are all intangible. [If] you go out and buy a manufacturing plant, you're buying big buildings; you're buying equipment; you're buying stuff that the bank can see. Most of the value of the broadcasting station is the license, and the license you can't sell. You can transfer it only with the permission of the FCC. So you don't own that license lock, stock, and barrel. When anybody buys a broadcasting station—it's easier today than it used to be—where if anybody buys a broadcasting station, you have to file a piece of paper in Washington and all that and get permission from the FCC and transfer the license. If you don't have a license, the assets are worth very little. I would say today, probably total assets of WISH are $5 million, maybe $6

million. But it would sell for over $100 million [because of] that license. It's better today, but in those days banks only wanted to loan where they had a sure thing. You know, they loan on your house, and they see a piece of property, and they can appraise it and they know that they can sell it for that. The bank couldn't recover the license if you lost your license. The bank couldn't recover it and recoup it, and they'd lose their money. Now, today they're doing more, but still it's tough dealing.

[My father] was well known civically . . . because he had started a television station, and that was a big activity at the time. He wasn't that well known before then. But he started a radio station and a television station, and it is like a publisher of a newspaper; they're pretty well known people. If a politician is going to run, he's going around calling on the media. You become important from your job. Everybody wants your cooperation. The newspaperman used to be a kingpin, but with the advent of television, his influence has come down and television's influence has gone up. The only difference in the case of a newspaper is [that] they're here forever. In television, the ownership was usually out of town. It wasn't at the time my father was here. They could see him, and so you get in that position of civic leadership for that reason, public appearance. When I was running the station, yes, I was probably [as well known as] Eldon Campbell at that time. He worked all the time, and he was well known. Now, he and I were the only two—you have Crosley—they changed managers every two years. I mean about the time somebody got acquainted with him, they put somebody else in. Well, that's tough on the guy, and it's tough on the station because no matter how good a guy he is—usually they're younger people and they come in here and the first job they've got to do is see if they can't get the station running right, and then they've got to do these other things, they can't call on a lifetime friend.

[As general manager] I always insisted that our people had to give both sides of a story. So, if we ran something and somebody was alleging something, you'd have to talk to the other person. Usually that was pretty effective. Once in a while they wouldn't respond. Most of the time they did. I mean for example, I've seen over the years where they will come out against the [Indianapolis] Water Company asking for higher rates without ever consulting the Water Company. It seems to me that you have an obligation to present both sides of that story. That sounds

John (Jock) Hay Whitney, McConnell, and C. Wrede Petersmeyer posed in front of the new WISH studios at 19th and Meridian Streets in the mid-1960s. WISH-TV/PHOTO BY RAY CONOLLY

McConnell "discovered" Debbie Drake in the 1960s. At a time when "reducing salons" were the craze, Corinthian Broadcasting Corporation syndicated her exercise show. DAVID SMITH

WISH's election coverage team in the early 1960s included (left to right) Dave Smith, program manager; Judy Harrison, copy writer; Marifrances Curtis, program secretary; Ray Sparenburg (standing), director; Richard Hickox (seated), news anchor; Mary Jo Peck, secretary; Joe Mingioli, director; Irving Liebowitz (seated), Indianapolis Times *editor/columnist.* CHARLIE CLARK

like a politician, "Take them out because they're charging too much money." But there's a new government regulation which forces them to spend the money, and they have no control over it and somebody in Congress passes the law and says you've got to purify your water to a higher degree than you ever had to purify it—that needs to be told. So I always tried to insist that we had that kind of fairness about it. In fact, I had him [the news director] do most of those editorials. That was his job. I never really felt very comfortable. Now Chapman did, but he was an entertainer. That was his stock-in-trade. I never felt real comfortable about doing that sort of thing. I never thought that I was particularly a good performer. That was not my stock-in-trade. I'd say on two or three occasions where I felt strongly, and I didn't want somebody else to get attacked, I would do it. I didn't mind exposing myself to criticism in that instance.

Hollywood has no morals and never had any. I saw the news last night and saw everyone talking about family values in the Democratic party now. Four years ago, when Mr. Quayle talked about it, it was obscene. I still recall in my mind, a CBS meeting I attended when Archie Bunker was so very big and I'm there. Norman Lear stood up for CBS television and said, "I'm going to be the first one to say the four letter "f" word on television," except he said the word. I thought to myself, "What a goal in life to be the first man to say it on the air." And, that's the attitude. I think half the problems we have today with the youth in our country have to go back to what they see on television. Everybody solves everything with a gun. It used to be that the good guy always won. They don't always win now, not even in the news. Because the entertainment industry or the movie industry will do anything for a buck—anything. I feel very strongly about that. I remember when I sat on the television code review board (we had a thing called the television code, to which stations were supposed to adhere). We had long meetings over the television code about the acceptance of personal products. When we put a Stayfree Mini-pads [commercial] on for the first time, we restricted it to what hours you could show it. Now, that's a laugh today, because anything goes. I'm not so sure that's good. I think we've brought our standards down so much in this country, everything goes. There are no rules anymore, and the kids are growing up thinking anything goes. I really believe that much of what's wrong with the country

today, much of what's wrong with that violence thing that we talk about all the time, goes right back to television. It wasn't happening when I was there. We didn't put those kinds of things on. Yes, there were guns. We had westerns for years. People shoot them up but that's not the same shoot-'em-up where people see people in their own settings doing it day after day. When a kid is growing up, how many murders does he witness a month? A good bit of the crime and violence we have in this country today is so many people think they can solve all of their problems with a gun. But they see them solve them every night on television, and the movies. I think you can put the movies right in the same view. It's all Hollywood. So you asked me about how I feel about it, I feel terrible about it.

I'm not one for highly regulating industry, but I think we've gone maybe too far the other way. I have for example, difficulty in understanding why the Commission—it was after I became less active in broadcasting—would allow anybody to own as many stations in the community as they want to. . . . Now, you can own three or four stations in the same community, and I don't know what the public value is. I still have difficulty with that. Why, a guy can own three [radio] stations in this community. It always used to be that the theory was that the more competitive voices, the better the service. Maybe that still goes that way. Maybe he owns three stations and competes with himself, I don't know. So, I'm not sure about the wisdom of that, but the government, whatever their wisdom was, or lack of wisdom, did it. I think part of the change in broadcasting has been brought about by the change of focus of government regulations. Back in the early days of broadcasting, we were very conscious of that because we had to have a certain percentage of this and a certain percentage of that on the air to keep our license. I'm not sure that's true anymore. I think you can do what you want to do, and if you don't violate any laws, you keep your license. Now, maybe when you talk about the American way of free enterprise maybe that's better. But, I think it does change the role of what you do. I guess there's a new requirement of public service. You can do what you want to, but you don't have to. Back in those days you had to have a certain percentage of it; so, we were probably more conscious about fulfilling that public service requirement which was put on by the government that gave you your license.

Bettie C. Engelbrecht (ca. 1990)

Bettie Engelbrecht

(1920–)

Bettie G. Engelbrecht married into the broadcasting business when she uttered the words "I do." Not only did those two words commit her to raising a family, keeping a household, monitoring the daily routine of a pig named "Hamlet," and teaching school all at the same time, but they also committed her to an enterprise that was more a "calling" than a radio station when her husband, John A. Engelbrecht (1913–1974), put WIKY on the air in 1947 in Evansville, Indiana. Broadcasting from a Civil War-era house atop Mount Auburn, WIKY serves the tri-state area of Kentucky, Illinois, and Indiana. From the earliest days of the station's existence, Engelbrecht was in charge of the public service component of a business that would eventually include AM and FM radio stations, a television outlet, and Muzak franchises in numerous markets. Listeners participate actively in the games and contests Engelbrecht organizes; Money Street, Look in the Book, *and* WIKY Word *attract diverse audiences. Never too busy to relate a story from the past, Bettie Engelbrecht is an active participant in WIKY's continuing success in the Evansville community. John Warner, a historian with Weintraut & Nolan, interviewed Bettie Engelbrecht in a crowded, chaotic lobby at WIKY in March 1997.*

John [A. Engelbrecht] came out of the navy and was excited about radio. He always had been. He had been in advertising sales with Keller Crescent Company and tried to talk Keller Crescent into buying a station that was for sale at that particular time. And they said, "No, we'll never be anything but a printing company." Of course, now they do TV commercials and everything else. But [John] came out and he said, "Well, I'm going to get a station one way or the other." And so he went to Washington. We ended up getting 820, which was a clear channel station, but we had to be off the air at 6:00 at night. It was a daytime operation, which was a little difficult to work with, but that was our first station. It was founded here in Mount Auburn—by that, I mean it started up here in the old Cutler home; we called it the old Cutler home in Evansville. When we went on the air, we said, "John, you never again are going to be on the air. You sound like you're giving code in the navy."

So then I taught school and would do things in the evening like help keep books (my father was the bookkeeper) and clean the studios and everything that you had to do when you were on a toothpick (and that's really what it was). We kind of begged, borrowed (and I don't think we did any stealing), but we did beg and borrow to make payroll and that sort of thing.

So it was a hard beginning, and we were trying to remodel the house; it was right after the war, and the people wouldn't get out. They were living here for free, so they just kept living

John A. Engelbrecht established his first station (WIKY) in the historic Miller-Cutler House in 1947. A fire gutted the building in 1981.

A youthful Bettie and John A. Engelbrecht put WIKY on the air two years after their wedding day (1945).

here. Finally one day, we just pulled the boards out from the second floor, and there wasn't anything to walk on so then they did move out. We moved in and lived here over the station and did live here until the fire, which was about twelve years ago.

So we lived at the station. We brought our son up here at the station, so he was very knowledgeable about what was happening in the radio business. I did all sorts of things for the station, and I did laundry Sunday mornings. I would get up and fix breakfast. On Sunday—I felt sorry for the Sunday morning man, and I'd fix breakfast for him, because I figured he wouldn't have a chance to get anything. In those times we didn't have the canteen sort of stuff either; if we had a good meal, I'd bring a meal down to the announcer. I mean it was just sort of like "old home week" all the time around here.

We used to have a kitchen upstairs, above the low space, over the studios, and people would ask John, "John, how do you enjoy your music?" And he said, "Well, if I hear some I don't like, I stamp my foot. And if they don't get it off, I'll come up and pick the damn thing up and break it."

We put our first FM in (they weren't in the cars yet), and they thought we were crazy to put FM in. Well, who's got it? So we put in the FM, and we started pushing our good music. We put evening music like "Serenade at Evening Time"— dinner music at 6:00 to 8:00 and that sort of thing. People would just listen to it; I mean they just loved that great stuff. And we pulled that audience over to that evening. For one thing we wanted to pull them off the evening because we were on daytime.

Marvin Bates

Bettie Engelbrecht remembered that Marv Bates began his thirty-year career in Evansville, Indiana, in 1947 at WIKY (owned by John A. Engelbrecht) and moved on to WGBF just two years later. Well known in the tristate area for his play-by-play of basketball, baseball, football, and even horse races, Bates was one of the few remaining sportscasters able to re-create away games from the Teletype machine. Drawing from a repertoire of more than sixty-five different taped sound effects, he simulated the atmosphere of a live game for his audience. This talent won him national acclaim when he appeared on Tom Snyder's show in 1975. That same year, Joe Garagiola originated his NBC baseball pregame show in Evansville just to feature Marv Bates. After WGBF was sold in 1975, Bates ended his working days as public relations director at the University of Evansville, his beloved alma mater. He died in a tragic plane crash in 1977 while traveling with the University of Evansville basketball team.[56]

COURTESY OF INDIANA STATE MUSEUM

There wasn't an audience [for FM]. We pushed and pioneered, and we talked; every time we talked to car salesmen, we'd say, "Now be sure you have FM in your car, because that's the future of radio." We kept pushing that sort of thing all the time. We were big pushers of FM. We called it stereo then; we literally played the same thing on the AM and on the FM.

Marv [Bates] started with us. (His wife was a third-grade teacher.) Anyhow, Marv would create the [baseball] games from the Teletype machine. It'd come in and he'd say, "He's on third; he's got an out," you know. And then he'd just tie the thing together—baseball games. We had sponsors, of course, and, in fact, people thought he was traveling around with the team. So he laid low when the team was some place, because he didn't want people to know how he was doing this. Of course, later it got out how he was doing it, but that's the way we had the ball games at first—re-created them . . . because we didn't get those big teams in here. And then, of course, we got our own team later and he left; I think he left us and went on to basketball. We always carried basketball. Now we don't, not now, but on our FM, we're carrying basketball, and of course we carry our school.

I make what we call the "green sheet," and it has all the [community service announcements]—not all, but the various activities are on it. I also do a *WIKY Word Call* [where] we use the name and give money. Of course, that's a contest, and it's not sponsored. It's a thing that we just do each day (it's sort of for the housewife, so to speak) where we call, and if they know the "WIKY Word," then we give them so much money that has built up.

Oh, we are big supporters [of community activities]. Girl Scout cookies, they come to us first. We were the first ones that gave out what date the Girl Scout cookies were going to be on. We really push them and we get all kinds of letters and thank-you notes because we help them.

We had big bingos in this town. It's a Catholic town. I mean it's a lot of Catholics, and they always have bingo games to keep the church going. And we always had to watch that; we could call it a "public party." There would be a public party here. Now, I can say "bingo" and nobody has ever said anything to us. Before, you had to be careful about how you said things. Now, when you see what you're seeing on TV, it's just atrocious, some of it. But that was the one word we had to be very careful about; you couldn't say bingo. You had to say public party. Everybody knew what a public party was, [so we'd] say, "Go to so and so on Saturday night where they have a public party. It will go on 'til midnight—high stakes." You could talk around it, but you couldn't say bingo.

And then we ran into an episode with the pig. One evening I came home from school and John—I could smell this horrible smell, and John had put a pig—not in the apartment, but at the other side, and put about two papers down. It was a darling little pig, a little white China pig. And John said, "We have to have this on the show, and we have to have it on every morning, Monday through Friday," because the company that was going to sponsor the show insisted the pig be there. Well, we didn't check into any pure food laws or that sort of thing at that time. I just got up every morning, and washed the pig and had an old sort of a garage extension on the building, and we'd take him out there and hold him in front of the heater, and he'd oink and carry on something awful. And I had him in harnesses, so they could lead him for awhile. It was up to one of the sales people to take him down to the Belvedere Café.

It was a promotion for [Weil] Packing Company. And this salesman wore butcher jackets with the names on the back, and we had a big audience every morning. Then Saturday mornings were particularly large. We had school-teachers, and we had everybody. We had a combo band play, and an organ and guitar and a saxophone, and some place during the show, why they would play, "Old MacDonald Had a Farm." Whoever they talked to then would pick, and take the pig, and when they stopped and said, "E-I-E-I-O," you punched the pig in the side and he would "oink-oink." So that's how he got the name of the "singing pig." People drove for miles to come into this *Breakfast Club* to sit there and hear that pig. Tommy Woods was the guy on the organ; he played piano and organ at the same time and sang. He was good. We had to have a little stage built up, and people just loved the show. We had all kinds of little contests going on—if you came with green hair on St. Patrick's Day and all that sort of thing, you know. It was silly, but it was really quite a popular show. But the pig was very popular and they would just run up there to see who was going to hold the pig, and punch the pig, and the pig would sing for them. When the pig got a little bit larger, we had a playpen to put him in. And finally the health department said, "We just don't think we need that pig here in the restaurant anymore." So we had kind of worn out the fact, and so we had a naming contest, and the name was Hamlet: to be or not to be a ham was the question.

We did a lot of remotes; we had a regular little remote van. We [also] had a guy that was called the "Curbstone Reporter," George Van Horn. He did a lot of that sort of thing, and he talked from the curbstone, so to speak; he got the man-on-the-street. We did malls, and we did openings of things, and we still do remotes. Remotes are a big thing with us now. We have one every Tuesday. There's a waiting list to get on. Joe Blair does the Tuesday, and then we have one almost every Saturday on WIKY, and WJPS also does lots of remotes. So we have four remote units down in our garage. Yeah, we do a lot of remotes. We'll be doing one now with Red Cross—Saturday remote for Red Cross, part of the flood effort for 1997, going through right now.

Charles A. Blake (ca. 1990)

Charlie Blake

(1927–)

A Hoosier by birth, Charles A. Blake attended Indiana University and the University of Evansville; his radio work began at IU's School of the Sky. His education was interrupted by service in the Communications Battalion in Korea. After graduation, he worked for two years as staff announcer at WSON in Henderson, Kentucky. He moved south to WTRL in Bradenton, Florida, for five years, first as an announcer and then as operations director. Financial considerations and a growing family brought Blake back to Evansville in 1957, where John A. Engelbrecht, a longtime acquaintance and owner of WIKY, gave him a job in sales and as an announcer. Blake guided the station through disasters as general manager. In 1981 the station was completely destroyed by fire. A few months later, a storm twisted WIKY's tower to the ground. In both instances, WIKY was back on the air the next day. Under Blake's management, WIKY became the number one rated station in its market. Laid-back and professional, with a distinct southern drawl and a tongue-in-cheek sense of humor, Charlie Blake has clearly enjoyed the broadcasting profession, so much so that he continues to work at WIKY even in retirement. John Warner, a historian with Wein-traut & Nolan, interviewed Blake in his office at WIKY in Evansville, Indiana, in March 1997.

When I was very young, some of the first efforts that I tried to do, as far as broadcasting was concerned, was to imitate Sid Collins when he was calling the Indianapolis 500 Race over there. And I got quite a reputation for that around the neighborhood, for re-creating from memory some of his broadcasts with guys like Ted Horn and Ralph Hepburn and some of those people involved, and even Wilbur Shaw and back to some of his earlier days. I went to school at Mount Vernon High School, where I graduated, and liked show business. I never thought a guy could make a living in show business, so I started out as a chemistry major up at IU. About the time I ran into qualitative and quantitative and organic chemistry, I decided that maybe it wouldn't be such a bad idea to get involved in the broadcasting, you know. My first experience with actual broadcasting was when I was in the service at Amherst College. You made a recording on one of the old acetate discs just about so big around and with just a little needle and everything, and when I heard my voice played back off this thing, I said, "Oh, my God, you've got to share this gift." And so that's how some of that started. I came back to school after the war, spent some time as a communications officer in Korea, and got some valuable experiences there. Came back and went to school at IU and immediately switched over into theater and speech and what radio department they had back in the late 1940s. Did some things on what they called their School of the Sky.

[Later in Henderson, Kentucky], I did everything that nobody else would do, and it worked out very well. I did some play-by-play, introduced live for programs and things like that, and then of course the usual disc jockey fare and doing news, and covering this story and that story. It worked out, too. It worked out very well. I did get a raise. Congress raised the minimum wage back in those years from forty cents an hour to forty-five cents an hour. That's how I got a raise. Then after a couple of years there, I got married and had the opportunity to move to Florida. A gentleman who had worked with me there in Henderson, Marlen Hager, who is still a friend of mine—I let him beat me in golf so he invites me back down to Florida. And Marlen called and said, "Do you want to come to Florida?" I said, "Hell, anything would be an improvement." So we went to Florida. We spent about five years in the Bradenton area and what was then WTRL 1490. Again, it was one of those jobs where we worked through the chairs from night man into day man, and early morning, and sales, and all those kinds of things. And if you're familiar with Florida at all, you know that a lot of times they like to compensate you with sunshine and palm trees and things like that . . . but there are a lot of fringe benefits as far as the climate was concerned. But my family was growing so fast, I had to come back up north and go to work in the real world and try to make enough money to feed those boys and some of the rest of them.

I'd been talking with John A. Engelbrecht two or three years. I'd come back up here on vacation because my family still lived around Mount Vernon and Wadesville, and John and I shared philosophies. And after two or three years of visiting with each other, he had an unfortunate incident. One of his employees was killed in an accident, an auto accident, and he managed to fill in for several months with people around the edges. That summer we talked, and John said, "Well, why don't you come up here and go to work for me?" And so I decided to do that. I have the original letter that he gave me, and I think he based it on some of my experiences. I had told him about doing everything but mopping the floors and everything, so that's about what that original letter of agreement included. I was going to do this, this, this, this, this, this,

this, this, and he hoped that I would become a valuable employee. And I thought it probably worked out very well.

I started out doing the morning show, and then after the morning show was over, I'd go out and try my skills at selling advertising time and counseling people about how to improve their business, and at the same time improve my business. So that worked out. I went through those chairs and worked into the management area. John was a pretty good guy. He would let me try almost anything I thought I was big enough to do. And, occasionally, he would deliberately let me go ahead and make some of those mistakes that became indelible in my mind. I never made those mistakes again. And I could tell later that he must have been chuckling while I was going through all of those throes and some of those things that we worked with. And from that point on, my personal growth came, and need for that came about the same time that these radio stations were reaching maturity. FM was coming of age and moving on, and so that's pretty well what worked out. We worked through all the chairs with sales and out of the programming into sales, and then into management and all that there. So that's kind of where we are at this point now. We've been able to step aside and out of the involvement of the day-to-day management of the radio station. I think I expressed to young John the other day that, "Hell, I'm starting to enjoy this business again, now that I don't have all those little sticky details after me," so it works out in that area. And that is a general summary of it.

John pretty much made [the formatting] decisions, but he was always careful to get a lot of input not only from staff but throughout the community. He had his own pretty good sounding boards, and he was well known and well liked around the area and so it worked out. He had a gentleman, Herb Simpson. If Herb was sandpaper, John was the match, and you rubbed those two together, and the sparks—ideas if you will—would fly. They worked a great deal together, and he advised us in some of our areas of advertising and promotion and several things like that.

This particular station [WIKY], because they had a lot of confidence in their own ability, we would do a lot of things correctly. And we weren't a big high-powered network station or anything like that. As a result, we were able to do more things that were—in other words, our time was our own. It didn't belong to the network or anything like that. We were in a position where we could be

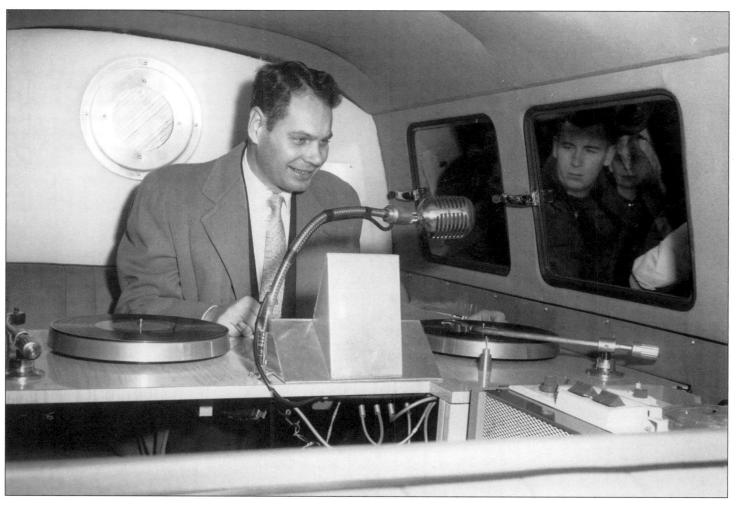

Blake, general manager of WIKY in Evansville, got his start as an announcer. Here he is shown broadcasting from the WIKY van.

Charlie Blake posed with a boat sponsored by WIKY and Risley Electric for "Thunder on the Ohio," an event that draws 75,000 to 100,000 spectators annually.

more involved with the community. Some of these innovative ideas and things that we brought into here—the *Spinner Sanctum*. This was a program where Ken McCutchan (one of my graduates here, now a historian, and he wrote the book [on Evansville]).[57] Ken and I worked together here for what ten or fifteen years, and he was one of the original announcers at the radio station when it went on the air in 1947. Ken had a Saturday afternoon program, and in conjunction with a local appliance and record store, he would preview some of their new records. If you liked that record you just called in. And hell, they would deliver that record to your door either by yellow cab or back in the days when the new Starlight Studebaker or whatever was there. Why hell, they'd drive up to your front door in one of those Studebakers, and I think it was Lloyd Studebaker here on West Franklin. They'd deliver that record. You could call up and say, "Hey, I want to buy that." And they went out. That was the early predecessor of, I guess what do you call that, the home shopping channel on television now.

But the style of programming that we were primarily involved with up until today has been pretty much a family oriented—we described ourselves in the tristates as a family radio station. [It's] never a problem when you have the caliber of people involved in the management that our radio stations have had through the years; there was never much question. Occasionally I'd have to caution one of the guys and say, "Hey, let's leave some of that material for Johnny Carson late at night," or some of these guys. And Johnny wasn't all that bad.

The general thought and feeling that [John Engelbrecht] expressed to me, not once but many times, was that, "You get out of the community what you put into a community. And the same thing," he said, "with a radio station; you get out of a radio station what you put into it." If you put the equipment, you put the people, you put the programming, and these things into it, you're going to get something out of it. We had, down through the years (prior to my being here and since), we've had some really talented people. But John was always pretty well on the cutting edge of the technology. The situation was a little different then than it is now, so that it was a little more affordable at that time. You've heard the story of the fact that we did stereo on radio back before the FM stereo system was invented. We would do one channel on the AM

station, and we'd do the other channel on the FM station. We had Sarkes Tarzian; his people made a radio that you could work off that. It made it a little problematical, because if you were listening on FM only, you only heard that one channel.

If you were listening on the AM and put the two together [FM and AM], then you had the full rich stereo in its original state at that point. Then later on, the Crosley system was invented, and we'd got it very early, so it pioneered right along. Same way with promotions and contests and things like that. John was one of the founding members of a group called the Association of Independent Metropolitan Stations. We were one of the smallest markets to be involved in it at the time. Houston and some in Philadelphia and New York—some of those guys are still around. We traded ideas, not only for promotion, but how you work with people, and ideas of what kind of programming was working where.

We worked with the county fair and the people out there, because, of course, this is the kind of people that we like to deal with and see the real backbone of America there and those folks in helping those areas grow. We worked with Mesker Zoo [Evansville] over here. I think we've donated an animal or two (we helped bring in the kangaroos). The public parks and the Mesker Amphitheater over here—helped promote them—helping to bring some of the bigger stars and things in here. We would work with some of the people who promoted those shows on damn near a public service basis just because that way they could afford to bring us the caliber of entertainment to the area, the Perry Comos or whatever (even though we would make a dollar or two out of the deal). But it helped them to promote those people, and we made it a more attractive place for them to come and put on their shows. So in any imaginable fashion that you can think of, we would get involved.

That [Westside Fall Festival], as you may be aware, or as you may not be aware, is the second largest street festival of its kind in this country, second only to the Mardi Gras down [in New Orleans]. From the very beginning WIKY promoted it. They have entertainment there, the booths and things, and many of the civic organizations, the church organizations raise their entire budget during that week down there by selling food and whatever up and down the line. There's about a six-block area on both sides of the streets; it's kind of like the ethnic food area that they have up in Chicago.

That's part of the responsibility, I believe. And I think that good broadcasters will continue to feel that way. The proceeds not only went into the individual groups, but the parent organization, the [Westside] Nut Club down there. The funds that they make, they contribute to the museum. And then of course there's another area, the philharmonic. These are the kinds of things. Even though it may not be a 100 percent compatible with our programming, we still support a number of these areas for the common good of all and to make our community a well-rounded community with a variety of interests. You don't have to run off to go to Chicago to see name entertainment. We've been able to help through subscription kinds of things where you've got worthwhile connections.

Service is what we're all about. I think it's always in the back of your mind. You know, it doesn't pervade every decision that you make, but you always come back and say "How is this going to affect our community service?" And it wasn't because there was any law. There is no damn law that says we have to run so much public service. But we do that because it serves a useful purpose for us, and we like to do it. But we're pretty selective on what we do, too.

I had the opportunity years ago to go to Chicago and get involved with an hour-and-fifteen-minute commute to work and an hour-and-fifteen-minutes home. That's good—there are other advantages and benefits there. The crime rate— I'm not sure how that really compares, but here, it's a fair-sized city, big enough that we can have certain of the cultural benefits, educational opportunities here with the universities and things that we have. Not much you need that you have to go someplace else to get, and that's fine. Of course, we always like to travel around, and I've done my share of it. If you come back home to a community like this (in fifteen or twenty minutes I can drive from one side of the town to another) and not really worry for life, limb, or property or getting run over out there in the traffic, that's a real benefit. I don't know how it's going to be after we get all the new plants and things in here in operation, but they're certainly welcome in this community. At this point [Evansville] is really experiencing a lot of growth and expecting some kind of growth for our radio station.

My philosophy on television is, "Hell man, I can make enough mistakes in the audio end of the thing, let alone to have to take care of other things." I don't need that. I mean, it's hard for a good lookin' guy like me to say something like that. I probably should have been on television. But in any case, that was it. But the focus was there, and at the time I was moving up, television didn't mean that much to me and, unfortunately, TV didn't mean that much to a lot of people, but there are still a lot of those who could use it, but I guess it may be here to stay. I'm not sure.

[Television] has made us [in radio] be more selective— made us think. We've had to maybe clean up our act a little bit. Well, hell, when you are the lone electronic alternative out there, you might get a little complacent by that. But certainly in the recent years you haven't had time or the opportunity to get complacent, because we've added more television stations, we've added more radio stations. Too damn many. You have to stay on your toes. If you don't, you're in trouble. That's one of the things we're working with now in adding this third FM station here. "The best defense is a good offense," said Marshal [Ferdinand] Foch or somebody.

When I was in Florida, there in the manager's office of that radio station, there was a poster up there, and I'm not sure if it came out of [The] New Yorker magazine or what, but here you see the conductor who's standing in front of a 250-piece orchestra, more or less. He's sweating, raving and rolling his hands over here. And here comes a guy running in on one side of the stage and he says, "Stop the music." He says, "The survey shows that nobody is listening." If you're in broadcasting, you've got to have enough ego to know that somebody out there [is listening]. Like I said, the first time I heard myself, on that acetate disc, "My God, I've got to share this." You know, a gift like this you've got to share.

Donald H. Martin, Sr. (1953)

DON H. MARTIN, WSLM

Don Martin

(1920–)

Perhaps some of Donald H. Martin, Sr.'s entrepreneurial spirit comes from his pioneering family, which includes the legendary Davy Crockett. Martin founded WSLM in Salem, Indiana, the town's first radio station, in 1952. He had majored in radio and drama at Indiana University and gained an understanding of engineering in the marines while helping to set up a radio station on the island of Guam during World War II. His knowledge of the Salem area, coupled with his experience in the service, convinced him that a station located in the rural area of southern Indiana had a future. From the beginning, his stations have featured a wide range of programs that appeal to all ages and interests. Through the years, Martin has experimented with a 50,000-watt FM station and cable television, always in search of what will work best in the Salem area. His son and daughter have joined him in the business, and at present the family owns WSLM-AM and FM and WHAN-TV 17. Don Martin's mom-and-pop enterprise in Salem is an excellent example of the vanishing breed of small-market stations in Indiana. His interviews took place in July 1996 in Salem.

Well, I'm not real sensitive about my age [laughs]. No, I was born in 1920 [in Salem], but it was about 1933 that I think I heard my first radio program. My family was pretty good at adapting to the depression, and we never ever went without a meal, and we had plenty of fuel. We lived on what you'd call a hobby farm now, but it was a livelihood then. My dad did take factory work in order to make ends meet, especially during the depression. But he farmed on the side when he wasn't at the factory, and he had a woods nearby and enough land to have cattle and hogs. I think cattle and hogs were the only thing, but we butchered our own meat and never, never were without meat. And my mother canned blackberries and garden stuff all summer. And as a result we ate just about as good in the depression as we would have without the depression. We had fuel from the woods there and kept warm all right. So the depression didn't hit us as hard as it might have. Some of the urban people got hit lots harder as the rule.

Well, it wasn't too long before I got interested in radio there, too, from my neighbor's radio. I moved to a crystal set which I earned by selling seeds, and I would get programs on it; it would come nearer to getting Cincinnati than it would Louisville. Although I liked Louisville programming, I'd have to go down to the neighbor's to get Louisville. But Cincinnati come in just like a boom, and I'd listen to WLW Cincinnati quite often on the crystal radio.

[Radio] came on, and the people out in the rural area of Salem, about everyone had to have a radio. It was a status symbol far back in those days . . . and those who didn't have a radio would come to their neighbors and listen to the radio. A lot of times they had to put the earphone in a big crock; everybody would get around it, and they would listen to the programs from the big power stations. There weren't any smaller stations at that time. All of them were 50,000 watts. Cincinnati even had 500,000 watts at one time until they had to change back to 50,000. But radio certainly did bring the communities together and they'd come to listen to pieces or subjects like—well, in our case here, old Jimmy Sizemore and his dad, Asher Sizemore. Anyway, Jimmy Sizemore was the star of the program, and they'd come to listen to him once a week. And they'd come to listen to *Lum and Abner* and to a lot of the other more or less sitcom comedies.

It seemed like instead of the newscast there, the comedy programs were more popular. They would come to hear the comedy shows more so than they would the newscasts, although our neighbors would keep up on the news and would let us know if there was anything of newsworthy interest. They'd let the other neighbors know. But they didn't flock in to listen to the neighbor's radio to the newscasters as much as I would have expected them to. Because nowadays news is pretty important. In those days, they seemed to be more casual about the news and wanted to hear the comedy programs. The entertainment factor was number one in our neighborhood at that time, I know.

World War II definitely did establish radio. And that may have been why I got my interest in radio, because I was sent overseas in the marines in more or less I guess you'd say the same thing as the signal company. Overseas, I made a razor-blade radio which I think I can still make and make it talk. The razor blade took the place of the crystal. And just a regular blade wouldn't do it, but an old rusty blade would be a detector similar to a crystal [because] we didn't have the crystal available. We just got around the headphones . . . and got results . . . off that razor-blade radio. We were in radar and in radio, and also did a little bit of work in programming it too. And we helped set up a radio station on the island of Guam, the first station there. And certainly all the people in the service would listen to the news on the radio—news from

home as well as news abroad. They had both national and international news, and I remember they would have more than one newscaster on it. They may be the first ones to invent having a dual newscast, because previously most of the newscast had been a single, just one announcer on it. But when they put two on there, it seemed to heighten the interest in it. I know our outfit that was listening to it on the outdoor theater speakers always was glad when they had two different announcers on it because it sort of made it more professional we thought.

That [experience on Guam] gave me the idea that if I could build one on Guam, I could come back to my own home town and build a station. Of course, I had taken radio and dramatics at IU, and it was mostly programming. But I got the engineering experience through the service. It made a complement, a pretty good complement for I knew about both the programming and the engineering, and it took both to operate a station in a small city. We may have been the smallest city in Indiana with our radio. I know what [the population of Salem] is now, about 23,000 now, but it was more like probably 15,000 or 16,000 in 1952. I know we were one of the smallest cities operating anyway. We started out with 250 watts and grew to 1,000 and then from 1,000 to 5,000.

There was more emphasis on news when I came back from the service than when I went in. I know there was more emphasis on the news; news and the comedy were, I guess, probably tops. They didn't do anything else. They hadn't started yet adapting to giving weather and traffic instructions on the car radios. They didn't start that until 1949 or 1950 when TV was making an inroad anyway.

I applied for [a license] in 1948 as well as starting teaching school in 1948. I applied for the license, but four and a half years later, something like that, the license came through. I had to have two hearings; my salary from the school there, although it was rather meager, was enough to help me go to Washington, D.C., for hearings. I went there for two hearings and won both of them.

There's a different economy now. I could never have started this station on a shoestring like I did then. Nowadays you couldn't do that. It was started on a shoestring. But back there you didn't have quite as much competition and many hearings. I went to two hearings. But now people would have to go to maybe five or six hearings in order to get a station. And hearings were real expensive then, but they're more expensive now. See these other stations have to have protection. And there's a lot more stations out there now.

I guess I had to be a daredevil, because it was whispered around town that some crazy man is trying to start a station in Salem [laughs]. I was a boy at that time, more or less, yeah. But anyway, they called it "some crazy man," I remember that came back to me, "is trying to start a radio station here." And then I went to one advertiser, just one in Salem, that said, "Well, the reason I'm not going to advertise with you is that I don't think a station will go in Salem." And I said, "Well, that's exactly the reason it won't go, if you don't advertise with me."

And I had to make another decision besides going with radio; I had to make a decision whether it was going to go AM or FM. A bunch of merchants came out and said, "You're putting in AM, Don, and you should be putting in FM." I said, "No, I know what I'm doing. I'll add the FM whenever it gets popular, because there are no FM radios in the homes right now. So why put in an FM station?"

We had a couple of investors at the very beginning. And I was real lucky that they got cold feet in the thing and sold out to me. I was glad, but I didn't know at that time how lucky I was. I was able to buy them out on contract, and it was the best thing I've ever done in order to end up as sole owner. I figured I could operate it as a one-man station if I had to. If it really came down to it I could have, although it would have been about a twenty-four-hour operation, to have done it. It would be real hard on a person to do it. Payroll is one of our biggest things. Ninety percent of our expenses is payroll, and I could have kept the payroll down; but never did I have to become a one-man station. But I knew in Salem that I could if I had to.

[We started] exactly on Valentine's Day in 1953. It was *BMI Magazine* that was coming out those days, and they latched onto the fact that we started on Valentine's Day and said, "Well, it should be called the 'Sweetheart of Southern Indiana.'"

[Radio in Salem] was pioneered by our family, and I don't know that anybody would ever have gotten the idea that Salem would support one. I think it had to probably come from within, somebody that was a native of Salem, because you had to have the confidence of the merchants. If somebody from outside would have come in they wouldn't have been able to start in with the confidence of

the merchants. Yes, I had visited with them [the merchants] and during that four and a half years [met] quite often and primed them for it, and they were looking forward to it and we started out—I don't know—we hardly operated any at all in the red. We started out pretty well in the black. I'd say you couldn't do that today.

I worked with the Chamber of Commerce and had done quite a bit, I guess romancing them before we started. And they come in pretty good. They started out buying newscasts first, of course. And they were right, the newscasts being pretty important. Then they started buying farm programs, second. And third then, some of them bought country music. I know some bands, local bands came in, country bands that wanted to get sponsors. And so I sent them out to some of our bigger sponsors, and they'd go out and see if they would sponsor you. They came back with the answer that the sponsors said, "Why should we sponsor a live band when we can buy music cheaper than that on the station?" So they'd buy the country music and didn't sponsor any live bands. But they came in order to get bookings for themselves, see. So we had studios full of live musicians every once in a while, and we did do a little bit of, I guess you'd say, selection to make sure that they weren't—well, just dogs. And also, I guess you'd say, didn't use bad language, stuff like that. We mostly had gospel groups, I think. We had some country, just straight country music, musicians still came. But they couldn't get local sponsors because local sponsors knew our price for sponsoring music and they wouldn't pay the talent fee.

Well, some of [the original programs] we still have even to this day. But we certainly had to adapt too, because we started out with I think too many—not exactly talk shows, but talk programs. Like we started out with the *Hoosier Schoolmaster,* and we even had this sponsored. But nowadays [we] couldn't go out and get a sponsor for an education program very easily. Just couldn't do it.

We eat lunch and go to meetings here with listeners and sponsors. So there is more of a personal touch than there would be in a big city. It'd take you a long time to get around to all of your sponsors in a large city very likely. But in our community, we meet them in civic meetings and community meetings and at the fair. See we have a booth at the fair, and the fair is coming up real soon here, the twentieth through the twenty-eighth of July. We have a booth there and give out souvenirs and meet the public. About three days out of the six or eight days, we're going to have a live broadcast from the booth and give out some door prizes. We pretty well mingle with the people that listen to us. And also, we're oftentimes set up next door to sponsors, and they get to know each other better too. So it's more of, I guess you'd say, interaction between the public and the sponsors with a smaller station than it is with a larger station.

We couldn't make it on all talk show, or all music show. We know our limitations, and we have to have a variety to get as many sponsors as possible in order to exist. So, specialization works in the bigger city, but it wouldn't work in our rural area. We have a *Memory Moments* program that we started with and it's been real popular all along. A lot of stations don't read obits [obituaries] at all, and some of them, if they do, they won't read them on a newscast; they'd have a special program for obits. But we find out that the people are listening for those obits and maybe our audience—that proved our audience is maybe more in the senior citizen line than it is anywhere. People will send in requests to play such and such songs in memory of maybe their husband or wife, or whomever. And that's where back in the days when we did that in 1953 they complained about, "He doesn't sing them as pretty as the other person sings them." They'd really call us on that, and it was the same record each time, you know, the same song. One we try to cater to is eighteen to fifty-four. But I think it's more like eighteen to seventy-four maybe. Anyway we've got all in between there. But if we'd shut out and quit doing the obits we'd have quite a bit of complaints, not only from our listeners, but from our sponsors too, because they sponsor the obits, knowing that they've got listenership on them.

We've kind of updated [the programming], and we find that we have a niche in bluegrass country instead of regular country, and we can get sponsors for bluegrass music now a little better than we could just for straight country. Other stations have told us, like a Columbus station—I'm not going to name the call letters—a Columbus station told us they listen to our station because we're the only ones that play bluegrass. We're close enough to Louisville; that's a bluegrass state, you know, down there. And so once in awhile we say we play bluegrass music for a bluegrass state, but it's also for Indiana as well as Kentucky.

But we're picked up in Kentucky, and we get mail from Kentucky.

We have to meet the requirements of the FCC. They require so much issues and answers. You're supposed to list your issues every month and also your programs that you air to answer, or I guess you'd say, respond to the issues. So we do that anyway, but especially now that they're checking all stations on the public issues versus your programming. We pick out issues sort of around certain things in the community. Well, we tried to keep a good reputation. I think we have one anyway. We did try to do community service or anything that would come up. We have a bulletin board program that's almost as popular as the newscast where we do community announcements free of charge about church meetings, Chamber of Commerce meetings, and lodge and civic organization meetings. That's strictly specialized but that program stays sponsored pretty well, too. Very seldom it's ever been without a sponsor.

We don't subscribe to Arbitron, but we do send in the diaries that they have. And we do get a pretty good rating with Arbitron. We also had bought some surveys which back up some of the things that we suspected pretty well—that certain programs were better than others, you know. And for awhile there, that *Memory Moments* program I thought was average turned out to be a number one program. Right now it's probably number three or four or something like that, because now our newscast rates higher. And our farm markets rate probably second and maybe *Memory Moments* third, or obits third or fourth anyway. But the sponsors go by our surveys, and they buy just about according to them, because it's pretty accurate.

Network Indiana is our state feed, and Agro America and USA News is our national feed. We have what we call local news network, and people out there call in when they see a news item, and we give a prize about every week. If their news tip warrants it we give—I think it's only five dollars cash, but they'll call in their news tips to get that cash money. And that's what we call a local news network. That's the public out there feeding us news mostly for I guess a prize or for getting their names on the air or something. But we stay pretty steady giving out a news tip per week to what we consider—and we let our staff judge it—what we consider the best news tip of the week, you know.

After learning from an IBA seminar that a searchlight could be a great sales booster, Don Martin invested in one and swore by it.

As part of its community outreach, WSLM sponsored a Little League softball team in the 1960s. Station owner Don Martin stood behind the team at right.   DON H. MARTIN, WSLM

Martin did everything around the station, including climbing the WSLM tower as shown in this 1963 photo.

DON H. MARTIN, WSLM

Well, of course, you may have to bow to some of the things that you wouldn't have to in some other business. The listeners are usually always right. Not always, but usually always. We always assume the listener is right just like they assume a customer is right in a store. And we've had some disgruntled listeners at times, thinking that we left maybe their memorial of of *Memory Moments,* when we didn't maybe. Or we got so busy we couldn't put them all on. They'll get disgruntled. But I don't think they get mad enough, angry enough to quit listening to us. I think they just want to voice their opinion to us at times if we fail to put them on; that's where we get the most complaints if we fail to put something on that they had wanted on.

And some of it is naive, and we don't make fun of them; we overlook it because they've not had any real experience, I guess you'd say, real city training in radio and its elements. When they call up and—this woman called up and said, "I want to speak to the governor." And we said, "Well, we had him on tape, but he's not here." And she said, "I know he is here. I heard him, and I know he's there." This woman wouldn't believe that he was on tape. So we finally told her. I said, "He is not here; we've got the tape here. I'll be glad to play the tape back for you or let you play it if you want to." And she got mad and hung up on us. And I don't know whether she stayed listening to us or not. But she never did believe that the governor wasn't there, and that we had him on tape that time.

You won't exist long if you won't accept responsibility to your listeners. Definitely you've got to become a part of the community and a member of it and the more clubs and organizations you get into—I've got my son into about the same ones I'm into. And [my daughter] Becky is in the clubs and organizations. You just have to have the personal touch in order to get the sponsorship. And that's what pays our bills as well as the employees' bill. So you have to really adapt and adjust to become part of the community. You can't be an outsider and stay an outsider, because an outsider wouldn't be accepted in our area.

Well, we had to grow into that confidence. It didn't start out quite that way where they would call in and ask for the announcements like they do now. They finally accepted us as being equal to a newspaper. At the very beginning there in the business meetings we'd go to—well, they'd talk local newspaper and we'd finally have to

bring up radio. But now they bring up radio as much as they do the newspapers. So they, after twenty-five or thirty years, they have accepted us on the same level as the newspaper.

We have three mobile units that go out and do remotes, and we do quite a few of them. It's become more or less an anniversary thing for a lot of the sponsors. On their anniversary they want a live remote from their business. And of course, on a new car showing, the car dealers want a live remote. And I found out the live remotes definitely put you out in front mixing with the public and mingling with the people. It's a two-way street. Not only do they pay for it, but at the same time you get to put your best foot forward in the community. There's a grocery store on their anniversary all the time that has a live remote and they look forward to it, and we look forward to it too. But it's pretty well sponsored and at the same time, you get to meet the public again and again and give away some of our station gimmicks.

We had at one time three airplanes, and we used them all in news. And I used to go to Chicago in my bigger one and sell advertising in Chicago. And it paid for itself. We used some of our planes for local news. And we'd fly to an area—and my farm director was often flying to farm meetings and farm field days and things like that. So we'd use all three of them. But it just finally boiled down to where we didn't have the staff to do it.

We bought [a] motorboat, I guess, to do some newsworthy stuff on the lakes and the Ohio River. We often went there when we had news stories during floods. And once or twice we would almost get hit by big boats. But I remember using it the most one time when a barge got stuck on the levee down there, I guess. Well, on a gate, one of the gates down on the Ohio River—a barge got stuck. And they were doing everything on earth to try to pry that thing loose, and it stayed there a long time. But we went down and covered it quite often, probably once or twice a day with our motorboat just to get the news from the crews down there. They finally did get it off. And not only that, we also ran our searchlight at night to keep the river safe for other barges so that, I guess, no other barge could hit it when it was lodged on the gate.

The searchlight was bought in 1968, and it was bought because of an IBA meeting where a seminar recommended that: if you can buy an old searchlight, it will help you sell your radio advertising. So I said, "Well, I'm going to try that and see." And I had to spend three or four years before I found a searchlight. Found one down in New Albany that was for sale. Had to be fixed up a bit, but believe you me, it has been superior in helping sell radio packages. We sold a big package once because we had it, and other stations, some of them bigger than us, had bid on doing a sesquicentennial in Crothersville, Indiana. And we all put our bids in, but we were the only one with the searchlight and we got the job because of the searchlight. Some bigger stations there, some from Columbus and Madison—we often rent our searchlight for their advertisers.

We've had some national reports; one of them, if you want to hear some more, when we broke into national news. Back about our very beginning—well, that was back in the days when all of them were naive, the people were. And they used us for finding such things as lost children, lost skunks even. We found a lost skunk for a lady. And this time a lost cow, that lady wanted, and she said she was desperate. She said, "I've got to have my cow. I've got to have my cow back. Will you please put it on the air right away?" Well, while we were typing that thing up, she called back and said, "I found my cow; I found my cow. There was a lady listening on the party line, and she knew where the cow was, and she told me." So we got scooped by a party line, the radio station did. And we printed up the story and sent it in the AP and UPI that we had at that time, and they put it on there and I guess all over the nation.

There were other things that we had locally that were more or less disasters eight years ago. We were the victims of a bombing scare down here. We had about eight or ten bombs and mostly labeled—mostly hung on the offices of attorneys. Attorneys seemed to be what they were trying to get at anyway. They hung these bombs on the sides of the buildings, and they had enough powder in them all right to blow the side of the building out, but they didn't have the right detonator in it. And thank goodness they didn't or Salem would have been kind of a rubble for awhile in certain places. That was one of the headlines that Salem made nationally. You could say it was infamous instead of being famous, but it certainly did attract attention. And Salem was known for that eight years ago. July 5th is when it happened.

One of the biggest changes for radio was when TV came. Until [radio] adapted, they said many a time, "Well, radio is dead. Television has got it all now. There's no need for radio; it's dead." [But] the theater of the mind is a whole lot more of a picture, a truer picture than the picture on the screen. The screen limits—you're limited by the picture on the screen. Now in the theater of the mind, there's no limit whatsoever. And believe you me, you can really have—I mean have imagination with just hearing rain on the program, or hearing drums beating. Your imagination is not limited in radio like it is by watching a picture on the screen. So there is some advantage to radio yet, and I don't think TV will ever equal that advantage. Therefore, I believe the radio will be here as long as TV is, or longer!

I learned somewhat from other stations about the [radio] adaptation, and from seminars. I went to IBA seminars every once in awhile to find out how to adapt. And then when they came out with methods of adapting, we'd do it too, like the other stations. Instead of having a—they had a lot more, I guess you'd say, road show programs, where they would give you information for radio in the car. In other words, they programmed for car radios a lot more then, because they knew they had a captive audience there, that they may not have in the homes, when TV might be on instead of the radio. So they started giving weather and road conditions and other things, and we did that too early of a morning, and also school closings that the TV has a harder job doing than we do. And things that TV couldn't do, we had to adapt to and learn to do and change over from maybe these comedy shows that made radio in the golden era.

We built a cable TV station in Salem. All the seminars we went to told us, "You better own your own cable system, because they're going to come into town and give you competition, the cables are." So we did build a cable system here in Salem in 1972. And we did do local origination on that. We did TV programs on that about thirty hours a week, and that also broadened the idea that I should go on in and build a TV station sometime. I know the public had asked us. They said, "When are you going to build TV? When are you going to go to TV?" And this kind of substituted for it, local origination. We had a TV program within the length of the cable [system]. Wherever the cable went in town, why they could get a TV program that we originated, local origination. But they were more

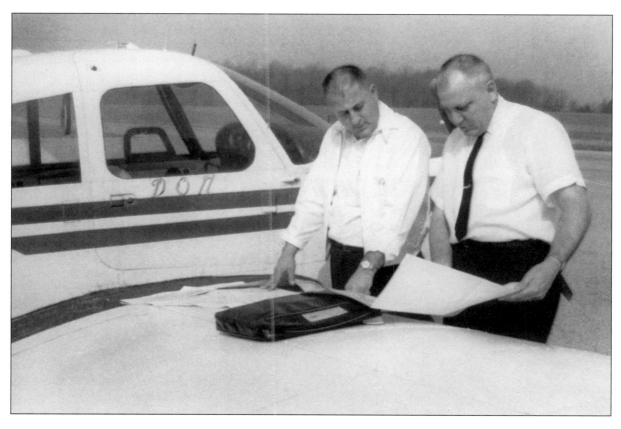

Don Martin plotted his flight plan with WSLM farm director Erwin Eisert. WSLM owned three planes in the 1960s, one of which was this Piper Cherokee.

At age seventy-seven, Martin continued to be active in the affairs of his stations.

interested in over-the-air TV, and that's what did come later. We were first to go ahead and apply for a different channel than what we've got now, but we're real happy with our Channel 17. We applied first for Channel 58 TV.

I don't exactly call myself a great entrepreneur, but I do think, and I did bring some innovations into it that might not [have] been brought in locally if somebody else had started this station. It took an awful amount of imagination that was fired by instructors at IU and the imagination that was fired by my drill instructors in the marines. So all of that combination, I think, went together to give me a little bit more diversity than possibly somebody else. And maybe my hometown was an advantage too, because people knew that I wasn't from a family that would normally stick them with advertising prices and also with advertising bills if they didn't ask for it or didn't order it. So it helped out being from this hometown. The fact that I'd been raised here and graduated from high school here and went away to college from here, and so forth, did help out, I think in getting basically started.

It's a family station here. My daughter does actually own the FM. I own the AM yet, and on paper she owns the TV station, but she's not got any investment in the TV. She's got it in the radio. [My son is] an engineer and a pretty good one, and he also climbs towers like I used to do. We've got that reputation in the Indiana broadcasters of being a family station, and we're not against it because it is true. And, of course, I'm trying to groom them to operate it whenever I can step out, and they're fairly ready; but I don't think they're quite ready to be pushed out of the nest yet.

I don't see any real change in [small-market radio] as far as becoming obsolete. I don't see it becoming obsolete. I think it's got its place alongside of the national radio and national TV even, because it's still more personalized. I don't know of any other niche in Salem I'd rather be connected with, because it's been my life since 1952 or 1953. And I hope it's going to be a life for my grandkids and my kids' grandkids.

Richard M. Fairbanks (ca. 1950s)

CHAPTER TWENTY-FIVE

Dick Fairbanks

(1912–)

With an ambition to become a newspaperman, Richard M. Fairbanks began his career at the family-owned Indianapolis News *before World War II. After the war, however, when the FCC ruled that no one operator could own both a newspaper and a radio station in the same market, he formed Fairbanks Broadcasting Company, which bought WIBC from the* News. *Fairbanks soon enlarged the station to 50,000 watts, and in 1960 his company signed on an FM station, WIBC-FM, changing its name to WNAP in 1968. Under his leadership, WIBC soon became the most successful radio station in Indianapolis. One of Fairbanks's proudest achievements is the founding of the Indianapolis Motor Speedway Network, which has broadcast the 500-Mile Race to listeners all over the world. A shrewd businessman, Fairbanks has expanded his empire far beyond Indianapolis. His company owns stations in Boston and Framingham, Massachusetts, and three stations in West Palm Beach and one in Fort Pierce, Florida. When Fairbanks's interview was conducted in July 1994, it was at his summer home in Indianapolis.*

I was born right here [in Indianapolis] in 1912. My grandfather, Charles Warren Fairbanks, who was the vice president under Teddy Roosevelt, was in the newspaper business until he died. He owned the *Indianapolis News*. (Politicians are frequently other things, too.) He actually got involved in newspapers—I read this someplace—in his youth. When he was quite young he worked for the Associated Press. But he got a law degree, and that was the end of that. His cousin, Delavan Smith—I think it was Delavan—was the publisher of the *Indianapolis News*, but he was also a part owner of it, and my grandfather went into the *Indianapolis News* because of family loyalties and because his cousin importuned him to come in and bail him out. So, that's how that started, oh, back in the 1890s, I suppose.

[My father] and a partner owned the *Anderson Herald* when he was young, before World War I. Well, I think he had the Anderson paper until he went into the army. Much later he acceded to the presidency of the *Indianapolis News* . . . through the deaths of his two older brothers. The *Indianapolis News*, I believe along with L. S. Ayres, owned the first radio station in Indianapolis. Now, this was a station that some guy built in his garage probably, and they put up the money for it. Nothing much ever happened. So when the depression came along, they just pulled out the rug and left. They said, "Well, we tried that, and it's no good."

Warren [my father's brother] had run the paper for almost twenty years, and it was during his tenure that the paper reached its greatest heights really—won two or three Pulitzer prizes—and circulation was miles ahead of everybody else. He did a very fine job. But when the depression came along, his philosophy of operating—I had no connection with this whatsoever—but his philosophy and mine are not the same. His idea was you just cut down on expenses. This was not unknown—not just in newspapers but in all industry during the depression, there were general cuts. You'd have a series of 10, 15, 20 percent cuts. And sometimes this works, and sometimes this doesn't. . . . Happily, I've never been in that exact situation, but I don't think that I would do it exactly that way. There are people whose philosophy is that you can always find somebody better and cheaper. And I heard those words actually used once. I don't believe this. I think you can find somebody better, and I think you can find somebody cheaper, but they don't go together.

There wasn't any question about [radio's growth during World War II]. That's how people got their news in those days, but paradoxically, there wasn't nearly as much news on radio then as there is today. Ah, they were feeling their way. They didn't know what they were doing either. In the same way that in the early days of television, your major network newscasts . . . were only fifteen minutes. That's all you got.

In today's radio and for the last twenty or thirty years maybe—twenty years anyway—program directors and program people have fought the commercial department. They don't want their beautiful programming interrupted [by] commercials, and without the commercials they're not going to have any beautiful programming. And so I go back to what we did with Armed Forces Radio—and I wasn't in Armed Forces Radio, but I had friends who were. We had these guys when we were in Guam struggling to pick up San Francisco stations. We had the same music on Armed Forces Radio, but they didn't have any commercials. So we manufactured commercials. We sold the service life insurance and this kind of thing—not real commercials, but they sounded like commercials. That made people much happier.

I remember at the *Indianapolis News* during the depression some women coming in and complaining because we weren't carrying enough advertising. We were very unhappy about it too, but that wasn't our choice. And people do this with radio and television today, consciously or unconsciously. I believe in it very sincerely.

I think that stations that run, and proudly proclaim that they don't run more than two minutes per quarter hour are kidding themselves.

When I got into radio it was supposed to be the end of the day for radio. Television was just starting up, and in 1948, I believe—Indianapolis being a little slow—had one television station come on the air. Channel 4 was assigned to Bloomington, but it came on around the same time. One little drawback—you couldn't pick it up. But Channel 6 came on, and people rushed to buy sets.[58] This happened all over the country. There was a freeze that went on in television construction in 1947—end of 1947—I think it was 1948, and there were no stations built for several years . . . because the [Federal Communications] Commission at that time thought that the only effective means of operating a television station was in what was known as the "low band." You'll never hear that expression today, but it was common then. That was channels 2 through 6. There is no Channel 1. Why is there no Channel 1? I have no idea. It has to do with physics, but I don't know why. There were a lot of people who wanted to get a television station, so the commission simply froze it, and they would accept no applications and wouldn't process any applications that they had. They just sat there, because they were going to figure out where they were going to put these channels. When they got through with it, they allocated channels not only in the low band but in the high band, which would be channels 7 through 13. *Nobody* wanted a UHF channel; that was the end, but they were allocated, too.

[I worked at the] *Miami Daily News* after the war for a year. I didn't come back to Indianapolis until 1947. The reason I came back is because the *News* was not doing very well. Having failed to interest Warren [Fairbanks] in broadcasting—I'm sure it's when my father was president and that was a rather brief tenure—I suggested to him that I had heard that WIBC—which I think was a daytimer at the time—was for sale. I said that we might as well buy this to protect our future. Well, some of the people who stayed on during the war did carry this on, and they did buy WIBC which by that time was full-time—oh, I think about 1942 or 1943.[59]

I found that the radio station was in the [Indianapolis] Athletic Club. This was all right except that they were paying rent there, and the *Indianapolis News* had about—I don't know how many floors—one, two, three, four floors totally vacant [laughs]. They owned the station; they owned the building, too. So it seemed reasonable to me to move the station into the building. And they did. In large part, the station was vaguely profitable in those years. They couldn't keep any of the money, and they couldn't keep any of the money in the newspaper for that matter because of the taxes that were in effect in World War II. So if we could move it into this building and charge them rent, at least the newspaper would get some rent out of it.

In 1947 I didn't intend to go to the radio station. I intended to go to the newspaper. The *Indianapolis News* and the *Indianapolis Star* were merged in 1948. The newspaper sold [the station] to me . . . so, I formed a company, WIBC, Inc.—a very clever title. When I bought it, it was still the Indiana Broadcasting Corporation, and the original owner named it. I used a family trust for financing, and that's why I brought [my cousins] into it since they had an interest in the family trust—fortunately, not as large an interest as I had.

I'd never been in a radio station before. But after I got here I figured out what to do. We had a radio station at the [*Miami*] *Daily News* that was run by a guy that I knew that used to work at the *Indianapolis News*, so I talked to him a little bit before I came back to Indianapolis—after I found I was saddled with this radio station. And then I went out and talked to people that I knew who had radio stations. Very simple.

In those early days, all stations, I think, operated with a circular antenna. The signal just went out in all directions. It was just as strong over here as it was over there. But, as they got more and more stations, they became more and more directionalized, so that you could put a station in New Albany and another station in Richmond on the same frequency—this is a little close—and you get involved in first adjacencies and second adjacencies and even third adjacencies. This is why they had to work out these very elaborate operations in order to get the stations on the air at all. In the early days of the Radio Commission, I don't think they had that problem because there weren't that many stations. I guess it may have been the Federal Communications Commission, but anyway, they finally came up with various classes of stations. WLW [Cincinnati], for example, is a Class 1-A. At one time, WLW, which still likes to call itself "The Nation's Station," had 500 kilowatts and was by far the most powerful station in the country.

I think WIBC was on two floors [of the Indianapolis News building]. Back in those days, I think they had two or three—three maybe—and a news studio. They performed up until the time I got there. We just put different shows together. The recorded music was so much superior to the music the musicians could put out that there was just no comparison. We got music from music producers. Well, in 1947, network radio was on a toboggan, but they were still programming several hours a day. They had soap operas. Many of the programs you see on television were on radio at night, and they had network news—fifteen-minute network news—two or three times a day. We had some news commentators from Mutual that we carried, but most of our news was local.

Well, [WIBC] wasn't doing very well. It was overpopulated, so I depopulated it. I cut a great many of them out. It wasn't all done at once. But I think a radio station probably, even in those days when it was inflated by unions, had too many people. As a small example—I couldn't do anything about this at the time—I think they had twelve or thirteen engineers. I don't know how many they have at WIBC today, but I'd be amazed if they had more than two.

[I kept] Chickie, Country Cousin Chickie. Easy Gwynn, I kept. Mike Dunn, I kept; he wasn't there for very long, but I kept him for awhile. Well, I kept Jim Shelton. He was there forever. Bill Fox, *The Fox's Den*. We were fourth in the market in 1947, and I would have said in 1948 we were possibly second, and in 1949—I'd say we were probably first—tied for first possibly. And from then on we were first. I just put on what I *thought* was going to go, and fortunately it did; management, solely and simply.

We concentrated on news—news and good programming and good personnel. There were certain people there who knew what they were doing. The only thing they didn't know anything about was news, and I simply went out and hired newsmen. That's not hard. It varies from station to station, but basically, most stations have a program director, and some have a production manager. It's a title I've never used. He sort of works with the program director. Basically, you have a program director, you have a sales manager, and you have an engineering chief. You may have a one-man staff, but that's your chief engineer.

Easy Gwynn was there from 1947 until probably 1963 or 1964. Finally, time passed him by. In the beginning, when he started out, it was sufficient to have a stack of records and just go in and ad-lib. Well, today, the morning show at WCLB [Boston] is basically two men. But then they have a third man who is supposed to be funny and a woman who does the weather. They have another woman—I'm not quite positive what she does—but this is a group effort. Probably on that one show they have more people than I used to have running twenty-four hours a day.

Jim Shelton was there when I got the station in 1947, and he was still with the station when I sold it in 1982. In the interim, he had progressed from being an entertainer into being a top salesman, as he was when I left. I'm not sure he ever wanted to stop being an entertainer, but he got more money being a salesman so he was willing to drop his shows, which were outgrown by that time. He invented *Pick-a-Pocket*. That was his main joy in life, really. And then he also did a record show in the evening. I can't remember what he called it. It was great for the 1940s and early 1950s, but it wasn't so good in the 1970s.

Same thing with Jack Morrow. He was there the same span of time as Jim Shelton, except that he had left the station and I brought him back I believe in 1947. He was a specialist in something that practically doesn't exist anymore. He did a lot of what we called P.I. These are commercials that are paid for by the number of inquiries that you got. P.I. stood for "per inquiry," and we stopped doing those, oh, sometime in the 1950s. After that, he did disc shows and eventually graduated, if that's the right word, from doing air work to handling affairs with the Federal Communications Commission.

The Haymakers were a hillbilly band; today it would be country. Tommy [Moriarity] was a musician, which Chickie wasn't necessarily. There was a guy by the name of Paul—I forget his last name. Paul and his wife, Sugar, were around for years off the air. People used them at parties as entertainers. But Paul was probably the best musician of the bunch. In fact, you might even say he was the only musician. Tommy Moriarity was good; he played the accordion. Somebody else played the clarinet. These were again off-the-air entertainers. On the air, Tommy still played the accordion, but he also tried sales. On the air—Paul Burton was his name—Paul played the same instrument but he called it a fiddle. Off the air, it was definitely a violin. A hillbilly band—that's what we called it in those days. It was a fiddle, an accordion—Chickie played the bass viol. I can't remember who else was in the group.

Sales then and now are so totally different that they are not really comparable, but the most effective salesman I had in the beginning was a man by the name of Watson [1947–70]. Kenny Watson came from a newspaper background. His father was a *Star* reporter in his youth but he had eye problems and was going blind. Kenny had to hustle even as a kid. He sold whatever there was available. When you sell radio, you're selling a concept, and he was very good at conceiving proper advertising vehicles for his clients.

Joan Evans was one of the very first women salesmen in the business. I don't say that she was the first, but she was one of the first. She was a secretary when she started, but she wanted to get into sales. Actually, I took her from being a secretary to do a woman's show. They don't have women's shows any more, but in those days we did. She sold her own show and branched off from that and sold all kinds of things. We scrapped her show, and she was the top salesman at WIBC from about 1960 maybe until she retired two or three years ago. People were fascinated with having a woman in sales. But today we have six radio stations and one of them has a sales manager who's a man, and just starting next week we have a sales office that will be handled by a man; all the rest of them are women. And if you go into a sales department, it's a rarity to find men. We have more in Boston than most stations that I know of. Basically, though, they're women. Women are more aggressive. Oh, much more aggressive as a rule, I would say [laughs].

Of course, there are a lot of women that are managing radio stations or radio groups. The president of CBS-Radio is a woman. There's a woman who is the manager of WENS and she is over the manager of WIBC and WKLR. So they have moved up the ladder. And this has nothing to do with EEOC [Equal Employment Opportunity Commission]. They did it purely because they had the ability to do it. EEOC says that you must hire women whether they're any good or not; and that isn't sufficient. For every one you hire, you should interview a hundred.

We have had very, very few people leave us. The atmosphere, I presume, is better. They like what they're doing. They like the way it's being done. We have had to kind of ease people out, but people have, by and large, stayed pretty much with us unless they got some big opportunity to go someplace. This has occurred, but not

Fairbanks, Fred Heckman, Bill Dean, and some of the WIBC office staff celebrate reaching their goal for the United Way.

Sid Collins, probably best remembered as the Indianapolis Motor Speedway Network's "Voice of the 500," later went into sales. Collins, a member of the Hall of Fame, died in 1977.

Richard Fairbanks gave the old building on Illinois Street to Butler University in 1981 when WIBC moved its headquarters to 9292 North Meridian Street.

"Big John" Gillis stood beside the WIBC helicopter from which he broadcast traffic reports.

very frequently. We still have people—up until the last couple of years—there were still people at WIBC who thought they were working for me.

Sid [Collins] wanted to be an entertainer, and when I got the station, he was running a show called *PM Party.* I can't imagine anyone naming a show that, but that's what they called it. It was live, so it wasn't destined to live very long. He wanted to do sports, because he thought it had a future maybe or glamour—I don't know which. Sid was a very bright guy, so he went out with a tape recorder and taped a couple of football games to show how well he could do them. He did do them well. Unfortunately, about that time I stopped doing live football games. So then he turned himself to sales. He thought maybe that's where the money was. He was a very effective salesman when he wanted to be, but his basic idea was to be a performer.

I started the Indianapolis Motor Speedway Network. In 1948 I bought the rights to the Speedway and broadcast it to two or three other stations in Indiana. Well, I carried it; as well as I can remember, in 1946, and 1947 it belonged to Mutual. I think in 1948 and 1949 I held the rights, and the first year I broadcast to three stations—next year to maybe four or five, all in Indiana. Then we decided, since everybody liked it, we might as well go national with it. So, this is what we did. We founded the Indianapolis Motor Speedway Network in conjunction with the Indianapolis Motor Speedway. Bought [the rights] originally from the Speedway, of course. They were certainly delighted with the whole idea, and we did it. And it seems to me that the Speedway paid us finally to do the race. Ah, and I've never thought they paid us enough, but that's beside the point. But they did pay us. We started in 1948 with Bill Fox doing the broadcast for us. He wasn't in very good health, so I put Sid Collins with him, and that's how Sid Collins got involved with race broadcasting and became the "Voice of the 500."

We had our own little network just in Indiana. Then in 1949 or 1950—I don't know when it was, but along in there somewhere—we set up a nationwide network. It was the biggest network in the world at that time because it was carried by the Armed Forces Radio Network. Wilbur Shaw, who ran the Speedway for Tony [Hulman] before he [Shaw] died, asked that we use people from the other Indianapolis radio stations and we did, same ones every year. A guy by the name of Gil Berry [Gilbert Berry] managed it from WIBC. You had pickup points around the track that

was all. Originally, we had one in the pits and, then I think we eventually went to two and one on each of the four corners. And we had a race driver in the booth after Bill Fox died, and that was quite a long time ago. We had a race driver in with Sid Collins. When we quit, when Tony Hulman died, whoever took his place in his company—not the Speedway—but his company decided that we were being paid too much for doing this. Why should we be paid when the Hulman estate had a radio station in Terre Haute. So they took it back, and they've done it ever since.

[Radio broadcasting] had two missions, I think. Which came first and which was the more important, I don't know. One of them was entertainment, and the other was information. And they exist today. The only difference is that you no longer find radio stations trying to be all things for all men. The closest you come to that are stations that call themselves "full service." And the full service radio stations are those that provide some music, some features like farm features, perhaps some news, maybe sports—depending on the station itself. They may have a talk program, and they also may not, but they cover a wide spectrum of activities. Most stations are concentrated on one area. It's no longer broadcasting; it's more accurately narrowcasting. You have to be a dedicated music lover, I think, to be able to determine whether a station is urban or "churban" or one of these strange words that they use. Modern music, to me, all sounds pretty much alike. I don't have to listen to it, and I don't. But to the dedicated aficionado, it's, I suppose, all clear as glass. They pick out the station they really like and then they go to the next station they like the most and perhaps to a third, but that's about as far as they go. There are others that stay with just one station, oddly enough. This distorts the ratings, but that's the way it operates today.

"Oh, the FCC." That's what I said when they used to dabble in things they didn't understand. They, at one time, proclaimed that you had to do so many hours of this and that and the other thing other than entertainment programming. This is nonsensical and ultimately it was dropped. But for several years this was law. I challenge you to find any radio station in the country that doesn't have placards on its wall proclaiming its dedication to public service. I think WIBC did more than most, but you get these awards. Any radio station gets awards. They're pitiful if they can't get an award. . . . I think public service programs, per se, are absolutely worthless. I think broadcasting in the public interest is fine. That was the thing that made WIBC great.

When the Commission tries to substitute its judgment for the judgment of the industry and/or the marketplace, then I think they're making big mistakes. And they do this periodically. In the recent administration—I guess it was [George] Bush—the chairman of the Commission launched a campaign to deregulate broadcasting. I think that was very constructive. This rescued a lot of radio stations that were failing, because it allowed a single entity to own two AMs and two FMs, I believe, in the same market provided they did not have more than 25 percent of the audience. This meant that a failing radio station could be picked up and rescued by a more successful broadcaster under something called an LMA, which is a local marketing agreement, and/or just bought. Then too, they also increased the number of radio stations and television stations that a single entity could own. Previously, the limits on the number of stations you could own was pretty strict—seven AMs and seven FMs. . . . Within the United States, within a given market you could own one AM, one FM; that's all. If, for example, WIBC wanted to buy WLW in Cincinnati, or vice versa, you couldn't do it by the old rules because there was an overlap. And these overlaps became pretty narrow. I wanted to buy WSAI in Cincinnati a good many years ago and was precluded from doing so because of the overlap. The overlap was so slight as to be unrecognizable.

Years ago, there was a Federal Communications Commission ruling called the "Mayflower Decision" that virtually precluded broadcasting stations, radio and/or television stations from editorializing. Then, after a few years and changes in the FCC, they decided that that was all wrong, that you *must* editorialize.[60] Well, that was fine, except that they then had something that was called the "Fairness Doctrine." If a newspaper comes out and writes an editorial saying that they don't like a pending piece of legislation, that's fine. Newspapers aren't under the Federal Communications Commission, and they're protected by the First Amendment. But if a radio station [editorializes], then you must court the competition. This is why I stopped editorializing. You must find a spokesman for the other side, and they can come in and have equal time. I don't mind somebody who objects to it having equal time, but to go out and search it down, that was too much, and I quit.

WIBC was sold in 1983, but we gave the Illinois Street building to Butler in 1981. I didn't specify—they could do what they wanted with it. I gave the Illinois Street building to Butler University at the time we moved out to 9292 North Meridian. We didn't have them simultaneously.

[My most important contribution to the industry has been] the Indianapolis Motor Speedway Network, because it was the biggest thing that ever happened in radio [and] because more people listened to it—all around the world. I went to the Speedway as a small boy. I was so engrossed with it that I always took a good book. When I grew up, I became a real fan. I covered the race for the newspaper. When I say I covered it, I covered one small segment of it, but I was part of the team. When I got the broadcasting rights for the Speedway, I took a great interest in it. I think it was a year later that—or the year after that perhaps—we set up the Indianapolis Motor Speedway Network. . . . Our broadcast was picked up by the Armed Forces Network. In the 1950s, 1960s, and 1970s for that matter, we had troops all over the world; so it went all over the world.

John F. Dille III (1997)
FEDERATED MEDIA

John Dille

(1941–)

The office of John F. Dille III is on the second floor of a downtown commercial building at the edge of Elkhart's business district in northern Indiana. Like his father before him, Dille heads what some have called "a small empire" of media companies. Dille began his career in journalism as a copyboy for the Washington Post *and then became a reporter for Thomson Newspapers, Ltd., with assignments in England, Scotland, and Wales. After a tour in the service, Dille returned to Indiana, where he worked for the* Mishawaka Times *and the* Elkhart Truth, *both of which were family-owned. While his father was primarily in the business of operating newspapers and television stations, Dille became involved in radio in 1971 when he was sent to "see what to do" with WMEE and WMEF in Fort Wayne, Indiana (the former WKJG stations). Success with the Fort Wayne stations led Dille into acquiring other stations. At the time of his interviews he was president of Federated Media, a thirteen-station group with locations in Indiana, Michigan, and Oklahoma. A soft-spoken and articulate interview subject, Dille is also a shrewd businessman who understands his markets and how to operate in the new environment of radio. He was interviewed in his Elkhart office in January and June 1996.*

I think radio (especially in the smaller markets around Indiana—rest of the nation for that matter) replaced the daily newspaper. Where daily newspapers could not survive, and shifted to weekly, it was the radio broadcaster who represented what the *Wall Street Journal* coined as the phrase "the daily diary of the American life," and that's really what it was. You look around small markets in Indiana. I can think of dozens of guys who were really the public record because newspapers, given their own cost structures, simply couldn't function in these places. These small-market radio broadcasters have—and God love them—that's the mom-and-pop, the fundamental fabric of this business, and we've all benefited.

[Today] it's a dying thing brought on partly by other forms. Cable has come along and changed the landscape for television, and I dare say radio, too, not only as a source of entertainment for the audience, but it's also shifted dollars around. Keep in mind in this discussion that there really are two tiers here: there are the listeners, and there are dollars. So, it's important that one think about that, as he or she contemplates these changes in the business. While cable has presented audience competition for television, the introduction of time sales on cable has really affected radio more than television, in my view. But all of it is more competition for these mom-and-pop people. The government changed the rules by allowing twice as many radio stations onto the band, or seemingly twice. I don't know what the real number is, but a significant number, a lot of which found their way into these small markets—they increased the competition. That came really in the form of Docket 80-90, for those doing any research, which was intended to do one thing, but really did another. Anyway, it increased the level of competition just within radio. Cable was just one more thing to distract any consumer's attention. And then, the change in the rules to allow duopoly really gave an exit plan for the mom-and-pop people, who simply couldn't do it anymore. The burden was too great. A lot of them have taken that exit door handsomely out of the business.

Tip O'Neill coined the phrase "everything in politics is local," and so it is with radio. Everything in radio is local. You spoke earlier of the influence on the staff twixt managers and owners. The owner may think he has some effect on the staff, but the truth is, it's the people at the station—and as it should be, for the reasons that I cited earlier. Everything in radio is local. Philosophically, I think that the closer the radio station is to the community, the better it is as a product for the consumer, but I also think the better it is as an investment. From the selling point of view, you're closer to the audience—not only listeners but your advertisers.

My great-grandfather was a educator, having founded Dixon College, curiously a place where Ronald Reagan got his degree. That was in Dixon, Illinois. But my grandfather then left Dixon and went to the University of Chicago and became fascinated somehow—and I cannot tell you how—I ought to do the research. How he got into the newspaper business, I don't know, but he came into the business as what was referred to as "a syndicate operator." He syndicated comic strips and entertainment features for newspapers called the National Newspaper Syndicate. He developed, among other things, one comic strip in particular, a science fiction thing which caught on in the 1920s and did well, called "Buck Rogers." (And served him and our family well until it started to come true.) My father was also in that syndicate business. Came originally to Elkhart, Indiana, calling on the *Elkhart Truth*. My father, at his father's bequest, went on the road selling these comic strips—Sam Snead golf columns and things like that. Anyway, he came to the *Elkhart Truth* and pitched comic strips and went on to the next town and so forth all around the country. As it happens, he had a fraternity brother whose family owned a piece of this newspaper.

By virtue of that relationship, they stopped him one day and said, "Do you know anybody who would like to be publisher of this newspaper? Our present fellow is about to retire" and so forth. And so he, sure enough, got I guess half a dozen candidates and in the course of that process, they said, "Well, we don't really like any of your candidates but we've come to know you. How would you like the job?" So, in 1952, he left his father and Chicago and came out into the wilderness—by his reckoning—to Elkhart, Indiana. . . . He came down here and began publishing this newspaper. Began as publisher. This newspaper was owned by the Greenleafs and the Beardsleys. Notable families in that the Greenleafs were the people who owned the C. G. Conn and related companies, the largest manufacturers of band instruments in the world, and Beardsley was the family that owned Miles Laboratories, manufacturers of Alka-Seltzer and other worldwide products. Both of those companies are now gone.

This newspaper has grown in proportion to the community. I think when he came down there its circulation was about fifteen thousand or something like that. It's twice that now, as is the community. And, I think you would learn that this newspaper was regarded as a pretty decent newspaper for its size. Then, in 1954 in response to marketplace activities, he decided he'd better put television on the air as a defensive move. Nobody knew that television wasn't going to replace newspapers.

TRC is Truth Radio Corporation . . . it's called "Truth." There are a couple of stories, but the one most often told—Colonel [C. G.] Conn, the fellow who founded this newspaper in 1889, was a Civil War veteran, a bugler, which was why he was in the band instrument business. He split his lip in combat or in a fight or something, and he had to make a mouthpiece that was different and that led him into the manufacturing. There was a Civil War monument being built, and there was a great argument about where it was to be and what its shape was to be. And whoever it was that prevailed, made Conn so sore that he decided to publish in opposition to whatever that proposal was, what was then called a "broadside," which was a one-page publication. Because he thought that the existing newspaper and those positions were something less than the truth, he thought that he'd print something he identified as "the truth." And so, page one exists down the hall here. You can have a look at it. But it's interesting.

GUARANTEED CIRCULATION
THIS WEEK,
14,000.

TRUTH

First Page: Editorial.
Second Page: Telegraphic News.
Third Page: Local News.
Fourth Page: Miscellaneous.
Telegraphic News up to 3 a. m. Each Day.

Vol. I. No. 1. ELKHART, IND., TUESDAY MORNING, OCT. 15, 1889. 4 a. m. Edition.

EDITORIAL TRUTHS

THE MISSION OF "TRUTH."

This initial number of the new morning paper to be published in this city shall now announce its mission. TRUTH must manifest itself in every word published, and no falsehoods shall be printed if the writer can avoid it. The editorial management must always investigate each item of news sent in for publication, and no intelligence of a personal nature shall ever be printed that cannot be fully substantiated by reliable evidence. The general character of TRUTH must not be political as politics are known, but the tenor of all political discussions shall be democratic, and as democratic principles are the people's doctrines this paper shall be known as the people's paper, and published in the interests of the laboring class, the mechanics and the middle class of people, which is generally known as the tradesmen and small capitalists.

No moneyed influence shall ever govern the policy of this paper, and no person rich or poor, shall prevent the publication of any article which the editorial management deems prudent to print.

Laboring men shall always find an earnest advocate in this paper, and the people who themselves do not feel the moral strength to announce their own rights can find a vindication by giving the information accompanied by a sworn affidavit, and no names shall be published or revealed, and the persons who are the perpetrators of outrages on the liberties and rights of the laboring man shall feel the power of TRUTH and shall know that the mission of this paper is truth and truth alone.

The industrial people of all classes shall be defended against the oppression of the demi-god, and the politician who attains this title by means of organized party politics to the detriment of the real interests of the intelligent voter, and shall know that his day is over in the city of Elkhart when the spring elections have passed, for the interests of the intelligent voter must and shall be protected and the machine politics of the demi-gods of all parties must be abolished, and the fearless and relentless manner in which TRUTH shall expose their organizations and pursue the organizers shall make them feel that truth is a power and that the voter's rights must be subserved and protected.

No man shall be permitted to oppress the laboring class without feeling this power, and if the wages of his workmen are cut down a reasonable excuse must be given or he shall be made the subject of a public investigation.

No man shall be a hypocrite in the guise of a christian follower unless his public and private life shall evince this sincerity, and his profession of goodness made evident by his life.

The slanderer shall be pursued if his scandal becomes a matter of public comment, and if his talk shall be injurious to the innocent and shall cause suffering from its heedlessness he shall be warned and exposed at the same time.

The mission of TRUTH shall be to expose public defamation and to protect well-meaning persons, and whoever reads this article will understand the serious nature of this warning.

To the well meaning person of all walks of life TRUTH shall always be a welcome visitor, and no comment is necessary to make them understand that they shall be protected from the assaults of the curious and the malice of the hypocrite, who smiles and smites, and who must be shorn of his smile and exposed in the true character which his evil life shall assume.

All the latest telegraphic dispatches up to three o'clock in the morning of the issue of the paper shall be published, and comments on all political questions and topics shall be free and without reserve.

TRUTH shall be published on Sunday morning, but all labor shall cease in the printing office at twelve o'clock Saturday night, and no Sunday work permitted except to circulate the paper. The Sunday issue shall be principally news of a religions character, and not of a political nature, except as refers to the events received in the telegraphic news. No assaults of any kind, either personal or political, shall be published in the Sunday issue, and as often as they can be obtained articles shall be printed from the different ministers and pastors of the churches in the city.

The publications of TRUTH during the week days shall appear at four o'clock each morning, and shall be circulated on the morning trains, and as soon as arrangements can be made an issue shall be printed for Goshen, South Bend, Mishawaka, Bristol and all the adjacent towns and villages.

TRUTH must not be misunderstood, and the persons who have reported that this paper was to be established in revenge and as a malicious undertaking shall be disappointed, for the motive will manifest in time, and as the first week's circulation is paid for wholly by the writer, he must be indulged in an honorable motive to vindicate himself from a wrong which would have ruined a person of less stern and determined purpose, and now that TRUTH has announced its mission let the reader surmise what that wrong is.

C. G. CONN AND GEO. W. BUTLER.

The contract which controls the business of the TRUTH printing office is substantially as follows: C. G. Conn furnishes $5,000 capital, and owns that amount of the office at all times. Geo. W. Butler manages the office and controls all of the profits of the job work which shall never exceed fifteen per cent. above the actual cost of the work, and all work done for C. G. Conn outside of the printing of three papers viz: The daily issue of TRUTH, the weekly publication of TRUTH and C. G. Conn's TRUTH shall be ten per cent. above actual cost. The entire control of the finances of the TRUTH printing office rests with C. G. Conn, and the entire management and ownership shall be explained at some other time. This is a brief synopsis of the business relations of C. G. Conn and Geo. W. Butler, and is published to notify the public that the solicitation of job work and advertising by Geo. W. Butler is authorized and that he should be so recognized.

The circulation of the daily issue of TRUTH shall be 2,000 copies for this week and after this week this number shall be increased or diminished as the demand justifies. The weekly publication of TRUTH shall not begin until November 1st, and the authentic circulation shall always be announced so that advertisers may rely upon the statements made by Geo. W. Butler. The issue of each paper may be relied upon, and as the advertisements shall be changed each day, each advertiser will see the benefit of this new form of a paper. Truth must be the advertising medium of this city and it shall be, because whenever desired the writer will write the "ads," for its patrons, and C. G. Conn is well known for his original manner of advertising and it shall manifest itself to all.

Advertising is not a study, it is a gift, and the man who copies fails, and he who has originality succeeds. Originality is sometimes called insanity by the envious, and whenever the people of Elkhart say that TRUTH has no method, and is not original its publication shall be stopped, for C. G. Conn needs the office in his own business, and Geo. W. Butler can always find job work when new type, new presses and new material are employed, and the printers and pressmen are skillful and engenious.

Newspaper writing with many has become a burden, and the only relief readers have from the balderdash class of ordinary journalism, is the neatly worded article which emanates from the flowing pen of the *Sturgis Mich., Journal* of Friday, October 11th, 1889:

"C. G. Conn, the noted manufacturer of band instruments at Elkhart, some time since, was converted to religion and has since got it into his head that it is his duty to reform the world, and with that end in view he will start a daily, weekly and monthly papers to be called TRUTH. G. W. Butler, of the Mennonite company, will have charge of the office, and is now in Chicago buying the outfit. Mr. Conn will be the editor, and in his prospectus he says that "the mission of this new TRUTH shall be to punish hypocrites of all classes, expose traitors to social and personal friendship in every circle of life, and to do away with Man-Gods, monkey-kings and impostors, and life shall be made a horror to some of these individuals. The paper is to be a morning paper, and will be printed on a double-cylinder press. This will make things lively, not in newspaper circles only, but in every way in that city. Mr. Conn seems to imagine that he is the protector of many people and things in that place, and the many unpleasant, if not dangerous things, will be said and done, goes without saying."

C. G. Conn is indeed converted, but has not got religion in the ordinary sense of the term, neither has he started out to reform the world, but he will make things lively and unpleasant for some persons and will not write anything dangerous. The editor of the *Journal*, reminds C. G. Conn of Balaam's ass, who brayed at his master, and the ass had a master? Yes, and Balaam had an ass.

Editor Fuller blossoms out quite as elegantly [illegible] the stick and hat are adver[illegible]ts and not graces. Fuller may be seen most any sunny day in front of the Bucklen picking the liquid out of his teeth, and the expression of his face is generally more Mr. Fuller than usual.

Notable events require notable notices, and were this issue of TRUTH to not notice the notable event of the noted Pratt, then he would *scarcely* be contented. Scarcely? —No, and why? Because that title is his by right; and the readers will smile when they think of his reply to a young man who desired a situation and wanted to know about the pay, and the philanthropist answered: "Well, young man, we pay *scarcely* any wages but a good trade." Since that notable event, which must have occurred some years ago, he is known among his employees as Scarcely Pratt.

Events that have no outcome are few, but this event has an outcome and an end, and the end is not here for Scarcely Pratt must some day explain that little event and acknowledge the title and not the name, for every person knows that Scarcely Pratt does not apply to the man but to the principle.

IS C. G. CONN INSANE?

ELKHART, Ind., Monday, Oct. 14, 1889.

I have carefully examined C. G. Conn, of Elkhart, Ind., as to his physical and mental condition, during four days I have been with him, and had him almost constantly under my observation.

I have seen him in his factory amongst his workmen; in his office with his accountants and clerks; in his family with his wife and child and on the streets with his friends and acquaintances.

I have applied to him all tests as to his mental condition, and I state as my honest and conscientious opinion that within that period, Mr. Conn has not manifested a single sign or symptom of insanity, but, on the contrary, he has been remarkably clear and lucid upon all business, political and social questions which were discussed between us.

From his own statements and the knowledge I have obtained from others, I am led to believe that within the past year, Mr. Conn has suffered from severe physical prostration, and from that has resulted a corresponding derangement of the nervous system, from which he has, in a great measure, recovered, and the improvement still continues.

With rest, recreation and the suspension of too active devotion to business interests, I believe within a few months, Mr. Conn will be fully restored to his former health and be able to resume the habits of an active business man.

(Signed) A. J. THOMAS.

The distinguished gentleman who makes the above statement is well known to practioners who have a knowledge of brain diseases, and his experience for the last ten and a half years as the superintendent of the male department of the Insane Hospital at Indianapolis should recommend him as an expert on all disorders of the brain, and also to give his statement the credence which rightfully belongs to a physician who is eminent in his profession as a specialist in brain disorders and mental afflictions.

The tests and examinations, except such as were made of the physical condition of the writer, were made without the knowledge of the subject, and although confidence in the result was sometimes lost, confidence in the ability and integrity of Doctor Thomas was always maintained, and had the doctor pronounced the writer insane even in the slightest degree, it was his full intent to close up his business affairs here in Elkhart and leave the city.

***

Doctor Thomas examined fully all the mysterious letters and writings which have been commented upon, and without an explanation eliminated them from the case entirely, but after the explanation given by the writer and the sure results which shall be accomplished by them in due time were explained, he laughed and seemed to think there was at least a method in the writer's manner of handling hypocrites, if not in the alleged madness.

***

It has been stated by Doctor Pixley and others that one symptom of the writer's insanity was the purchase of the farm north of the city, and to Doctor Thomas this purchase did have a bearing in the charge of insanity until the writer showed him the engineer's report on the immense hydraulic power to be developed there some time, and then that charge fell to the ground.

***

Doctor Pixley also advanced the theory that the house the writer is building on this farm was another indication of insanity or *paresis* as he calls it, and when the writer explained that he had been married to his *now* loved wife twenty years, and during that time he had squandered thousands and thousands of dollars, and had lavished thousands of dollars on other women, and all this time this faithful and loving wife had waited patiently, as only a true and affectionate wife can wait for the sunlight of love to dispel the cloud of bitterness and sorrow which had so long darkened the home of the writer, and that sunlight came with the reformation of the writer, and with that sunlight came the resolve and the determination to build the long looked for house, and although it will probably cost about *seven thousand dollars*, it shall make a happy home, and the maligners who have attempted to incarcerate the writer in an asylum for alleged insanity shall in time see their own folly and their own punishment.

***

Once when in Arkansas on a hunting trip, and while under the influence of liquor, the writer bought 160 acres of land for $250, and when he had reformed, this land was sold again for $200, at a loss of $50. Doctor Pixley advocated this transaction as another evidence of paresis.

***

For the past two and one-half years the business of the writer has increased in magnitude and in profit, and many old debts have been paid, the wages of the workmen advanced, land bought, houses erected, and no money expended in [illegible] and drunkenness, and this was another indication of the writer's insanity, so says Dr. Pixley, and he told the Rev. W. D. Parr that he had been watching these indications during the above mentioned time.

***

The Review Printing Company have never taken an invoice of stock and material nor rendered an accounting for five and a-half years, and because the writer insisted upon this accounting, and because he did not believe the affairs of the company were legitimately conducted, and because he arrested Charles H. Chase, an alleged charge of insanity was made against him and sworn to by Dr. C. S. Frink, and an effort was made to have him taken care of, and a special detective was placed over him, and he was watched and hounded by a republican poll worker, and a bill was presented to the City Council by City Marshal Needham, and the following explains itself:

CITY OF ELKHART,
To S. S. BRODE, Dr.
Sept. 25th, to 14 days at $1.50........$21

Having examined this bill we approve the same.

E. GOLDTHWAIT, Mayor.
PERRY S. TURNER, City Attorney.
JAMES H. STATE, Prosecuting Atty.
C. C. NEEDHAM, Marshal.

Minority report of Committee.

ELKHART, IND., Oct. 9th, 1889.

Your committee respectfully report that the above bill was contracted for detective service in a matter over which we have no jurisdiction and it is therefore not approved.

C. H. CLARK,
Claims Committee.

By referring to the minority report of the committee it will be seen that Councilman C. H. Clark was the only man on the Claims Committee who had the nerve to face the storm of the Mayor, City Attorney, Prosecuting Attorney and City Marshal, and he did it manfully, and is a man for his manliness. The vote of the Council shows on the minutes of the City Clerk as follows:

"Mr. Clark of the Committee on Claims, reported adversely upon the claim of S. S. Brode for services and a motion to allow the bill was *lost* as follows:

"Ayes—Beardsley, Evans, Hill, Moyer, Newman, Shafer,

"Nays—Clark, Johnson, Miller, Rinehart and Slear."

As it requires a two-third vote to carry a motion to expend money from the city treasury this motion was lost. Councilmen Moyer and Shafer, the majority of the Claims Committee, being ashamed to make a report, voted to pay the bill.

Councilmen Beardsley, Evans, Hill and Newman shall be mentioned by the writer later.

***

This shameful treatment of the writer by the officers of this city whose names are seen on the bill of Sid Brode is now a subject of investigation, and the blame shall fall upon the rightful owners, and justice shall demand a recognition of a peaceful citizen's right. The recognition of this scandalous proceeding by the councilmen who voted to pay an infamous steal from the city treasury shall receive further mention to-morrow, and the citizens of Elkhart shall thus want to know why money shall be employed to pay republican poll workers to watch and follow and hound a respectable and law abiding citizen.

THE Democrats may carry Virginia, but if they do it will be because Mahone and his "forest meetings" at night were outgeneraled, a conclusion not likely to be entertained. These night meetings are a novelty and wholly new in that they are held in the woods at night without any political machinery—simply a neighborhood visit, and they are held in every precinct. If, as is reported, the great readjuster has 4,000 voters for a landwehr at $5 per head, it will carry the State handsomely. This is a revised edition of "blocks of five," and a great deal easier handled and more potent.

C. G. Conn, Elkhart, has now decided to have two experts stay with him two weeks to test his sanity. If they decide him insane he will go to a private asylum.—*Indianapolis Sun, Oct. 9, 1889.*

Yes, and the experts have been here and they are residents of Indianapolis, and were Dr. A. J. Thomas and his estimable wife and lady, Mrs. Thomas, who sojourned at the home of the writer until the doctor was convinced that no insanity occupied the same residence, and now he has gone back to the home of insanity, the State Hospital for the Insane.

Artistic Crayon Portraits.
We invite your special attention to the quality and prices of our crayon work. Strictly one grade—the best.
BUTLER & KNOX,
Blackburn Building.

Charles G. Conn went to the trouble and expense of printing this broadside (later the Elkhart Truth*) to proclaim that he was "not insane."* FEDERATED MEDIA

He presents the mission statement, if you will, of the newspaper, and as a sidebar story, points out that he is not insane. Shakespeare might have said, "Methinks he protesteth too much."

[My father] saw [television] as the twin effects of both a competitive threat and a marketing opportunity. He was a gadget guy, and he liked stuff like that. So, even though he was worthless as a technician, he loved gadgets. To tell you the truth, in his office there are still instruction manuals I know he never opened. [So, the first radio station was] WTRC, and it went on the air in 1931, although he was not here. It came with a newspaper—sort of a little station in the back of the newspaper. Nobody even cared much about it, except those who operated it.

He bought WKJG television, which was an NBC affiliate in Fort Wayne in 1957. It had two radio stations with it, WKJG-AM and WKJG-FM. Really it was Hilliard Gates who ran it from the day my father bought it until the day my father sold it, 1957 to 1971. Somewhere in there also my father was in contest with Tony Hulman for a television station in Terre Haute.

My father was an assembler of things, and rather than get in a big fight (I think, this is really the truth of it) rather than get in a big fight about the cable franchises here in South Bend and Elkhart, he went to Franklin Schurz of the *South Bend Tribune* and Father Joyce at the University of Notre Dame and said, "Why don't we team up on this deal? We are the logical people to do this, rather than get in a big fight over these franchises." In these days we were all going around these little communities getting franchises to hang cable on the poles, which required a franchise.

That main thing I think was the power. So anyway, the point is they did agree, and so they formed a thing called Valley Cablevision. In subsequent years, my father, through his activities as chairman of NAB, met Al Stern, who was chairman of NCTA [National Cable Television Association], and they became pals and formed a new company called Television Communication Corporation [TVC] and bought our Fort Wayne television station. It was the first product thing that the cable company, TVC, had bought. It had been a cable company.

He thought cable was a coming thing, just as he had thought television was fifteen years before, or seventeen years—whatever it was. That had the effect of allowing

him to straddle television and cable. TVC then finally went into Warner Communications. Now, it's Time-Warner. Went through all those little steps which are unimportant—Garden State Bank in New Jersey, whole bunches of crazy steps. Anyway, that had the effect of carving him out of television and hooking him up with cable and leaving stand-alone, two radio stations in Fort Wayne, which is how I got into the business.

[After attending] Colby College in Waterville, Maine . . . I went to Washington as a copyboy on the *Washington Post*. Actually, the *Post* had just merged with the *Washington Times Herald*, which is interesting only in that *Times Herald* had employed a young female photographer (who used to stop by to see her cronies at the *Washington Post* following the merger) named Jacqueline [Bouvier Kennedy] Onassis. I would have been in Washington during the Nixon-Kennedy campaign. I tell my kids I was in Washington when Eisenhower was president, and, of course, they think it goes Washington, Jefferson, Lincoln, Eisenhower.

I had the great good fortune of hooking up with the Associated Press, and I got a work permit to go [to England]. I sat in a booth and transcribed copy, which came through from the continent through the London Bureau. I was just really a typist, and then managed to get away from there and hook up with Thomson Newspapers, again as a copy kid and a police reporter (like a court reporter). So, I was in Cardiff [Wales]. I was in London and Cardiff and Sheffield and Newcastle [England] and Aberdeen [Scotland]. It was a great experience for a young man. Then, I went to Paris, and I can't speak French worth a damn so I couldn't keep a job very long. Anyway, I came back here, and I went in the service. I can remember being at Fort Benning [Georgia] and seeing all of those helicopters. Nobody quite knew what was going on, at least at my level. We were all moving out. Eleventh Air Assault was hooking up with a First Cavalry Division in Fort Riley, Kansas, to make the First Air Cav, the first big unit sent in by [President Lyndon] Johnson.

I missed Vietnam twice. . . . I came back to Indiana; got married—one of my motivations to leave active duty—got married, and came back to work for the *Mishawaka Times*, which was operated by the *Truth*. And then, subsequent to that—actually the *Mishawaka Times* closed in 1967, I guess. By then I was over here at the newspaper. So, I

An announcer posed in the WTRC studio at the Hotel Elkhart for this photo in June 1941. In the early years of broadcasting, hotels in small- and medium-sized towns in Indiana rented unused space to radio stations as a way of advertising their facilities. FEDERATED MEDIA

WTRC's first transmitter was located near its tower on the outskirts of Elkhart, Indiana. John Dille II bought equity in the station when he became the publisher of the Truth *in 1952.* FEDERATED MEDIA

was off the editorial staff. I was doing promotions and production things.

By [1971] I was general manager of the newspaper here in Elkhart. There came these two radio stations [WKJG-AM and FM], and somebody said, "Well, why don't you go down there and see what to do with these things?" Like I knew. And so, I did that. It was an opportunity to have a hands-on experience, and what do we do with these radio stations that were nothing? They amounted to nothing. We hired a fellow named Bert Sherwood, terrific guy. I mean, a *terrific* guy who was briefly in Fort Wayne, who really put us on the air in the form of WMEE and WMEF. Top 40 and beautiful music (industry terms) were formats at that time. MEE was Top 40, and MEF was beautiful music—"easy listening" was a term developed later.

[We changed call letters because] believe it or not, it's hard to say WKJG. It's easier to say WMEE, WMEF (actually, they're not particularly easy to say either, but that's why) and because the television station was keeping its call letters. We wanted a separate identity for these rock-and-roll radio stations. We were, from the product point of view, competing with another radio station, WLYV, for the Top 40 audience, the kids. MEF was beautiful music, and there had been no beautiful music station in Fort Wayne. It was a relatively new format, which is the Montovani and Hollywood Strings and stuff that's gone south since. But those were very successful formats in Fort Wayne in the early 1970s. MEE—its call letters are alive today, although now over on the FM side.

[Changing call letters] is easy. You just say to the Commission, "We'd like to change." These call letters are available, which you get from a list. We'd like to do it. They look at it to make sure there were no conflicts without taking someone else's, and they say, "Fine." Those two call letters, as it happens, came from two Coast Guard ships, hulls that were assigned but not built.

We had two [radio stations at Fort Wayne], and they were stand-alones; so they required the attention. Radio station here (WTRC) is the WIBC or the WGN of Elkhart. It is the daily public record for radio for this market. WCMR is a competitive radio station then which is Clarence Moore Radio which had a religious—Ed Moore runs it now, a fine guy. They are also in the equipment manufacturing business.

My very first [acquisition] was in Grand Rapids. We bought WJEF from John Fetzer—John E. Fetzer, to be exact. Soon thereafter we bought WCKY from the *Washington Post*. WCKY stands for Covington, Kentucky. It was put on the air by L. B. Wilson, who was a longtime, famous broadcaster. That acquisition was followed by an FM acquisition in Grand Rapids, and a second acquisition in Cincinnati—this time an FM, WWEZ.

In those days you had to declare your format as a part of the license transfer procedure and CKY had been acquired by the *Washington Post* from the L. B. Wilson estate. They were really after the television stations in Jacksonville and Miami. They had this little radio station, which L. B. had put on the air many years before in Cincinnati. They didn't know what to do with it and really weren't radio people. So, they sent a guy out to Cincinnati, said, "Just keep us out of trouble." So, he had put a huge amount of news and public affairs like 25 percent (you had to describe your percentages in those days) which is an extraordinary amount—twice the normal, maybe three times the normal—and music which wouldn't offend anybody. It was actually a format which subsequently might have been referred to as "music-of-your-life" (another term you'll hear in your travels), which is big bands and Frank Sinatra, and Perry Como, and Rosemary Clooney, who, of course, was a Cincinnati local. Nick Clooney was our morning guy at WCKY when we took over the station. (I think his son, George Clooney, is now a popular television [actor]. I don't keep track of that, but he's a fine guy. He looks like his father; he's got his looks.) Anyway, we said that we'd like to play country music. We thought Cincinnati needed some country music. This is 1974 that we made this decision. WMAQ in Chicago had just gone country, and it was the first of the new generation of country radio stations. *Urban Cowboy* was about that time—hadn't yet happened, but was about to. So WMAQ was the first really big AM station to change formats to country music. There had been some before—WJJD and others around the country that had done really country western music—Sons of the Pioneers, and western. Country-country is guitar in nature and not so much banjo. Country western is like Sons of the Pioneers, and Gene Autry, Song of the Purple Sage and all that kind of thing. It was great stuff, but different.

In telephone research you could say, "Do you like country music?" The answer would be, "No," but you could hear country music being played in the background. There were a lot of jokes about that in the business. It was not cool; it was not hip; it was not okay to be a country listener. *Urban Cowboy* changed that.

So, we thought we'd try to be a clone—we didn't use those terms—of WMAQ, which had really met with some significant success. But this was very offensive to the people who had enjoyed Frank Sinatra. The notion of hearing Waylon Jennings instead of Frank Sinatra was just absolutely an anathema. There was a newspaper columnist who just stirred and stirred this thing. We didn't know it but the disc jockeys were on the air saying, "If you don't like this proposed change" (which is another way of saying that we're not going to be a part of this sort of thing, because we're probably going to get fired) "write to the Commission." So, fifteen hundred people did. So many letters and so much commotion that Bill Gradison, then congressman, called for a congressional hearing of the matter of CKY's format. Well, it is preposterous. Anyway, it was out of that case and a couple of others akin to it that the Commission concluded privately [that] they had no business in the content regulation portion of the broadcasting activity. But I recall Dick Shiben, the bureau chief, then called me up and said, "How would you like to take this case to the Supreme Court?" And, I said, "Well, it scared the hell out of me." Anytime you get a call from the Commission it's frightening, at least to me. But I said, "No, I don't want to; we can't do that. No, I don't want to do that." Anyway, about that time they decided they had no business doing that, and they removed those questions. They subsequently granted the transfer on Valentine's Day of 1976.

We now have several [talk radio shows]. I didn't complete the list of our acquisitions, but we now own WOWO, for example. It is all talk, or nearly all talk. TRC is all talk. Our AM in Tulsa is all talk, the AM in Grand Rapids is all talk, and our other AM in Cincinnati is all talk. But while there was news-talk before in WINS in New York—"Give us twenty minutes and we'll give you the world" was the phrase that really brought all-news radio into the forefront and then derivatives followed. That was news. It was Rush Limbaugh who really is the easiest benchmark to the rebirth of AM radio and the birth of talk radio. And now, there are a number of stations across the land that are news-talk and stations that are just talk, not so much news. Given the nature of the listener, talk is a "foreground-listening" thing, when the listeners are listening to what's being said, as opposed to the music format where sometimes it can be a bit of a background thing.

Actually there may be people in Fort Wayne who hate us, because they blame us for the potential signal restrictions, which may be placed on WOWO. But for anybody who's been in Indiana, particularly any broadcaster, WOWO is one of those stations, one of those granddaddy stations that people grew up with. WOWO went on the air in 1926—it was one of the first stations in America (not the first, of course, but one of the early ones) and has had only four owners in all of that time: the people who put it on the air, Westinghouse, there was a ten-year period with Bob Price, and then ourselves. We are the second Hoosier owners, the first being the people who put it on the air, Main Auto in Fort Wayne. So we were pleased to return it to Hoosier hands for whatever that might account for. So, it was both an emotional decision and a financial decision. We thought that news-talk was a worthwhile format and provided a genuine public service and therein a business opportunity.

[WOWO] was sold—but only briefly—to a second New York company, which had a radio station in New York, WLIB on the same frequency. Price sold it to a company called Inner-City Broadcasting. They bought it for the purpose of really turning it off so that they could increase their power on their station in New York, as I say, on the same frequency. I called them up when I learned this and said, "Wait a minute. Why should we do this? Why don't we work out some kind of an arrangement so you raise your power enough to cover New York, but we retain enough in Fort Wayne to cover our market, which really is Ohio and Michigan and Indiana (if you think about the agricultural folks) and maybe forgo listeners in New York and Massachusetts and places like that since there really aren't many there now anyway." It's a fun thing to do, but it isn't really like it was in the 1930s. And they said, "Okay." So, that's what we've done. They will curtail our signal headed on a line from Fort Wayne to New York. But we'll pull back in that direction. And they will fill the void left by the departure of our signal.

In the 1970s . . . talk began, but it didn't find its way to fruition till the early 1980s, and you've heard this discussion from others called Docket 80-90 wherein additional

As chairman of the IBA Legislative Committee, Dille spcarheaded a trip of broadcasters to Washington, D.C., to meet with Indiana's congressional delegation in June 1981. Here Dille expressed his thoughts to Senators Richard Lugar and Dan Quayle at a breakfast hosted by Lugar. FEDERATED MEDIA

John (Jack) Dille II, a role model for many Hoosier broadcasters, foresaw the dominance of television. He put WSJV-TV (W Saint Joe Valley) on the air in the mid-1950s and purchased WRJC in 1957. He later became involved in cable in the South Bend–Elkhart area. FEDERATED MEDIA

John Dille III made a point at an IBA meeting in the 1970s. Dille served as president of the organization from 1979 to 1980. FEDERATED MEDIA

radio stations were created? Had the effect of increasing inventory which had the effect of decreasing, in the end, profit. Profit is not a dirty word. Broadcasters were then so squeezed, some of them lost money. I should say, many of them lost money by the end of the 1980s and early 1990s. . . . In this country, we thrive on competition. It's a very good thing. But there comes a point where—and it's hard to, given the way that we're geared [with our] capitalist economy—but there really is too much competition. Because these are licenses that the marketplace can't really behave as freely as it could. We're in a free market because of the strictures of the government.

[When] you could only own one station and [the FCC] created more of them, [this] caused more people to come in the business. If there was a license, it was hard to get; that led to sort of a fanaticism to get into the business. That overpopulated the business. So there wasn't enough money to go around—not enough of the advertising revenue to go around to the radio stations. So there wasn't enough revenue per station. . . . That squeezed profits and caused people to automate via satellite—less local—and that was in many ways a degradation in the quality of the product. In some ways it's an improvement, but that's another discussion.

Because there were so many stations trying to survive, they sought every smaller niche, and in some cases it drove the creative juices to present a product that super-served a smaller audience, but it did super-serve them. Anyway, that then led to a rules change. You could own two [stations], which had the effect of some synergism, some savings, so that one operator could operate two stations as efficiently as one and for almost the same cost. That was the first step. It also in its way reduced the ferocity with which the competitors attacked each other. The subsequent Telecom Bill, which was February of 1996, now allows operators to own three or four stations, and in some cases five in a larger market of any one service, FM or AM. That further consolidates the business. Doesn't reduce the number of radio stations, but it does reduce the number of owners which further reduces this ferocity. Doesn't change the competitive aspect but it does make a more sane approach to business, which I think will have the effect of—because profits will return once again—allowing an operator to be more creative in his product, if he can afford to do it. The government, in setting up their rules, really ought to assure that the public is served by a range of services—which they have done and which they intended to do—but not constrain the owners.

In reflecting on the role of broadcasters in the community, Dille said, being involved in the community is simply good business. I don't just mean being involved in the United Fund and United Way and all those charitable organizations or service organizations, but providing that informational source to the community is good business. It costs more, but I believe if you do it right, you will enjoy the benefit of increased revenues, such that it covers any increase in cost. That's certainly what we've done in Fort Wayne at MEE, and K105. We have the advantage of being able to share in the data from the news gathering organization with this sister station, and the community benefits from that.

At WOWO . . . they billed themselves as "The Voice of a Thousand Main Streets." I always liked that line. And in that way WOWO did bind together those listeners from across the land in a common experience of listening to the radio. As today, we can—setting aside your views of a person—listen to Rush Limbaugh. There is a common experience listening to him across the land, as there is in television. I mean the *Johnny Carson Show*, everybody was, "Did you hear what Johnny Carson said last night?" And Letterman's Top 10 lists are repeated on the radio the following morning. I don't think radio wants to be one thing to all people. I suppose on the one hand, [each station] might think it great if it could have all of the listeners. I'm not sure that's really a very good idea, as an economic argument. Radio is local, that's its value.

Jeffrey H. Smulyan

Jeff Smulyan

(1947–)

As a young boy, Jeffrey H. Smulyan was always fascinated by broadcasting. After graduating from the University of Southern California Law School, he returned to Indianapolis in 1973 to operate WNTS, a small AM station in Beech Grove owned by his uncle. A consummate entrepreneur, he realized his boyhood dream when he founded Emmis Broadcasting Corporation in 1980. The new company's strategy of purchasing and turning around weaker stations proved highly successful, and Emmis expanded rapidly into major markets in the 1980s, including New York, Chicago, Washington, D.C., and St. Louis. Smulyan, who describes broadcasters as having "a unique compact" with the public, has a reputation for effectively identifying and evaluating the tastes of his audiences. He has a wealth of knowledge about broadcasting in Indiana and a strong sense of pride in its history. His commitment to Indianapolis is evidenced by the location of the new headquarters of Emmis Broadcasting downtown on Monument Circle on the very site of the Canary Cottage, a well-known landmark for local broadcasters. Smulyan was interviewed in his office in January of 1997.

I think, if you had to summarize my career, I just probably love doing something that nobody else can do. I love doing deals. If everyone else can do it, we probably think "Okay, we love creating a new format, a new strategy for the business, a new idea out of the business."

I was born here in 1947. I went to school here on the north side, Eastwood Junior High School and North Central [High School]. I went on to school in California at USC. I went to undergraduate school there and stayed for law school, and then decided to come home and get involved in the radio business. I was going to get a masters in radio and TV and somebody said, "Go to law school and get a law degree and specialize in broadcast law." It was great advice; being a lawyer allows you to sort of understand how to allocate among competing interests.

I think if there was a "golden era of radio" in Los Angeles, it was probably the late 1960s or when a lot of these modern formats were taking shape, when it made the transition from mass, truly mass media—nationally distributed networks—again before TV. Once TV came about, radio transformed itself; it had to become the niche business. Some of the things that were developed—talk radio in Los Angeles in the 1960s, Top 40 radio, sort of the modern principles of Top 40 radio, album rock radio, progressive radio—some of those things developed in L.A. So being in L.A. at that time further fueled my interest. I just always was fascinated by it.

I always loved it [radio]. Every kid likes rock and roll, Top 40, and I used to listen to Top 40 stations here and everywhere, and it was a big part of my life. I always thought it was a much

Smulyan appeared with Wayne Cody on his Sportsline *show in Seattle.*

Smulyan and "friend" mug for the camera at his home.

more creative medium than television. TV in those days, you turned on the switch and got whatever CBS was sending down the line. In radio, you sort of created your own format, you marketed it, you found your niche, you sold it, and it was just fun . . . a lot of imagination.

Smulyan's father was an entrepreneur in Indianapolis whose cousin owned WNTS, a small news-talk daytime station in Beech Grove. They encouraged Smulyan to come back and run it. He operated the station from 1974 to 1979 and employed his contemporary, David Letterman. I'm biased. I think David is the most brilliant guy in America, but you had a radio station run by a twenty-five-year-old guy trying to communicate with the audience of talk radio which is basically sixty-year-old people. And he had a cult following of twenty-five to thirty year olds who thought it was the funniest thing of all time. But you had sixty year olds who thought, "This guy's crazy!" In those days everybody was worried about the communists, and I used to get calls, "You've got a Bolshevik working for you." "What do you mean?" Somebody called in one day, and said, "Dave, I think there's communists in Carmel." And of course, Dave said, "I think we ought to give them Carmel. The schools are overcrowded, and you can't find parking spaces. I think we've got to give them Carmel and hold the line at Nora." Well, you know, guys of my generation think this is the funniest thing they've ever heard. But sixty year olds who come from a different view of the world think, "This man wants to see [the Russians take over our community]" you know . . . and so we had a lot of that, but it was hilarious. David is unbelievable, but it was not a fit for that audience . . . he was too hip and too young.

I was running the station myself . . . and so I never really had a day-to-day mentor. There were people in this state, John Dille—I don't want to say he's a big brother, because he's not that much older than me, but just somebody that I just respect tremendously. I mean, I just think the world of John. John is a, you know, a sort of little older contemporary. He's somebody that I can always talk to about anything, and we've been on the NAB [National Association of Broadcasters] together and the RAB [Radio Advertising Bureau] and just talked.

Emmis was always sort of my dream company. It's the Hebrew word for truth. . . . It started really as one radio station that was a turnaround; it was a start-up, if you will. And we did that over and over again, and we were very

successful. We did it with the financial technique of debt in those days, because you could buy something that had no cash flow, and if you created a lot of cash flow, you could then apply that to service the debt on the next station . . . but you had to improve the operations dramatically. As the financial climate changed, and as the industry became more mature, it was harder to do those things. We had a major home run with [radio station] WRKS New York in 1994, when we bought something with $7 million cash flow . . . and immediately doubled the cash flow. But that's rare in this day. And I think we adapted to a different world, and a different capital structure by paring down our debt and attracting capital from the public. Yet, I think through all this time, one thing that we demonstrated is that we've been fortunate enough to attract people who really can manage radio stations as well as anyone, and businesses. I think the magazines, our two city magazines [*Indianapolis Monthly* and *Atlanta*], probably perform as well as any in America. So I think if you look at Emmis, it has had its ups—it was a sky rocket from 1981 to 1989. It suffered from 1990 to 1992, reversed itself and went back and from 1992, now to 1997, it's had pretty nice growth.

Now it's a mature company. Now we have different issues. Now our growth is structured a little bit differently, but we think it can be a major company. You know it has about a half a billion dollars in value now, and we believe that it should be a multibillion dollar company by the turn of the century if we do our job.

We like to think that our corporate culture sets us apart. We have some guiding principles; we call them the "Ten Commandments of Emmis." Never jeopardize your integrity. Have fun. Don't tear down your industry; build it up. Don't take yourself too seriously. Never get smug about anything in life. Be rational. Be good to your people, and get them involved, and I think to believe in yourself. I think that hopefully is the message that ownership can communicate to its employees, that you create an attitude, an atmosphere where people have fun. This will never be an autocratic company. It will be a company where people can take risks and make mistakes and know that they don't get fired for them, that people can feel good about their work and good about their jobs. We believe very strongly that the company of the future is a company where people feel they have a stake in not only the ideas of the company but also the ownership of the stock in the company. We probably have more employee shareholding in this company than anybody in American broadcasting, and we're proud of it.

We [broadcasters] have a unique—what they call "a compact" with the public. We get our license from the government, and even though we buy them from other people, they were originally given by the government free. Now, as a friend of mine always says, "If the airways are free, why did you pay $10 million for this radio station?" But it's a unique situation. It's unique, especially in a world where we have cable, and we have now satellite broadcasting. The over-the-air broadcaster is really the only entity that doesn't charge the public anything. And I think it's a situation that's worked well. When you look at models for communications of the future, most of them, whether they come on phone lines or satellite or cable require the consumer to pay something. But the over-the-air broadcaster has a unique role in that he distributes universally to everyone. All you have to do is buy a radio or TV set. You don't have to pay a monthly fee.

I think that originally from the government, that was the notion of serving in the public interest. And while people might think it's passé to talk about public interest responsibilities, you've created several generations of broadcasters in this country, especially here in Indiana, who have taken that responsibility to heart. At the heart of almost every broadcaster I know, there's a belief: sure we have to make money, and you can't ever take care of your employees or your shareholders, or anybody, if you're not profitable. [However, we can be financially successful and still improve the quality of life in our communities.]

I think that by operating for profit, you have to be reflective to what the public tastes are. On the other hand, if you merely reflect the public taste, you can't educate and inform them. And I think that's why the idea of subsidizing public broadcasting makes sense . . . sometimes you have to recognize some things aren't demanded by the public. You have to go outside and get someone to subsidize education and information. That's why I believe in public broadcasting. We have to subsidize educational programs for children, because when you dictate it, it's very difficult in a marketplace to solve that.

There's also a feeling that we have a larger responsibility to serve the public good, to get involved, and I think we have. I'm very proud that most of the broadcasters I know, especially the people in Indiana, going back from the earli-

est days of WFBM and WIBC, felt that it was their obligation to improve the quality of life here. It's mandated, yes; it's mandated to generally serve in the public interest, but I think people realize, and this is something that maybe goes less to altruism than anything else, that most broadcasters realize that being involved in the community is just good business.

You know people always worried in the government that if you didn't have certain responsibilities—when I started you had to have "X" amount of public affairs a week, and license ascertainment and everything; now it's much more laissez-faire. But most broadcasters haven't abandoned it. They have abandoned news on a lot of FM stations and children's programming on certain TV stations, because I think what you find is that the market dictates what you do. WIBC is the place people go for news; so we don't have much news on WNAP or WENS, because we find that those listeners go for entertainment. On the other hand, I would tell you that most stations—most entertainment and music stations—have found that while they do less news than they did twenty years ago, they're much more involved in public affairs.

We do things in our community for—I mean last year we did a radiothon for Riley Children's Hospital and raised several hundred thousand dollars in a few days. It was tremendous. We do something called "Knowledge Is Power" in Los Angeles, where we've raised millions of dollars. Involvement, getting involved in the community, [is] getting our listeners involved in improving the quality of lives of less fortunate people. When we had WFAN, Don Imus, who was considered to be one of the most off-the-wall, offbeat, crazy, sarcastic characters of America, raised millions and millions of dollars for a radiothon and does it every year for the cancer ward of a hospital.

[The role of government] has changed, and I probably have a unique perspective. I'm sort of the original child of the 1960s, moderately liberal Democrat, who has sort of arrived at the notion that while government can do good things, that government also can be oppressive and sometimes gets involved where it just doesn't understand the issues. I think that if government could create a relatively free marketplace that you will see a pretty good system of broadcasting. There is regulation that's important, and that sounds like a oxymoron that any broadcaster would say that regulation is helpful, but obviously you need technical

Smulyan sits on a balcony of the Emmis Broadcasting Corporation building with a view of Monument Circle behind him.

limitations so that you don't turn on your television and three guys are coming in over Channel 8 in the morning. Or five people are at 1070. The government has to fulfill those roles.

I also think that the government is realizing that the communications landscape is so diverse today. . . . The public decides what works and what doesn't and what it wants. . . . You don't have to worry that one broadcaster can determine public opinion. . . . Well, even if Saddam Hussein bought the NBC-TV station in Indianapolis, he might start out by saying, "I'm going to be able to dictate that only pro-Iraqi news is carried." That's obviously the ultimate extreme, but the fact is that in about three weeks, when his manager said, "Look, people don't want pro-Iraqi news. You know, you're losing your ratings." He'd say, "Well, we have an investment to protect." That's taking it to the extreme, but the fact is that the marketplace dictates what we do.

All communications have narrowed. I mean, when I started you had three TV stations in most markets and an independent. And now you've got seven or eight over-the-air stations. You had no cable, and now you've got seventy cable channels in most areas. We probably built this company on a premise that you can never stand in the way of an idea if its time has come. And the idea of its time had come—FM radio. The first station I ran was an AM. And we felt that with FM you would see greater coverage and greater fidelity, because AM had been carved up so much that in every market there were really only one or two stations that could cover the market. The reason we feel so strongly about WIBC as the only real viable AM station here, is because it's the only one that covers most of the marketplace.

WIBC was an asset to this community, an important part of the community, and Randy Odeneal, who ran Sconnix and who oversaw WIBC when they bought it, and I were friends. But I said, "Randy, I've got to tell you, if you lived in Indianapolis, you wouldn't allow this to happen. This station is just—to me, it's an embarrassment." We thought it was very strident, very divisive. Listen, we carry Rush Limbaugh, and we carry some controversial talk shows, and I understand that there's an audience for that. But this is a radio station that was a real asset, a real resource to this community, and I felt that they were destroying it. And so we stepped up. I tried to buy it for a couple of years, and we finally bought it and I have never regretted it.

When we bought WIBC, they had a building up north and we have this one here. Our leases are up soon on both, and we debated, and we thought why don't we just build our own building, because we're now going to have three stations and a magazine. Probably, when all is said and done, we'll buy a couple more here. . . . [Shortly after this interview, Emmis purchased WTLC-AM and FM.] And when we were getting ready to make a decision to build on the canal, the city said, "You know, we have this one spot on the Circle; it would be linked to the [Circle Centre] Mall." And we said, "Well, there's no parking." And they said, "Well, we'll put in a parking garage," and they really made us an offer that we couldn't refuse.

We knew it would cost a little bit more to build on the Circle, but the idea of putting radio stations on the Circle really intrigued us. It really goes back to the history of the industry. There was radio—the Canary Cottage on the Circle. If you look at the old *Pick-a-Pocket* show with Jim Shelton, it was on the Circle. The WIFE *Window on the World* was tremendously successful. And we thought if you can do all of that on the Circle, and make it a focal point for broadcasting. . . . One of the things we are working on with the city is the old WIBC sign—that dates me—the news reader on the old Blue Cross building at Illinois and Market Streets. And I remember when I was a little kid going downtown and walking around downtown and seeing the latest news from the WIBC newsroom on that sign.

We think that this communications center can be a great focal point of the city where there's always something going on. We think that there will always be broadcasts from our on-Circle studios. Even though the main studios of each station will be up in the building, we'll have "windows on the world" on the first floor whether it's WIBC's morning show or promotions that we do for WENS or whatever; we think it will make it very exciting.

I think this is a great place. I take great pride in Indiana. I have a great affinity for the original pioneers in this business. I think they really sort of met the ideals of what broadcasting is all about, whether it's the Fairbanks or the Time-Life people. . . . But I look at the history of this town, and the state, you know, WOWO in Fort Wayne and [W]SBT in South Bend, and I just take a great sense of pride about the legacy that they've left. And hopefully some day people will look at us and say, "They carried on an honorable tradition."

Concluding Commentary

From Tommy Longsworth who creates visual images of a bygone era to Jeff Smulyan's impassioned analysis of business today, the narrators of this book provide a glimpse into an industry that has affected every American's life. In their own words, these twenty-seven narrators convey a sense of collective responsibility to the people of the Hoosier State. Their lives are part of its history. Some of the older narrators were born into a world that was vastly different from that of today. It was a time before world wars, and an era in which ideas were transmitted through the written word or through personal, verbal contact. It is through the words of the men and women of this book that the transformation of technologies, of political views, and of social values unfolds. Each interview is unique, yet all of these narrators experienced the same social, economic, and political tugs and pulls as broadcasters in other areas of the country. They are all part of the same story.

That is not to say that these men and women all viewed their responsibility to the listening public in exactly the same way. The context of each person's life shaped his or her perception of the public interest. Some of these narrators spoke eloquently of the sense of working for the public good. Others had difficulty expressing their personal interpretations of the public interest and instead spoke of the federally mandated definition or the "code" of the National Association of Broadcasters. However, their actions demonstrated a cognizance of ethics and responsibility that was far beyond their ability to articulate. For all, the collective vision of "in the public interest" was integral to the manner in which they functioned in business. Before the accolades for the profession become overwhelming, however, we must qualify the emerging vision of the public interest, for there certainly are broadcasters who did not pursue it in the same way or with the same strength of commitment.

More than anything, these stories reaffirm the primacy of the local and the personal in people's recollections. The years surrounding the depression are most telling. Broadcasters who lived through this era remembered little of the hardship except as it touched them personally. For example, they recalled local church broadcasts in that era, but not the national programs of the radio priest Father Charles E. Coughlin in which he questioned whether capitalism could survive. If there was a larger social message in these local programs, these broadcasters were unable to retrieve it from the recesses of their memories or they had been unaware of it at the time. It had not touched them personally.

For those who wish to learn more about the profession than could possibly be conveyed between the covers of this book, the complete oral history transcripts are reposited at the Indiana Historical Society Library and the Indiana State Museum. The stories of these broadcasters are many times longer than the excerpts presented here. Those who read the entire transcript will find that sometimes the interplay between narrator and interviewer reveals much about their lives and careers and other dimensions of the public interest that could not be included here. At other times, there are insights to be gained through what is said as well as what is left unsaid, through what is remembered and also what is forgotten. For example, on surface questioning, broadcasters typically remember little about conflict at their various stations; the past has been sanitized in their memories. It is only through subsequent, more detailed questioning that nuances of conflict become evident.

At times the passion of these narrators explodes across the pages of these oral histories, as they speak of subjects about which they care deeply and about which there are unresolved issues. For example, many of the broadcasters who were active in television in the 1970s were asked to respond to a published quote by Hilliard Gates in which he stated that programming standards were being set on the East and West Coasts and thus did not reflect the values of the Midwest. Retired broadcasters concurred with this, sometimes vehemently. Broadcasters who were active in the profession and those who had recently retired tended to take a less extreme approach, expressing the belief that Gates was correct in his assessment but that the situation had moderated somewhat. While some might assume that age had produced an intolerance toward a more liberal society, careful reading of the complete oral histories suggests that the situation is more complicated and warrants, perhaps, another, more directed project focusing on values in broadcasting.

Space and narrative format have necessarily limited the content of this book, but the oral histories themselves will provide fuel for other books and inspiration for other undertakings. As these broadcasters have related their life stories, we have learned who they are, their goals and aspirations, and how they perceived their public responsibility in relationship to other broadcasters. It is a tale strikingly simple and yet filled with complexity, with all the human contradictions and unresolved issues involved in the public interest. It is a story with an untold and unwritten ending, for the broadcasting profession continues to explore the boundaries of its "unique compact" with the public.

Endnotes

1 K. D. Ross, "As I Remember," unpublished manuscript, n.d., 22; K. D. Ross, "The Birth of a Station," n.d.

2 Erik Barnouw, *A Tower in Babel: A History of Broadcasting in the United States to 1933* (New York: Oxford University Press, 1966), 289.

3 Programming designed for a specific segment of the market.

4 Richard R. Zaragoz, Richard J. Bodorff, and Jonathan W. Emord, "The Public Interest Concept Transformed: The Trusteeship Model Gives Way to a Marketplace Approach," in *Public Interest and the Business of Broadcasting: The Broadcast Industry Looks at Itself*, Jon T. Powell and Wally Gair, eds. (New York: Quorum Books, 1988), 27–28; Robert L. Hilliard and Michael C. Keith, *The Broadcast Century: A Biography of American Broadcasting* (Boston: Focal Press, 1992), 49–51.

5 Barnouw, *A Tower in Babel*, 203; John R. Bittner, *Broadcast Law and Regulation* (Englewood Cliffs, N.J.: Prentice-Hall, 1982), 352–60.

6 Powell and Gair, eds., *Public Interest and the Business of Broadcasting*, 23–29.

7 Ibid. and Donald J. Jung, *The Federal Communications Commission, the Broadcast Industry, and the Fairness Doctrine, 1981–1987* (Lanham, Md.: University Press of America, 1996), 1; Hilliard and Keith, *Broadcast Century*, 236.

8 Hilliard and Keith, *Broadcast Century*, 200, 213, 222, 235, 240.

9 David Lowenthal, "History and Memory," *The Public Historian* 19, no. 2 (spring 1997): 32.

10 Walter Donaldson, "How 'ya gonna keep 'em down on the farm after they've seen Paree?" 1919, Sheet Music Collection, Special Collections Library of Duke University Library, Durham, North Carolina.

11 Fred Zieg, owner of WOWO.

12 Westinghouse purchased WOWO and WGL from Zieg in 1936.

13 The name "Jane Weston" was used by many women who hosted the popular women's program in Fort Wayne. It is likely that the name "Weston" was a takeoff on "Westinghouse."

14 Jay Gould began broadcasting at WOWO in 1941, performing forty-five years at that station. Often paired with WOWO broadcaster Bob Sievers, he was known primarily for his association with *The Little Red Barn.*

15 Chris Schenkel, a native of Bippus, Indiana, got his first radio job in the summer of 1942, working as an announcer at WLBC-AM in Muncie. He returned to Purdue University that fall, but did not return to broadcasting until after graduation and military service. He was among the first announcers of football on television in the early 1950s. Perhaps he is best known for his association with the *ABC Professional Bowlers Tour*, on which he appeared from 1962 until the program's final broadcast in 1996.

16 Hall of Famer Jim Mathis started his career as host of a children's show on WTTV and later moved on to WFBM Channel 6 as its sales manager in the 1960s and 1970s.

17 Geisler is referring to the Emmis Broadcasting Corporation.

18 Bill Kiley was a member of the sales department at WFBM.

19 *Indianapolis Star,* 6 November 1964; Burk Friedersdorf, *From Crystal to Color: WFBM* (Indianapolis: WFBM Stations, 1964).

20 Walton refers to the Bank Holiday (6–14 March 1933) during which President Franklin D. Roosevelt suspended all banking activity.

21 In 1915 musicians and music publishers sought to protect unauthorized and uncompensated use of their works on radio by forming the American Society of Composers, Authors and Publishers (ASCAP). In addition, radio stations formed their own opposition to ASCAP in organizing Broadcast Music, Inc. (BMI) through the NAB in 1939.

22 NBC had two radio networks, NBC Red and Blue, until 1943 when the FCC required them to divest themselves of one. NBC Blue became ABC.

23 "Television—Invented in Indiana?," *Mature Living in Indiana* (winter 1988): 3–4.

24 *Indianapolis Magazine* 16, no. 2 (Feb. 1979): 23–24.

25 Wilbur Shaw, a three-time winner of the Indianapolis 500-Mile Race, later became president and general manager of the Indianapolis Motor Speedway Corporation.

26 Ray Wilkinson, a friend of Martin in farm broadcasting, operated a farm network in North Carolina.

27 *Indianapolis Star,* 14 Nov. 1963; 7 Feb., 13, 18 May, 14 Sept. 1964; 17 Sept. 1965; 6 Mar., 1 Apr., 7 May 1966; 1 Feb. 1975; 8 June 1976; 4 Apr. 1977.

28 Later ABC.

29 The estate of William Kunkle owned WKJG at this time. Ed Thoms, Lester Popp, and Charles Schust purchased it. Ed Thoms became general manager, and Gates was his assistant. In 1957 John Dille II bought the television and radio station.

30 Dave Nichols, *Fort Wayne,* Nov. 1978, p. 20.

31 Russell Pulliam, "Eugene C. Pulliam," in *The Encyclopedia of Indianapolis,* David J. Bodenhamer and Robert G. Barrows, eds. (Bloomington and Indianapolis: Indiana University Press, 1994), 1151–52.

32 Information from Indiana Broadcasters Pioneers' Hall of Fame induction speech by James R. Phillippe.

33 Hugh Kibbey was WFBM program manager at the time.

34 *This is Vincennes: WAOV,* p. 194; *Indianapolis Star,* 20 Sept. 1939.

35 The navy's V-7 program served as a precursor to actual naval service. Men were trained in this program and were assigned to specific duties.

36 Stewart Center, formerly Memorial Center, named for R. B. and Lillian Stewart. The change in name came during MPATI's stay in that building.

37 *Perspective,* Purdue University, (summer 1997).

38 Howard Caldwell, "Broadcasting," in *Encyclopedia of Indianapolis,* Bodenhamer and Barrows, eds., 18.

39 *Fort Wayne,* Nov. 1978.

40 Howard C. Caldwell, Sr., was the CEO of his own Indianapolis advertising agency for nearly fifty years.

41 Harvey Weir Cook (1892–1943) was born in Indiana and came to Indianapolis in the 1920s. The Indianapolis International Airport was originally named for Weir Cook in 1944.

42 Selected awards to Channel 6 from this period include: Radio Television News Director Association Award for editorials on civil rights (1964), National Press Photography Association's News Station of the Year (1966), Alfred Dupont Award for documentary series on lack of public housing in Indianapolis (1966), Sigma Delta Chi Distinguished Service Award for editorials that ended open dump burning in Indianapolis (1967), Peabody Award and Saturday Review Magazine Independent Television Award for the documentary *The Negro in Indianapolis* (James Hetherington, researcher/writer, 1970).

43 Herman B Wells was president of Indiana University from 1937 to 1962, and has served as the university's chancellor from 1962 to the present.

44 Other investors included: Thomas Mathis, Francis J. Feeney, Jr., John Chittenden, John J. Dillon, Anthony M. Maio, and Patricia Welch (*Indianapolis Star,* 7 Dec. 1967).

45 GIPC, Greater Indianapolis Progress Committee.

46 Gary Todd was a longtime WIBC morning personality.

47 Al Hobbs was at WTLC from 1971 to 1993.

48 The old WIFE occupied the 1310 spot on the AM dial previously occupied by WISH. WIFE later became WTUX, and is now WTLC-AM.

49 Paul C. Major replaced Al Hobbs as WTLC general manager in 1993.

50 G. Gordon Liddy, a talk show host.

51 Brown's column, "Just Tellin' It" appears weekly in the *Indianapolis Recorder*.

52 WISH-Radio made its formal broadcast debut on 2 Aug. 1941.

53 Frank E. McKinney, Sr., formed Universal Broadcasting Corporation in 1947 and purchased WISH-FM for $554,000. In 1948 Bruce McConnell became a majority stockholder in Universal and once again ran WISH. *Encyclopedia of Indianapolis*, Bodenhamer and Barrows, eds., 1398.

54 J. H. Whitney & Company, a New York banking house. According to McConnell, Whitney would buy CBS only because he was the brother-in-law of CBS's chairman, William Paley.

55 The Corinthian Broadcasting Corporation was formed November 1956 in New York City.

56 Information from Indiana Broadcasters Pioneers' Hall of Fame induction speech by James R. Philippe.

57 Kenneth P. McCutchan, *At the Bend in the River: The Story of Evansville* (Woodland Hills, Calif.: Windsor Publications), 1982.

58 WFBM, 30 May 1949. WTTV, 11 Nov. 1949.

59 The *Indianapolis News* purchased WIBC in May 1944 and moved it from the Indianapolis Athletic Club to the Indianapolis News building in December 1945. When Eugene Pulliam bought the paper in 1948, Fairbanks took over WIBC operations entirely.

60 In 1941 the FCC ruled in favor of the Mayflower Broadcasting Company which challenged the license renewal of a Boston station. The resulting decision forbade editorializing, but was overturned in 1949. The FCC had decided instead to encourage controversial programming, given that stations provided "all sides of the issue." That ruling was the genesis of what became the "Fairness Doctrine." Hilliard and Keith, *Broadcast Century*, 95, 121–22.

Select Bibliography

BOOKS

Anderson, Benedict. *Imagined Communities: Reflections on the Origin and Spread of Nationalism.* London: Verso Books, 1983.

Barnouw, Erik. *A Tower in Babel: A History of Broadcasting in the United States to 1933.* New York: Oxford University Press, 1966.

————. *The Golden Web: A History of Broadcasting in the United States, 1933 to 1953.* New York: Oxford University Press, 1968.

————. *The Image Empire: A History of Broadcasting in the United States from 1953.* New York: Oxford University Press, 1970.

Bittner, John R. *Broadcast Law and Regulation.* Englewood Cliffs: Prentice-Hall, 1982.

Blum, John Morton. *V was for Victory: Politics and American Culture during World War II.* San Diego: Harvest/Harcourt Brace Jovanovich, 1976.

Brinkley, Alan. *Voices of Protest: Huey Long, Father Coughlin, and the Great Depression.* New York: Knopf, 1982.

Carothers, Diane Foxhill. *Radio Broadcasting from 1920 to 1990: An Annotated Bibliography.* New York: Garland Publishing, 1991.

Carr, David. *Time, Narrative, and History.* Bloomington: Indiana University Press, 1986.

Cohen, Lizabeth. *Making a New Deal: Industrial Workers in Chicago, 1919–1939.* Cambridge [England] University of Cambridge Press, 1990.

Ditingo, Vincent M. *The Remaking of Radio.* Boston: Focal Press, 1995.

Flannery, Gerald V., ed. *Commissioners of the FCC, 1927–1994.* Lanham, Md.: University Press of America, 1995.

Friedersdorf, Burk. *From Crystal to Color: WFBM.* Indianapolis: WFBM, 1964.

Gitlin, Todd. *The Sixties: Years of Hope, Days of Rage.* New York: Bantam Books, 1987.

Gluck, Sherna Berger. *Rosie the Riveter Revisited: Women, the War, and Social Change.* New York: Penguin Books, 1988.

Graebner, William S. *The Age of Doubt: American Thought and Culture in the 1940s.* Boston: Twayne Publishers, 1991.

Halberstam, David. *The Fifties.* New York: Fawcett Columbine, 1993.

Hilliard, Robert L., and Michael C. Keith. *The Broadcast Century: A Biography of American Broadcasting.* Boston: Focal Press, 1992.

Hilmes, Michele. *Hollywood and Broadcasting: From Radio to Cable.* Urbana: University of Illinois Press, 1990.

Hobsbawn, Eric, and Terance Ranger, eds. *The Invention of Tradition.* New York: Cambridge University Press, 1992.

Jackson, Kenneth T. *Crabgrass Frontier: The Suburbanization of the United States.* New York: Oxford University Press, 1985.

Jung, Donald J. *The Federal Communications Commission, the Broadcast Industry, and the Fairness Doctrine: 1981–1987.* Lanham, Md.: University Press of America, 1996.

Krattenmaker, Thomas G. *Telecommunications Law and Policy.* Durham, N.C.: Carolina Academic Press, 1994.

Lipschultz, Jeremy H. *Broadcast Indecency: F.C.C. Regulation and the First Amendment.* Boston: Focal Press, 1997.

Lipsitz, George. *Time Passages: Collective Memory and American Popular Culture.* Minneapolis: University of Minnesota Press, 1990.

Lowenthal, David. *The Past is a Foreign Country.* New York: Cambridge University Press, 1985.

Marsh, Dave. *Louie, Louie: The History and Mythology of the World's Most Famous Rock 'n' Roll Song.* New York: Hyperion, 1993.

Powell, Jon T., and Wally Gair. *Public Interest and the Business of Broadcasting: The Broadcast Industry Looks at Itself.* New York: Quorum Books, 1988.

Schudson, Michael. *Watergate in American Memory: How We Remember, Forget, and Reconstruct the Past.* New York: BasicBooks, 1992.

Susman, Warren I. *Culture as History: The Transformation of American Society in the Twentieth Century.* New York: Pantheon Books, 1984.

Terkel, Studs. *The Good War: An Oral History of World War Two.* New York: Ballantine Books, 1985.

———. *Hard Times: An Oral History of the Great Depression.* New York: Pantheon Books, 1970.

Tunstall, Jeremy. *Communications Deregulation: The Unleashing of America's Communications Industry.* Oxford: Basil Blackwell, 1986.

United States Senate. *Broadcasters' Public Interest Obligations and S. 217, the Fairness in Broadcasting Act of 1991.* Washington, D.C.: U.S. Government Printing Office, 1992.

Zelizer, Barbie. *Covering the Body: The Kennedy Assassination, the Media, and the Shaping of Collective Memory.* Chicago: University of Chicago Press, 1992.

ARTICLES

Bennett, Tamara. "Primaries Yield Profits for WTLC: Selling the Black Vote." *Indianapolis Business Journal* (21–27 May 1984): 1, 17.

Berman, Christine. "Media Moguls." *Indianapolis CEO* (August 1995): 9–16.

Bodnar, John. "Power and Memory in Oral History." *Journal of American History* (March 1989): 1201–21.

Brown, Duncan H. "The Academy's Response to the Call for a Marketplace Approach to Broadcast Regulation." *Critical Studies in Mass Communication* (September 1994): 257–73.

Caldwell, Howard. "Broadcasting." In David J. Bodenhamer and Robert G. Barrows, eds. *The Encyclopedia of Indianapolis.* Bloomington and Indianapolis: Indiana University Press, 1994.

Ehrlich, Matthew C. "The Competitive Ethos in Television Newswork." *Critical Studies in Mass Communication* (June 1995): 196–212.

Gillis, John. "Remembering Memory: A Challenge for Public Historians in a Post-National Era." *The Public Historian* (fall 1992): 91–101.

Gruley, Bryan. "Wave of Radio Deals Face Antitrust Scrutiny." *The Wall Street Journal* (8 October 1996): B1.

Harton, Tom. "Robert McConnell: Retired Channel 8 Head and Silent Civic Leader Begins Second Career at Helm of Indianapolis Water Company." *Indianapolis Business Journal* (6–12 July 1987): 12–14.

Horton, Gerd. "Radio Days on America's Home Front." *History Today* (September 1996): 46–53.

"Interview: John Dille, Skip Finley, and Herb McCord." *Radio Ink* (22 May–4 June 1995): 34–38.

Kukolla, Steve. "Major Drums in Fine-Tuning for WTLC-AM and FM." *Indianapolis Business Journal* (26 April–2 May 1993): 10A, 33A.

Lang, Kurt et al. "Collective Memory and the News." *Communication* (1989): 123–39.

Lowenthal, David. "History and Memory." *The Public Historian* 19, no. 2 (spring 1997): 31–39.

———. "The Timeless Past." *Journal of American History* (March 1989): 1263–80.

McChesney, Robert W. "Off Limits: An Inquiry into the Lack of Debate over the Ownership, Structure, and Control of the Mass Media in U.S. Political Life." *Communication* (August 1992): 1–19.

McGlone, Robert E. "Rescripting a Troubled Past: John Brown's Family and the Harpers Ferry Conspiracy," *Journal of American History* (March 1989): 1179–1200.

Nichols, Dave. "25 Years of TV in Fort Wayne." *Fort Wayne* (November 1978): 18–27.

Nora, Pierre. "Between Memory and History: Les Lieux de Memoire." *Representations* (spring 1989): 7–25.

Peters, John Durham, and Kenneth Cm el. "Media Ethics and the Public Sphere." *Communica ion* (August 1991): 197–215.

Petranoff, Robert. "A History of Broadcasting in Indiana." *Indiana Business and Industry* (September 1963): 22–24.

Pierce, Paul, ed. "The Friendly Voice of Indiana: The WIBC Story." *Air Pockets* (July 1955): 8–16.

Rivera-Sanchez, Milagros. "Developing an Indecency Standard: The Federal Communications Commission and the Regulation of Offensive Speech: 1927–1964." *Journalism History* (spring 1994): 3–14.

Rogers, Kim Lacy. "Oral History and the History of the Civil Rights Movement." *Journal of American History* (September 1988): 567–76.

Sanders, Donald G. "Watergate Reminiscences." *Journal of American History* (March 1989): 1228–33.

Shortridge, Norm. "Meet the Gang at the Speedway Radio Network." *Indianapolis Magazine* (May 1974): 43–52.

Stamm, Keith R. et al. "The Contribution of Local Media to Community Involvement." *Journalism and Mass Communication Quarterly* (spring 1997): 97–108.

Taylor, Chuck. "While Change is Certain, Local Radio Has Little to Fear from Digital Satellite Radio." *Billboard* (26 April 1997): 81.

NEWSPAPERS

Elkhart Truth, Fort Wayne Journal-Gazette, Indianapolis News, Indianapolis Recorder, Indianapolis Star, Indianapolis Times, Jasper Herald, Muncie Evening Press, South Bend Tribune.

INTERVIEWS

Hale, Michelle. "Senior Lawyers Project: Interview of Mr. Willard B. Ransom." Indiana Historical Society Manuscript Collection, BV 2620.

Weintraut, Linda. "Senior Lawyers Project: Interview of Mr. James Beatty." Indiana Historical Society Manuscript Collection, BV 2620.

Hall of Fame

The Indiana Broadcasters Pioneers Hall of Fame was founded in 1981 as a joint project of the Indiana Chapter of Broadcast Pioneers and the Indiana Broadcasters Association, which had been founded in 1948. The Hall of Fame was spearheaded by Reid Chapman, president of the Indiana Chapter of Broadcast Pioneers. Eighteen charter members were inducted in the Hall of Fame in 1981 at the spring convention. As of September 1998 the roster included sixty-seven broadcasters.

1. Marvin Bates
2. Charles A. Blake
3. Joseph Boland
4. Donald A. Burton
5. Howard C. Caldwell, Jr.
6. Eldon Campbell
7. Tom Carnegie (Carl Kenegy)
8. Reid G. Chapman ("Chuckles")
9. Dee O. Coe
10. Sidney Collins ("Sid")
11. Albert Wayne Coy
12. William Crawford
13. Madelyn Pugh Davis
14. G. Christopher Duffy
15. Capt. William C. Eddy
16. Joseph Edwards
17. Leonard J. Ellis
18. John A. Engelbrecht
19. Richard M. Fairbanks
20. Philo T. Farnsworth
21. Robert W. Flanders
22. H. Gilbert Forbes
23. Gerald R. Fordyce ("Gerry")
24. George A. Foulkes
25. William C. Fowler
26. Harry Frankel ("Singin' Sam")
27. M. Wayland Fullington
28. Hilliard Gates (Gudelsky)
29. Marthabel Geisler
30. Jay Gould
31. Gordon Graham
32. William T. Hamilton ("Tom")
33. Ann Wagner Harper
34. Frederick William Heckman, Jr.
35. Robert L. Hoover ("Bob")
36. Helen H. Huber
37. John Carl Jeffrey
38. Durward Kirby
39. Howard D. Longsworth ("Tommy")
40. Donald H. Martin, Sr.
41. Harry Martin (Harold S. Modlin)
42. James B. Mathis
43. C. Bruce McConnell
44. Robert B. McConnell
45. Donald Menke
46. Edwin C. Metcalfe
47. Jack D. Morrow
48. Waldemar Albert Nehrling ("Wally")
49. Bazil J. O'Hagan
50. Daniel Park
51. Robert M. Petranoff
52. James R. Phillippe
53. Kneale D. Ross
54. Christopher Schenkel

55. Franklin D. Schurz
56. Frank O. Sharp
57. James Shelton
58. Robert S. Sievers ("Bob")
59. E. Berry Smith
60. Lester Graham Spencer
61. Betty Chadwick Sullivan

62. Elmer G. Sulzer
63. Sarkes Tarzian
64. Carl W. Vandagrift
65. Ralph Luke Walton
66. Martin R. Williams
67. Hilda C. Woehrmeyer

Acknowledgments from the Indiana Broadcasters Pioneers Foundation, Inc.

I t has taken the better part of a decade to bring *"In the Public Interest"* to a successful conclusion. During this time, many individuals and companies both inside and outside the broadcasting industry contributed funds to the project, while others spent endless hours to make this book a reality. We are grateful to them all.

With a project of this size and duration, there are always a number of individuals, companies, and institutions that deserve special mention. Early on, the Indiana Historical Society, our publisher, awarded the Foundation a Special Project Grant to conduct the oral interviews. Jeff Smulyan, a modern-day broadcasting entrepreneur, graciously hosted an organizational luncheon in his home and gave a generous donation to help get the project rolling. Helen Campbell, a true pioneer in her own right as a radio songstress, helped provide the initial impetus with a substantial donation. Helen worked tirelessly over the years on the Foundation advisory committee, and at a financially critical point she again gave a generous donation to help keep the project on track.

The Indiana State Museum and its curator of history, Dale Ogden, offered support and guidance over the years. The Indiana Broadcasters Association provided ongoing monetary and moral support. Toward the end of the process, the IBA board, under the leadership of its president, John Newcomb, financially guaranteed the completion of the book. During the final three years, Linda Compton and Gwen Piening added this project to their duties with the IBA and helped in untold ways, from keeping our records to providing meeting space and generating publicity. The Farm Bureau Insurance Company made a substantial donation specifically designated for the distribution of a copy of the book to high schools in the state of Indiana, thereby guaranteeing that students will have the opportunity to learn about the impact of broadcasting upon the lives of Hoosiers.

Over the years, our historians, Weintraut & Nolan, easily could have moved on to other projects; however, they stayed the course. Thank you, Linda Weintraut and Jane Nolan, for a job well done. A huge thank-you to the hard-core members of the Foundation advisory committee who met month after month, year after year, to bring this work to completion. People such as Reid Chapman, Ken Coe, Jim Phillippe, Helen Campbell, Dick Lingle, Jim Hetherington, Howard Caldwell, Dave Smith, Bob Petranoff, and Ken Beckley proved with their time and effort that this truly was a labor of love.

Finally, our congratulations and thanks to the Indiana Broadcast Pioneers who inspired this project and brought it to life. Without their vision, cooperation, and support, this chronicle of the rich history of broadcasting in Indiana would not have been possible.

MICHAEL J. CORKEN
President, IBPF
1 October 1998

Indiana Broadcasters Pioneers

"Honor Roll of Donors"

Gugliellmo Marconi Donors
($25,000 and over)

Helen Campbell
Indiana Broadcasters Association
Indiana Historical Society

William S. Paley Donors
($10,000 and over)

Emmis Broadcasting Corporation
Indiana Farm Bureau Insurance

H. V. Kaltenborn Donors
($5,000 and over)

Broadcasters Foundation, Inc.
John F. Dille III
Fairbanks Foundation, Inc.
Indiana Chapter of Broadcast Pioneers
E. Berry Smith
Wabash Valley Broadcasting

Philo T. Farnsworth Donors
($1,000 and over)

Artistic Media Partners
Ken Beckley
Reid G. Chapman
Cinergy (PSI Energy)
Duncan's American Radio, Inc.
IPALCO
Indianapolis Motor Speedway
Marian McConnell
McGraw-Hill Foundation
Don H. Martin, Sr.
James R. Phillippe
Chris Schenkel
WEHT-TV Evansville
WFBQ-FM/WNDE-FM, WRZX-FM
WLFI-TV Lafayette
WSBT Stations South Bend

C. Bruce McConnell Donors
($500 and over)

Howard Caldwell
Mrs. Alex M. Clark
Ann Wagner Harper
Durward Kirby
Robert B. McConnell
Earl and Sylvia Metzger
Robert Petranoff
WHHH-FM
WNDU-TV South Bend

Eldon Campbell Donors
($200 and over)

Tom Carnegie
Michael Corken
William C. Fowler
James and Melva Freeman
Daniel J. Henn
Ruth Hiatt
Klaehn, Fahl & Melton Funeral Home

Dr. James R. Platt
Roehling Broadcast Services
David Smith
WBKS/WIRE-FM/WJZY-FM/WAV-TV
WFIE-TV Evansville
WFMX-FM/WGLD-FM/WGRL-FM
WFYI-FM
WIKY/WJPS/WABX-FM Evansville
WISH-TV Indianapolis
WRTV 6 Indianapolis
WTHR-TV Indianapolis
WWKI-FM Kokomo
Hal Youart

Don Burton Donors
($100 and over)

Ball State University Foundation
Jinsie Scott Bingham
Mr. and Mrs. Charles Blake
Russell J. Dodge
Joseph Duncan, Ph.D.
Leonard Ellis
George Griffith
James Hetherington
Jim Hinga
Indiana Basketball Coaches Association
Indiana State University R/TV/F Program
Stephen Ingram
Gordon Johnson
Alice McMahan Hendricks Leppert
Dick Lingle
Howard D. Longsworth
Paula MacVittie
Jack Messmer
Meyer Broadcasting Corporation
David Miller
Frank Moore
National City Bank
Network Indiana
Jerry Newsom
Robert S. Sievers
Dean Spencer
WANE-TV Fort Wayne
WBCL-FM
WEJS-FM
WEVV-TV Evansville
WIBC-AM
WICR-FM
WLBC Muncie
WLQ -FM/WRIN-AM
WMEE-FM Fort Wayne
WNAP-FM
The WNDU Stations
WNTS-AM
WOWO-AM Fort Wayne
WRCR-FM
WTBU-CH 69
WSJV-TV
WUEV-FM

Sid Collins Donors
($50 and over)

ASCAP
John R. Atkinson
Jerry L. Ayers
Bomar Broadcasting Corporation
Barbara Boyd
The Cromwell Group, Inc.
Dearborn County Broadcasters
Marthabel Geisler
Casey A. Heckman
Byard Hey
Jefferson High School
F. Robert Kalthoff
Robert King
Edwin C. Metcalfe
Dr. Joe Misiewicz
Bazil J. O'Hagan
James Rogers Trust
John Schuler
Thoben VanHuss & Associates
Irene Walters
WFLQ French Lick
William Gerald Willis
WPTA-TV Fort Wayne
Lloyd Wright
Xavier University

Helen Huber Donors
(under $50)

Dick Baumgartner
Harold Benson
Mr. and Mrs. Charles Boswell
Robin Bright
Crossroads Communications, Inc.
Myron Dickinson
Dan Edwards
Carl Erskine
Mr. and Mrs. Thomas Fowler-Finn
John A. Guion
Fred Heckman
David Johnson
Dr. Richard Juergens
Charles O'Donnell WRTV
Dr. Marvin Priddy
Gerald Sargent
Charles Schisla
Joe Sexson
William Stearman
Allen Steere
Mary and David Tyndall
Jack E. Weicker
WNJY-FM
WROI-FM Radio

Some of the gifts of the above donors were given in the memory of the following individuals: Hilliard Gates, William "Bill" Fowler, Don Burton, Eldon Campbell, Mary Hulman, Paul Roberts, William Leppert, Emmett DePoy, Francis A. "Jake" Higgins, and Peter Reilly.

Index

Engelbrecht, Bettie: oral interview, 239–42

Engelbrecht, Bettie G., *see* Engelbrecht, Bettie

Engelbrecht, John, 246

Engelbrecht, John A., 239, 241, 242, 245, 246, 248

Equal Employment Opportunity Commission (EEOC): and radio licenses, 95, 97, 266

ESPN, 119

Ethics: and broadcasting, 131, 132, 189, 213–14, 218, 225–26

ETV (Educational TV): funding of, 152

Evans, Joan, 266

Evanston (Ill.), 203, 205

Evansville (Ind.), 148, 245; radio in, 45, 47, 125, 225, 239, 241; television stations in, 178; news coverage of mayor's death, 180; growth in, 249

Evansville Bosse High School, 47

Evansville Central High School, 47

Eyck, Sidney Ten, 75

Face the Nation, 216

Fairbanks, Charles Warren, 263

Fairbanks, Dick, 93, 94, 137, 138, 225, 263; buys radio stations, 95; and commitment to station's community service, 97; oral interview, 263–70

Fairbanks, Richard M., *see* Fairbanks, Dick

Fairbanks, Warren, 263, 264

Fairbanks Broadcasting Company, 85, 263, 288

"Fairness doctrine," 2, 270

"Fairness Report," 2

Fall, Bill, 71, 73; oral interview, 147–52

Fall, Joyce, 147

Fall, William R., *see* Fall, Bill

Farm broadcasting: radio and, 79, 82

Farm markets: and radio, 68, 254

Farnsworth, Philo T., 70, 72

Farnsworth Television & Radio Corporation, 70

Federal Communications Commission (FCC), 185, 221; and regulation, 2, 3, 4, 16, 24, 26, 38, 144, 188, 237, 278; and community service in broadcasting, 17, 104, 254, 269–70; and concept of public interest, 73, 83, 95; assigns television channel to Indianapolis, 73; freeze on television applications, 82, 264; and WIFE license renewal, 94;

revokes WIFE license, 94; and radio licenses, 95, 104, 106, 143; and television licensing, 95, 108, 116, 117, 119, 129, 166; grants permission for television station in Fort Wayne, 108, 166; grants license to WAOV, 143; and signal restrictions, 148; and concern with monopolies, 148, 150; and frequency assignments, 150; mandate for local programming, 155; and code for public interest, 156, 225; and digital television, 175; and WTLC ownership dispute, 214; and regulation of ownership, 225, 263, 281; and broadcasting licenses, 234; establishes various classes for stations, 265; and deregulation of broadcasting, 270; and radio and television editorializing, 270; and change of radio station's call letters, 277

Federal Radio Commission (FRC), 144

Federated Media, 225, 273

Fein, Jessie, 147

Fetzer, John E., 277

Fibber McGee and Molly (radio program), 16, 38

Fidelity Bank (Indianapolis), 232

Film Daily (newspaper), 68

Fine Arts Society, 214

First Amendment, 2

First Baptist Church (Fort Wayne), 54

Fitz and Fellows, 56

Fitzsimmons, Guy, 56

Flint (Mich.), 185

Floods: radio coverage of, 30, 49, 51, 163, 242, 257

The Flying Scot (book), 111

Foch, Ferdinand (Marshal), 249

Forbes, Gilbert, 38, 78, 82, 90, 92, 117, 140

Ford, Betty, 210

Ford Foundation: and television financing, 73; sponsors program, 147; funds educational programming at Purdue (MPATI), 150

Forrest, Frank, 139

Fort Benning (Ga.), 276

Fort Riley (Kans.), 276

Fort Wayne (Ind.), 11, 17, 114; radio stations in, 11, 19, 29, 30, 53, 56, 61, 63, 78, 99, 108, 111, 232, 273, 277; cable television in, 68; and television manufacturing, 70, 73;

professional basketball team in, 103, 104, 113; and television, 108; radio and television stations in, 161, 166, 276; first television channel on air in, 168; listeners are unhappy with WOWO signal restrictions, 278

Fort Wayne Journal-Gazette, 53, 56, 99, 106, 108

Fort Wayne Magazine, 108

Fort Wayne National Bank Building: radio station in, 166

Fort Wayne Pistons (NBL team), 99, 103, 104, 113

Fort Wayne Zollner Pistons, 113

Fox, Bill, 265, 269

Friendly Neighbors (soap opera), 16

The Fox's Den (radio program), 265

Framingham (Mass.): Fairbanks Broadcasting owns station in, 263

Franklin Securities, 175, 177

"From Franklin to Frost" (educational program), 152

Franklin Volunteer Fire Department, 140

Frost, Robert, 152

Gabby the Duck (Harry Martin's sidekick), 75, 80

Gable, Clark, 90

Gair, Wally, 3

Galbreath, Dick, 12, 56

Gamble, Bob, 198, 200, 203, 204, 205, 206, 209, 210

Gandhi, Indira, 200

Gandhi, Mahatma, 200

Garagiola, Joe, 242

Gardner, Earl, 12, 14

Gaston, Hazel, 40

Gates, Hilliard, 71, 72, 127, 276, 292; oral interview, 99–109

Gates, Rae, 103, 104, 109

Geiger, Miss _____, 89

Geisler, Marthabel, 37, 79; oral interview, 37–42

General Electric, 1, 53

"Get Out the Vote" (radio campaign), 216

Godfrey, Arthur, 166

Golden Dome Productions, 189

Golden's Men's Wear (Fort Wayne), 56

Gospel Temple (Fort Wayne), 54

Gould, Jay, 17, 53, 56, 57, 67, 68

Gradison, Bill, 278

Grand Hotel (Vincennes): WAOV located in, 162

Grand Ole Opry (radio program), 67

Grand Rapids (Mich.), 278